CUBA WITH PEN AND PENCIL

LOST AND FOUND

THE CLASSIC TRAVEL SERIES

"La siempre fiel isla."

CUBA WITH PEN AND PENCIL

by

SAMUEL HAZARD

"It is the most beautiful land that eyes ever beheld."—Columbus

Signal Books
Oxford
2007

This edition published in 2007 by
Signal Books Limited
36 Minster Road
Oxford
OX4 1LY
www.signalbooks.co.uk

First published in 1870
Introduction © Richard Gott, 2007

A catalogue record for this book is available from the British Library

ISBN 978-1-904955-20-7 Paper

Cover Design: Baseline Arts
Design & Production: Devdan Sen
Cover Image: Samuel Hazard
Drawings: Samuel Hazard

Printed in India

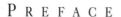

PREFACE

Some of the chapters in
this book were written
in Cuba, amidst the
beautiful scenes they describe,
which will account to the reader
for what may appear to him as too
glowing descriptions.

As for the rest, the author
feels he owes a debt of
gratitude to at least the
climate of Cuba.

The fall of the year in
which our great war closed found
the writer with a constitution
impaired by disease engendered
during his service in the army, and
ordered by his physician to a
southern climate.

Almost indifferent where he went,
but having pleasant
memories of a
previous visit to
Cuba, he went there.
From the
moment he landed,
he gained new life,—

such was the wonderful effect of that delicious climate.

Like many others, he was "killing time" in Havana, supposing, from the lack of information and of books, there was nothing specially interesting outside of Havana, when fortunately he came across a little volume in Spanish, now out of print, called "Manual of the Island of Cuba."

It is safe to say that had the author not found that book these pages would never have been written; but with this volume as his guide and teacher as to what was to be seen in the whole Island of Cuba, he spent his time during his stay on the island wandering from place to place, studying the people and their habits, and picking up where possible, views and illustrations; or, where there were not to be had, resorting to his own pencil or the assistance of the photographer.

The liberality of the publishers of this volume enables the author, therefore, to place before his readers the best of these illustrations; and believing that as "actions speak louder than words," so do cuts tell more than descriptions, he, wherever possible, permits the illustration to tell the story.

"The general reader," says Livy, "cares little for the antiquities of a people." With this in view, the author has given only sufficient of the general history as may satisfy the majority of readers; but for the benefit of the more profound student of Spanish colonial history, he appends a list of valuable works pertaining to the Island of Cuba, of most of which he has made free use. To Don Jose Garcia, de Arboleya, author of "The Manual of the Island," the reader is indebted, as is the author, for the principal *facts* in this volume.

In concluding these few words of preface, the author cannot do better than to use the words of an old writer in saying: "An useful work needs no indelicate recommendation, nor can a bad one be supported by it, although a sonorous patron might happen to help the sale."

Such as I have I give unto the world, with a heart conscious of upright intentions; and I readily confess I am more disposed to do them the (Cubans) real service than to flatter.

If the reader find me imperfect, it will be some little apology that I am but a man."

Germantown, September 1, 1870.

L I S T   O F   W O R K S   P E R T A I N I N G   T O   C U B A
U S E D   O R   Q U O T E D   I N   T H I S   V O L U M E

Prescott's History of Mexico.

The Works of Humboldt and Bonpland. Paris: 1808–9.

Irving's Life and Voyages of Columbus.

Llave del Nuevo-Mundo. Por Arrate. 1 tomo.

Historia Economico—Politica de la Isla de Cuba. Por Lasagra. 1 tomo.

Historia Fisica, Politica y Natural de la Isle de Cuba. Por Lasagra. Nine large volumes, en folio. Con preciosos laminas iluminadas.

Descripcion y Vista de los Prinipales Ingenios de esta Isla. 1 tomo folio marquilla, con hermosas litografias iluminadas.

Dr. Wordiman's Travels in Cuba.

May's Almanaque Mercantil para el ano 1870. Published in Havana.

Guitera Historia de la Isla de Cuba. Dos tomos. New York. The best work for the general reader published.

Nuevos Elementos de Geografia e Historia de la Isla de Cuba. Por D. José Maria de la Torre. Havana: 1863.

Compendio de la Historia de Cuba. Por Emilio Blanchet. Matanzas: 1866.

El Cocinero Cubano. Por J. P. Legran. Havana: 1864.

Fairholt's Tobacco and Tobacco Pipes. London.

The falls of the Rosario

INTRODUCTION
by Richard Gott

Samuel Hazard was a nineteenth-century American writer and artist who travelled to Havana in the middle of the 1860s and soon became embroiled in the task of recording his impressions of Cuban life and society—with pen and pencil. The Cuba he came to was still a wealthy province of the Spanish Empire, its immense riches based on the production and export of sugar—and on the labour of black slaves imported from Africa. The Atlantic slave trade was still in operation and slavery itself was not formally abolished in Cuba until 1886. Yet times were already beginning to change. Many American visitors like Hazard could see that the power of Spain was crumbling, and they fondly imagined that the island might soon be theirs.

This was still the era of America's "Manifest Destiny", the doctrine first developed to justify US expansionism, formulated by a journalist writing in 1845. America's task, declared John O'Sullivan, was "to overspread the continent allotted by Providence for the free development of our yearly multiplying millions." The United States had already "overspread" much of the continent by mid-century, and many people assumed that Cuba was high on the list. Louisiana had been gobbled up in 1803, Florida in 1819, and the former Mexican territories of Arizona, California, Nevada, New Mexico, Texas and Utah in 1848. An American adventurer, William Walker, was to seize Nicaragua in 1856.

For America's southern states, controlled by slave owners, the acquisition of an important slave state in the Caribbean would have strengthened their position in their arguments with the North. While O'Sullivan had made no direct reference in his expansionist writings to the independent states of Central America and the Caribbean, he had been made well aware of the arguments in favour of acquiring Cuba. His sister was married to Cristobal Madán, a wealthy Cuban sugar planter exiled in New York who led the Cuban campaign for annexation.

The arguments of the Cubans like Madán were simple. Spain had been chased out of most of Latin America in the 1820s, and the Madrid government had been in a state of prolonged political crisis ever since. Cuba remained the jewel in the Spanish crown, and the principal source of its wealth, but there was no certainty that Spain could hold the island for ever. Trends in trade and commerce, as well as the permanent facts of geography, were drawing it ever more closely into the US ambit.

Yet many members of the Cuban elite of sugar planters and slave owners remained reluctant to abandon the Spanish connection. They were fearful that the country's majority black population—of both slaves and free blacks—might one day overwhelm the whites and establish a black government on the lines of the black republic set up on the island of Santo Domingo during the French Revolution, in what today is the republic of Haiti. This was the "great fear" of those times, and to many of the slave owners the possibility of an alliance with the slave states of the United States seemed a providential outcome to the imagined dangers and uncertainties that lay ahead.

American readers were largely unfamiliar with both the history and the contemporary reality of the island that might suddenly become theirs, and part of Samuel Hazard's aim in writing his book was to fill this obvious gap. In the final pages he reveals his own political position in broad support of annexation: "We have wandered together over the beautiful island of Cuba, looked at its lovely scenery, mingled with its mixed population, dipped a little into its antiquities, history, and productions... [and] perhaps you may be able to answer the question often asked: 'What sort of a place would Cuba be if she did belong to the United States?'"

Hazard had his own answer prepared: "Cuba with a free government, *plenty of ice*, and a large immigration, would become a wonderful garden."

For a nineteenth-century observer Hazard had produced a splendidly twentieth-century image. In the years after the US invasion and occupation of 1898, and notably in the 1920s and again in the 1950s, Cuba did indeed become an American garden. It developed into a playground for the wealthy American settler and weekend visitor, a place where gamblers and drunkards mingled with beautiful women, and where indeed there was "plenty of ice", tinkling in glasses permanently replenished with local rum. Hazard could not have foreseen such scenes of decadence, nor could he have been held responsible for them, yet the magnetism of the island was already attracting many of his countrymen in his own century.

Americans had been moving to Cuba in increasing numbers in the forty years before Hazard arrived in 1865, and many leading Confederate figures took refuge there at the end of the Civil War in the very year of his visit. Large numbers of "refugees from New Orleans" had taken up residence in the capital, reported the US consul in Havana in 1866. They came accompanied by their personal slaves, and many were to remain. Anthony Trollope, an earlier visitor, had already noted in 1859 that "Havana will soon become as much American as New Orleans." These southern exiles joined the nearly 3,000 US citizens already based on the island permanently, and the 5,000 or more who came each year to work under contract. Many Americans, like Hazard, came to spend the winter months in a warm climate or simply to convalesce. His well-presented and knowledgeable guide book would not be short of readers.

More than 2,000 US ships docked each year in Cuban ports. They called at the smaller harbours of Matanzas, Cardenas, Sagua la Grande, and Trinidad, as well as at Havana and Santiago. Most travellers, like Hazard, found it easier to move around the county by sea rather than by land, and even the ships that sustained Cuba's coastal trade were usually built in the United States and owned by American trading firms. American entrepreneurs were everywhere, operating trading companies and railway lines, and buying up sugar plantations and sugar mills, and coffee estates. American firms owned iron mines at Juraguá and copper mines at El Cobre. Visitors could find American-run boarding houses in every town, and worship at

Protestant churches serviced by American pastors. By mid-century, the US had become Cuba's most important trading partner. While 65 per cent of the island's sugar crop went to the United States, only 3 per cent was shipped to Spain.

The belief that Cuba's future lay with the United States was widely held in both countries. Successive US presidents had actually offered to purchase Cuba from Spain. President James Polk told the Madrid government in 1848 that he was prepared to pay $100 million for the island, and President Franklin Pierce increased the figure to $130 million in 1854. US diplomats in Europe called on Washington to seize the moment, echoing the fears of white Cubans about possible black rule: "We should be unworthy of our gallant forefathers and commit base treason against our posterity if Cuba were to be 'Africanised' and become another Santo Domingo, with all its attendant horrors to the white race, and suffer the flames to extend to our neighbouring shores, seriously to endanger or actually destroy the fabric of our Union."

America's financial offers were firmly rejected by Spain, and the government in Washington abandoned the idea of a negotiated transfer. But freelance US adventurers believed that the island was militarily vulnerable and could be captured easily. One recent military expedition had taken place in August 1851 when Narciso López, a former Spanish officer and provincial governor in Cuba, had sailed from New Orleans and landed to the west of Havana with several hundred men. Readers of *Cuba with Pen and Pencil* are reminded of the bleak story of the capture and execution of López and the leaders of his band, in spite of the energetic protests of the British consul.

★

Samuel Hazard had first visited Cuba as a young man of 23 in 1857, a few years after the López expedition, and he returned to research his book in 1865. Little is known of the details of his short life, but he was born in Philadelphia in 1834. He was the son of another Samuel Hazard (1784-1870), an American archaeologist and antiquarian, also from Philadelphia, who had travelled widely in Asia as a young man, and devoted much of his later life to the production of innumerable volumes of the *Annals of Pennsylvania*. His son's familiarity with Philadelphia is apparent in his reference to Elisha Kent Kane, a well-known Arctic explorer from his home city who had died in Havana when staying there in 1857, the year of Hazard's first trip.

Hazard's book about his Cuban travels was eventually published in 1870, signed off at Germantown, near Philadelphia, on 1 September. A few months later, in February 1871, he was to travel to Santo Domingo and to Haiti to write a second book with a similar theme: the US acquisition of Cuba's neighbour. He went as a newspaper correspondent, visiting the island at the same time as a three-man US government Commission led by Andrew Dickson White. The Commissioners had been sent out to examine conditions in the Dominican Republic, and to report on its admission into the Union. Hazard's second book, *Santo Domingo, Past and Present: With a Glance at Haiti*, which was published in 1873 [reprinted by the Editora de Santo Domingo in 1974], details the history of the island as well as the activities of the Commission. It has a similar spread of attractive illustrations as his volume on Cuba. (The project to acquire the Dominican Republic was defeated in the US Congress, and nothing came of it until the twentieth century when the US Marines occupied it between 1904 and 1916).

Apart from the occasional autobiographical reference in Hazard's two books, indicating for example that he once visited England, little more is known about this elusive writer. He was to die in 1876 at the relatively young age of 42.

Hazard clearly belonged to that section of American society that hoped that Cuba would soon be free from Spanish rule, not as an independent state but as an addition to the United States of America. Yet in practice, when he came on his second visit to Cuba in the autumn of 1865, the prospect of US annexation, long canvassed over the previous two decades, was effectively dead. Hazard tells his readers that he had returned to Cuba on doctor's orders, for he had fallen ill after taking part in the campaigns of the American Civil War which had just ended. Although this might not have been obvious to

Hazard, he had arrived at an important moment in the island's history, for, with the defeat of the South, and the formal end of American slavery two years earlier in 1863, the notion of a union of slave states was no longer at the top of the agenda.

Groups within the Cuban elite had begun to consider other policies, and some revived the old slogan of "Cuba Libre", with its call for a free and independent Cuba, free from both Spanish colonial rule and from the threat of US annexation. In September 1868, Carlos Manuel de Céspedes assembled a rebel band of sugar planters and tobacco barons at his farm near Manzanilla and issued the so-called "Grito de Yara", a declaration of independence.

Hazard had arrived in Havana just as the island was about to explode into what was to become a bitter, ten-year struggle for independence, but he had already returned to Philadelphia by the autumn of 1868 when the first signs of Céspedes' rebellion were detected. By that time he was writing up his travel notes and preparing the sketches for this book, as well as copying many of the prints and photographs that he had obtained on the island.

His evocative and detailed description of Cuba in the 1860s makes little reference to the political situation and maybe he did not want to alarm his readers. He does refer briefly to "the troubles in the island" and he remarks elsewhere that Havana could well be described as "a military city". He writes how "at every corner, you meet a soldier, before nearly every office there is a guard..." And on a visit to the inland town of Camagüey (or Puerto Principe), he hints at its significance in the independence struggle: "Its sons have had a greater or smaller share in almost every revolution that has taken place in the island. It has now received its baptism of blood in the cause of liberty for 'free Cuba', having sustained a siege, been attacked and almost starved out..."

In Trinidad, too, his reflections on the delightful evening parade in the town's central square are interrupted by thoughts about the human cost of the war. "Since these lines were written how changed has been the fate of many of those same promenaders. To some— fathers, mothers, and sisters—have come sorrow and mourning; to others—men, brothers, fathers and husbands—wounds, exile, or death. Alas! And alas! Is it all for naught that those brave hearts have laid their hands upon the staff that bore the banner of liberty, only to give another illustration of the motto, 'dulce est pro patria mori?'" Or, as Fidel Castro would frame the sentiment nearly a hundred years later, "Patria, o muerte, venceremos."

Hazard seems to have had a premonition that the rebellion was not going well—and he rightly hints that the rebels would have a difficult and perhaps disastrous time ahead. Indeed, after a long and bitter struggle, and the death of Céspedes and many of the other leaders, the Cuban rebels were driven to negotiate a cease-fire in 1878. A fresh generation, led by José Martí, renewed the rebellion in 1895, only to be pushed aside when the Americans invaded the island in 1898, defeated the Spaniards, and seized victory for themselves.

Hazard's references to the independence war were clearly added at the last moment, and there is no reference to the political troubles in both Madrid and Havana that accompanied its early months, when revolution in Madrid sparked off a counter-revolution in Havana. So although his book was not actually printed until 1870, it is basically an account of Cuba "before the deluge", an almost nostalgic snapshot of a society and a way of life that was about to disappear. He was an exceptionally observant traveller.

Like many visitors, Hazard was captivated by Cuba, and his book is a most excellent and complete guide to every service that the traveller might require. He reels off the names of the hotels and restaurants, the parks and public gardens, and explains where to swim and what kind of carriage to hire. He knows where to find good food, and takes the reader to the fish-market as well as to the stalls selling vegetables and fruit. He reveals where to get oysters for breakfast ("they have the briny and somewhat coppery taste of the French oyster"), as well as where to buy *helados*, *refrescos* and *dulces*.

He provides details about telegrams and the price of postage ("ten cents on all letters going out of the island for each half-ounce"), and reveals the frequency of delivery (twice daily "generally 7am and 3pm") and its speed ("six days to go from Havana to Santiago de Cuba, to which place it goes partly by rail and partly by horse"). He gives special instructions to the American community anxious to retain links with home: "Letters for the United States are best mailed at the Consul's, or at the offices of the steamers of mercantile houses, who generally have a private mail-bag by each vessel."

Hazard is an energetic and entertaining travel companion, with a fund of amusing stories and anecdotes, but he is not perhaps immediately likeable. Typical of many Americans of his time, and indeed of many of the Cubans that he meets, he is outspokenly offensive about blacks. "Did you ever see anything more disgusting than that great negro wench?" and he describes his washerwoman, "a large clothes basket on her head, a colossal cigar sticking out from beneath her thick lips, while she walks along, majestically trailing an ill-fitting, loose dress... She is free, too; and, as many others of them do, puts on airs..."

He is often absurdly patronizing about women, although he tells an entertaining (and modern) anecdote against himself when he encounters a young woman who dreams of life in the United States. She asks of him whether "everyone is free there now, Señor?"

> "Oh, yes," I replied, "we have no negro slaves there now."
> "No, no! Señor; you don't understand me. I mean the women, too, — are they not free?"
> To which I was obliged to reply they were, and only we poor men were their slaves.
> "*Es muy bueno*, Señor; it is not so here."

Like all good journalists before and after, Hazard pillaged as many Spanish texts as he could find to provide a reasonably coherent picture of the island's past. Inevitably he relied largely on the work of Spanish journalists like José García de Arboleya, a prominent supporter of the Spanish cause, and that of the renowned Spanish botanist Ramón de la Sagra. But many of the sharp comments are his own, and his intimate descriptions of the processes involved in sugar and coffee production, as well as the fabrication of cigars, are exceptionally vivid.

What gives his work its defining attraction are the cascades of delightful illustrations. Although many are shamelessly pillaged from the works of others, the effect is one of unalloyed pleasure, capturing on almost every page the island's peoples and its architecture at the height of their fame and fortune.

Richard Gott is the author of Cuba: a New History, *published by Yale University Press.*

1898 · America invaded

"The Queen of the Antilles!" Yes, and a beautiful queen she is, with the sapphire and emerald waters of the Gulf, sparkling 'neath the glories of a tropic sun, washing her stony feet in angry spray; or, where her golden shores stretch out, rippling in gentle waves upon the sandy levee, as though murmuring in low but passionate tones the love notes of the South.

Ah! Carissima, indeed!

Cuba! the land of the cocoa and the palm,—of the golden banana and the luscious orange,—well may the hearts of thy sons and the dark, lustrous eyes of thy maidens glow and glisten with pride at the praises of thy sunny isle!

How few Americans there are that have formed any correct conception of "Life in the Tropics!" To the generality of us, Cuba suggests the idea of heat and yellow fever, of venomous reptiles and insects, slaves and sugar, oranges and ever-blooming flowers,—an idea in a great degree erroneous.

Few, indeed, can realize that, leaving the snow-clad hills of New York harbor in the depth of winter, in three and a half or four days they will be sailing over the placid waters of the bay of Havana, under a tropic sun, which even in mid-winter rivals that of our own land in its season of dog-day heat, and will see around them the verdure-clad hills, with the graceful palm and cocoa-tree clear against the pure blue sky of the beautiful isle, so truly called "the most precious jewel of the Spanish crown."

Yet there are many Americans who, each year, either for purposes of health, business, or pleasure, flock to Havana, all glad to avoid the inclement weather of the icy north; and even with all their traveling it is difficult to get any reliable information as to what preparations one needs to make before starting; unless, indeed, some of one's acquaintances have been there, and even then it is very limited.

To him, therefore, who has any intention of making a visit to the Island of Cuba with the purpose of staying there some time, of traveling over the island, and of really enjoying its beautiful scenery, its oddities of manners and customs, or even of trying its numerous medicinal waters, I recommend to pick up a little Spanish, even if it be only enough to ask for something to eat, to give directions about luggage, and such other every-day necessities as occur to the traveler in any land.

The Cubans themselves are not a traveling people, and, to use the words of one of their own authors, "have little fancy for traveling, be it on account of the bad roads, that now, thanks to the zeal of the government, of the Junta de Fomento (Improvement Society), and of the good patriots, are disappearing with the advent of steamboats and railroads, or be it from the love with which the localities where we are born and pass the first years of our infancy inspire us,—where exist our interests, and where gather round our sweetest memories." Few foreigners go much away from Havana or Matanzas, or perhaps Cardenas, and the people have not yet learned the necessities of those who travel for curiosity or health; and therefore to us, accustomed as we are to have our traveling made easy, many things will seem hard, uncomfortable, and strange, unless one is able by a few words of Spanish to smooth away the rough peculiarities of places and people not accustomed to a traveling public. And yet, with all the inconveniences and peculiarities that the traveler experiences after leaving Havana, he is compensated, in my opinion, for all of these by the perfect novelty of the sights and scenery he meets with, and by the extreme change in the manner of life he is accustomed to, although he may leave behind him some greater conveniences in quitting the prominent places like Havana and Matanzas, where, after the novelty of the streets, the architecture of the houses, and the odd appearance of the stores, etc., are worn off, he is reminded of the city life of his own land constantly. The social life of the better classes is much the same, the world over; they eat, and drink, and visit pretty much as they do in all the great capitals of the world.

But it is in such towns as Trinidad and Santiago de Cuba, and in such pretty villages as Guines, San Antonio, and Guanajay, or among the coffee-places of the Vuelta Abajo, and the sugar estates of the Vuelta Arriba, that the stranger sees the original habits and customs of a people who are always loth to change; and it has been truly said that Cuba is more Spanish than Spain; for here it is out of the world, in some degree, while there effort is made to keep up with the new ideas of the day.

In the country and towns of the south coast, too, the air is somewhat drier during the season of the northers, which, for invalids, is most important.

A more kind-hearted, hospitable people than the Cubans, particularly to "Los Americanos," it would be difficult to find; no trouble is too great for them if you can make them comprehend the *purpose* of what you desire; and the "oiling of the palm" is just as effectual amongst these primitive people of the interior as in more civilized lands.

Many of the people speak English, a great many French,— which, in fact, is the household language in some parts of the island,—and many of the young men one finds have been regularly educated in the United States.

In arranging money matters, unless one is very extravagant indeed in his daily expenditures, five dollars gold per day is a very fair allowance for ordinary expenses while on the island for simply living and traveling; while, of course, if one desires to be extravagant or make purchases, there are just as many ways of getting rid of money as in other places.

The provision for these expenses can best be made by a letter of credit. As exchange on London is generally at a premium in Havana, a bill of exchange even up to ninety days on some well-known house can be disposed of to advantage; as, however, there is not the same system of banking in Havana as there is with us, the best arrangement for the general traveler is to take a letter of credit on some well-known house in Havana. He will then only have to pay for money as he uses it, he has no trouble in carrying money with him, and such houses will furnish letters of credit to other parts of the island, which is a great convenience.

An amount of silver in ten-cent pieces, which pass readily as the "real sencilla,"—say from twenty to fifty dollars' worth, will be found very convenient for the thousand and one daily expenses of the traveler, small change being scarce. Other silver coin it is not advisable to take, since our twenty-five cent pieces pass for only twenty cents (*peseta*), and the half dollars (*medio peso*) for only forty cents. American gold passes readily, being generally at a premium of seven or eight per cent; and if you can supply yourself with the Spanish doubloons at their intrinsic value of sixteen dollars they will pass for seventeen dollars in Cuba, as that is their value fixed by the government to keep the coin in the country.

Letters of introduction to business men in Havana are really not worth the paper they are written on, no matter by whom written, or in whose favor given; for the merchants receive such hosts of them that it would be impossible, even had they the inclination, to show attentions to the bearers. Many amusing incidents I could give of persons with really strong letters, presenting the same under the impression that at least some ordinary civility would be shown them, when *au contraire* they were astonished by the very blunt question addressed to them, without preface, of—"Well, what do you want?"

Letters to planters or citizens will be found very useful, and are generally well and politely received, particularly those to the owners of sugar and coffee estates, than whom a more hospitable, kindly people it is hard to find. They are generally very glad indeed to entertain you at their places, if they themselves are living there; or if not, and you desire to visit a sugar estate, are kind enough to forward you, with a letter, to the administrator of the estate, who constantly lives upon it, and will take good care of you.

Clothing for a stay on the island needs to be of the very lightest summer kind; and one can wear, almost without intermission, linen clothes, or a light suit of summer woolens. As to an overcoat or heavy clothing, although I was six months on the island, in every part, including the mountains, and experienced some of the "northers," I never had occasion to remove mine from the box in which I had placed them on leaving New Orleans.

The nights during the winter months are quite cool and

agreeable for sleep, but the middle of the day is always warm, the average temperature in Havana being about eighty degrees. Clothing, particularly linens, of all kinds can be purchased, of the best kinds and makes, in Havana, and at very reasonable prices; and ladies informed me there were certain styles of dresses that could be much better purchased there than at home, some of them being made specially for the Cuban market.

A suggestion, prompted by experience, I would here make to any one intending to leave the traveled routes (as in fact it applies as well to the towns, where they have no baggage carts), and that is to have one's baggage in the shape of good sized valises (*maletas*), for these can be easily handled, can even be put in the car with the owner, and in the country, strapped on the back of mules or horses, which is the only mode of transportation the people are familiar with.

If the traveler is an invalid, and proposes to go to other places than Havana and Matanzas, it will be well to provide himself with an air-pillow, and, if he cannot sleep on a somewhat hard bed, an air-mattress also. Few of the hotels even in Havana are provided with mattresses to the beds, and the pillows are generally stuffed with hard cotton or hair, the beds being a simple sacking bottom, covered with a linen sheet. This may seem, at first, a great hardship, accustomed as we are to our patent spring-mattresses; but I assure the reader they are much cooler and, after a little experience, as comfortable for that climate as are mattresses. Half a dozen towels will not be found amiss, as at some of the smaller places the supply is somewhat short. And in speaking of invalids who are very far gone with any organic disease, very few indeed are ever very much benefited by a stay on the island, any more than that they avoid the inclemencies and changes of a northern winter; though there are cases in which some wonderful cures have been effected, particularly in the Island of Pines.

For the overworked man of business, however, the debilitated or weakly person, or one whose system has from some cause or other become reduced, the climate and scenes of Cuba will work wonders; and all such cases generally go back at the end of the winter completely restored.

But the poor consumptive, who has left it till it is too late for anything in this world to do him good, only comes out here to have his high hopes entirely dispelled, particularly when he finds so many of the ordinary comforts to which he is accustomed, and which are so necessary to the invalid, entirely unheard of.

It is safe for the stranger to visit the island any time after December, though January and February are the gay months, and he can remain until even the first of June, though in May they have it very hot indeed, and also some little fever amongst the shipping.

If it is necessary for the invalid to leave home in October, before the winter of the north sets in, he can visit the island with safety, but will find it pleasanter to go directly to some of the "places of *recreo*," as they are called, near the city,—which are simply pretty villages, such as Guines, Marianao, and Puentes Grandes, where good accommodations can always be had.

There is, however, not much to be done or seen before January, if one wants to make simply a pleasure trip of it; for at Christmas almost all the families visit their estates and distribute presents to the hands, making a week's regular holiday of it; after which the grinding season begins on the sugar plantations, and the business of the town becomes quick and active.

Carnival season, the week before Lent, is the jolly season of the year, when everybody gives up to the spirit of pure enjoyment and mischief; and it is then the Habañeros are seen unbending from their usually dignified manner, and giving loose rein to their tastes for balls, masks, and spectacles.

Holy Week, the closing of the Lenten season, has also its attractions in a country so thoroughly Romanistic as Cuba; and the processions and ceremonies of the church, some of which are carried on with great solemnity and splendor, will interest the Protestant traveler.

Many persons make the trip to Havana and back solely for the sea voyage, from which they derive great benefit, simply staying over one steamer. I have known business men in New York, who would not tear themselves away until actually sent away by their doctors, take the voyage out, remain ten days in Havana, and return thoroughly recuperated men,—so wonderful is the effect of the sea air in the Gulf Stream, and the immense let-up afforded by the entire change of customs, scenes, and language at Havana.

As the steamers are large and well patronized, their accommodations are of the very best class, and one is always sure to find pleasant company on board with whom to while away agreeably the short passage, of even four days.

On leaving New York, the best steamer is undoubtedly the "Morro Castle," which has made the trip in three days and fifteen hours; but all the steamers of that line are excellent boats.

There is a good line of steamers from Baltimore, and about once a month one from Charleston; and there is also a line of steamers from Philadelphia, that make the trip in five days for less price, though with fair accommodations. The steamers from New Orleans, which leave generally once a week, are very excellent boats, making the trip in from two to three days, and enabling a person to leave the north in October, spending the early winter in the south, and gradually, as the weather gets colder, going as far south as New Orleans, where he can take one of these boats, and reach Havana just at the right season to enjoy the Christmas holidays.

The moneys used in Cuba are very easily understood with a little study, and every traveler should make himself perfectly familiar with the names of the coins, as nothing is used but gold and silver, and most of that is Spanish, with small American money as change.

The following is the table of the coins as used :

Medio sencilla,	.5 cents,	The American	half-dime.
" fuerte,	6¼ "	"	sixpence.
Real sencilla,	10 "	"	dime.
" fuerte,	12½ "	"	shilling.
Peseta sencilla,	20 "	"	quarter.

or any Spanish or Mexican coin of that nature that has *no pillars* upon it.

Peseta fuerte, twenty-five cents—any Spanish or Mexican coin that *has* upon its face the *Pillars of Hercules*.

Medio peso,	$0	50	Silver.
Un peso,	1	00	Gold or silver.
Escudo,	2	12½	Gold, Spanish.
Doblon,	4	25	"
Media Onza,	8	50	"
Onza,	17	00	"

It will be seen from this table that there are two kinds of coin,— the "sencilla" (simple) and the "fuerte" (strong). Money sencilla is that of the Spanish stamp, which differs from the others in *not* having on one of its faces the pillars of Hercules; while the money "fuerte" is that *small money* which *has* the columns, the half dollar and dollar, though they may not have the columns, and also any silver money of any of the South American states except Chili, which has been at a discount.

Although with us the *doubloon* is generally understood to mean the seventeen-dollar piece, in Cuba it is always called *ounce*, and when they speak of the doubloon (doblon) they mean a four-dollar-and-a-quarter piece.

Passports should always be obtained before leaving for Cuba, and it is best to get United States passports (not individual state passports), and have them visèd by the Spanish Consul resident at the port one sails from; by doing this the traveler will be saved some delay and perhaps some annoyance, as he can then, immediately on arrival, get his landing permit from the authorities without any trouble, through the interpreter or hotel runner who attends to this matter for the guests after landing.

Since the trouble in the island, the authorities are more strict, and require a passport to be shown for every passenger desiring to land; and for this reason it is now the custom for the purser of the ship to take up the passports with the passage tickets, the boarding-officer at Havana collecting the former when the steamer arrives.

Letters to be safely delivered should be directed to one's banker, or, better still, to the care of the American Consul-General at Havana; and the American traveler will be wise, immediately on his arrival, to pay his respects to our courteous Consul-General, Thomas Biddle, and inform him of this circumstance. His office is No. I Obispo street, which runs along-side the "Plaza de Armas," down to the bay. The postage should be carefully attended to.

Every one will find useful a capital little book called "Guide to English and Spanish Conversation for the use of Travelers," published at Paris by Hingray, and to be had at any of the foreign book-stores. It is a pocket volume, and can be used to advantage by those even who do not know Spanish.

It will assist the traveler vastly, on his arrival at Havana, if he studies a map of the city before reaching there, as he will find, by a proper conception of the true direction in which the streets run, he can save himself many squares in going from place to place.

NOTE.—The following lines run regularly from the United States to Havana :

Lines			Agents in Havana
Bremen Line, from New Orleans,	fare gold,	$30	Upmann & Co. 64 Calle de Cuba.
Atlantic Mail S. S. Co., N. Y.	"	60	Drain & Co., 12 Mercaderes St.
Baltimore Line, from Baltimore,	"	50	R. O. Williams, 26 Mercaderes St.
Atlantic Coast M. S. L., N. Y. and N. Orleans,			D. McKellar, 76 Calle de Cuba.
N. Y. & Mexico Mail Line, from N. Y.			
(Sisal and Vera Cruz,)			Zaldo, Feffer & Co., 25 Obra-pia
Alliance Line, U. S. M., from New Orleans.			
This line stops at Cedar Keys, Tampa,			
Apalachicola, and Pensacola, Florida.			Lawton Bros., 13 Mercaderes St.
Phila. & Southern Mail, from Philadelphia			
and New Orleans,			A. D. Strauss, 2 Mercaderes St.

With a pleasant companion, the above instructions attended to, a comfortable stateroom, and a kind Providence to send soft and favorable winds, I trust you will have with me a truly "*bon voyage.*"

"We left behind the painted buoy
    That tossed at the harbor-mouth;
And madly danced our hearts with joy,
    As fast we fleeted to the South.
How fresh was every sight and sound
    On open main or winding shore!
We knew the merry world was round,
    And we might sail forever more.

Warm broke the breeze against the brow,
    Dry sang the tackle, sang the sail;
The lady's head upon the prow
    Caught the shrill salt, and sheered the gale.
The broad seas swelled to meet the keel,
    And swept behind; so swift the run,
We felt the good ship shake and reel,
    We seem'd to sail into the sun."

                —TENNYSON.

"Blessed be the man that invented champagne!" must be the exclamation of every sea-sick traveler who, after suffering torments equal to those of Dante's "Inferno," begins to recuperate sufficiently to think he could "take something light."

"Even Mahommed," says the Turk, "forbidding in the Koran the use of wine to his followers, saith nothing of champagne; therefore drink I devoutly to the prophet;" for which reason I think the old boy of a prophet, whose venerable beard his followers swear by, must have been himself, at one time or another, sea-sick, and discovered some deliciously cooling brand, only more ancient than the "Veuve Cliquot" of to-day.

It was with some such thought as this that the insinuating suggestion of the steward, "Try iced champagne, sir!" met with a ready assent, and under the miraculous effects of which I found myself, for the first time in three days, on deck, enjoying the balmy air and beautiful skies off the coast of Florida.

"Will make Cuba in the morning, sir," is the captain's reply to my inquiry; and so I stroll forward to watch the porpoises as they race along with the steamer through the blue water, or amuse myself watching the tiny mariner, the nautilus, as it floats lightly on the wave.

With night comes the never-failing pleasure of leaning over the vessel's stern with some charming fair one, watching the ever-sparkling beauties of the phosphorescent light in the vessel's wake, and enjoying that indescribable pleasure of a tropical night at sea.

"Cuba is in sight, sir; can see it through your window," says the steward, rousing me up as I lay dozing on the morning of the fourth day out; and, turning over in my berth, there, sure enough, are seen the hills of Cuba, and the indistinct outlines of the Morro Castle—looking, as I see them through my window, like some beautiful painting to which the oval of the dead-eye forms a frame.

We are fortunate in arriving so opportunely, for, had we arrived the previous evening after sundown, though it were still daylight, we would have been compelled to lie outside all night, as no vessels are allowed to enter after evening gun-fire, at sundown.

There are the signals flying in the morning breeze from the watch-tower of the grim Morro Castle; and as we approach more nearly, we distinguish our dear old bunting, rivaling with its stars and stripes even the bright sky and sparkling waves.

And now we have before us a full view of Havana and its surroundings—the Morro Castle to the left; to the right, the city, with the fort of La Punta (historic, too) on its extreme point—the white,

Havana

blue, and yellow colored houses, with their red tiled roofs, looking fresh and bright in this breezy January morning.

Still later, we are passing within easy stone-throw of the grim-looking Morro, from whose frowning battlements the sentry hails as we go swiftly by; there, to the left, the white walls on the abrupt hills of the Cabañas fortifications; to the right, again, the bay side-walls of the city, with the roofs of houses and towers of churches piled up in close proximity; and there, fresh and green, like an oasis in the desert of stone houses, the small but pretty Cortina de Valdes, looking so invitingly cool in the shade of its trees; some of the other Paseos in the outer portion of the city being marked out by the long, regular rows of green trees that stretch away until they are lost in the distant buildings.

How one's heart leaps at such a quaint, novel scene as this! Havana, around whose walls cluster so many memories of the once haughty Spanish Dons, whose foundation dates back nearly two centuries before our own noble country was settled; what visions of gold-laden ships, of wild, reckless, murderous freebooters, expeditions of gallant early adventurers and discoverers, and more lately the realization of numerous passages of Irving's and Prescott's glowing descriptions, come flooding upon one as he sees for the first time this apparently beautiful city!

Still swiftly gliding on up the bay, passing as we go the Spanish men-of-war and vessels of all nations sailing in and out, we see to great advantage this far-famed beautiful bay; a turn to the right, and we see the long line of covered wharves, with the shipping of the world lying side by side, waiting the completion of their cargoes; to

the left, the white walls of still another fort—the Casa Blanca—that commands the city, and farther on in front of us we see the little town of Regla, with its immense warehouses of solid stone and corrugated iron for storing the sugar of the island, as substantial and handsome in their structure as any the world can show. And now we are at anchor.

The custom-house officers come on board, and the steamer is surrounded by a perfect fleet of small boats, that are a cross between a market-wagon and a scow, from which rush a horde of hotel runners, all expatiating upon the merits of their particular hotels, some of them in the most amusing broken English.

These boats, by-the-by, are afloat what the "volante" is ashore; and as the traveler must needs use many of them if he wishes to see anything of the bay and surroundings of Havana, I give below the usual rates allowed for carrying passengers by the "Regulation tariff for small boats in carrying passengers and baggage in the port of Havana."

For crossing from La Punta to the landing (opposite) of the Morro, 5 cents for each passenger.

From the same point to any vessels anchored near the entrance of the bay,10 cents for each passenger.

Any ordinary trip from the quay on one side to the landing on the other, in the narrow part of the bay, 5 cents.

From the general landing (Caballeria or other) to any vessel anchored in the bay opposite, 10 cents.

From the general landing to vessels anchored above the docks (floating), 50 cents.

From the general landing to the storehouses at Regla (a very pleasant sail), 40 cents.

From the general landing to the anchorage for foreign vessels of war, 20 cents.

For each small valise, 5 cents.

For each trunk, 12 cents.

The passenger who keeps a boat waiting for him while on board ship or ashore, pays at the rate of ten cents for each extra quarter of an hour.

Wet or stormy days, or at night, the boatman has a right to exact *reales fuertes* in place of *sencilla*.

Small boats are not allowed to carry more than five passengers, or the large ones ten!

"From ten and a half o'clock at night until the firing of the signal gun at daybreak in the morning, no boats will be allowed to pass in the bay." The traveler is, however, on all long trips, advised to make a bargain with the boatman, using the above as a guide that he is not overcharged.

The custom-house officers being now on board, we are asked for our passports, which is probably the last we shall see of them, unless we afterwards go to the passport bureau and inquire therefor, the which, with some delays and the payment of four dollars, we finally get. With the experience of a former trip in view, I keep mine in my pocket until I arrive at the hotel, where I get the runner of the hotel, who generally has some friend at court, to get the document properly arranged, thereby saving much trouble.

When first I visited the island, I gave up my passport, never showed a paper, and left the island without passport or trouble; but in those days they were either indifferent or careless. At present this is all changed, and it is perhaps best to comply strictly with the instructions given in the accompanying permit, which will be procured at the hotel on giving up the passport.

WARNING

This permit must be presented to obtain the baggages, which can be landed every day, Sundays and holidays included, from sunset till sunrise, provided the consignee of the vessel has obtained the necessary permit from the collector. Should it contain any articles subject to duties, these will go to the custom-house stores to be dispatched according to the ruling dispositions; and if it were to take place at irregular hours, or on feast days, they will be put in a safe place until office hours.

This permit must likewise be presented to the owners of the house or establishment where the passenger goes to stop, so that he may give the necessary advice to the police.

This permit will enable newly-arrived foreigners to transit in all directions during one month from its date. It will also enable, during the same time, to fix residence in every place in the island; according to it, its presentation is always necessary before the Capitan de Partido, Comisario o Celador respective. After that period, a *pase de transito* is required to travel over the island.

Shipwrecks and military or public functionaries who come appointed to the island or transient on commission service, will pay no fees for this permit.

The want of a passport, or of the compliance to these regulations, implicates a fine of ten dollars.

In Havana, passengers are allowed to land only at the special wharf designated for that purpose alongside of the derrick, where these permits will be distributed and the baggages be examined.

No passenger will be allowed to enter the city without subjecting to these requisites, and will be obliged to justify its fulfillment by presenting the permit and the mark or sign which the custom-house agents put to the respective packages after inspection, to the officer at the door of the said landing office.

No foreigner is allowed to reside more than three months in the island without procuring a *carta de domicilio*, which he will obtain by a petition backed by the Consul of his nation.

Nobody, whatever be his rank or class, is exempted from obedience to the ruling government, and police regulations, and ordinances.

Having made up our mind before leaving the steamer as to which hotel we proposed to patronize, we point out our baggage to the runner of that hotel, who will take charge of it, and we shall have no farther trouble about it, except to pass it at the custom house on landing. The runner has also a boat, into which we go, and have no trouble about fares, the which are settled for, and with the baggage charges will be found in his hotel bill "all right."

Now comes the fun. The passengers crowd into the little boats, a pile of baggage is stowed forward, the sail is set and away skims the little tub to the custom house, each one trying to get there first.

Arrived there, the voyageur has his first experience of a *Cosa de Cuba* in the shape of a stalwart negro who takes a trunk, no matter how large, from the boat, places it on his head, and in the most nonchalant manner walks off with it to the examining office as though it were a trifle instead of a trunk on his brain, if he has any at all of that organ. The officers are very easy and polite in their examination of baggage, passing everything almost with a merely nominal examination, particularly if the keys are politely and readily produced.

And now we are in Havana, and free to go where we like, notwithstanding those two military statues at the door, who look at us so fiercely as we go by.

Outside the custom house will be found hacks, which for twenty cents will carry the traveler where he wants to go, if he desires to ride. If he has studied the map, and wants to walk to his hotel, he will enjoy that more than anything he can do; for it seemed to me things looked more particularly strange and odd when I first landed than they would have done had I become accustomed by degrees to the strange sights and scenes.

Havana! shall I ever forget the agreeable, yet strange, impressions made upon me by thy walls, when, in the full blush of youthful vigor, landing at the custom house, years ago, my foot first trod a foreign soil?—impressions which now, after this lapse of years, and even after months of suffering, are in no wise marred by a second visit, but rather strengthened in their pleasurable emotions. Still the same sights, the same novelties—the clattering of a foreign tongue, the narrow streets, the handsome stores, with their entire contents exposed to view. The variegated awnings, being stretched from wall to wall across the streets, while keeping off the sun, give a strangely pretty yet bazaar-like appearance to them. Still the same funny names of stores—"Palo Gordo" (fat stick), "Leon de Oro" (golden lion), "Delicias de las Damas" (ladies' delight), etc. Here, as we go by the "Café Dominica," which used to be the great resort, we will stop and try *una cosa de Cuba*, which goes under the name of *Refresco*, and is a

Café Dominica

cooling drink of some kind, pleasant to the eye and yet more agreeable to the taste, and while sipping which we can take our first lesson in Havana life.

But here we are at our hotel, and plenty of hotels there are to satisfy every taste and purse, though somewhat different from our great caravansaries like the "Continental" or "Fifth Avenue." To me, however, the ease and comforts (or lack of such, as we know them) of the "Hotel Telegrafo" or "Santa Isabel," are more acceptable with their *café con leche* or chocolate at early morning, their eleven o'clock breakfast of luscious fruits and cool salads, and their abundant and pleasant dinners at five or six o'clock. After dinner comes the delicious drive on the "Paseo," where magnificent equipages, lovely women, and well dressed men, added to the beautiful surroundings of stately, graceful palms, and avenues of tropical trees, make up a scene that will vie with anything the world can show, the day ending, maybe, by a charming stroll in the magnificent grounds of "El Jardin

Botanico," at the Governor General's, where, at no expense, and without let or hindrance, one can wander for hours at a time through a garden that in its luxuriant magnificence of trees, fruits, and flowers rivals anything the eye has ever seen in America.

But as we are studying Havana life thoroughly, we will devote our next chapter to their hotels.

HOTEL LIFE IN HAVANA

"*Café solo o con leche?*" (coffee with or without milk) is about the first thing one hears of a morning in a Spanish hotel, as "Boots" puts his head in at the door to make the inquiry; and as, to make use of a common expression, "you pay your money and you have your choice," you will very quickly decide, if you want to get into Cuban ways, to have it thus early in the morning *con leche.* My reasons for this are that in Cuba the custom is, on first rising, to take only a cup of coffee or chocolate, with a bit of dry toast or roll, which satisfies the appetite until the regular breakfast-hour of nine, ten, or eleven o'clock; and experience has taught that coffee *with* milk on an *empty* stomach is better than the coffee without (or *café noir,*) which is best as a digestor *after* meals. Fruit, also, in the morning on rising is used, and is very palatable; but I think a little experience will show that the Cuban fashion of *beginning* the breakfast with fruit is best.

As the same aphorism is relatively true as regards hotels, the traveler is advised to post himself up as to their relative merits; and to assist him, I have devoted a chapter to those in Havana, all of which I have at various times tried myself, or have had friends try whose judgment I could rely upon for a "character."

But, if any unfortunate traveler should put his foot on Custom-house quay, of Havana, with the expectation or hope that he will find a Fifth Avenue or a Continental Hotel, either within or without the limits of the city, he will be most grievously disappointed.

Havana, city as it is of quite two hundred thousand inhabitants, with abundance of travel at certain seasons of the year, does not boast of one first-class hotel, as we understand the word, though there are several where the traveler, if he is not too particular, can be tolerably comfortable.

There is no giving the reason for this,—the fact is so, and though there are numbers of excellent restaurants kept by Spaniards and French, yet there is but one hotel that I know of kept by those people that is more than passable.

The city is large, there are constant arrivals of people from other portions of the island, and in the winter season there are crowds of travelers from abroad; and yet, if you discuss the matter with a Cuban, he will only shrug his shoulders, and remark, "It won't pay."

But what more can be expected from a city that does not possess a chimney in its whole vast extent of private dwellings? Who ever heard even of a *house without a chimney*? They don't need them here, you say? Well, how do you account, then, for the absence of the other things?—you can't say they don't need them. I mean—oh! I remember now—"modern conveniences," they call them.

Most of the hotels that are worth anything are due to the enterprise of Americans, and some have shown great ingenuity in adapting buildings not intended for such purposes into tolerably comfortable hotels. For some time there was no attempt made to keep an hotel on the American plan; but, thanks to the enterprise of Colonel Lay, a very pleasant and courteous gentleman, from New

Hotel Santa Isabel

Orleans, the Hotel Santa Isabel was opened, with meals and rooms, as far as circumstances would permit, in the American style.

Afterwards, securing the former palace of the Count Santovenia, he fitted it up in thorough American style as a first-class hotel.

In some respects this is the most desirable hotel in the city, as the rooms are large and airy, the house having one front on the Plaza de Armas, where the band plays every evening, and for ladies, a great advantage—that of being waited on by people of their own sex; for, funny as it may seem, in Cuba the chamber-*maids* are all *males*. English is also the language of the house, and people of every taste can be accommodated as to their meals, while the location is in some respects very desirable, being near the American Consulate, and opening upon the bay, where all the life and bustle of this great port can be seen. To my taste, it is too far down in the old city, known as "inside the walls."

The building occupied by this hotel exemplifies one of the peculiarities of Havana life; for even when it was occupied by the Count Santovenia and his family, the upper rooms where they resided being fitted up and furnished in the most elegant manner, yet the first story was occupied as stores and warehouses, very redolent, as I remember, of fish and oil.

In the new city, known always as "outside the walls," when they were all standing, is probably the best Cuban hotel on the island. This is known as the "Hotel Telegrafo," or Telegraph House, and was erected especially for hotel purposes.

It is most beautifully situated in the most convenient part of the city for pleasure, being opposite to the military parade known as the "Campo de Marte," on Amistad street, near the Paseo, the best cafés, and the Tacon theatre.

They speak all languages there, and—a very great advantage—it is well supplied with baths, and one can take meals *à plaisir*.

The Hotel Inglaterra and restaurant, at the "Calle del Prado," is also a very excellent house, probably more particularly so for gentlemen, as one can there take a room and use the restaurant *à la carte*. It is delightfully situated on the Paseo, near the Tacon theatre and fronting the Parque Isabel, where the military band plays every

View in the Parque Isabel showing the Hotel de Inglaterra, Tacon, etc.

night, and is probably in the most lively part of Havana.

From its balconies, most lovely views can be had of the entrance to the harbor, as well as extensive views of the "Prado;" and my memories of some of these on moonlit nights are never to be forgotten.

Hotel de Europa, on the Plaza de San Francisco, is a hotel which, under the *régime* of Mrs. Almy, was as well and favorably known as any in Havana; but it has now gone into the hands of a Cuban. To me, it always partook of the nature of a large boarding-house; and being deprived of some very necessary conveniences, as well as owing to its situation in the old town on the edge of the bay, I was never tempted to stay there long, even with the inducement of its generally having the best of company. For those who like quiet, listless life it offers many advantages.

Experience has shown me that the ordinary American traveler will do well in any of the above hotels; but for me, being possessed of a large amount of curiosity, I prefer to seek out the more peculiar but interesting native hotels.

People making a long stay in Havana can be very comfortable in seeking out some of the large boarding-houses kept mostly by

American ladies, where the terms are very moderate, the meals at regular hours, and the feeling more home-like. Among them are Mrs. Almy's and Mrs. Tregent's, both good houses, where the charges are from thirty-four to fifty dollars per month for lodgings and board of two meals per day, according to room. At the best hotels, the charges are from three to five dollars per day, and this may or may not include wines, which in this climate are almost a necessity; and among the native and French restaurants *vin ordinaire* or *vino catalan* is always served as part of the repast, whether that be breakfast or dinner.

There are several smaller hotels of an inferior kind that only charge two dollars per day, but not having patronized them, I am not prepared to speak of their merits to the traveler.

The most comfortable way—and certainly the most independent way—for a single man who desires to stay some weeks in Havana, is to rent a furnished room, and live at any one of the numerous cafés. By doing this, one lives a great deal better, a great deal cheaper, has a room to himself from which he is not disturbed by an influx of guests, and can come and go when he pleases. Rooms can be obtained of many private families, and at the following places at about thirty dollars per month, furnished: Hotel St. Louis, next to the Hotel de Inglaterra, on the Paseo Isabel—excellent; Aguila de Oro, a Spanish house, with restaurant attached, where one can get most excellent breakfasts—Spanish only spoken—corner of San Ygnacio and Obispo streets.

If the traveler wants to be very quiet and comfortable, in a very nice, airy situation overlooking the ocean, the Morro, and the entrance to the bay, there is a quiet, decent house, owned by a South American, but kept by a German woman, who speaks a little English, and of course German. It is one square from the Paseo Isabel, No. 78 Ancha del Norte, known as Hotel San Felipe. I lived there several weeks very pleasantly, being desirous of enjoying the sea baths, which are right alongside the house, and convenient enough to slip out of one's bed-room in slippered feet, *en déshabille*, at early morning, and take a most refreshing and invigorating plunge in old ocean.

At all places of this kind it is just as well to have it distinctly understood that you are to have your *café con leche* in the morning, attendance, and a proper supply of toweling and clean bed linen; otherwise the supplies in this respect may fall short.

The very best café or restaurant for persons having rooms in the above way is the "Restaurant Français," kept by a Frenchman,— François Garçon,—in Cuba street, No 72, between Obispo and Obrapia streets, in the centre of the city. It is a place frequented by the best of the young foreign merchants, who have their club-tables there.

The *cuisine* and table are unexceptionable, being in the French style; and in no place in the Island of Cuba have I found better or more reasonable living. The charges are quite high enough, if you only take separate meals; but you can make a permanent arrangement at not over fifteen dollars per week, or fifty-one dollars per month, including the *vin ordinaire*, or fair French claret; or, if one wants finer grades of wine, he can obtain them at fair charges; the system is *à la carte*.

The same arrangement can be made, at a little less price, at the restaurant of the Hotel de Inglaterra, but the kitchen and service are not quite so good as at the establishment of "François."

In the street of San Rafael, nearly opposite the Tacon, are several excellent restaurants, mostly in the Spanish style. The "Tuilleries," at the corner of Consulado and San Rafael, is more French than Spanish, where they get up very nice *petits dîners*, and the bills likewise. There is a saloon upstairs for ladies, and it is the only decent one I know of, except François', where ladies can go.

The "Noble Havana," one of these, is celebrated for its shrimps (*camarones*), and particularly shrimp salads.

The "Crystal Palace" is also a very good place, and scattered throughout the city are other places that *look* very tempting, but as they make use of Spanish oil and some garlic in cooking, the traveler is not advised to try them.

The good God, O reader! protect you from some of the indigestions, that in my curiosity and the desire to obtain information I experienced in some of these places; and I can assure my reader that he will not come to grief in any of the above places if he is anything of a voyageur, should he be tempted to visit Havana.

Moonlight view

But if, in opening his room door he should see the "heavens above," or while waiting to have his room assigned him, should hear the clerk say "on the roof," the traveler need not feel alarmed, for choice rooms are sometimes on the roof, called in Havana the terrace; and there it is very pleasant to go and sit, late at night, and smoke the cigar, enjoying the breeze from the sea, and the balminess of the midnight air.

There, in very warm nights, whole families spend their time, and often, while sitting thus, will be heard the sound of the guitar or the music of voices from some neighboring roof.

My room at the San Felipe opened on a gallery that led upon a roof, from which you looked out directly upon the sea,—to the right, the Morro Castle, with its flaming light, and then far away to the west the mysterious line of coast as it lay in shadowy contrast to the moonlit sea. *Ah! que hermosura!* I shall not soon forget those lovely nights.

chapter four

BATHING AND RIDING
IN HAVANA

*Pleasures of a bath after sea-
sickness; Baths, warm or cold;
Changing clothing; Some habits
peculiar to Cuban women; Good
bath-houses; Marble tubs, etc.;
Baths at hotels; Campos Eliseos,
or Elysian Fields sea-bathing;
Bath-tubs hollowed out of solid
rock; Sea-bathing in a norther;
Effects of the water; The bathing
season of the Cubans; Cuban
ladies at the sea-baths; Happy
faculty of Cuban negroes and
horses for sleep; Riding in
Havana; The "Volantes"; Their
drivers; The "Victoria"; Livery-
stable carriages; Private
equipages; Pleasures of volante
riding; Tariff of charges; Don't
fight with hackmen.*

I know of nothing more refreshing, after landing from a
sea voyage, in this warm climate of Cuba, than one of
their *baños calientes* or *tepidos* (hot or warm baths),
particularly if the voyageur has been prostrated by sea-
sickness.

Securing a room at the hotel, after a warm walk
from the quay, still clad in the thick clothing of the
north, it is pleasant, before making the necessary
change of raiment suitable to this climate, to have a
bath as a preparation for the lighter clothing required by
the nature of the climate; apropos of which, it is well to
caution the stranger against dispensing entirely with
woolen under-clothing, as every one will be healthier by wearing
guaze or flannel next to the skin as a precaution against the drafts
which, from the nature of the houses, prevail.

Until lately, most of the hotels and many of the private houses
were unfurnished with the luxury of baths, which in this climate
might be thought a necessity; but now, the principal hotels have
baths, in addition to which, scattered throughout the city, are some
very well arranged and comfortable establishments (*baños publicos*) of
this kind, which are well patronized by the males of Havana, and
which, for a moderate sum, offer every luxury in the shape of good
attendance, marble tubs, tiled floors, and cleanliness in every respect.

In the use of these baths, I speak of the males of Havana, as I was
not able to learn that they are much used by *females*; in fact, there
seems to be a diversity of opinion even among the Cubans
themselves as to the habits of cleanliness of their *women*.

Of course, in matters of this kind, touching the habits of the fair
sex, my authority must be second-hand; but I have been frequently
informed by lady foreigners, long time resident in Cuba, that the only

performance of this kind gone through with by the Cuban women, in the country and small places, is the dampening of a corner of the towel with *aguardiente*, a species of rum, and rubbing with it the face and neck.

As, however, the habits of well-bred people are the same pretty much the world over, the *ladies* and the majority of the females of the larger places are more particular in this respect, I presume; though I confess to being much astonished when, in conversation with a lovely Señorita, she informed me that only during the *temporale* (bathing season) did she ever commit any such indiscretion of bathing, as our women understand it, and then in medicinal waters only; her other ablutions being confined, I understood, to a weekly wash. Her explanation of this wash was rather astounding to my thus far unshaken ideas of cleanliness being the basis of health, and was based, I think, upon climatic influences; but it was only when she repeated, in the most earnest manner, "No! no! Señor; I say water is very bad for the body," that I felt bound to *bow* my assent to her theory, whatever I may have really thought.

There is this difference, which it is well that the stranger should adapt himself to, in their mode of bathing, as I believe from experience it is much the best in this climate,—and that is to take the baths warm or tepid.

Accustomed as I was to the invigorating influences of my daily cold baths, it was some time before I could reconcile myself to warm baths in a warm climate; but I believe that is considered sound practice by the medical fraternity, inasmuch as there is no reaction after a warm bath to set the blood flowing too rapidly, and to excite the skin into a state of perspiration. Be that as it may, one is much cooler for taking his baths tepid (*caliente*) in this climate in the afternoon, the custom being to take the morning bath before breakfast in cold water, and the afternoon bath before dressing for dinner as above.

Inquiry at one's hotel will enable the traveler to find out where are the best baths; but I give for convenience the address of a few considered best.

Inside the walls, opposite the Belen church, corner of

Compostella and Luz streets, is a most excellent place, with barbershop attached; and it is a perfect treat, after a warm walk, sight-seeing in the city, to enter a cool place like this, with its tesselated floor of marble, prettily painted tiled rooms, into which the high main hall is divided, and clean looking marble bath, and enjoy *un baño* before dinner. The charge is usually thirty cents.

Bath room

On emerging from the water, it is universally the custom in Cuba to throw over the person a large linen sheet before applying the towels, and it has a decidedly agreeable as well as beneficial effect.

Down town, at 45 Cuba street, is another excellent place, while outside the walls are the baths of the superb place, "El Louvre."

But the sea baths, of an early morning, are, after all, the best to my fancy, particularly for the invalid, notwithstanding the Cubans assure him "it is death."

This arises from the fact that when we Americans are in Havana it is *their* winter, while it is really equivalent to *our* summer; and the water being that of the tepid Gulf stream, it is warmer than the atmosphere on coming out of the bath; but to us, I think, it is only perceptible when there happens to be a cold norther blowing, and even then, any evil effects can be guarded against with a flask of "cognac." At all events, I bathed every day while I was in the city, and some of the most glorious baths we had were when a stiff norther was blowing that would send the surf and spray dashing far enough over our heads, and even over the roofs of the bath-houses. These baths are situated upon the rocky shore, at the end and left of the Paseo Isabel; there are several of them, but the best are those nearest to the Paseo, and bearing the singular name of *Campos Eliseos* (Elysian Fields).

At this point, the waters of the Gulf roll in upon a shore composed of a species of coral rock, and from this rock these baths

Sea baths

have, at great expense, been hollowed out. There are quite a number of them under one roof, of different sizes,—from the *baño reservado* (private bath), to the *baño publico*, a large place where any one for a *real* can have a swim. They consist generally of basins, about twelve or eighteen feet square, and about eight feet deep; the water in them being kept at an average depth of about five feet by the narrow opening in the solid rock, on the water side, and on a level with the calm sea. This opening permits the flow of the sea in and out, thereby keeping the water in the basin perfectly pure, while at the same time it is small enough to prevent the ingress of any voracious monster of the deep, of which it is said there are plenty outside the rocky walls.

The water in these baths is as clear as crystal, permitting the bottom to be seen distinctly, except at times when there has been a storm, when the sea breaks over the top of the rocks, making a most superb bath of foaming, boiling surf. The present proprietor informed me that about thirty thousand dollars were expended upon these baths, and that they were made about twelve years ago, the great labor being performed by negroes and convicts. They are rented out each season (which generally begins for the Cubans about April 1st, and lasts until October), for the sum of three thousand five hundred dollars. Although in winter time the sheds that cover these baths are usually taken down, owing to the high sea and northers at times, yet there is always sufficient protection for the bather; and I am confident this sea bathing did several of us as much good as the pure Cuban air itself; for it is said these waters of the Gulf are much more strongly impregnated with iodine and salt than are our sea waters, a fact which after some of our baths was very perceptible, by the sort of stickiness felt upon the person; so much so, that it was our habit always after the sea bath to bathe our faces in fresh water.

The usual charge for these baths, supplying towels, and a slight bathing dress, is forty cents for each bath, or twenty cents where the bather finds these articles himself.

It is quite amusing to see on a morning during the *temporale* in April or May, when the weather is hot enough to make even the Cuban women think a bath will be refreshing, even if not healthy, the quitrins and carriages driving down here with their loads of Señoras, generally accompanied by a female servant, to take their sea bath; this they do while their conveyances wait for them, and the driver, with the happy faculty of the Cuban negro, immediately drops into a doze, the horse following generally the driver's example.

To see the curiosities of Havana and its neighborhood properly, there is necessarily involved, in addition to a large expenditure of shoe-leather, much expenditure of *reales* and *pesetas* in cab hire.

Although there are few passenger railways in Havana, yet from the abundance of all kinds of public vehicles it can not be said that they are missed much, since, if it is desired to go to any particular spot, all that is necessary is to wait in front of your hotel or at the corner of the street, and inside of three minutes you will have your choice of perhaps a dozen vehicles, that are constantly passing in every direction, and which, for twenty cents, will carry you to any part of the city.

These comprise various kinds and styles; but the one most in use today, and the latest novelty, is the "Victoria," a very comfortable four-wheeled affair, with seats for two, and in front, a seat upon the box for the driver of the one horse

La Victoria

required to draw it. All of these vehicles are the property of one or two owners, who rent each conveyance out to its driver for the sum of six dollars and twenty-five cents per day, the owner feeding the horses and keeping the equipages in repair.

Such is the constant busy travel, that there is always a great demand for them, even at what would seem a high price, in comparison with what the *caleseros* (drivers) are allowed to charge the passengers; and yet the owners told me they could rent out a greater number still, each driver, at that rate, making from two to four dollars per day.

Wherever you go in the city, you see a constant stream of these carriages going in every direction, without and with occupants; those that are not occupied have a little tin sign hanging over the box, "*Le alquila*" (to hire). One of the owners of a line of these carriages had made over $100,000, and was desirous of selling out and going back to his *belle France*, from whence he originally came.

Although the popular name of the "volante" has made it familiar even to the foreign mind, there is in fact a great mistake about that conveyance,—since the volante proper was a different affair in times gone by, and is to-day, from what is now called volante, which in truth is really the "quitrin." The old volante is now almost extinct, or used simply by some businessman to drive to and from his place of business, or is found in a very dilapidated state in some of the

Old Volante

interior towns of the island. It, like the volante vulgar, is a two-wheeled affair, with long shafts, which rest upon the horse or mule, upon whose back sits the driver in a clumsily made big saddle. The shafts have one end resting upon the axle, the other upon the horse, on the same principle as the poles of the old-fashioned litter; and the volante body is also on the same principle, being with its huge leather springs, constantly in motion from side to side. The main difference between the two vehicles is, that the old volante does not lower its top, which is

permanent, while the volante or
quitrin of to-day permits of the
top being lowered or raised at
pleasure,—a great improvement
and convenience. As public
vehicles in Havana, these are
fast giving entire place to the
carriage and the Victoria; but,

Volante as it is

the private quitrin is, and always will be, one of the *cosas de Cuba*, for
it is the only vehicle used on the bad roads by the families in going
to and from their places, while in the city it is splendidly adorned
and decorated with silver-platings and rich stuffs,—the most elegant
and handsome affair in which the Señoritas can take their airings,
and show off their handsome persons.

It is amusing sometimes to see these long-poled conveyances
attempt to turn one of the corners in the usually narrow streets of the
old town. It is a matter of considerable difficulty, the horse and rider
appearing as though they would have to enter some store-door to get
out of the way of the volante behind it, and is the occasion of much
hard swearing. In 1857, when I was there, the volante was the only
conveyance seen; and now, on the contrary, one sees carriages of all
kinds and styles, of as fine and striking appearance as anything in
Central Park.

But the volante or quitrin of the
livery-stable is, *par excellence*, another
affair, as any one will find out to his cost
who orders one innocently from the stable
without inquiring its expense. When,
however, he sees it drive up with two fine
horses, the *calesero* in a stunning red livery,
covered with gold lace, high boots coming
almost up to his waist, and the horses
decked out in harness that reflects the sun
from a hundred silver-plated buckles,
rings, and knobs, he begins to have a
glimmering that this is going to cost

El Calesero

something, and must "be settled" for.

On the public stands can also be had two-horse carriages, usually very comfortable barouches, and used generally for a party of four or five for a drive on the Paseo. The livery-stables, also, furnish very handsome carriages of the same kind, which with the two-horse volantes, can be had at all times by applying at *the hotels*, as *they* generally have some particular stable at which they get carriages. The prices are in all cases quite high enough.

A two-horse volante for a drive of an afternoon,—say from four to seven o'clock,—costs at least eight dollars and fifty cents, and as much more according to the time you may arrange for; a two-horse carriage, to carry four, costs about the same; and I have known twenty-five dollars paid for a carriage to go some distance in the country and return the same day. If it be desired to take a carriage from the stand, the charges are much more reasonable, and it is quite as good for the purpose of sight-seeing, unless one is desirous of making a splurge upon the Paseo amongst the many other handsome affairs. The following are the regulations and tariff prescribed by the *Gobierno Politico* of Havana.

"Owners of carriages for rent are required to provide their drivers with a sufficient number of tickets for the purpose of delivering one to each person that rents the vehicle, in order that if there is any dispute he may rectify it by calling on the Chief of Police, situated in Empedrado street, corner of Monserrate. Passengers are advised to pay any over charge demanded, since on reporting it at the above office, the amount will be returned, and the driver fined." (?)

Public carriages are required to have posted up in them the following list of prices:

FOR TWO-HORSE CARRIAGES

For a journey within the city to the limits of Aguila street, with one or more passengers,	4 reals.
For a journey to the limits formed by Jesus del Monte, Cerro, Castle del Principe, and San Lazaro, one or more passengers,	one dollar.

For each hour that the carriage is occupied in driving
round, for one or more passengers,   one dollar.
     On wet nights, or other nights after ten o'clock, double the above
prices are allowed.

ONE-HORSE CARRIAGES (VOLANTES OR VICTORIAS),
WITH SEATS FOR TWO PERSONS

For a journey not occupying over half an hour,	2	(sencilla)	reals.
For a journey not occupying over one hour,	4	"	"
For half a day, that is understood as being more than 3 hours,	20	"	"
For an entire day, that is understood as being 8 hours,	40	"	"

The stranger is advised never to ask "how much?" of the driver,
at the end of the journey, as the moment this question is asked, he
instantly suspects you to be a "green one," and demands double fare
accordingly; whereas, in getting out, if you simply hand him the
proper amount as fixed by the tariff, he goes quietly off, without
remark, thinking you are an old hand. Give him but the opportunity,
however, of thinking you are "fresh," and he will protest, by all the
saints in the calendar, and in the most excited manner, that such a fare
(his proper one) is ruin and robbery for him.

     Cabmen appear to be the same the world over; and I shall not
soon forget an amusing episode that took place on our first departure
from Havana. One of these fellows, of an early morning, had carried
us to the depot, and upon settling with him I gave him double fare in
consideration of his putting our trunks in his wagon. This was a
proceeding so unusual, that he immediately thought I must be a
novice indeed, and demanded double the fare already paid him. I
politely declined to comply with his request, on the ground that I had
already paid him double; whereupon he stormed and swore that he
was being robbed, very much to our amusement and that of the
bystanders. I could not resist laughing in the fellow's face at his cool
impudence, which aggravated him so much that he thrust the fare
back into my hand, vowing he would take nothing.

     I thanked him very kindly, and, with the utmost gravity, told him

I would drink his health, and raising my hat to him, politely bade him good-by; and, showing my ticket, was about entering the cars, when the fellow was so taken aback at this peculiar way of meeting him, that he rushed at me, holding out his hand, and remarked, "Ah, you are an American; give me what you please!" upon which I returned him his gift, and left him with a smile upon his countenance, and the remark, "A pleasant journey to you, sir;" when, had you seen him five minutes previously, raving and lamenting, you would have truly thought he really meant what he said.

If any one should happen to reach the city of Havana in the evening, and leave it again at an early hour in the morning, without an opportunity of seeing anything in detail, and afterwards be asked what were his impressions of the city, I am sure his reply would naturally be, "Bells, sir; nothing but bells, sir!" Hardly has the day begun to break, which in Cuba is at a very early hour, when the newly-arrived traveler is startled from his delightful morning doze by the alarming sound of bells ringing from every part of the town. Without any particular concert of action, and with very different sounds, they ring out upon the still morning air, as though for a general conflagration, and the unfortunate traveler rushes frantically from his bed to inquire if there is any hope of safety from the flames which he imagines, from the noise made, must threaten the whole town.

Imagine, O reader! in thy native town, every square with its church, every church with its tower, or maybe two or three of them, and in each particular tower a half dozen large bells, no two of which sound alike; place the bell-ropes in the hands of some frantic man, who pulls away, first with one hand and then the other, and you will get a very faint idea of your first awakening in Havana. Without apparent rhyme or reason, ding, dong, ding they go, every bell-ringer at each different church striving to see how much noise he can make, under the plea of bringing the faithful to their prayers at the early morning mass.

Being thus awakened, it is useless to think of again going to sleep; for it will take some days for the uninitiated traveler to get accustomed to these bells, to which he might truthfully exclaim: "Sleep, there is no sleep; the bells (not Macbeth) have murdered sleep;" and if he is wise, he will avail himself of the cool hours of the morning to make his first inspection of the "city sights." Fail not, then, as soon as your toilette is completed, to order and dispose of your *café con leche*, which must be your sustenance until the breakfast hour of nine or ten o'clock, and sally out for a stroll.

Let us first saunter through some of the principal streets most interesting to a stranger, and these are in the old town,—Ricla, Obispo, and O'Reilly, running down to the bay, and Mercaderes crossing them at right angles, which, if the reader has at all consulted the map, he will feel somewhat familiar with as running through the heart of the city; and I quite envy any novice the peculiar sensations of first going through them of a warm day, when the sun is hot enough for the awnings to be stretched across the street from house to house, formed, many of them, of bright, gay colors, which give a strange but shaded appearance to the narrow streets. Even after weeks of residence, I never was tired of strolling through any of these streets, noting the curiosities and oddities of their architecture, the funny names of the stores, and the curious but attractive way of exposing their goods to the public eye,—not as a general thing in shop windows, but by having the whole store open to the gaze of passers by.

Although early in the morning, the town seems to be quite alive, with men only (for we meet no women), and the volantes and carriages are dashing by as though it were mid-day in our cities. Let us now leave Ricla street, with its sides lined with handsome stores of every variety of jewelry and dry goods, and beautiful fancy things, and even that funny looking store at the corner, which is devoted entirely to the sale of wax tapers of all colors and sizes, from the little taper to the immense pole of wax, looking much like a small hitching-post, with its curious designs painted all over it, all of them for sale to the devout. Now, turning Mercaderes street, we go up a long, well built street, not so full of stores as the others, but still a place of great business, as we can see from the offices and large warehouses. Here we are at Obispo street. Now look out there, and see what a picture of life and bustle that is. This is one of the liveliest streets in town, its sides lined with the most attractive stores all the way out to the old walls of the city, where the passengers through the street seek egress

Obispo street

by means of the gates or *Puertas de Monserrate*; extending at the other end down to the Caballeria quay, at the water-side.

Note now this scene of life, looking down the street. That fine large building on the left hand side, occupying the whole of the square, and quite grand in its architecture,—that is the Captain-General's palace, and the open space you catch sight of below is the "Plaza," or public square; while the building, large and white, that you see at the end of the street, is the former palace of the Conde de Santovenia, one of those combinations of elegant private mansion with filthy store-house peculiar to Havana; for while you see that all the first floor inside of that noble looking arcade is devoted to business and trade,—rented out, maybe, to half-a-dozen tenants,— the upper stories, used formerly as a palatial residence by the aristocratic Count, vying in its interior elegance with any of the private residences in Havana, are now used as a hotel.

Let us take that victoria, and pass up O'Reilly street, equally celebrated as the others, and which also runs alongside of the Governor's palace out to the walls of the city. Here, at the corner of Mercaderes again, is the celebrated café of "Dominica," which, in days past, was the fashionable resort for ladies and gentlemen to get their "*frescos*" and "*helados*" (drinks and ices), but which is now for that purpose old-fashioned, though still patronized by the merchants "down town" during the day, and by the fair ones when they want to purchase the "*dulces*" or sweetmeats candied, for which this place is celebrated as being the largest and best manufactory on the island, and whose products in the shape of bon-bons, dulces, candied fruits, and all manner of sweet things are sent to all parts of the world, having in Europe particularly a great reputation. The café is simply a large marble-floored room or saloon, with a pretty fountain in its centre, and filled with small tables, seated at which you can have your "fresco" *à plaisir.*

One thing will strike the stranger curiously in this old town of Havana, and that seems to be that there is no particular locality specially devoted to the residences of the "best society;" for right alongside a private dwelling, with its trim and neat appearance, may be found some shabby-looking establishment used as a warehouse. Again, you look into a neat hall, on one side of which stands a very handsome gig and carriage, maybe, and you think it is a first-class livery stable or carriage shop; when, in casting your eyes to the other side of the same hall, you see fine large rooms, handsomely furnished, where, perhaps, are seated members of the family who occupy the house.

I was in a constant puzzle, on first visiting Havana, in regard to private residences, for there seems to be no "west end,"—at least in the old town. People of the best class live here, there, everywhere,— some up stairs, and some down, some *in* warehouses, others *over* warehouses and stores.

I remember very well the feeling I had when, wishing to present a note to its address in person, as a social matter, I thought I had made a mistake on finding when arriving at the designated spot a sort of dry grocer's shop, with barrels, casks, etc., scattered around the entrance.

I was, however, reassured when I saw a negro, in a "stunning" livery, harnessing up in the court-yard two richly caparisoned horses. So, plucking up courage, I addressed an individual in the corner of the front hall, busily making cigarettes, and who turned out to be the porter of the house. He directed me to a flight of solid stone steps on one side of the court-yard, which on mounting I found led me up through painted halls into some very handsome galleries overlooking the *patio*, when I had an opportunity of presenting my note in the most agreeable way. *Cosa de Cuba*, indeed!

Dwelling entrance

One cannot help thinking, though, in this queer old town, that the people originally must have lived at daggers' points with each other, or were called upon to resist attacks from some feudal lord, anxious to raise the "tin;" for every house almost is walled like a fort, the doors are thick enough to resist a battering-ram, while every window, even to those on the roof, is barred like a prison, as though the occupants expected to be called on at any moment to resist invasion.

Now let us take a dash outside the walls, to the Paseo Isabel, that stretches outside the old city walls in a wide, handsome street, extending down to the sea, being known as the "Prado" in that part of it lying beyond the Tacon theatre, towards the ocean.

This Paseo is, in some respects, the finest in the city, being wide, well built on both sides, laid out with walks and carriage drives and long rows of trees, and having upon it some of the principal places of amusement; nearly all the gates of the city, when the walls were standing, opened onto it, and it is the general thoroughfare between the old and new town.

In 1857, there were five rows of shady trees all the way down the Paseo, but they have been torn down, in part by a tornado and in part

El Paseo de Isabel

by the authorities, and others, yet small, put in their place; the street has also been lately beautified in several places by the making of new improvements. Fountains are scattered at intervals along the street, some of which add a fine effect. There are other paseos on the bay side of the city, where it is pleasant to go and get the fresh air from the sea, morning and evening.

Beyond the Paseo Isabel is the fine "Calzada de Galiano," a handsome paved highway, with long rows of well-built, striking looking houses, most of them with pillared fronts.

Leaving this street, crossing on our way the "Paseo Tacon," we pass over into the busy street of "Calzada del Monte," one of the strangest, busiest looking streets in the new city, stretching as it does from the city gates past the "Campo Militar," out beyond the Bridge of Chavez, until it finally brings up in the little village of Jesus del Monte, one of the suburbs of Havana. In the city, it is lined with stores and buildings, some very fine, others small, and as you get out farther, there begin to be seen very pretty rustic retreats or summer-houses.

View of the Calzada del Monte

There is also the "Calzada del Cerro," one of the finest streets in the city; the street of "Belascoin" extending out to the sea, and upon which is situated the "Plaza de Toros," and more than all, the beautiful drive, known by its various names of "Tacon," "Reina," and "Principe."

It will take the traveler two or three days to get accustomed to the directions and novelties of the different streets in a town like Havana, where everything is entirely different from what he is accustomed to, and where he can wander about, hour after hour of a morning, finding new novelties at every step, and hardly ever meeting a female on foot,—unless a negress,— noting the fact of the barred windows, which would give to the houses a prison-like appearance, were it not that the bright colors in which they are painted have nothing of the sombre air of a jail, and behind which may occasionally be seen some bright-eyed Señora, in not the most careful toilette in the world. Then the volantes with their curious shapes, drivers, livery, harness, etc., the peripatetic tradesmen with

Cuban Window

their strange cries, and the general bazaar-like appearance of some of the streets attract the eye.

As, however, I found there were so many beautiful paseos and streets to see, I determined it was best to go about my sight-seeing systematically, and therefore divided into daily trips my plans for seeing everything; and if my reader so desires, he can, by casting his eye on a map of the city, accompany me in my walks and drives. To make it additionally interesting, I give here some facts relating to the history of Havana, which I have been at some trouble to gather and translate from Spanish sources,—facts which give extra interest to different localities.

The city of "San Cristobal de la Habana," capital of the Island of Cuba, and one of the first cities of the New World, is situated upon the bay of the same name, but called originally "Careñas" (place of repair). The foundation of the city dates as far back as 1574, but tradition says not in the place it is at present located, but upon the other side of the island, at the place or neighborhood now known as Batabano, and where, it is understood, it existed in1519, when Hernando Cortes started from there on his grand expedition for the conquest of Mexico. Various authorities state, however, that on the banks of the river Mayabeque, that empties into the bay of Batabano, about fifty persons, on the 25th day of July, 1515, settled the town, which, in honor of the day of its erection, or more likely in honor of the great discoverer, they called "San Cristobal," but more lately Havana, from the district in which it was situated. Its location was doubtless selected from the fact of its being a favorable spot from which to carry on a commerce with the South American countries. It would appear that those tormenting insects, the mosquitoes, were the primary cause of the town being removed; for it is stated, on good authority, that they were so thick, and the fevers so bad from the general unhealthiness of the locality, that the town was transferred to the other side of the island, at the little bay and place known then, as now, by the name of Chorrera, about one mile west of Havana, and constituting now one of its suburbs. Diego Velazquez, the conqueror of the island, has the honor of first establishing the town, while Sebastian Ocampo, on his voyage of circumnavigation of the island in 1508, put into the bay of Havana for the purpose of repairing his vessels; and from its excellent natural shelter and facilities, he gave it the name of Careñas (or careening place.)

Velazquez, in removing it here from Chorrera, gave it the name of "Llave del Nuevo Mundo" (key of the new world), from its position for trade and commerce in the newly discovered region of America; and it is today said to be the eighth commercial city in the world.

During its early history, Cuba was subjected to the attacks of the buccaneers or pirates, composed of English, French and Dutch, who attacked, with fire and sword, the Spanish possessions in America; and finally, being sustained by their governments, they came into possession of Jamaica, Hayti, and other of the islands. On one of these expeditions, in the year 1528, they attacked and captured Havana, and setting fire to it, reduced it to ashes. On account of this, the Governor, Hernando de Soto, who was at the then capital of the island, Santiago de Cuba, came to Havana, and upon arriving there, immediately proceeded to put the town in a state of defense, beginning with the erection of the fort known as La Fuerza. This at once gave importance to the town as a fortified place, and at which ever after stopped all the vessels on their way to and from New Granada, or Spain, as Mexico was then called.

In 1551, such was the fear of invasion by these pirates, that the head authorities of the island, being requested to live at Havana, issued the order "that no man, under penalty of a fine, should take off his sword night or day; that no tavern should keep in or out of the house more than one pipe of wine; that labor being scarce, and there being many negroes going about peddling oranges, plantains, etc., this was forbidden under penalty of whipping and imprisonment."

In 1555, Jacob Sores, a celebrated pirate, penetrated into the city, and not satisfied with sacking the church and various houses, attacked the fortress, whose commander sustained himself three days, and only surrendered because part of his garrison were killed and the balance wounded. Sores and his people committed great outrages and murders, and after their departure other pirates arrived and committed excesses. The town was threatened, in 1585, by Drake, but finding it better prepared for resistance than he had anticipated, he withdrew without attacking it. It was from Havana that De Soto sailed, in 1539, on his expedition for the conquest of Florida, and from which he never returned.

In 1589, Philip II ordered two castles to be built for the protection of the town from the pirates. These were the "Bateria de la Punta," and the Morro Castle, or "Los Tres Reyes" (three kings). Their erection was directed by a celebrated Italian engineer, Juan Bautista Antonelli. To pay the expenses of this work, the gold chests of Mexico were required to furnish the means, as well also, from that time, to maintain the garrisons of both forts and La Fuerza, which now amounted to three hundred men. Antonelli also built an aqueduct from the river Chorrera to Havana to supply it with pure water.

In 1592, these forts were still uncompleted, though they were hurried forward on account of the fears that Drake, who had left England for the purpose of raiding upon the Spanish possessions, might make his appearance.

It is curious in this connection to refer to the authorities of the time for descriptions of the appearance of Havana, the houses of which are described as being of straw and wood; all had small gardens, and many of them were protected by double rows of a thick prickly shrub; generally speaking, the furniture consisted of benches and seats, of common woods, without backs. In every "*sala*" there was a religious picture of some saint, before which they constantly burnt lights. The rich lighted their houses by lamps from Castile, filled with olive oil, while the poor simply made use of the common tallow candle. When night came, the streets remained in obscurity, in constant possession of runaway negroes, mountain dogs, and craw fish, which latter are said to have invaded the place in fabulous numbers.

If it was actually necessary for a person to go out on any business, it was always with an armed escort, and bearing lanterns. Even Humboldt, in his visit so late as 1800, describes the streets as being unpaved, filled with mud, and in wet weather almost impassable, and only to be traveled in carriages or on horseback.

During the reign of the Captain-General Cabrera, from 1626 to 1630, the three fortifications of Havana advanced considerably, though they were often threatened by pirates and others; and in 1628, the Dutch admiral, Jolls, threatened them from August to September.

During the command of Juan de Prado y Porte Carrero, the English took possession of the city, appearing off the port on the 6th of June, 1762, with a fleet of two hundred vessels, under the command of Sir George Pickock, with an army of fourteen thousand men, in command of the Duke of Albermarle. The place was somewhat unprepared for them, but in spite of this it made a good defense, particularly the Morro Castle, which was finally taken by assault, after the springing of a mine by the English, on the 30th July. They then took possession of the town, the 14th of August being the day on which the city capitulated. By this success they captured nine frigates of those that had remained in the bay, the three others being sunk at the entrance to block the channel. The English had control of the city for a year, remaining in possession, however, only of the coast from Mariel to Matanzas; but on the 10th of February, 1763, it was restored to the Spaniards in exchange for the Floridas. On the 10th of July, they took their departure, which was celebrated by the Spaniards for the succeeding eight days with great rejoicing.

A number of hurricanes have, at different times, done great damage to the city, particularly the one in 1768, known as that of St. Theresa; and in 1810, there was another one, in October, that caused immense damage,—more than sixty vessels, anchored in the bay, were destroyed, while fields and houses suffered much.

In October, 1864, there was one that did immense damage all over the island, destroying entirely some of the handsomest gardens, fruit trees, etc.

It may be interesting to know that, in 1768, France having ceded to Spain the territory of Louisiana, Don Antonio Ulloa had gone to New Orleans to take possession of the town; but he was received in such a mutinous manner that he was compelled to return to Havana, where Marshall O'Reilley organized an expedition, and went over and took possession quietly of the town, bringing back with him some of the principal citizens whom he had arrested as ring-leaders, placing them in the prison at Havana.

In 1771, Havana as well as other Cuban ports was declared open to the commerce of the world in certain articles of grain, etc., used as provisions, the ports of Seville and Cadiz having been the monopolists of all of the trade with the island. In 1781, there was also a grand expedition that sailed from Havana for the capture of Pensacola, then ceded by France to Spain; and from these two periods the prosperity of the city seems to have commenced.

In 1802, the 25th and 26th of April, a fire consumed in Havana one hundred and ninety-four houses, and left houseless some ten thousand people; but as there was in the same year an order issued prescribing regulations for building, it is probable that there was a good result and improvement from this catastrophe.

Of all the governors who have been in command of the island General Tacon seems to have been the best, doing the most to improve the island, and particularly Havana; making laws, punishing offences, and establishing some degree of safety for its inhabitants. It is reported of him, that he is said, like the great King Alfred, to have promised the Cubans that they should be able to leave purses of money on the public highway without fear of having them stolen. At all events, his name is cherished by every Cuban for the good he has done, and paseos, theatres, and monuments bear his great name in Havana.

There is a story current in Havana, of which I cannot answer for the truth, but which has been so very nicely told in "The Nation," as translated from the work of Von Sivers, a German traveler, that I give it here verbatim:

"Miralda Estalez was a beautiful young girl of Havana, who, after the death of her parents and of her brothers and sisters, found herself sole heiress of her father's house and cigar-shop. She was but sixteen years of age, but the sorrows of her early life had tinged her character with a certain melancholy, which, however, did but enhance the charm of her beauty. Her shop soon became the universal resort for cigars. The idler as well as the busy merchant never failed to make a detour through the Calle de Comercio when they wanted a cigar, and often when they did not want one. She treated all her patrons alike, showing none of them the slightest preference, until at length it was generally said that she specially favored a young boatman named Pedro Mantanez, who plied between the Castle Morro and the Punta.

The Count Almante, however, one of the gayest cavaliers of Havana, paying no attention to the report, persisted in considering himself her favorite, without observing that she was as affable towards everybody else as towards him. For days he sat chatting with her, and when at length he fancied that the proper time had come, he entered her shop one evening, and smoked a cigar, and kept her in conversation till the other neighboring shops were closed, and the streets were deserted. As soon as he thought himself safe from intrusion, he made his explanations, offered her whatever sum she asked for her present shop, and put at her disposal another shop in his palace in the suburb Cerro, where she could carry on her business, if she would live there as his mistress. Instead of replying to the proposal, the girl mentioned the name of another shop where they sold better cigars than she did, and expressed the hope that in future the Count would supply himself there. Almante, thinking she was in jest, came nearer, but Miralda, who seems for a good while to have feared such an event, drew a dagger, and, with flashing eyes, bade him beware; and he retreated. The girl breathed freer then, and congratulated herself on being released from her persecutor. But several days only had elapsed when, in the evening, a squad of soldiers halted at her door, and the officer accompanying it commanded her in the name of the law to follow them. Unconscious of guilt, she did not dare to oppose Tacon's orders, and so obeyed. But when she found that they had passed by the prison, and were taking her out of the city, her fright was extreme, and she entreated them to tell her where they were going. Silence, however, was the only answer she obtained till she arrived at Almante's castle, in the Cerro, where the Count, with a smiling face, received her, and expressed the hope that she would relax her obstinacy. Miralda answered only with a gleam of her dagger as she entered the apartment prepared for her. There she remained several days alone, refusing the visits of the Count, in the sure hope that Pedro, to whom she had related Almante's persecution, would discover the place of her concealment. He did discover it, and, disguising himself as a monk, obtained access to her, when they resolved to appeal to the justice of Tacon.

Pedro at once repaired to the Governor, who gave him a ready hearing.

"Is Miralda your sister?" he asked, with a gloomy expression, as Pedro finished his story.

"My betrothed," replied Pedro.

Tacon then bade him come nearer, and, holding up a crucifix, commanded him, with a look that penetrated to his very soul, to swear to the truth of what he had said. Pedro knelt and kissed the cross, and swore. Tacon then told him to wait in an adjoining room, with the assurance that his affair would soon be attended to. In the course of a couple of hours, Miralda and Almante were brought before the Governor.

"You have abused the uniform of the police for the abduction of this girl?" he said to the Count.

"I was so rash as to do it," replied the latter; "I cannot answer for it before you."

The supreme judge in a moment—"At present I ask you, upon your honor, has violence been done the girl?"

"On my honor, none."

Tacon then wrote a note and despatched it; and, after the examination had been continued and the answers compared with one another in their presence, Pedro, a priest, entered, and Tacon commanded him to perform at once the ceremony of marriage between Miralda Estalez and the Count Almante. In vain did the Count protest, and appeal to his nobility; in vain did Pedro entreat it might not be. Miralda stood as if bereft of her senses, and before one of the party concerned could recover his presence of mind, the ceremony was over. Almante was then commanded to leave the castle, while Miralda and Pedro were directed to remain. Tacon then went on quietly with the other business before him. But half an hour had hardly elapsed, when the officer on guard entered.

"Is my order executed?" said Tacon.

"Yes, Excellencia! Nine bullets passed through the Count's body as he rode round the corner of the street you mentioned."

Tacon then turned to the priest and said, "You will see that the legal announcement is made of the marriage just performed here, as well as the legal announcement of the death of Count Almante, with the addition that, on account of the want of relations to inherit, his widow becomes sole heiress to his property and his name."

Miralda and Pedro were then dismissed with the benevolent injunction to attend to the further prosecution of the case for themselves.

This is in strong contrast with the late General, of whom I have the following from personal knowledge. When I first arrived at Havana, I signified to a lady friend, long resident in the fashionable quarter of the Cerro, my desire to meet some of the lovely Señoritas in her neighborhood; whereupon she informed me that she would give me a "*tertulia*," at which I might see some of the beauties. The arranging of this placed her in an awkward predicament; for at one of the neighbors' houses, where were one or two of the pretty girls, the mistress of the house was living with an official high in authority, as his wife, but yet bearing a different name from his. My friend, not desiring to offend any of her neighbors without cause by leaving them out of her party, called on her, and with English candor told her the purpose of her errand,—that she would be delighted to entertain her with the rest of her neighbors, if she was certain that she quite understood the position of the Doña; but that in her country, when ladies were married they generally bore the same name as the husband. The poor woman burst into tears, and amidst sobs and tears told her the following:

Her husband being very much in love with her, after meeting her several times, had applied to his chief and brother officer, the

Captain-General, for permission to marry.

"Marry!" said the Governor, "Carajo! what a fool you must be to think of such a thing! Have as many wives as you like, but don't marry."

The official insisted that he was truly in love with a pure woman, whom he desired to marry.

"Pooh, pooh!" said the General; "look at me,—I have all the wives I want, and I am not married; and I forbid your marrying her." Whereupon the official came away, somewhat down-hearted; but love getting the better of him, he and his inamorata went down into the country, and were married privately; and taking a copy of the certificate, he sent it, unknown to the Captain-General, with his application to the Queen for permission to marry, the which, not having yet arrived, he was afraid to publicly give his wife her proper name, and to which she was entitled. It would therefore seem that the Captain-General has unlimited power over those in the island.

But to return to Tacon: he certainly did do wonders. Beginning at the root of evil, he finally established his authority all over the island; for the Governor of the Eastern department, having refused to recognize his authority, he sent an expedition of 3,000 men against him. Lorenzo the insurgent, not being able, however, to prevail upon his troops to fight against their brother soldiers and the authority of the Captain-General, therefore fled the island. This matter being settled, Tacon proceeded to put other things in order by issuing the strictest and most severe laws, particularly against the national vice of gambling at the game of "Monte."

As the results of these measures were highly beneficial to every one, it is not for us to judge harshly of measures which would at any other time seem despotically severe; but when we read that in a city like Havana it was not safe to walk the streets after dark without an escort, that the roads were not safe to travel, and communications, unless in large parties, were therefore stopped from one part of the island to another, and that known murderers stalked abroad publicly without fear of molestation at the hands of the bribed authorities, it must be confessed we must join with the Cubans in their belief, that Tacon was indeed *un hombre muy grande.*

Hurricane of 1846

It was during his career that the first railroad was completed, under the direction of the "Junta del Fomento." He established night-watchmen, a police corps, and a fire department.

On the 10th day of October, 1846, the most violent hurricane ever known upon the island took place, the barometer during the day falling very rapidly, and the wind beginning to blow from E. N. E., increasing to a violent gale, accompanied by rain, and augmenting its force up to ten o'clock in the morning. In its course it destroyed one thousand eight hundred and seventy-two houses, sank one hundred and eleven coasting vessels, one hundred and five others, besides seriously damaging sixty or seventy more; destroying completely the Coliseo theatre in Havana, besides a total number of five thousand and fifty-one houses, while hundreds of persons were injured or killed, the country between Bahia Honda and Sagua la Grande being in many places laid waste, though Havana seemed to be the centre of destruction.

And now, to-day, notwithstanding the attacks of pirates, of fire and sword, and of hurricanes, Havana is a well built, large city, and very attractive to the stranger. Its streets are mostly paved with stone, but, having no gutters, are very wet during the rainy season, though during the winter, when travelers mostly go there, they are in very good order. Being cleaned at night by a force of negroes, all of the refuse of the city after twelve o'clock is set directly upon the narrow side-walk beside the doorways; it is, therefore, advisable for the benighted traveler to take to the middle of the street to be out of harm's way. The police system, with the military guards, seems to work very well; for, though I have passed through some of the loneliest portions of the city late at night, I was never disturbed, nor did I ever hear of any particular cases of robbery or assault; but since the troubles in the island, this has somewhat changed.

Excepting on the quays, at the water side, the old city was surrounded by stone walls, bastions, and forts, to which are attached a great degree of historical interest, as they date back, portions of them, from the earliest history of the town. The moats in late years were all occupied with vegetable gardens, bath and store-houses, and used for other than military purposes; while the grim, grey old stone walls stood still solid, and, I may say, useless, with their ten bastions and seven entrances on the land side, while on the water side several batteries and bastions looked out upon the bay. Thus, as the city has grown so immensely, it is well they have been mostly pulled down.

On the other, or east side of the bay, there is also a considerable population, under the shelter of the principal series of fortifications which stretch from the entrance to the upper end of the bay, comprising the Cabañas, the Casa Blanca, and little town of the latter name, as well as the busy place of Regla. This bay of Havana is a noble bay indeed, not so extremely large either, but having good depth of water and being so completely sheltered from the storms. Its channel or entrance is about one thousand four hundred yards long, and about three hundred and twenty-five in width, and the harbor is composed of three almost distinct bays, bearing the names of Triscornia, Marimeleña, and the Fondo, or depth of the bay between Guanabacoa and the castle of Atares. The water is of such depth that vessels of the largest size can be moved to the quays; and it is quite a novel and interesting sight to wander along these well-built wharves,

under the shelter of the roofs supported by iron columns, which serve
to protect both the merchandise and the merchants from the sun and
rain, and see the long line of bowsprits almost touching the walls of
the edifices facing and upon the quay.

The situation of the city is such, being in some degree a
peninsula extending into the bay, that the streets generally run at
right angles to the bay, and would, if it were not for their narrowness,
receive the benefits of the different breezes; but this narrowness is an
advantage, when in the middle of the day, the sun gets so hot that one
is very glad to take shelter on the shady side, the shadow of the
building not permitting the sun to penetrate entirely into the street.
In addition to this, the awnings can be more easily stretched from
house to house, making quite a cool, pleasant promenade. Here, for
instance, is a portion of O'Reilly street, looking down which you see
the old tower of the venerable church of Santo Domingo, while above
one's head nearly all the way are these fancy awnings, bearing the
signs of the different stores opposite which they are stretched.

Havana, whose government is confined to its jurisdiction, which
extends to all the villages and suburbs within a certain distance, as
well also as to the Island of Pines, is the capital of the island, and the

O'Reilly street

headquarters of the jurisdiction of Havana, as also of the governments, political and military, of the Western department. It is the residence of the Governor Superior, the Captain-General; of the Superintendent General, the Diocesan Bishop, the General Commandant of the Marine, the Intendente of Royal Property of the whole island, and of the "Royal Audencia Pretorial." It has a literary university, collegiate seminary, preparatory schools, and two meteorological observatories, besides various other public institutions of science and learning, and comprises within its actual limits the little towns of Casa Blanca, Regla, Jesus del Monte, Arroyo Polo y Cerro, while there are a number of small places that pass as the suburbs—as Puentes Grandes, Marianao, Guanabacoa, etc.

The total population, according to best authorities, is one hundred and ninety-seven thousand, a large share of which are blacks and mulattoes, free. The inhabitants, as a general thing, appear to be as polished and well dressed as in the most civilized cities of Europe; yet as a rule, the women are so only in appearance, being, many of them, though the possessors of large means, very illiterate; but of course, it is here, as with the best society everywhere,—there is a higher class exceedingly refined, and well educated either in the United States or abroad.

Generally, the men appear to be intelligent and well informed, though I must confess to being surprised at the want of knowledge of—in fact, the indifference to, the peculiarities and places of the island. Every young man's ambition seems to be to go "north," while the women look upon the United States as a country to be dreamed of as a fairy vision, where life and liberty are to be really enjoyed, or as one sweet innocent inquired, "Every one is free there now, Señor?"

"Oh, yes," I replied; "we have no negro slaves there now."

"No, no! Señor; you don't understand me. I mean the women, too,—are they not free?"

To which I was compelled to reply they were, and only we poor men were their slaves.

"*Es muy bueno, Señor*; it is not so here."

First morning in Havana

Cocoa milk

MARKETS OF HAVANA

IT is always a matter of interest to the traveler in any land to know how and from where the supplies of food for the people generally come; and this is best seen by a visit to the public market-place, where not only the material with which they are fed can be seen, but a great deal may be learned of the manners and habits of a certain class of the people themselves.

Therefore, as fruit is said to be best in these warm climates before breakfast, we will stroll down to the markets, and while doing a little inspection duty, make an investment in some of the fruits of the country.

The most convenient one inside the city is that of the "Mercado de Cristina," in the Plaza Vieja, situated at the corner of Teniente Rey street and San Ygnacio. Here, in the centre of a hollow square, the sides of which are formed of ranges of stores of all classes, faced by an arcade, is one of the great marts for the sale of vegetables, fruits, and meats for the supply of the city. It is a large stone building apparently, though really a simple quadrangle, open to the sky, occupying the whole of a square, and was erected in 1836, during Tacon's administration, the model governor of the island.

The arcade of stores is filled with shops of all kinds, but principally occupied in the sale of such "notions" as will please the country people or the negroes, while the Plaza is filled with immense piles of onions, and cabbages, and sweet potatoes, which are the principal productions of the island in the vegetable way; and there are smaller piles of oranges, green mangos, pine-apples, and other tropic fruits, new in name and appearance; clusters of the plantain, or banaña, as we call it, of various colors, and pyramids of the green cocoa fruit meet the eye at every turn, all presided over by dusky

Mercado de Cristina

negroes in all varieties of costume, or swarthy Cubans, the native country people. These come in from the surrounding country with their products, raised upon the small *estancia* in the neighborhood of the city. Here and there, too, may be seen the patient donkey, with his load of green fodder, giving comic life to the scene. Of these market-places Havana possesses four,—the one we are now in, and another known as "Del Cristo," inside the walls; while outside are those of the Place de Vapor, or Tacon, and of Colon. The only two worth visiting being this one of Cristina and that of Tacon.

The plantain, of which we see such large quantities exposed, is the vegetable upon which the lower classes depend for food, and which is cooked in various ways; and with the *"tasajo"* (jerked beef, or fish), constitutes the diet of the poor. Of the many delightful vegetables that grow in such abundance in our summer season there is not a single one to be seen. Of berries of any kind there is not one raised upon the island, as far as I have seen, owing to the great heat which burns them up, it is said. The market presents a very different appearance from one of ours, with its profusion of everything arranged in the tidy looking stalls, and presided over by clean looking venders. Here it is very different; a great proportion of the market people are negroes, most of whom are free, and such a chattering as they keep up, particularly the women, who are scolding, laughing, or railing at each other in the most deafening way. It is very amusing to walk along in front of the little tables, or more usually the piles of fruit on the ground, and buy some of the queer-looking fruits you see, and which are totally unheard of by the names which the negroes give them, many of them, nevertheless, being quite palatable. The little banaña and the orange are, however, the most agreeable of all, tasting

very pleasant and cool in the early morning before one's breakfast; but there are others that are very luscious when eaten perfectly ripe and in season, and which the market people will gladly tell you all about, as soon as they find you are a stranger,—particularly an "Americano."

The choicest of these, after the luscious pine-apple, orange, and banaña, are the delicious "*anon*," the "*sapote*," and the "*mamey colorado*," the latter

Fruit seller

sometimes called "angels' sweetmeats;" any of which, if they happen to be in season, will please the palate of the stranger, if he is fond of rich, luscious fruits; many persons find them too rich and sweet.

Having heard so much of the milk of the cocoanut when drank fresh from the green fruit, I seize this opportunity to get a new experience of a *cosa de Cuba*; and, negotiating for a good large one, for which I pay *un medio* (five cents), the negro takes a huge sharp knife, and slices off for me the top of the fruit, in which he punches a hole from which I am to drink. Seizing it with both hands, I raise it to my mouth like a water-jar, and empty the contents, as I think, down my throat; and sweet, cool, and pleasant it certainly is to the palate, only this is rather an awkward and inconvenient way of drinking it, as I find on examining my shirt front, which has received a good share of the contents.

A much more convenient way is to carry the green cocoanut to one's hotel, and there, pouring out the milk into a big glass, add plenty of ice and a little brandy, and it makes a delicious drink,— sweet and wholesome,— pronounced capital as a diuretic.

Strolling through the market, one sees every variety of Cuban peasant and negro,—many of the latter coming into town only to bring a small quantity of the sugar-cane, which is bought and eaten by the people with great zest. Then, in going through the stores surrounding the market, one sees innumerable strange sights and articles, a busy throng of buyers and sellers of all kinds of merchandize, of oddities and antiquities of architecture; and, perhaps, heard above all the din and bustle, are the loud nasal tones of the lottery-ticket vender, calling out in his protracted high key the number of the tickets he has for sale.

From here we will stroll over to the fish market, or "Pescaderia," as it is called, and see another *cosa de Cuba*. This is situated over on the other side of the town, on the bay side, and we reach it by going directly along the street Mercaderes, on the lower side of this market, which comes out directly opposite the fish-market, in Empedrado street.

It is a well-built stone building, with the lower portion open on the side facing the street, and supported by pillared arches, which give the place somewhat the appearance of an arcade. In the interior, as permanent structures, in lieu of tables, are square stone forms with tiled tops, upon which the fish, fresh from the sea, are exposed for sale, and which are of great variety many of them resembling ours,— such as the flounder, and bass, and one something like the blue-fish. All the fish on the coast are very fine, with some few exceptions,—as the *pez espada*, *gato*, *picna*, and some others that have the peculiarity of making persons sick, or poisoning those that eat of them.

Of all the many species (and there are said to be one hundred species and more), the *pargo* and the *rabi-rubia* are the best, being somewhat scarce, except during the prevalence of north winds in the

Fish market at Havana

winter season, when they sell as low as twelve cents per pound. The shark, small and large, in pieces or whole, may also be seen here for sale, under its name of "*tiburon*" the which abounds in these waters, and from it is extracted the oil. It is very fierce, and many accidents happen each year from persons recklessly going in to bathe in some of the bays frequented by these creatures, who attack the swimmers without hesitation, and gobble a leg or arm, or maybe the whole person; the little ones, that are called "*cazones*," are eaten.

Their fish are not all brought from along the coast, but many of the larger fishermen have properties on the coast of Yucatan, and bring the fish from there, as also from Florida and the Tortugas. Generally, however, the first come from the coast in the neighborhood, many being caught just off the bay; and if the traveler desires to try the sport, any of the boatmen around the Punta can put him in the way of going out.

At the little village of Chorrera, directly on the coast and about two miles from Havana, is, however, the great fishing place for this district, and one can go out any time, taking the passenger (horse) cars

Real Casa de Beneficencia

at the station opposite the Tacon theatre, and going out there. The cars leave every hour, take about half an hour to go, and return the following hour; fare twenty cents. On the way out, the traveler passes through a portion of the city he is not otherwise likely to see, that is parallel with the coast, passing by, also, the large charitable institution, the Real Casa de Beneficencia, at the corner of the street Belascoin. This is a flourishing institution, being an asylum for destitute orphans and the prevention of vagrancy, by putting all vagrants therein. It was established during the time of Las Casas, in 1790-96, and in 1802 enjoyed the protection of the Marquis Governor Someruelos, who at one donation bestowed twenty-five thousand dollars. It is a fine, large building, and has beautiful grounds.

The village of Chorrera itself is a small place, celebrated as being the first site of Havana, and as being the place where the English attacked and landed, the commanding officer of the fort or castle blowing it up and retiring. There is now a queer looking tower, with portcullis, still there for protection, though the Fort Principe commands the place.

It is rare indeed that a meal in Cuba is served without fish, for even in the interior some of the streams are abundantly supplied. It is stated by one of the old authors that that was the reason all the settlements were located on the coast of Cuba by the early inhabitants, in order to be convenient to the supplies of fish.

El Manati

In connection with the inhabitants of the deep, there is one that they have in Cuba, known as the *manati*, a species of sea-hog, somewhat resembling those met with in Florida,—different from the sea-calf or cow,—that frequents the mouth of the rivers, and even mounts up on the earth. From its flesh they make *tasajo*, its oil is useful and medicinal, and from its skin canes are made that are very beautiful but very expensive.

Of the shell-fish there is a great variety,—amongst them the lobster, the craw-fish, and (best of all) the shrimp, both salt and fresh water, which is *par excellence* the most delicious thing they have on the island, being as tender and resembling the white meat of the crab. They are eaten simply boiled, and served cold with a little salt, or made into a delicious salad. Some of them are quite large, and resemble a lobster-claw, are considered very wholesome, and used in great profusion all over the island. *Camarones*, bear in mind, is the name for them in Cuba, and they are identically the same as those we have south.

The Cuban oysters are quite small, and it would take a dozen of them to make one of our noble York river oysters or chincoteagues; but they are nevertheless very good, being very appetizing, eaten at breakfast, as they have the briny and somewhat coppery taste of the French oyster.

To finish up the morning's walk before breakfast, let us take a victoria out to the other market of Tacon,—unless, indeed, you want

La Punta after a norther

to turn the corner here, go up those old stone steps, and take a stroll along the Paseo de Valdes, which is cool and shady at this hour in the morning. Then, too, perhaps at this end near the steps, we may see some odd kind of fish we have not seen in the markets, for this is also frequented at times by fishermen, who do a small trade with the negroes, cutting up the small fish, even into quarters and halves, to sell to those villainous, filthy looking negroes, who are probably too lazy to work to buy themselves better food.

On our way out, since it is a fine, breezy morning, and the sea is coming in heavily, we will pass by the Puerta de la Punta, and see the surf beating on the rocks in a most beautiful, violent way, dashing the spray high in air. This is always the case after a norther; and it is a most attractive sight, either after or during one of these blows, to come out here on the point, and see the ocean worked up into a state of fury, entirely different from its usually calm, placid appearance; and here, just outside the gate, is always to be seen a lively party in that cove-like place with the gravelly shore,—for here gather, of a morning, some times as many as a dozen or more negro drivers, with

Malojero—Guajiro

their two and three horses each, and entirely naked, except a short pair of pants. They swim the animals into the salt water, which is most excellent for them. It is a jolly sight, when the sea is rough, to see these fellows, laughing, shouting, and singing, enjoying their bath on horseback, the sea breaking clean over them at times, and the horses bracing themselves against the shock with their hind quarters to the waves.

The odd looking building you see in the back ground is the old Bateria de la Punta, and the end of the new building is part of the government ordnance shed; the circular-looking iron affairs scattered along the shore being the old-fashioned sugar-pans.

And now for the Plaza de Vapor, which is a market very similar to that of Cristina, known more generally as "Mercado de Tacon." It is situated at the corner of Galiano and Reina streets, or *calzadas*, the name generally given to fine wide streets like avenues. This market is rather better in appearance than the others, being elevated some distance above the ground, and is two stories in height, with very good sized stores around its four sides, with the portico facing on the street, the market itself being inside the square.

Here we have the opportunity of seeing to advantage special types of the lower class of Cubans,—countrymen as well as citizens. Here, for example, is the *malojero*, who comes from some distance in the country simply to bring that load of *maloja* that he has on the back of his horse, and which is the product of an inferior kind of corn that does not run to seed, and is raised with so little trouble that these lazy fellows prefer to let it grow on their places rather than trouble themselves to plant crops that require cultivation and attention.

The *guajiro*, or small property-owner from the country, is also seen here in his glory, with his varied stock of produce, seeking a market.

There is rather greater profusion of fruit here, but the meat carts with their uninviting loads are in appearance bad enough to take one's appetite away, as he sees these sides and quarters swinging to and fro, or piled up one upon the other in these small carts which bring the beef from the *mataderos* on the outskirts of town, no butchering being allowed within the city limits.

The shops, and in fact the whole market, present the same general appearance as the others; if you see one you see them all, with, perhaps, this difference—that there is always a great variety in the colored human nature, which at times presents itself very grotesquely to one's notice.

One of the best and pleasantest ways of getting an idea of Havana within the walls, and particularly that portion of it lying on the water side, I found to be to hire a carriage by the hour, and start early in the morning, or, if more convenient, after an early dinner in the afternoon, when the sun is sufficiently down to make it cool.

There is always this disadvantage in going anywhere within the old city in the afternoon,—that almost the entire general business of the city is confined to this portion of it; and as most of the mercantile houses do no business after four or five o'clock, that portion of the city at the water side does not present as lively an appearance as in the early hours of the morning, when the business community, taking advantage of the freshness and coolness, attend to most of their business out doors and upon the quays, which thereby present a much more stirring and active picture to the stranger. On the contrary, outside the walls in the afternoon all is life, fashion, and pleasure.

We direct the driver to enter the city by the extreme north gate, known as La Puerta de la Punta, which is the entrance at the extreme end of the city on the bay, and where commenced the walls of the old city, which are here entered by an ordinary stone arch, some twenty-four feet long, the sides of which were casemates for storing artillery implements, etc., while the top of it formed a battery *en barbette*, with terreplain, stone rampart, and a slope leading up from the ground; while mounted for defense were some half-dozen rusty, old-fashioned carronades that would be no earthly use in case of need; across from it can be seen the Morro. Inside the gate and extending along the

Morro Castel and Punta Gate

street, parallel with the water, quite up to the Maestranza, is a stone covered way, with a stone parapet to serve as breastworks in case of need. Outside the gate and to the left is the landing quay, or the point used for landing and embarking timber, horses, etc., and a good place whence to start for the Morro Castle, there always being a boat or two there. Continuing down Cuba street, we come to a fine, large building on the left hand, evidently a modern affair, built of brown stone, and several stories in height. Here are the offices and officers' quarters, and in fact the head-quarters of the artillery, known as the "Maestranza," or Parque de Artilleria. Keeping on down past the building, we come to the street Chacon, turning into which to the left we can go inside the arsenal belonging to the Maestranza, where is a large supply of ordnance of various kinds, and a number of old bronze cannon, bearing some very antique inscriptions and strange names, such as the "Peacemaker," the "Thunderer," etc. Immediately opposite to this is the entrance to the Paseo de Valdez, which extends along the bay side to Empedrado street. We direct the carriage to meet us at the other end, and then find it pleasant to stroll down the walk. Though the Paseo is not now in the best order, it has still a pretty row of trees, stone seats, and always a delightful breeze, and commands a fine view of the fortifications across the bay. At the entrance there is a sort of an arch and fountain erected, which, though now in sad repair, has been in its day quite handsome, and, as its tablet informs us, was erected by the corps of Royal Engineers, in 1843, the slab upon which is the inscription being marble from the Isle of Pines, and on the top of which are grouped different symbols of the military and particularly the engineer profession. Here, of an early morning, it is pleasant to stroll, if you have nothing better to do, and hear the music of the military bands performing inside the walls of the Cabañas opposite, and which comes softly and pleasantly mingling with the breeze of the ocean, which is only a short distance off.

Entering the carriage, we drive through the street Tacon, passing the Pescaderia and the Intendencia, which is directly in front of La Fuerza, the oldest fort in the city, and around which cluster many traditions of antiquity, of assaults and defences, and attacks of pirates and enemies. Desiring to enter and see it, we pass around into the barrack yard on O'Reilly street, and are permitted to go through it. It is still a star-shaped bastioned fort, having a good line of fire upon the entrance and the bay, and having fine, large quarters near it for the troops.

This old fort dates back as far as the time of Fernando de Soto, the conqueror of Florida and discoverer of the Mississippi, who, being governor of the island, gave orders to the engineer, Captain Aceituno, to build, in 1538, this fort, allowing for the purpose the sum of $4,000,—the which was paid by the inhabitants of Havana and Santiago de Cuba, for the purpose of having a fortified place on this side the island. It was completed six or seven years after it was commenced. At the beginning, it was simply a quadrilateral of walls of double thickness, twenty-five yards high, with arched or casemated terreplains, and a bastion in each angle, the whole encompassed by a foss. In subsequent years, it has suffered various reforms, but still is of the general form as when first erected.

The portcullis and the barracks of the troops were erected in 1718 by Don Guazo, the then governor-general. De Soto's wife, it is said, died here, after waiting many years for news of her gallant husband.

La Fuerza

The statue on the top of the castle is that of an Indian, who (so runs the legend) was the first to receive Columbus on landing. Opposite is the public square, known as the Plaza de Armas, and on the west side of that is the residence of the Captain-General of the island.

The large building adjoining the square of La Fuerza, is the head-quarters of the military governer of the city, the official who grants permission to visit the Morro Castle and Cabañas, at the written request of the consul.

In the lower part of the same building are the "Administration and Treasury" of the Royal Lottery, as also the Monte de Pieté, which latter charitable institution makes loans at eight per cent upon pledges of gold and silver, and is supported by the government with a capital of $80,000.

The sentries and guards on duty at these two places are worthy of a little attention from those fond of military matters. They are generally picked men, whose "get up" is quite unimpeachable when on duty during the day, being clad in a uniform of pure white, with trappings, "neat and gay," of red cloth, and who, in their comfortable linens, look "natty" and soldierly.

Passing around the square to the lower or east side, we come to what is known as "El Templete" (little temple), at the corner of Ena street.

Tradition relates that in 1519, on the removal of the city to its present site, there was celebrated under an old ceiba tree the first mass in commemoration of this event; and upon this same spot was erected, in 1828, the present temple to perpetuate it. It is a substantial stone building, not very large, erected in imitation of a Grecian temple, with a portico and pillars, standing some distance back from the street, from which it is protected by iron railings connected with heavy stone columns, the whole resting upon a solid base of stone. Within this railing stands the stone column that marks the spot where the old tree grew.

El Templete

Only once a year is it open to the public, and that is on the 16th of November, the feast of San Cristobal; but there is really nothing within it to attract the stranger, as it contains simply a bust of Columbus, and two or three ordinary paintings.

We now direct the driver to "Plaza de San Francisco," which is between the streets Lamparilla and Amargura, facing the Quay de Caballeria, and reached by passing through Officios street, running in front of the custom house.

As we enter the square of San Francisco, the old yellow building at the left hand corner is the former "Hotel Almy," now "Europa," probably one of the most celebrated in its day of any in the city. It was

Plaza de San Francisco

there that Dr. Kane, the arctic explorer, died, the hotel occupying the second story over the warehouse. On the opposite side of the Plaza, the antique, worn looking building is the old church of San Francisco, which has had its formerly sacred halls turned into a custom house store-room.

This old church, it is said, was in its day the best church in the city. It was consecrated in 1737, and shut in 1843. Its tower to-day is the most elevated one in the city, the immense weight of which is supported upon the arches of the principal doorway.

It is a singular looking old building, and has undergone some changes since its occupation for business purposes. The towers have been despoiled of their bells, and an additional door knocked in its side. The front of the church, in the narrow street Officios, can not be seen to advantage; but in the niches, of which there are two, one on each side of the front, there are queer old statues, in stone, of monks, one of whom, from his peculiarity of attire, is readily perceived to be a Franciscan.

As one looks at these *hard* old boys, that have stood here for so many ages, he is struck with the thought of what capital sentries they have made. Posted, each one of them in his niche, like a sentinel in his sentry-box, they have stood here, doing that which they were placed here to do, without any relief ever passing around in so many years to make a change for them. There they have stood, year after year,—aye, scores upon scores of years, too,—and seen these portals, that once swung back only for the entrance of the devout and prayerful, open for the entrance of the worldly, with their bales of goods; there, calm and immovable, they have seen the busy throngs of ages past go by, and yet still they stand impassive and inanimate as in days of yore, as the busy throng of to-day still goes by, many of whom, throwing but a casual glance at these stolid old fellows, perhaps know not, and care less, that this was the first place where their mothers' mothers knelt and prayed. Though the world has changed, though governor after governor has come and gone, though the small group of houses that once was the original town has grown into a vast assemblage of what is now a fine city, though other churches have been erected,—aye, even amid the roar of the tempest and the lashing of the stormy waves which in the wild fury of a tropical storm have dashed almost to their very feet,—there they stand still, not a muscle changed or a position altered since they were first posted in their stony guard-houses, on guard.

Passing through the handsome iron gateway which separates the square from the quay, you enter upon the landing, known as the "Caballeria," being a portion of the continuous wharves that extend from the Castillo La Fuerza to the marine barracks and quarters, and the whole of which is devoted to shipping purposes. Here, any morning, you will find a busy throng of merchants, clerks, etc., talking, and smoking, and driving their bargains,—for this is, in fact, the Exchange,—while the active portion of the business is done by sturdy negroes and swarthy laborers of many climes.

The whole series of quays is covered so completely with roofs that one may walk a considerable distance free from exposure to the sun, amusing oneself in examining the variety of vessels—of which there are crowds, side by side—from every nation in the world.

In this ocean-loving city of Havana, boatmen take the place of the persistent cabmen who assail one the moment of coming from a depot. Here, the moment you put your foot upon the quay, every boatman imagines you must want a boat, and a crowd gathers round you immediately, each vociferating the name of his boat, and you have considerable difficulty in getting away from the swarthy, piratical-looking fellows who cease not to accost you with—"*Quiere bote, Señor?*" all desirous of securing you for a *paseo* on the water.

The quay of the "Machina" is next in order, adjoining that of the Caballeria; and on leaving the square of San Francisco, it is just as well to tell the driver to go to "El Correo," the post-office, which is at the foot of Ricla street, and just above the Machina.

Before the doorway of the "general delivery" at the post-office is the "Commandancia de la Marina," or the quarters of the commanding officer of the marines, with the marine sentries on guard at the door, the street between the two buildings being covered in by an archway.

The general mail for all the island is daily, and closes generally each day at 4.30 P. M. It takes six days to go from Havana to Santiago de Cuba, to which place it goes partly by rail and partly by horse; between small places and towns with no railroad facilities the mails are only twice a week. Letters for the United States are best mailed at the Consul's, or at the offices of the steamers or mercantile houses, who generally have a private mail-bag by each vessel. Every letter that is put in the post-office requires Spanish postage stamps, as follows:

On the island, each half-ounce, five cents; city delivery (of which there are two deliveries daily, generally 7 A. M., and 3 P. M.), two and one-half cents. The boxes marked "Correo," are to be found in various parts of the city. Ten cents on all letters going out of the island for each half-ounce. Letters must be asked for by number and not by name, for the reason that, after the arrival of each mail, lists are made out, and the names, with a corresponding number, stuck up in glass frames in the post-office; and the stranger, by looking over the list, and seeing there his name, asks for the *number* set opposite.

And now we are catching the fresh breezes from the bay on the Quay de Machina, or machine wharf, which is the landing used for the men-of-war, and is, in fact, a naval storehouse on a small scale.

Machine Wharf

The objects that will probably interest the stranger here are the state barge of the Captain-General, a very large and gorgeous affair of a boat, as also the very diminutive garden, about the dimensions of a good-sized parlor, seeming to be made simply to see how small a garden can be. It is quite pretty, though, with miniature walks, shrubbery, and flowers, and also a fountain containing gold and silver fish, the whole affair being surrounded by an iron railing, and guarded by some nautical individual, who takes great delight in showing you through, particularly if one tips him a trifle *para beber*. It is really a curious place from its wonderful smallness; add to which there are two of those most ridiculous looking birds, the flamingos, which seem to be retained here as pets. They were the only ones that I saw on the island, although there are numbers found in different parts. They are of a delicate pink color, shading off into a yellowish white, with very long necks, which they are constantly contorting in the most ridiculous manner; and with their short bodies resting on their long, bony legs, they look as though they were mounted on stilts, from which they keep bowing and nodding at each other in the most laughable way. Just beyond the quay of the Machina are the ferries for crossing over the bay to the little village of Regla, where are the wonderfully large storehouses for storing the sugar, and which are seen in the engraving on a previous page; also, the depot of the railroad for Matanzas, and for Guanabacoa. The boats run every five minutes to the other side, the fare upon which is ten cents each way. They are exceedingly well built boats, having all been made in the United States (as in fact are nearly all the steamboats in Cuban waters), and are kept in very good order, more so than most of our ferry lines. If one has nothing better to do of a morning, it is quite a refreshing trip to go and return on one of these boats, since there is a fine view of the different portions of the bay, the shipping, and the city; add to which there is always a fine breeze felt on them when in motion.

Flamingo

Stretching from these ferries, almost continuously, are what are known as *paseos*, or promenades. They are a species of boulevard, in fact, running parallel with the bay, laid out in trees and a well made walk, with solid stone wall, erected at the water side, and fountains and stone benches scattered at intervals throughout their length, some of the former being very pretty and tasteful in their designs.

The first and most imposing of these paseos is that of the "Alameda de Paula," erected, in 1802, by the Marquis Governor Someruelos. It is also called Lalen O'Donnell (after the marshal of that name, who was inspector of the island), and is situated between the quay De Luz and the bastion of "Paula," overlooking the bay. It has seats of stone, trees on the land side, and a breastwork on the water side formed of a balustrade composed of plaster concrete, with ornaments of the same, alternated by iron railings. In the middle there is a semi-circular *glorieta*, or stone look-out, furnished with seats, behind which is a handsome stone fountain, having in its centre a marble column with military trophies and national symbols in very good taste.

Alameda de Paula

Next to this one is that of the "Paseo de Roncali," from which one has a fine view of the upper part of the bay, with the castle of Atares in the background, and fine views of the surrounding country. This is a beautiful place of a moonlight night to get a view of the bay, but is not much frequented. This castle of Atares that you see in the centre of the bay is said to be the one where young Crittenden and his fifty fellow-prisoners,—all young men from the United States, who had come out in the Lopez expedition,—had been captured, and were there shot, being brought out, twelve at a time, compelled to kneel down, six at a time, in front of the other six, and thus were all gradually murdered. A noble story is related of old Mr. Crawford, the then English consul, who, disgusted as every one else was by the inaction of our consul, Mr. Owens, when seeing these poor fellows shot down, went to the authorities, and told them that these massacres must cease; that though these men were Americans and filibusters, they were yet human beings, belonging to the Anglo Saxon race; and that, if the shooting did not cease, he would throw the English flag over them on the score of humanity. All honor to such a

Castle of Atares

noble, brave spirit! and I am glad to say it was appreciated by the Americans living at the port at the time, for they presented him with a handsome set of silver.

As a matter of curiosity, to see what is understood by a navy-yard in Cuba, it is well to pay the "Arsenal" a visit, where is at once the naval dock, navy and store yard, situated at the extreme south-western corner of the town, just outside the walls where they commence at the water side. It is entered from the city by the Puerta del Arsenal, and with its pretty officers' quarters and green trees, looks quite attractive from the outside. At present, it certainly does not amount to a great deal, though it has ship-houses, docks, machine-shops, and other things peculiar to naval construction. In days past, however, the arsenal of Havana was very celebrated. In 1722, they began building vessels of war, and quite a large number were built; and the vessels obtained such a good reputation from the excellent quality of wood used that an arsenal was, in 1728, regularly constructed, and finished in 1734.

In 1766, the "Santisima Trinidad" was constructed, carrying one hundred and twelve guns, and in the same year the arsenal was rebuilt, having been damaged by the English in their taking of the town.

Cannon were also cast at one time, of bronze, the copper being furnished on the island from the Cobre mines; but everything in this way seems to be at a stand still, the yard deserted, and no work of any important nature being carried on. The dock is capable of docking a vessel of one thousand tons, and their engine is of only twenty horse power. Everything is very different from the bustle and life and extent of our navy-yards, and even the excitement of the Chilian war did not seem to rouse up any new life in this department.

And now we will finish up our morning by returning by the way of "Los Ejidos," a street running inside and parallel to the old walls. Here were some of the most interesting features about Havana, giving it that old air of walled antiquity, and offering some attractions to the student of history in the events so closely connected with their construction. Some are still standing, in tolerably good order, though they all have a somewhat dilapidated look, and are all to be torn down. A good smart cannonade would knock them to pieces very quickly. They are of not much use now, for they may be said to be in the very heart of the city, and would be of no avail in a strong attack against the city, as a city, except as a *dernier resort* for a small body of men. Guards were, however, still mounted at some of the gates, and cannon yet frowned from the grass-grown battlements; and the moat, with time and indifference, had become filled with all manner of structures,—even truck gardens being laid out in some of them.

These gates and walls used to be of great interest to most travelers, as they were, for so many, many years, connected with the history of the old city of Havana; and though as walls they no longer stand, yet the expression has become so familiarized that one still hears " inside the walls" and "outside the walls" freely used.

When this improvement of laying out their sites in new buildings has been completed, it will be a great improvement to that part of the town, consolidating the entire city in appearance; but in our engraving of the city we have still retained their outline, as marking out the historical old, from the new.

Tierra Gate

As portions of these walls are still in existence, and the trenches also, with their nondescript appearance, it may not be amiss to give here some historical facts pertaining to them.

Some of the gates were constructed with an eye to architectural beauty originally, but are now among the memories of the past. The best of them, I think, was the Puerta de Tierra, near the Ursuline convent, on Sol street, which still looks well, and had a somewhat imposing design. The gates of Monserrate were probably more used than any other of the gates, there being two of them,—one of egress, and the other ingress, for the busiest streets of Obispo and O'Reilly

As early as 1589, under the superintendence of the Governor and engineers Lejada and Antonelli, these walls were traced out, destined to take an important part in the defense of the town from the repeated attacks of the pirates, and have lasted nearly three centuries. In 1633, under Flores, they were regularly begun, and in 1740, were in great part finished, except the covered ways and the ditch, which were not completed until 1797. In 1664, Flores' successor, F. Davila Orijon, finding that the public exchequer was short of means, decided not to continue them with the same solidity with which they had been built, and therefore made them thinner, with supports. In 1670, however, they were continued in a solid manner, there being employed upon them as many as nine thousand *peones* at a time, contributed by the planters, who were desirous of seeing the town made safe. They were continued through the years, with slight interruption, from 1680 to 1687. In 1695, under Diego de Cordova, they extended the fortifications of the capital, completing the chain of walls from La Punta to the Tenaza and the hospitals of San Francisco; and in 1702, under De la Vega, the walls were considered finished; but they still, in 1724, under the command of Martinez, worked upon them, completing those from La Punta to San Telmo, from El Angel to the bastion of La Tierra, and from the angle of the Tenaza to the collateral bastion. In 1789, it was found that a portion of the walls had suffered from the washing of the water, and it would be necessary to strengthen them, which was done by breaking up half the principal walls, and strengthening them from both sides. They now remain solid throughout.

Old city walls

THE CHURCHES OF HAVANA

If the old adage be true, that "the nearer the church the farther from God," then I fear much the Habaneros have no hope of future salvation; for to almost every square in the old city, within the walls, there seems to be a church of some kind, to many of which are attached religious societies or organizations.

The priesthood and the church have probably a greater share in the life of the Cubans, particularly with the female portion, than anything else that goes to make up the sum of their simple daily life; and as one strolls along the street, he is met at almost every turn by some priest of some particular order, either in shovel or three-cornered hats, or, perhaps, like a stout old Franciscan,—whose vows prevent him from having anything *comfortable* in this world,—forced by the heat of the sun to forget his resolution of baring his head to the elements, and sporting an enormous palm-leaf, that answers the purposes of both hat and umbrella. I was considerably interested, after a while, in studying out the peculiarities of   the wearers of the different hats, and I finally came to the conclusion that the shovel hats were a badge of good living,—for nearly all their wearers were stout, jovial, hearty looking priests,—while the three-cornered ones had a young, thin, unfed, Oliver-Twist-like look about them (though these hats all have their particular meanings, according to the order to which they belong).

The superior authority of the secular portion of the Cuban church is the Captain-General, as Vice Royal Patron, and as his deputy in the Arch-bishopric of Cuba, the Commanding General of the Eastern department. There are attached to the church a number of dignitaries of different grades, all drawing salaries in proportion to their rank; while the government of the church is divided into four vicarages and forty-one parishes, the grand Cathedral being situated in the town of Santiago de Cuba. Besides the churches actual, there are a number of convents, monasteries, etc., belonging to the different orders of St. Domingo, San Francisco, Jesuits, San Augustine, etc., etc.

The Cuban church, in comparison with that of other countries is said to be poor, especially in the Arch-bishopric, the temples needing the magnificence and those church ornaments that the traveler on the continent of Europe admires so much. Notwithstanding, in some of the principal towns there are a few imposing structures, interesting from their great antiquity and ancient style of architecture, while upon special occasions the services carried on are tolerably rich and imposing.

There is a regular tariff of prices to be charged for all such ceremonies as in a more Christian land are thought to belong to the duties connected with the church. A baptism, for instance, from one dollar upwards; a burial five dollars; and marriages, masses, and prayers for purgatoried souls in proportion,—the poor being attended to without charge.

The church has charge of the cemeteries now, the burials in old times taking place in the church itself, since it is only in consecrated ground a true Catholic can rest in peace; and up to within a few years it was never permitted to a heretic, dying in his unbelief, to be buried in any of the cemeteries for the above reason. Since then a provision has been made for the interment of strangers.

These cemeteries are generally composed of a series of stone niches, in rows like (if I may use the expression) so many bake-ovens, and the burial in which (each niche containing only one body) costs from thirty to one hundred dollars; there are also vaults costing as high as three hundred dollars.

The feast days (*dias de fiesta*) are very numerous, and, with the Sundays, that are also considered as such, make great inroad upon the working days of the year. The legal feast days, with necessity of hearing mass and ceasing all manner of work, are called in the island two-cross days (*dos cruces*), and are marked thus, ‡, in the almanacs; and others on which work is permitted, but the obligation of hearing mass required, are called days of one cross (*una cruz*), marked thus, †. Besides these, there are other days —*feriados*, or days of shutting up the courts, on which the different tribunals do not work; also, days on which souls are drawn from purgatory (equivalent to All Souls' day), marked *anima*. Add to these the regular holy days, and as each town and village has its Patron Saint's day, which is also strictly observed; days in honor of the reigning sovereign, consort, their parents, and the heir to the throne, called *besamanos*, at which all the principal officials, in full dress, are required to pass before the Captain-General as representative of royalty; it will be readily seen that the working days in the year cannot be very numerous, it being computed that there are only two hundred of such days in the three hundred and sixty-five.

The first church that the traveler from any land (and particularly we Americans) will desire to visit, is the Cathedral, not from any great beauty of itself,—though it is, perhaps, the most interesting church edifice in the city of Havana,—but since within its walls lies ensconced beneath a simple slab all that remains of him who gave to the world, from his combined wisdom and courage, not only a new continent, but also a new theory of a world—Columbus.

This old church, now the most magnificent one in the city, is very odd indeed, seen from the outside. It stands facing an open square, at the corner of Empedrado and San Ygnacio streets, in the extreme north-eastern part of the city. Constructed of a peculiar colored brown stone, now blackened by age, it has no great beauty in its exterior architectural design; but yet, with its two queer old towers, its facade of pillars, niches, cornices, and mouldings, it is a striking looking edifice. It was erected in 1724, for a college of Jesuits, who at the time, occupied the site where now is the palace of the Captain-General. It is composed of the church edifice itself and the capacious buildings adjoining for the use of the priests of the order. It was, in November, 1789, constituted into a cathedral; has one large doorway in the centre, and two smaller ones, one on each side of that, with a solid stone piazza, reached by short flights of stone steps, at its front. There is also a side entrance by means of a stone court, on the other

Old Cathedral

side of which are the dormitories of the priests. I made several visits to this old church, and upon one of them, in the middle of the day, when the church was closed, we were taken through the church by the rear entrance, and shown the *vestiari*, or robing-room of the priests, where superb robes were carefully put away in immense chests of drawers, in a room in the rear of the choir. Our guide on that occasion was an uncleanly individual, with a "cross-eyed" expression of countenance, who would insist on trying to describe the church to us, in most horrid French and English instead of his native Spanish, which so impressed us with the idea of his abilities and position, that we came very near not tendering him the usual gratuity,—an unpardonable mistake, had we committed it.

The church is shown to strangers at any hour of the day, by inquiring of any one of the priests you meet in the courtyard, and it is also open every morning and evening for mass; though it is best seen, I think, in the morning, when the soft sunlight comes into the building, giving good effect to the shadows and shades of the massive pillars and arches; while the kneeling devotees serve to illustrate the great size of the structure by comparison.

The grand altar is very handsome, as is also the choir in the rear. The carving of the stalls is exceedingly fine, being done in polished mahogany, in very light and graceful designs. At intervals around the church are several very beautiful altars, formed with solid pillars of mahogany and cornices and moulding of the same material, richly gilt upon the most prominent parts. Each one of these altars is devoted to some particular saint, and boasts of some very good altar-pieces, copies of Raphael, Murillo, etc.

The grand object of interest however is the "Tomb of Columbus;" and it is astonishing how many people there are who come to Havana that are ignorant of the remains of Columbus being in the precincts of Havana,—having been transferred from the place of his death.

History tells us that Columbus died in Valladolid, Spain, on Ascension-day, the 20th of May, 1506; that his body was deposited in the convent of San Francisco, and his obsequies celebrated with funeral pomp in that city. His remains were afterwards transported, in 1513, to the Carthusian Monastery of Seville, known as "Las Cuevas," where they erected a handsome monument to him, by command of Ferdinand and Isabella, with the simple inscription, borne upon his shield, of—

À CASTILE Y LEON,

NUEVO MUNDO DIO COLON

In the year 1536, his body and that of his son Diègo were removed to the city of St. Domingo, in the island of Hayti, and interred in the principal chapel. But they were not permitted to rest even there; for on the 15th of January, 1796, they were brought to Havana, and interred in their present tomb, amidst grand and imposing ceremonies, participated in by the army, navy, and church officials, and an immense concourse of spectators. To use the words of a Spanish author: "Havana wept with joy, admiration, and gratitude at seeing enter within its precincts, in order to guard them forever, the ashes of Cristobal Colon."

The ashes, it is understood, were deposited in an urn, which was placed in a niche in the wall, at the entrance and to the left of the chancel of the cathedral. Over this has been placed a slab of stone, elaborately carved, in a stone frame, and representing the bust of Columbus in the costume of the time, a wreath of laurel around his head, and symbolical emblems at the foot of the medallion, upon which is inscribed, in Castilian :

> "Oh, rest thou, image of the great Colon,
> Thousand centuries remain, guarded in the urn,
> And in the remembrance of our nation."

Well may the question be asked: Where, then, were all the muses when they inscribed such lines as these?

One morning, after making the accompanying sketch, I became so lost in thought in trying to realize the great lapse of time since these ashes, now lying dead and useless within the urn, had been the heart of Columbus, beating with the pride and hope of new discovery,

Tomb of Columbus

that I did not notice the church had been closed, and I was left alone with my sketch-book and my meditations. I tried a door or two, and found them all fastened, and was beginning to think I might have to spend the day there, when, fortunately, there appeared from out the chancel a negro attendant, accompanied by a very nicely dressed youth whom I took to be one of the acolyth. Having satisfied their curiosity with my sketch-book, I mentioned to them my desire to leave those hallowed walls for the most convenient place of breakfast; whereupon I was desired to follow through the chancel and out by a room or two to the inner gate, which was unlocked for me. Here, desiring to reward my darkey attendant, I bestowed upon him several reals, never dreaming of the nice young man's accepting any gratuity, and to whom I bowed my serious respects as he stood, with much dignity, at the door; but he, having no such scruples as I had endowed him with, placed his hand upon his breast, and said, "Señor, I too; you certainly will not forget me, sir;" whereupon I "settled," and departed, having learned the lesson, that "palm oil" is good in more ways than one. I' faith, one is accustomed to pay to enter a show, but they don't often charge to let one out.

Another church is Santo Angel, a small, old church, at the corner of the streets Los Cuarteles and Compostella. There is nothing there to attract the stranger; but its old-fashioned tower is almost the first one he sees in coming in sight of Havana, it being close to the walls, in the upper portion of the city. Coming down Compostella street, at the corner of O'Reilly is the queer old church of Santa Catalina, built in the year 1658, and to which is attached a nunnery, I believe. The church itself is not remarkable in its architecture, being one large hall, without pillars or arches, and with but few paintings; the

Tower Santo Angel

cloister partition is, however, a fine piece of carved mahogany, the altars are very gorgeous in white enameled paint and gilding, with paper flowers, and over one of them is the recumbent figure of the saint after whom the church was named.

At the corner of Aguiar and Empedrado is a very old church indeed,—that of San Juan de Dios, being built in 1573; otherwise, there is nothing remarkable about it. It has the usual number of altars, etc.

San Felipe, at the corner of Aguiar and Amargura streets, is rather a small church, but possesses a number of handsomely decorated altars;—the principal altar-piece is a very fair painting. Attached to this church is a large library, mostly of religious works, however.

The church of St. Augustine, corner of Amargura and Cuba streets, is worthy of a visit, since it is a large church, belonging to the third order of Franciscans, and it is in many respects a curious church. It was built in 1608, and has a great many richly decorated altars. The altar-piece over the grand altar is one mass of paintings in gilt frames, representing a variety of subjects of a scriptural character; it has also some *alto relievos* of the Crucifixion. The roofs of many of these churches are well worthy of attention on the part of the visitor, since many of them are made, with a great deal of skill and ingenuity, of different woods, and some of them of curious designs.

During carnival season, there is posted up, in conspicuous places, a notice to the faithful that they may go and sin for a certain time, under certain restrictions. It strikes one as rather odd to see upon the doors of churches a placard like the following:

"Pious invitation, that directs to the faithful of this city his Extreme Excellency, Señor Bishop Diocesan. Desiring his Illustrious Excellency to afford to his very much loved faithful ones the spiritual practice of doctrines, with the greatest abundance possible, for the salvation of their souls, he has ordered that there shall be two missions in this capital during the present Holy season. His Extremely Illustrious Excellency makes known to all and to each one of the faithful that goes to hear the word of God in this Holy season, that he concedes to them *forty days of indulgence* for *each time* that they thus do so, and also, as special apostolic favor, a *full indulgence* to those that attend *four* sermons in said missions, and confess and worship devoutly; all of which," etc., etc.

That is very liberal, certainly, on the part of his Excellency.

The Church of Santa Clara is a large and capacious church, at the corner of Sol and Cuba streets, without any remarkable peculiarity, other than that it is the wealthiest nunnery in the city,— unless we except that it has, of an early morning, many beautiful devotees, who, as is generally the custom, select that hour for attending mass. None of the churches are provided with pews or seats, as with us, and only in a few can you find one or two long benches, placed length-wise in the church, for the accommodation of, generally speaking, the male portion of the community, who do sometimes attend. The ladies are usually accompanied by their servants, who, entering the church with them, carry an elegant rug, of fine material and beautiful colors, which they unroll, and spread upon the stone floor for their pretty mistresses to kneel upon and say

Church of Santa Clara

their prayers, while many of them carry, also, a light, cane-seated chair, which is placed convenient to the rugs, for their mistresses to rest themselves upon from their kneeling posture, and at their leisure to gaze round the church to see who of their acquaintances, male or female, are in the church, while they keep up the never-ceasing and graceful movements of their beautiful fans.

The Belen church, at the corner of Luz and Compostella streets, occupying nearly the whole of the square, is remarkable as having the largest dome and tower in the city. Although the church edifice itself is not very large, the whole square is occupied by buildings pertaining to it. It and the hospitals belonging to it were erected, in 1687, by the bishop of Compostella, who, as the authorities of the time relate, was an exceedingly intellectual, amiable, and charitable priest. It has or had attached to it a school for girls, and the seminary of San Ambrosia. The front of the church is somewhat curious in its architecture, and stands back some distance from the street, being reached through a small but luxuriant garden, in which may be seen a number of the tropical plants and trees peculiar to the country. It is now the Royal College of Havana, and open to visitors. Probably the only other church in which the traveler will be interested is that of "La Merced," on Cuba and Merced streets, it being a very large and imposing

Belen Church

structure, with a very venerable and antique pillared front that looks as if it had been exposed to the elements for a thousand ages, so dark looking and frayed is the stone from the effects of the weather and age. They were making a large addition to the chancel when I was there, erecting a dome and beautifying the interior in various ways, so that it will probably rival any church in the city; though I should much prefer it in its respectable antiquity of appearance. It has many handsome altars, and some old paintings, one of which, a very large one, on the wall at the left-hand side near the chancel, I was very much interested in—giving as it does a *miraculous* history of its patron Saint "Merced," or Mercy. These old, wonderful church legends always remind me of the *fairy tales* of my youth, and I read them, therefore, with eagerness. This may amuse the reader also, since it is somewhat historical, and *not noted* in the works of any of the biographers of Columbus that I have read.

It is a large, old painting, representing in the foreground a group of Indians, each one of whom resembles a Peruvian Inca, but in no way the simple natives that Las Casas describes were found upon the island. In the centre of the picture a wooden cross is seen, upon the arm of which is seated a female figure, with an infant in her arms, while in the background is the figure of a priest, behind whom are gathered a number of Spanish soldiers. I tried for some time to understand what it could mean, and finally succeeded in finding, down in the corner of the picture, upon a scroll, the following inscription, in old Castilian, which, being freely translated, saith:

"The Admiral, Don Christopher Columbus, and the Spanish army, being possessed of the 'Cerro de la Vega,' a place in the Spanish island, erected on it a cross, on whose right arm, the 2d of May, 1492, in the night, there appeared, with her most precious son, the Virgin, Our Lady of Mercy. The Indians who occupied the island, as soon as they saw her, drew their arrows, and blazed away at her; but, it appearing that they would not stick, the Spaniards took courage, and, falling upon the Indians, killed a great number of them; and the person who saw this wonderful prodigy first was the V. P. F. Juan," etc., etc. (?)

There are a number of other churches, but they offer nothing particular, that I know of, to the curiosity or interest of the traveler, though I question if there is not something in almost every one of the churches in Cuba that will strike the Protestant traveler as odd or curious; whether it be the highly decorated altars, the remarkably adorned figures of saints, the queer-shaped confessionals, looking, some of them, like old-fashioned easy-chairs, the peculiar architecture, or the appealing mottoes of the poor-boxes, to say nothing of the tottering and strange looking old people, of whom one always finds a number, white and black, either sitting or praying, in every church. As for me, the churches were a never-failing source of amusement and interest, either to see the service or the pretty women, or hear the music in the soft hour of vespers.

The confessional

chapter nine

OUTSIDE THE WALLS

For a simple drive outside the walls, on the Paseo, in order to see and be seen, the afternoon hour of five or six o'clock is decidedly the best; but for combining pleasure with the business of sight-seeing, give me the cool, breezy hours of early morning, even though one does not then expect the pleasure of seeing the bright-eyed occupants of the elegant quitrin on his journey.

The driver is directed to start with us from the end of the Prado, which opens directly upon the sea, with the Morro Castle opposite, on the other side of the entrance, while close at hand is the queer old fort of La Punta, originally a bastioned, star-shaped fort, now somewhat rambling in its form. This is, also, one of the antiquities of Havana; for on the very spot where it now stands landed the pirate, Robert Baal, when he attacked and burned the city, in 1543. San Salvador de la Punta, which is its original name, was begun at the same time as the Morro, and by the same engineers, in 1589, and finished in 1597.

To the left of the Prado, directly on the sea, can be seen the various sea baths. Now facing toward the city, we begin our journey down the street Prado, or Paseo Isabel, a wide, capacious street, arranged as a boulevard, with rows of trees in the centre, beneath which are, at intervals, stone seats, and a promenade for foot-passengers, and on each side of this again, the drives for carriages. The sides of the street are occupied by rows of fine buildings,— private dwellings, many of them,—with pillared porticos, and tasty fronts, of white or blue. This drive was first begun in 1771, and in 1772 was first opened. In 1797, under Santa Clara, it was extended, and several fountains erected upon it, and in Tacon's administration it received some improvements.

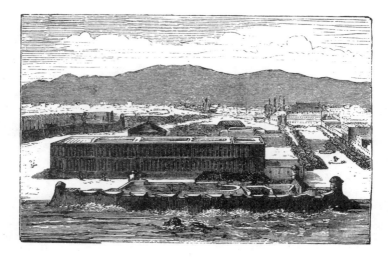

The Royal Prison

After leaving the Punta, the first building that we notice is the large yellow one to the left hand, occupying a whole square. It is the Royal Prison, and general head-quarters of the council,—singular combination,—the front on the Paseo, being used as quarters and offices, while the rear part, facing towards the walls, is the public prison for malefactors. This was also erected in 1771, and is in the form of a hollow square, the court-yard of which is used by the prisoners for exercise; and they can be seen any day through the iron-grated gates or windows, as well also as much of the prison as one wants to see. The student of physiognomy will find some interesting subjects at these windows any day, about twelve o'clock, when the prisoners are sometimes allowed to receive, through the gratings, packages from their friends, being first inspected by the sentries always on guard in the narrow, barred passages which separate the outer and inner world. The large open space beside the dungeon is used as a parade-ground; and it was here that the unfortunate Lopez met his death, dying like a brave man, after the unfortunate expedition, which, induced by the promises of the Creoles, he had conducted to Cuba, and in which he was defeated. Here, in the presence of a vast body of troops, on the 1st of September, 1871, he was garroted, his last words being: "I die for my beloved Cuba."

Scattered along the Paseo, at different intervals, are various fountains of stone and marble, many of them of very handsome design, and a few of them of some antiquity, though nearly all of them appear to be dry. On the right-hand side of the Prado, No. 86, is the Gymnasium and Fencing School, where is the best gymnasium in the city, with a very excellent instructor in Lewis' system of calisthenics, and dumb-bell exercise, as well also as a good French master-at-arms. The Cubans are, many of them, very fine gymnasts; and of a morning, from seven to nine, there is generally a very good class exercising under the supervision of the instructor, who speaks English. To the left is the theatre of Villa Nueva, a rather poor affair, and used mostly as a French theatre, or for the smaller Spanish dramatic companies. It is built of

Fountain

wood, principally, and never seems to be well filled, though I saw a most excellent French company, from Paris, performing there to very slim audiences. It has now become a historical place, from the fact that it was here the troops fired on the audience while attending a representation, during the present troubles.

On the Prado, opposite the gates of Monserrate, is what is known as the "Parque de Isabel," a portion of the street being laid out with grass plots, gravel-walks, trees, and handsome iron settees, while in the centre is a marble statue of Isabel II. Opposite to it, on the western side, is one of the finest blocks of buildings on the street, in which are situated the Hotel de la Inglaterra, Café St. Louis, and at the corner, El Louvre, the café for ices and sherbets, *par excellence*.

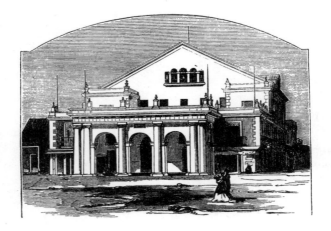

Tacon Theatre

On the corner of the street San Rafael, opposite the Louvre, is the Tacon Theatre, a not very imposing building from the outside, but the principal one of the city, and very handsome in the interior. It was constructed in 1838, during the command of Tacon, the governor-general, whose name it now bears, and was in great degree built by convict labor.

Nearly opposite the Tacon theatre is the depot of the horse-car railway that runs out to the village of Chorrera, on the north-western portion of the city.

Next, beyond the Tacon, to the right hand, is the "Paradero de Villa Nueva" railroad depot, from whence start the cars for Matanzas, Batabano, and Guanajay. It is some distance back from the Paseo, is a well built edifice of white stone, with iron railings in front, and every convenience for the traveler in the way of waiting-rooms and baggage shelter; and from the many trains on the different roads that start from here, presents always an animated scene.

Opposite this, and directly on the Paseo, is the large square known as the "Campo de Marte," or field of Mars, where the troops are generally in the habit of exercising early in the morning, or during the winter about two o'clock in the day. It is a square somewhat in the

form of a trapezium, with its longest side about
two hundred and twenty-five yards in length,
and surrounded by an iron railing upon a base of
stone, combined with pillars of stone at regular
intervals, and upon the top of each one of which
is an iron bomb-shell, of large size, by way of
ornament. It has four principal entrances, closed
by iron gates, upon the top of the posts of which
are placed bronze mortars; and as the columns
are large and well built, the gates have a good
effect. They are called after the distinguished
men who bore the names of Colon, Cortes,
Pizarro, and Tacon, the latter being the founder
of the square, which at various times has

Gateway

suffered considerable damage from the tornadoes. It is now repaired
and beautified.

Directly opposite the square, in the centre of the Paseo, is the
beautiful Glorieta, and fountain of India, surrounded by noble *palmas
reales*. The fountain is a work of considerable beauty, carved out of

Fountain of India

Carrara marble, and erected at the expense of the Count of Villa Nueva. It is one of the most beautiful of the public fountains, and does equal credit to the taste and heart of the patriotic citizen who erected it, and is an example which some of our millionaires, who hoard their money to no earthly good, would do well to follow in beautifying their native cities. The beautiful avenue in which this is situated is also part of the Parque Isabel.

Nearly opposite the fountain, on a small paseo leading from the Prado, is the Circus, and on the other side of the Campo del Marte is the magnificent private residence, or in fact palace, of the Aldama family, which was one of the richest in Cuba, and owned a number of the finest sugar estates in the island, but since confiscated, owing to the family having interested themselves in the rebellion now going on in the island.

Directing now the driver to the Paseo de Tacon, we turn into a fine, wide street, known as the Queen's Street, or "Calzada de La Reina," which runs from the Campo del Marte to the Calzada de Belascoin, when it continues on out to the Castillo del Principe, bearing from Belascoin street the name of Paseo de Tacon.

The Queen's Street is a fine wide street, upon which there is generally seen more life of an afternoon than on any other, although on some portions of it the buildings are not so fine as in the other streets. At its junction with the Paseo Tacon, there commences one of the prettiest drives about the city, having double rows of trees, with a promenade for foot passengers, and a fine, wide carriage-drive, which is the fashionable one of an afternoon, and where the splendid equipages of the Habaneros may be seen to advantage. At different intervals along this Paseo there are fountains erected, statues, and *glorietas*; and of a fine day, with its beautiful women, elegant equipages, and long rows of shady trees, it presents a perspective and near view perfectly charming. The Marquis of Someruelos, then governor, did much to improve this Paseo, erecting, in 1802, the statue of Charles III, which is said to be the finest piece of art in the island. Tacon also did something towards its improvement, and one of the columns bears his name inscribed thereon. To the left, just after entering the Paseo Tacon, is the depot of the railroad running to the

Avenue of Palms

pretty villages of Marianao and Puentes Grandes. On the right hand, and nearly at the end of the Paseo, is a fine gateway, giving entrance to the beautiful gardens known as the Botanical Gardens (*Jardin Botanico*), and adjoining which are also the beautiful gardens belonging to the country place (*Quinta*) of the Captain-General, known as "Los Molinos." These are all so very beautiful and interesting that the stranger will, if he have time, want to pay them several visits, both morning and evening, as they offer more attractions than any public place I know of pertaining to Havana. Even in the middle of the day, when it was too hot to go anywhere else, I frequently took a volante there, and found it a cool, pleasant, shady place, in which to pass the mid-day hours. They are open day and night, and any one is allowed to enter and stroll through the beautiful walks, shaded and surrounded by most exquisite tropical flowers, shrubs, and trees. Nothing can be more delightful, of a warm morning or evening, than a saunter through these magnificent grounds, rivaling in their beauty, luxuriance, and novelty any garden that we have in the United States. The best plan, on a casual visit, is to leave your carriage at the entrance of the Botanical Gardens, and direct the driver to meet you at the entrance to the Quinta, some distance above; and you can then, after strolling through the gardens, pass into those of the Captain-General, and, enjoying them, sally out by the magnificent Avenue of Palms that leads from the gateway to the house. In the Botanical Gardens there are specimens of most every tropical plant, and directly in the centre is a large stone basin, filled with the finest water-lilies, and in the middle of that a rustic fountain, made of shells.

Passing from these gardens, you enter those belonging to the Quinta, which are somewhat larger, and contain some very beautiful walks,—one of which, nearly one hundred yards long, is as complete a lovers' walk as the most ardent pair could desire. It is formed of the rose of the Pacific ocean (*mar Pacifico*), growing to a good height, and covered with flowers of a light pink color, the bushes forming a handsome green and fragrant arch over the head of the pedestrian. There is an artificial fountain or cascade, formed, also, by permitting the waters of a small creek to pass over artificial rocks, which form

underneath a damp, and, it must be
said, unattractive cavern; while the
waters are carried off by a canal, upon
the surface of which rest the pleasure-
boats of his Excellency, the banks
being shaded by the overhanging trees,
and inhabited by some curious breeds
of ducks. An aviary or two there are
also, filled with some species of doves
of different kinds, while in the centre
of the gardens stands the comfortable
house of the Captain-General, and the
buildings pertaining thereto.

Rose Walk

The avenues of palms in these gardens will strike the visitor with
astonishment, as something surpassingly graceful, beautiful, and
majestic; while he can study to advantage the cocoa and plantain
trees, with which the gardens are filled. The whole place would be
perfect in itself, in the way of a garden, were it not that it has been
necessary to run a railroad through the middle of it, the noise from the
passing trains of which breaks at times inharmoniously upon the ear
as one saunters enjoyingly through the fragrant and otherwise quiet
paths. The gardens seem to be divided off under different names, as
may be seen by the sign-boards, at different places, designating the
gardens of San Antonio, the Queen, the Wood of the Princess. A
military guard is in and about the gardens all the time. It has been the
custom for the Captains-General to spend their summers here; but it
having got abroad that the place was unhealthy, it has not been so
often occupied lately, the Governors going out to Marianao or
Puentes Grandes. Be that as it may, it is a lovely spot for the stranger,
on his winter visit, to stroll into and pass his time agreeably, whether
sauntering through the shady walks with some lady friend, or
smoking his fragrant Havana 'neath the stately palms.

From these gardens, if the traveler is anxious for exercise, he can
mount up to the fort upon the hill, known as the "Principe," and from
whence there is a good view of the surrounding country, always
provided the sentry will allow him to pass. The fort itself is small,

Continuation of the Paseo Tacon

though somewhat old, having been built, in 1763, for the protection of the village and bay of Chorrera.

I must confess it is hardly worth the trouble of mounting up the steep hill, as one has better views of the town in more convenient places.

Leaving now the Quinta, we have a very pretty view of the continuation of the Paseo, with its rows of trees that shade the road so nicely, and which have attained such a luxuriant growth that it makes this, with reason, one of the most charming portions of the afternoon drive of the Habaneros.

Turning again into a fine, wide avenue, known as the "Calzada de la Infanta," we drive over to a long, handsome street, known as " El Cerro" (the hill), and leading out to a little village of that name.

It is a very handsome street, about three miles long, lined on each side with the beautiful and comfortable residences of the fashionable and wealthy, for whom this with its surroundings is the principal place of residence, particularly in the summer.

Here is an ample field for the study of tropic architecture, hardly any two houses being alike, yet all with the same general plan, very different indeed, from our ideas of comfort, and yet, probably the best plan that can be adopted for this climate.

Not only on the "Cerro," but everywhere in the cities, is the stranger struck by the peculiarities of this Cuban architecture, with its enormous windows, without a particle of glass, but grated with strong iron bars, the single story of height, the tremendous doorways, their massive doors studded, many of them, with numerous brass knobs and decorations, all bearing the appearance of having been built for defence from outside attack.

Upon the Cerro, the houses are modernized somewhat, having their stables and carriages in their rear, and in front, stone piazzas, elevated some distance above the level of the street. Passages are not at all frequent in the houses, and the principal entrance opens directly into large and cool halls, which are in fact rooms and furnished as such, laid with marble-tiled floors, and connected with the rooms beyond by large arch-ways. These halls are usually the dining-rooms, where always there is a breeze from the open court-yard or through the wide *sala*, or parlor, at the entrance; the whole being devoid of curtains, and exposed to the eye or curiosity of every passer-by. The ceilings are uncommonly high, and the houses are, without exception, open on the interior side to the *patio*, or court-yard, which affords, even of the warmest days, a chance for some air.

This *patio* takes with those in the cities the place of our gardens; all the rooms open onto it, and where there is a second story, a gallery runs around the entire square, having either blinds or fancy colored awnings for protection from the sun's rays, which have full scope in the open centre of the square.

This secures a free circulation of air, a shady place in which to sit or walk, and very often, when the *patio* is laid out with walks, flowers, fountains, and orange, pomegranate, or mignonette trees, a charming place in which to dream one's idle hours away, or flirt desperately with "*las bonitas Señoras.*"

In the vicinity of the Cerro there are a great many very beautiful places or residences known, as "Quintas," which the stranger will generally be permitted to inspect by "making it right" with the gardener or porter of the place, more especially if the family are not there.

The charming place to the right of the Cerro, formerly known as the Bishop's Garden, but now the residence of the Count Peñalver, is one of the most attractive of these, a superb avenue of the mango tree, celebrated as bearing the most luscious fruit on the island, being particularly worth seeing.

Here are also to be seen some superb specimens of the cactus, which in Cuba grows to an immense size, and possesses great strength, for a plant of this kind, in its branches, some of which will bear a man seated on them. In the trenches around Havana are also other fine specimens, which have a very odd appearance at times from the large quantities of fine dust that settle on them.

On our return, we pass through the "Calzada Galiano," one of the finest streets in the city, and always having new charms for me, with its width, pillared porticos, and regular architecture, to say nothing of the constant life there visible.

At the corner of Aquiar and Empedrado streets, is the station of the horse-cars that run through the best portions of the city out to the Cerro, for twenty cents, thus giving the stranger a pleasant way of seeing the whole route at his leisure. The cars run every five minutes, move fast, and are not over-crowded.

Large cactus

chapter ten

HAVANA FACTORIES, LA HONRADEZ, SHOPS, ETC.

"And what does La Honradez mean?" the curious reader will ask; to which question I will reply that, as regards the mere definition of the word, it signifies Honesty; but as to its special meaning, with the prefix "La," it means the name of the most curious and interesting factory in Havana. And for what? Simply as the manufactory of the paper cigar, so universally smoked in every Spanish country.

Wherever one goes in Cuba, the cigarette meets him at every turn, more so even than the cigar; for, in the cars, between the acts in the opera house, in the mouths of pretty women, between the courses of the dinner, and even, I might say, at the very portals of the church-door, one finds the delicate, fragrant, paper cigar.

Let no traveler imagine, therefore, that he has "*done*" Havana, if he goes away without seeing the place where is made this peculiar institution of the country, and which is as well known as the Governor's palace, under the name of the " Royal and Imperial Factory of La Honradez."

This establishment occupies a whole square, from Cuba to San Ygnacio street, corner of Sol, and in its general arrangement, intelligent manner in which its business is

La Honradez

conducted, and the great spirit of enterprise possessed by its proprietors, would do credit even to us Yankees.

Entering the building on San Ygnacio street, one finds himself surrounded by the offices and counting-houses of the establishment, arranged in a handsome and business-like way, and where he is received by a very polite usher, whose business it is to show the stranger through the establishment. He is then requested to register his name in a book kept for that purpose, and quite as large as a hotel register, in which every one that enters the place is required to write his name; and, after going through the factory, is requested to make any remarks he pleases, touching the method and peculiarities of the manufactory, according to the impression made upon him.

From this portion of the house, communication is had with the other parts of the factory by means of the telegraph, arranged in a very simple way, so that the office is in direct communication with the chiefs of the different departments, without the loss of any unnecessary time in running backward and forward from office to factory.

From thence one is taken into the carpenter-shop, where are made all the boxes, barrels, etc., in which is packed the finished material, whether of cigarettes or smoking tobacco. The lower saloon, or machine room, contains machines adapted to various purposes; the most novel of which is, perhaps, the press for stamping brands upon wood, which, instead of being burned in, is by a very ingenious process printed, giving a much better impression, without the roughness or imperfections of the branding-iron, while at the same time the operation is much more rapid.

The barrel department is very curious,—one seeing barrels turned out by steam, with great velocity, and though in such large numbers, yet perfectly air and water tight.

The machine for cutting the *picadura*, the fine tobacco employed in filling the paper cigars, and the hydraulic press for compressing the tobacco for exportation, in blocks as solid as wood, are all interesting to see in operation.

On the second floor is a complete printing-office, in every branch of typography and lithography, constantly engaged upon work of the

Magneto-electric machine for engraving

factory, printing their circulars, labels, views of the factory, wrappers, and the millions of the beautifully colored and tastefully designed papers that enclose the cigarettes in packages of twenty-five.

In the lithographic, drawing, and engraving room, I saw what I had never seen before in any other establishment, and which, I am told, is an entirely new discovery—the process of drawing, on stone by chemical action and machinery. This is the machine known as the "Magneto-Electrique Machine," the invention of Mr. E. Gaiffe, a Frenchman, and which took the prize at the World's Fair and others. This machine, which has for its principal organ electricity, is the first that has been practically put in use, in this sort of industry, since the days of Franklin, the discoverer of electricity. The principle of the machine rests upon the interruption of the currents by a composition, or isolating ink, of which the design upon the matrix is composed.

By a circular motion of both the surface to be engraved on and the graver, and with the assistance of an electric magnet, pointed with a diamond, a complete and perfect drawing can be made without requiring any human assistance.

The special advantage of the machine is, that henceforth the designer will be able himself to engrave his works without their passing through the medium of the engraver or the lithographer, who often, in following the text, cannot reproduce the peculiar touch of the artist; while with this invention, the design being made by the artist himself, the machine, with the electric fluid, acts in place of his hand, though upon the work as drawn out by him.

In the number of patterns of envelopes for the paper cigars they are very rich, possessing some two to three thousand patterns, many of them of most beautiful designs. But the most interesting room to me was the one in which the cigarettes are filled, and where Chinese

Cooley making cigarettes

workmen are employed in that occupation. Each workman has a small table to himself, at which he folds, fills, counts, and does up in packages the little cigarettes; and it is astonishing what facility and dexterity they acquire from long practice in handling and counting these small bits of paper.

I watched the movements of one whose business it was to enclose twenty-five cigarettes in a package, just as we buy them, and this he did apparently without counting them; and yet by a movement of his fingers he would tell if there was one or two more or less, with surprising accuracy, and apparently simply by the sense of touch. The usher informed me that they rarely or never made a mistake. It is a curious sight to see these Asiatics, clad in their blue dungaree clothes, some of them with heads entirely shaven, some with their pig-tails all twisted up, while others, who are not so careful, permit their hair to grow out until it looks like a big black brush. All are, however, scrupulously neat and clean in their persons and attire, and are required by the rules of the establishment to keep so. The dormitory where these people sleep is a model of neatness and good order. Each man has a cot to himself, with neat coverlid and pillows, and everything about the room is required to be kept in the neatest manner possible. Around this room may be seen many curious articles of Chinese life and habits,—musical instruments of various kinds peculiar to Chinese art, gambling boards (much used by them), etc. All the workmen are required to wear a uniform hat, with the name of the factory upon the band, and, in fact, the whole establishment is run with a degree of military precision and system quite remarkable. For the Chinese, who are contract laborers belonging to the proprietors, there is quite a system of punishments in the shape of fines imposed; the severest being those imposed upon the smokers of opium, who for each offense have to pay the large sum of seventeen dollars, and for gambling, they confiscate all their capital, the amount so levied being invested in lottery tickets for the benefit of the Chinese generally.

There is a watchman employed at this establishment whose business it is to visit, each hour during the night, every portion of the building; and in order to secure the perfect discharge of this duty, there is a species of detective clock, that communicates by telegraph with all the rooms, and on entering each room the watchman must touch the button that communicates with the clock, and which thus shows if he attends to his duty. There is also, in this establishment, a curious fire machine, by which fires can be extinguished immediately by the use of soda-water, and which is known as "*el aniquilador.*" This is a simple machine, with a receptacle hermetically sealed, of variable capacity, full of water saturated with carbonic acid gas, charged to its greatest capacity, a pipe, to which is attached an elastic tube, and at the bottom a key perfectly adjusted. The high pressure of the water makes it discharge itself, the moment the key is turned, with such force that it extinguishes by its projection as well as by its essential qualities of water and gas.

It is computed that the average daily production of these cigarettes is two million five hundred and thirty-two thousand, and which find their way to all parts of the world, being, as they are, made to suit all classes of taste and smokers, some of the paper being united with rice or coffee, pectoral, perfumery, corn, etc. The receiving and examining room is one of the most interesting in the building. Here, when the cigarettes are made, they are put up in large, round

Packing cigarettes

packages, examined, labeled, and packed away in barrels, or piled up in enormous quantities to supply a constantly increasing demand.

The laborers employed in making these apparently trifling little things are not only the hands working at the factory, but in addition there are about fifteen hundred of the soldiers of the garrison of Havana, who take this means, in their leisure hours, of adding to their scanty pay. Besides these, almost every porter at every house occupies himself with his little box of cigarettes, devoting his leisure and otherwise loafing hours at the grand doorways, to the acquisition of more "*dinero.*"

This firm also manufacture cigars, and their snuff has, I believe, a great reputation; but for this I cannot vouch from experience, as I should have to answer "No" to even the following poetically inscribed question of a snuff-taker:

"Knows he, that never took a pinch,
Nosey, the pleasure thence which flows?
Knows he the titillating joys,
        Which my nose knows?
O nose! I am as proud of thee
As any mountain of its snows;
I gaze on thee, and feel that pride
        A Roman knows."

I have not half enumerated the attractions of this place,—they must be seen to be enjoyed; and now-a-days no one, in visiting Havana, fails to go to the "Honradez," which is the property of Messrs. Susini & Sons, who are very affable, kindly, courteous gentlemen, very successful in their enterprise. There is a regular day, I believe, for general visitors through the establishment, but foreigners are always made welcome, and courteously shown through the factory; ladies particularly receiving great attention from the gallant owners.

On leaving the building, you are desired to enter your opinions of the establishment in the register, opposite where you have recorded your name; and you are also somewhat astonished to find yourself presented with a package of cigarettes, prettily done up in a fancy wrapper, upon which is printed your name, "in remembrance" of the proprietors,—the whole having been done during your visit through the factory. This is one of the few places where it is offensive to offer a gratuity to the guide.

The register in which visitors record their names would drive an autograph-hunter crazy with delight, were he able to secure it; for here are registered not only the names but the opinions of some of the great notarieties in all parts of the world,—distinguished in war, art, literature and science,— some of whom are quite amusing in the tenor of their remarks, the French and Spanish having a great deal of "highfalutin" in them, while those of our own people are plain and practical as the people themselves. The one recorded by the Hon. W. H. Seward, formerly our Secretary of State, on his visit there a few years since, is happy in its practical flight of fancy, and reads as follows: "Am deeply impressed with the successful manner in which the proprietor has combined *West India* production with *American* invention, *European* talent, and *Asiatic* industry."

The attempts at first smoking the cigarette, by the novice, are highly amusing; and to be able to prepare and roll one for smoking is

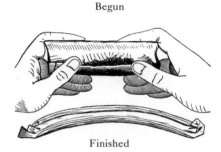

Begun

Finished

quite an art, the most skillful being the Señoritas, with their delicate hands, though all the Cubans are very expert at it. For the benefit of the uninitiated the following method of rolling the cigarette is given. The upper fold of the wrapper is rolled back, always taking care to open the ends well before doing so; to wrap it firmly and well, the thumbs and fore-fingers should be in the position shown in the picture. Now, by gently pressing the roll with the thumbs up against the fore-fingers, which remain steady, the whole is neatly and firmly folded, and then being bent somewhat in the middle, the fold uppermost, it remains perfectly firm during smoking, being grasped in a firmly-delicate manner towards the mouth-end with the thumb and fore-finger only. It is quite laughable to see how long it takes one before he acquires this knack of rolling the cigarette, and many of them have I spoiled before getting my smoke.

Cigarette holder

The Cubans, men as well as women, are very graceful in their movements with the cigarette, and you can tell a thorough-bred exquisite as well by the way he handles his cigarette, as you can by the way he draws on his gloves. The most elegant of them have what is called a *tenaciua* (tongs), made out of silver or gold, and of very graceful design and shape; one end with small claws, with which to grasp the cigarette, and the other with a small ring, to put over the finger. It is useful as well as ornamental; as to smoke the cigarette without one of these either stains your fingers or damages your gloves, which, in these days of two-dollar "Bajous," is a serious matter.

I do not wish to influence my lady readers when I say that nearly if not quite all the ladies in Cuba smoke cigarettes; if not habitually, then at least *poquito*; and it is quite the proper thing to do, if you happen to be with the ladies in the railroad car, to present your *cajilla* of cigarettes to them, being quite sure that the elderly ones of the party will often accept, with a courteous "*Gracias, Señor.*"

There is sometimes manifested in this country, at state dinners, an affectation of Cuban customs which is quite amusing. I allude to the fashion of smoking cigarettes between each course; a fashion which, I am sure, had its origin only in the brain of some club-swell, who has never seen the Cubans at home.

Usually with the cheese and jelly (in Cuba universally eaten together) are served cigarettes, and with the coffee, which ends the repast, cigars are served and smoked; but at no time or place, in my experience, have I seen this practice of indiscriminate smoking between every course indulged in by any one.

The above factory is about the only one of any particular interest to visit; but Havana does yet a large business in the manufacture of articles sold in the shops, while the different branches of mechanical trades are well represented. Carpenters and coopers find plenty of occupation from the large business done in sugar boxes and hogsheads on the neighboring plantations, while building is constantly going on.

The manufacture of carriages is quite an extensive business, though confined more particularly to the building of the native volantes, quitrins, and victorias; many of the best of the superb carriages and curricles one sees being brought from America. These quitrins and volantes are some of them very expensive affairs, costing five hundred dollars each and upwards, lasting with regular service from eight to ten years, though the commoner kind used for hire cost only two or three hundred dollars, and do not last more than three or four years.

The business of the harness-maker in this city of gorgeous equipage display is a very extensive one, and I used to find great amusement in examining closely some of the sets they have for sale. They are wonderfully rich in stitching, plated buckles, rings, and fancy mountings.

Most of the shoe-makers are, I think, Frenchmen, and there are a good many of their stores scattered throughout the city, making very nice shoes, too. Those made by the natives for rough use are very durable, and principally worn upon the island. There are still, though, a large number of shoes imported each year from the States.

Havana is particularly rich in jewelry and silver-ware stores, and they are among the most attractive stores one sees upon the street, their rich interiors of glass cases, filled with *bijouterie*, and shelves lined with handsome silver, being perfectly open to the eye of the passer by.

Iron mongery, arms, locks, etc., are generally imported from England, and some from the United States, and there are no factories of them upon the island; matches, however, are entirely supplied of their own manufacture.

Of the smaller trades, there seems to be an innumerable quantity of tailors, milliners or mantua makers, hatters, perfumers, artificial flower makers, and furnishing stores; many of this class of people are French women, and I am told they have the business of the *modistes* entirely in their own hands.

The system of shopping here is very different from anywhere else, and it is principally the custom for the dress goods people to send their wares to the homes of their customers; and this is usually the best way for ladies stopping at the hotels, particularly if they have no one to do the translating for them. Most of the stores have clerks who speak English, and they are very polite and obliging on coming to the hotel.

Ladies in shopping, in Havana, very seldom leave their volantes to enter the stores, but the articles are brought to them at the sidewalk. Their excursions of this kind are generally early in the morning or in the evening.

Lady foreigners usually find it a pleasant occupation to drive around among the stores, and examine the articles, always provided they are escorted by gentlemen or elderly ladies, as, I am sorry to say, the manners of the Habaneros are peculiar in this respect, and they are not so respectful to women as they might be; permitting themselves, on some occasions, to act in a grossly insulting way to young ladies, who, unfamiliar with the custom, happen to ride together. They get taught a sharp lesson though, sometimes, and by the fair ones themselves.

I knew an American lady, remarkable for her fair complexion and great beauty, who was seated in her volante while her companion had stepped into a store for a purchase, when a *gentleman* stepped up and saluted her, at the same time, leaning forward, attempted, with the greatest familiarity, to take a flower from her hand. Frightened, but very angry, she, quick as thought, laid the back of her hand over the young man's face, who, utterly taken aback, stooped to pick up his fallen hat, uttering some savage *carrambas* and *carajos*, which were cut short by the opportune arrival of the lady's gentleman escort. I need hardly say matters were soon fixed.

In shopping it is well always to remember that custom permits of the store-keeper asking more than he expects to get for his wares, and it is never wise, therefore, to pay what is asked.

"What is the price of this hat?" I asked.

"Six dollars,—very cheap."

"Whew !" (with a long whistle), "I'll give you three."

"Couldn't take it, sir, —cost me nearly six; may have it for five, though."

(Starting to go out), "I'll give you three and a half."

"The señor may have it for *four*; and that (with unmistakable earnestness), is the lowest;" thereupon I became the owner of the *sombrero*.

Havana is noted for the elegance of its fans and the beauty of certain kinds of lawns and organdies, and particularly of piña cloth, which, in highness of color and lightness of texture, I can compare to nothing but butterfly-wings. In buying any of these things, they sometimes seem very cheap for a dress pattern; but it must be remembered the Cuban *vara* or yard, is quite three inches shorter than the English.

The bookstores I always found pleasant places to visit. The assortment of books, in some of them, is very good, especially in foreign books, illustrated works, etc.

The great charm of Cuba for the traveler from the United States is the entire change of appearance of matters and things from what he is accustomed to. From the time of landing at Havana, with one's mind filled with the Spanish life as described in Irving's "Alhambra" and "Granada," or as written in Prescott's works, there is an additional pleasure of seeing, verified with one's own eyes, those peculiarities of houses, climate, and people, described somewhat in those works.

From the moment of entering the bay of Havana, where one sees the city before him, with all its oddities of colors, and shapes, and styles of its walls, with an occasional palm or cocoa tree to give a marked type to its appearance, to the time of turning his back upon the luxuriant Coffee Mountains of the east, or sugar-cane clad prairies of the valleys, there is one constant charm of novelty, and very often ridiculously so.

The first thing that strikes the novice, in wandering through the old town of Havana, is the solidity of the buildings and the narrowness of the streets, the smallness of the sidewalks of which will cause him at first some considerable annoyance in stepping off into, perhaps, the muddy street, for the purpose of giving the "right of way" to some pedestrian, who is keeping to the right, "as the law directs;" or, when disgusted with the constant getting out of the way, he takes to the middle of the street, and is suddenly punched in the ribs by the shafts of some

A little punch

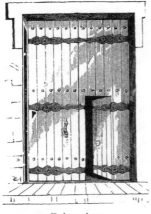

Cuban door

volante, whose driver has gauged his pulling-up so nicely that he just avoids running over you.

Then the houses, hardly ever more than one story high,—never more than two,—with their tremendous doors and windows; when, if the door is open, you see a handsome flight of stone steps, perhaps, leading to the upper story, the walls all gaily painted in white and blue, or yellow; the entrance probably taken up with a gorgeous quitrin, or perhaps a handsome carriage, according as to whether the family are wealthy, and occupy the whole house, or only well off, and keep the upper stories, renting out the lower ones, which are probably filled with merchandise. Notice, now, this great door to the large and showy mansion. It is shut; but see how resplendent it is with brass decorations, latches, hinges, door-plates, or studded with quaintly shaped, brass-headed bolts, which, with the shining handles to the solid wooden leaves of the door, give it a "(k)nobby" appearance in more senses than one.

And then the absence of the "dear creatures," too, whose pretty feet and lovely figures we are so constantly in the habit of seeing upon our own streets, that I am afraid it is not until we reach a place like this, where ladies never walk upon the streets, that we begin to appreciate the kindness and loveliness of our fair pedestriennes at home. Is it wonderful, then, that an American, with his national character for impudence, should follow in the steps of the courtly and stately Spaniard, when he sees a pair of lovely eyes peeping at him from behind the curtain of the barred window, and, doffing his hat, should exclaim, with antique gallantry, "Señorita, I put myself at your feet," or "the surprising beauty of your lovely eyes will not permit of my passing by, Señorita, without doing them homage?"—grateful if he is rewarded, as he always will be, by bright glances from the dark-haired damsel, who, with a stately smile, utters her *"Gracias, Señor,"* in return for what she deems only due tribute.

Here's a contrast! Now mark that great negro, with his ridiculous looking wheelbarrow, appearing as though it had come out of the ark, such is the simplicity of its construction; the negro himself, without head covering, with as little clothing as the law allows (if there is any law in such matters), generally ragged pants, and a portion of a shirt only.

"Gracias, senor"

The contrast

Here we are in the ever busy street O'Reilly, which, like Obispo or Ricla, one never gets tired of wandering in. Do not imagine for a moment, if you want to find any particular store, that you must ask for Mr. Smith's or Mr. Jones's establishment; oh, no, *amigo mio*,—these people do not generally travel under their own names; but, like a hotel, stick up something that is unique, expressive, or easily remembered. As a consequence, you have "The Nymphs," "The Looking Glass," "The Little Isabel," the "Green Cross," which you see gets its name from the big Maltese cross, built into the wall of that corner store, and hundreds of other funny, curious, and expressive names.

Just look down that street, this hot February day. See those fancy colored awnings, stretching across all the way down, to keep the warm sun away from our heads; those handsome shop windows, or the

The Green Cross

stores themselves, in fact, with their shelves almost upon the street, all reminding one of the descriptions of Eastern bazaars, were it not that the well-dressed men that are scattered through the non-coated, cool-looking people, show the presence, in a civilized land, of capital tailor's work.

And now, while intent upon the sights, you hear a shout of "*Cuidado! cuidado!* " (take care), behind you, and, jumping out of the way, in the expectation that your last hour is come, you are convulsed with laughter at the cause of your alarm, in a most ridiculously small donkey pulling a big cart, while upon the back of the donkey, perhaps, are piled a dozen folded blankets or cloths; upon top of which, again, is a great cumbersome saddle, big enough, and heavy enough for a French cuirassier. Poor little devil! He has just twice as much load as is necessary to carry, but the plucky little fellow goes sturdily along as if it was all right. Now, turning a corner, we are suddenly taken aback by a negro girl, with a white child in her arms, out for an airing, I suppose, from the *fresco* nature of the apparel,

which consists of just the amount of hair usually found on the heads of children, and which probably the novice thinks is a little too airy for the public streets of a city like Havana. *N'importe*, my friend; you will get used to worse things before we part than that trifling *cosa de Cuba*.

"Halloa! what's up now, in this narrow street we are going through?" you will ask, as, looking ahead, you see it

Donkey-cart

completely stopped up with a mass of green vegetable matter that is coming down on you with hardly any perceptible propelling aid; however, now it is near, you descry the long-eared head of a small donkey, or perhaps a Cuban horse, almost buried under a load of green fodder, piled upon and beside him in such manner that nothing is to be seen except the head and feet of the little fellow, who, while thus buried, has not even the satisfaction of a quiet little chew of the material that

A tight squeeze

surrounds him, for his mouth is muzzled up in a curiously netted muzzle of twine. This fodder constitutes, with corn, the only food given to horses in Havana, and is all brought in from the surrounding country on the backs of mules, sometimes ten or twelve in number, strung together like a lot of beads, head and tail. No oats are raised, or grain of any kind, in the island, except the small sweet ears of Indian corn which is grown everywhere, and the stalks of which, with the tender tops of the sugar-cane, make up the only food to be had for horses.

Milk horse

There's another fellow, bawling out, at this early hour, something he calls "*leche, leche;*" and which we find to be milk he is carrying around in those immense tin cans, stuck away in the straw or palm panniers hanging over his horse's back, and which, with the hot sun and the motion, would soon get churned to butter, or rather oil, the latter being the way they use it on the island.

Peripatetic Chinois

Again is heard a peculiar clattering, as if crockery was being hardly dealt with, and which is found to proceed from the hands of a peripatetic "Chinois," who takes to the street for a market for his wares. Here he is, now, a regular thorough going "John Chinaman," who, after having served out his time as a Coolie on perhaps some large sugar estate, has become imbued with the ambitious desire of being a merchant, and no longer remaining in his hard working way of life as a "*trabajador*" in the hot sugar fields. Having saved sufficient money from his hard earnings, or, what is more likely, made his capital by gambling with his more verdant and less fortunate fellows, he has started in trade, with a bamboo yoke carried over his shoulders, and pendant from the ends of which hang two large, round baskets, filled with crockery of all kinds. Clad in thin, wide pantaloons, a blue dungaree shirt, with a broad palm-leaf hat on his head, and his feet thrust into loose, heelless slippers, he perambulates the streets, seeking to tempt the cautious housewife into purchasing something of him,—not by the dulcet sounds of his voice (which sounds like a turkey-gobbler), but by the insinuating music of the wares themselves, emitted in a peculiar sound and way by the half-dozen saucers he carries in his hand, and which he is constantly throwing up gently, and letting them fall one upon the other with a sharp, continuous, rattling sound that will bring the indolent housewife quickly to the window, if she wants anything in that line. No danger of his breaking them in this way of making himself known, for the Chinese are celebrated for their sleight of hand, and this is evidence of it.

Now we hear the fruit-venders crying out their wares, as they walk beside their pannier-loaded horses. "*Naranjas, naranjas, dulces*," (oranges, sweet oranges), he cries; which, in the season proper for them, you can buy of him, the largest and ripest kind, for a *peseta* (twenty cents) the dozen, or less,— as well as other fruits of the country. Although the oranges are ripe all the year round, there seems to be a profusion of them in the early Spring months, unless, as is the case some years, they are somewhat scare from the tornadoes having destroyed many of the trees.

Poultry vender

Look at this ridiculous sight,—that fellow, a poultry-dealer, going up the street there ahead of us, mounted upon his donkey, his feet projecting out in front, while he is high up on the pack that holds his large, square panniers of chickens, which he has brought in from the country to dispose of, and which he carries safely in the baskets, corded over the tops with a net work, or more frequently a cloth, the *pollos* sticking forth their heads from time to time, and doubtless wondering, as they keep up their cachinating, why their master is thus treating them to this morning's *paseo*.

Dulce-seller

Now we meet a "*dulce*" seller. As a general thing they are neat-looking mulatto women, rather better attired than most of the colored women one meets in the street. They carry a basket on the arm, or perhaps upon the head, while in their hands they have a waiter, with all sorts of sweetmeats,—mostly, however, the preserved fruits of the country, and which are very delicious, indeed,—much affected by ladies.

We need not have any hesitation in buying from these women, as they

Paisano

usually are sent out by private families, the female members of which make these *dulces* for their living, the saleswoman often being the only property they own, and having no other way (or, perhaps, too proud, if they have,) of gaining a livelihood.

Here's another fellow, this time, a "Paisano," a regular raw, fresh countryman, who probably has a little place of some five or six acres somewhere near the city, and who raises a little of everything, himself being the salesman, and seeking his market in the small streets outside the walls. He is not so green as he looks, with his great straw hat like an umbrella over him as he sits perched up there. Try to chaff him while you purchase your oranges of him, and you'll find him as "wide awake" as his hat.

Here is something that won't strike you quite so agreeably. Did you ever see anything more disgusting than that great negro wench,—a large clothes basket on her head, a colossal cigar sticking out from between her thick lips, while she walks along, majestically trailing an ill-fitting, loose dress (probably the only article of apparel she has on) after her slip-shod strides? She is free, too; and, as many others of them do, puts on airs, occasionally, if you pitch into her for spoiling your clothes, that you have rashly trusted to her to wash for you.

Well, I might go on describing "lots of things" that one sees; but this will give the reader an idea, if he doesn't go there himself; and if he does, he will probably see as much or more to interest him. I must not forget, however, the most important street sight or cry, without which no description of Havana would be complete. I refer to the sellers of lottery tickets, of whom there are all sorts and kinds, and of both sexes and various ages, that you meet everywhere,—in the cafés, at the door of the churches, at your hotels, and at every place of amusement,—in fact, you can hardly move without meeting one of these people.

Lotteries may be said to be the curse of the Cubans; for every one, from the highest to the lowest, from the small child hardly able to walk (who has its ticket purchased for it), to the tottering, feeble man or woman; the poor, ignorant, filthy negro, or the dainty, elegant exquisite; the humble, hard working washerwoman, and the elegant, indolent, rich young beauty,—all, all of them are equally interested in the lottery, proportioned, not by the prices of their tickets, but by the extent of their hopes, according as they want the money to enable them to cease work, commit some new piece of extravagance, or dip into some other excitement.

There can be no doubt that the universal indulgence in this practice has a fearful amount to do with the indifference and indolence of the people to any higher aims than just to live. The few dollars that are made, over and above the daily wants of the middle and lower classes, all go in this way, in place of being put away for some future need, or some present increase of industry. The whole community is demoralized on this point, and even strangers become infatuated with the excitement on hearing that such and such a person drew a prize, or that such a new, large commercial house got a lift when they started of fifty or one hundred thousand dollars (this is true) by a prize in the lottery.

Here now is "Ramon," perhaps better known than the Captain-General, —a strange odd-looking dwarf, not much if any over three feet high, broad shoulders enough, and head remarkably large;—a native, as he informs me, of Porto Rico, aged forty-five years, and follows this as a regular vocation. His head is actually too large for his

Ramon

body, and he is therefore compelled to support the weight of it by carrying a stick up over his shoulder, in the manner you see in the picture, upon which to support this vast weight of cranium, if not brains, while his thick, bushy beard gives him rather a fierce appearance. Take him altogether, he is quite an object, aside from his being an illustration of the lottery-ticket vender.

But not only such persons as Ramon are occupied in this business. Now and then, in addition to plaintive women or loud-talking men, you come across the "swell," who, in elegant attire, and with courteous address, solicits you to buy the ticket he offers you, politely assuring you it is just the number to draw the grand prize. Watch him now, as, being asked for some impossible number, he places his eye-glass, and begins to run over the numbers he has, until suddenly it strikes him that he has been "sold" himself; and turning to you, he calmly tells you he hasn't *that* number, and bows himself off to some more speculative "lot."

Imagine, now, one of those noisy fellows that constantly perambulate the street, crying out, in strong, high tones, at the same time managing to give them a deep nasal sound, as he cries out in the full, round periods of the beautiful Castilian tongue, "*Loteria! Loteria!* a good number,—number twenty-five thousand nine hundred and fifty-one!"

The lottery is a government institution, and from it the exchequer receives as much as from any other source of rent, since it takes one-fourth part of the sum put up as capital. The treasury emits annually about five hundred thousand tickets, at seventeen dollars per ticket, in nineteen series of tickets, each series of twenty-seven thousand tickets. At each of the drawings, which number about twenty in a year, three-fourths of a proportionate sum into which the capital is divided are distributed among the players in about the following proportions:

One ticket of		$100,000
"		50,000
"		30,000
"		15,000
"		10,000
Six tickets of	$2,000	12,000
Ten "	1,000	10,000
Sixty-two "	500	31,000
One hundred and forty-three	400	57,200

In the drawing, which is open and public, they put twenty-seven thousand tickets, numbered from one to twenty-seven thousand, in a globe, and in another, two hundred and twenty-six tickets that represent the foregoing prizes. A child draws from the globe one of the numbers, and another child from that of the premiums, calling out in a loud voice, and noting the prize corresponding to the number drawn; thus, as soon as the two hundred and twenty-six numbers are drawn, the lottery terminates.

They consider, also, as entitled to premiums of six hundred dollars, each one of the tickets that have the two numbers before and the two numbers after the one that draws the one hundred thousand dollar prize, and as worth four hundred dollars, each one of the sixteen tickets of the same nature of the fifty, thirty, fifteen, and ten thousand dollar prizes.

Baker

In order to put the lottery within reach of every one, they sub-divide a large number of tickets, into sixteen parts, at one dollar each, and a fraction, and the premium corresponding to this fraction of the ticket is paid in proportion.

The dealers in the tickets are all licensed, and are required to wear the brass badge in a conspicuous place upon the front of their coats.

Yet one more *cosa de Cuba* we meet before entering our hotel, and that is the "Panadero," or baker, who supplies us with our "staff of life," and a very excellent one it is, too; for I think I can say that the whole time I was in Cuba, whether in country or town, I never ate a piece of bad bread, or rather roll,—for the bread is never made into loaves, as with us, but simply into bakers' rolls, well baked, and quite light.

This fellow you see here is the "*mozo*," who accompanies his master, the baker, through the streets, to dispose of his supply; or, if he has a regular set of customers, goes alone from place to place, carrying his load of bread, not, as with us, in a hand-cart, but on his apparently insensible cranium, the bags pendant from his arms being made of plaited palm-leaf, and filled with rolls, which are left as ordered.

Mozo

HAVANA BY NIGHT

> "Quand on fut toujours vertueux
> On aime à voir lever l'aurore."— Gozlan

"Paris, town of the north, should be seen by the light of torches and of the gas,—it is its *rouge*. * * From the hour that it is lit up, its inhabitants appear as though they commenced to live."

Substitute Havana, city of the south, for Paris, and the above description will be just as apropos; for, with a large proportion of the people of Havana, and particularly the fair sex, their day begins in the evening (*tarde*).

During the day, as a general thing, the streets are peopled simply by those who are necessitated to go forth upon their special business, and few natives either walk or drive out for pleasure until the evening hour, which must be understood as corresponding to our afternoon. After five o'clock, one may begin to expect to see something of life; for, at that hour, the Paseo begins to teem with life and animation, to be filled with promenaders, and handsome carriages and quitrins, with their beautiful and richly-dressed occupants, who, during the previous portions of the day, have been "killing time," most probably, in dowdy dishabille, listlessly lolling in rocking-chairs, with no other effort made than that of fanning themselves, and assisted in the above occupation, perhaps, by an hour or two's *siesta* in the middle of the day.

But now their hour is come. After submitting themselves to their hair-dressers (for the Cuban ladies' coiffure is always a work of elaborate art and beauty, and, it must be confessed, they display great taste in making up the hairy covering that nature has bestowed so bountifully upon them), they are ready to be admired.

Military Promenade

One sees them, then, on the Paseo, generally two ladies together, in a quitrin, or, if in a carriage, a party of ladies, with a beautiful child or two,—the former with no covering upon their heads but that so magnificently bestowed by nature, in the shape of "tresses, dark as raven's wing;" the horses of their conveyance marshaled by a swarthy negro, gorgeous in gold-laced livery, boots that come up to his waist, and decked with silver spurs. Or, perhaps, it is a superb turn-out in the shape of a barouche or drag, with liveried footman and coachman, and the most stylish northern-bred horses of the largest size. Sometimes one may see worn by the ladies the far-famed Spanish veil,—not often, however.

It is a lovely sight, indeed, this evening drive out the Paseo Isabel, Reina, and Tacon, when the delights of the tropical evening may be enjoyed to their fullest extent. The beautiful women, dressed with extreme taste in their highly-colored stuffs, the well dressed men, the striking and richly decorated equipages, with their liveried servants,—add to which the soft air, fragrant with the rich perfume from the tree mignonette, and the tropical character of the surrounding trees and scenery,—have a particularly pleasant and soothing effect upon one accustomed to continued residence in the north.

The quitrin seems just the vehicle for these rides on the paseos. It is large and roomy, very easy in its motion, and occupied generally by two persons; but the private ones have a small extra seat fixed to

Quitrin

the other, so that three ladies can ride together, the front seat being usually occupied by either the youngest or prettiest of the party; and it is from this, I presume, that the ladies always speak of this seat tenderly as that of *la niña bonita* (the pretty child).

There is a vast deal of etiquette amongst the best of the Habaneros, and in nothing is this more forcibly shown than their custom for gentlemen always to sit on the left of the lady, in riding; and while two ladies and one gentlemen (he always sitting on the left) *may* sit on the same seat, two gentlemen and one lady cannot, without infringing the laws of *haut ton*.

Now as the day rapidly changes into dusky night (for there is little or no twilight), the lights spring up in every direction. Long rows of gas-lamps upon the paseos, around the fountains, and in the shops, give a particularly brilliant and, I may say, fairy-land-like appearance to the scene.

The cafés now become resplendent with lights and alive with people; the grand theatre Tacon opens its doors, and is also ablaze with light; the old-fashioned watchmen (*serenos*), with their spear-headed poles and their little lanterns, are posted at the corners of the streets, and everything is life, bustle, and animation. These watchmen are also a *cosa de Cuba*, being originally instituted by Tacon in his sweeping arrangements to establish law and order; and if they were not a better lot in his day than they are now, they could not have been of much use, except for show. They are, many of them, stout, jolly-looking fellows, clad in thick coats, with a belt around the waist, in which is some old-fashioned pistol; and they sensibly select, particularly late at night, the softest piece of curbstone they can find at the corners of the street, until it comes time, which it does every half hour, for them to get on their feet, knock their staves upon the pavement, or, perhaps, give a long whistle, and then carol out, at the top of their voices: "Twelve o'clock, and all's well,"—night serene or raining, as the case may be. As their prevailing cry is *sereno*, from the fact that the nights, year in and year out, are usually clear, they themselves have been dubbed with this name. Now just imagine yourself occupying a corner house, with four of these fellows, one after the other, coming down to your corner and kicking up this row, just as you want to turn in, maybe at an early morning hour, and you will have a faint idea of how pleasant it must be.

One night when they bothered me so much that I couldn't sleep, I tried coming out on the balcony and offering to stand the "beer," if they would just miss a song or two till I got asleep; but, as the old fellow could not see it, and got a little "huffy," muttering something about "*officiale*," I gave it up.

Suppose now, reader, we make a night or two of it together, in a quiet way, and then you will be able to "go it alone." Let us, then, after our pleasant drive (sometimes dusty) on the Paseo, stop at El Louvre, on the opposite corner from the Tacon, and get our cool *refresco* of *naranjada*, which having leisurely finished, we light our *Londres*, and stroll slowly down Obispo street to the Plaza de Armas, opposite the Governor-General's palace. Notice now the pretty effect of the stores as, brilliantly lit up, they reflect from their thousand and one articles a variegated and dazzling light. Mark, also, the volantes at the doors, with their dark-eyed occupants, who have taken the cool hours of the evening to do some shopping, perhaps *en route* to hear the music.

See the difference in the number of people in the streets now and at the same place at mid-day. Everything is now gay, brilliant life, except where, peering through the barred windows, the curtains of which are now drawn entirely back, you are permitted to look into the cool halls, floored with tiles or marble, and see the inner life of the people as they sit receiving or ready to receive their friends.

Notice the peculiar manner in which the chairs are placed. You see two rows of chairs, parallel to each other, and, perhaps, a large rocking-chair at each end, or very possibly all are rocking-chairs. No carpet is on the cool floor, except a rug in front of the above chairs, where the sitters' feet will rest. People these same chairs with two or three pretty girls, presided over by an elderly lady, and you have Cuban social life. If you are a visitor merely, you see them there any time after five o'clock; if you are a lover, still the same. No more freedom or liberty will be allowed you than to call just in that way on your *inamorata*,—no snug little talks, no charming strolls, either *à pied* or *à cheval*. No, sir; if you want to squeeze your dulcinea's hand, you

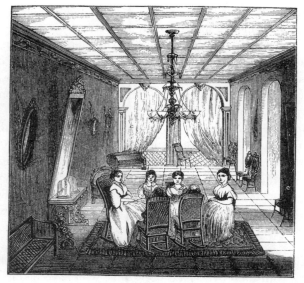

Saloon of Cuban dwellings

must do it, staring mamma in the face; and as for anything farther—unless—well, perhaps, you can try it some of these days.

The signal

"And cautious opening of the casement showing
That he is not unheard; while her young hand,
Fair as the moonlight, of which it seems a part,
So delicately white, it trembles in
The act of opening the forbidden lattice
To let in love."   *   *   *

Here we are at the Plaza de Armas, which is the principal public place of the city, occupying the square between O'Reilly and Obispo streets, and in front of the palace. It is a prettily laid out quadrangle, around the sides of which are stone seats, backed by an iron railing, the pavements of stone, and within its limits four gardens, separated from each other by four streets, which meet in the centre,

The Governor's Palace and the Plaza de Armas

forming a *glorieta,* or inner circle, in the centre of which has been erected a statue in marble of Ferdinand the VII, of Spain. The gardens are filled with shrubbery and flowers, while the ever stately *palma real* adds grace and beauty to the scene.

Directly opposite the western side is the palace and residence of the Captain Governor-General, the principal official of the island. It is a large, yellow, stone building, with the upper stories on the front built over a stone colonnade, which gives it a good architectural effect. Through the centre of the building there is an archway opening into the *patio,* or court-yard, around the four sides of which are the interior windows of the building, the entire edifice being devoted to the residence of the Captain-General, his staff, and the necessary offices below for the transaction of the public business.

Around the square are some very beautiful and curious trees, which have stood here for many years, in spite of the storms and tornadoes that have at times ruined or damaged some of the palms. They are a species of banyan tree, known as the Laurel of India, and an evergreen, I believe.

The reason that this square is the most popular place of resort, in addition to its being near the palace, is, that on every evening one of the military bands of the garrison performs here for the public benefit and the satisfaction of the commanding officer. This evening concert, known as the *Retreta* brings out a great many people of both sexes,— the ladies in their carriages, who drive around and around the square in the intervals of the music, or receive the attentions of their beaux; while the gentlemen, strolling through the square, smoke their cigars, or rest quietly in some of the many chairs furnished to the public by private enterprise, each chair costing five cents without limit to time.

Sometimes the ladies, if they have a male escort, leave their carriages, and promenade around the square. I must confess, however, that I was struck by the want of attention shown by the men to the ladies at the square. It is very rare indeed that you see gentlemen approaching the carriage, and chatting in a familiar, friendly way with the ladies, as is the custom in America. The ladies lean back in their seats in the most indifferent, stolid manner, without any apparent enjoyment, and as if they were going through with it as a ceremony; very different from the jolly time our lively American girls would have, had they such lovely opportunities and places for flirting at their command.

Every evening, a few moments before eight o'clock, a detail from some regiment, consisting of a sergeant's guard, and the band, generally numbering some fifty or sixty instruments, march into the square, and take up their position in the main avenue leading to the palace, standing at "rest" until the tap of the drum in the neighboring barracks gives a warning of retreat; they then stand at "attention," awaiting the signal gun from El Morro; immediately after which the band begin their performance, the guard, meanwhile, standing in open order, with ordered arms, at attention, until the music ceases; during the intervals of which they are allowed to rest. The music is generally very fine,—the selections being in good taste for occasions of this kind,—the principal operas furnishing the airs. At nine o'clock precisely, the bugles and drums in the different quarters signal the tattoo, and it being ended, the guard and band march out into the street directly in front of the palace, and play there just one more tune, as a special compliment to the Captain-General, and to let the people see that, while they play a whole hour for the public, he only exacts one tune specially for himself. This ended, the troops file off to their quarters to the sound of the quick march, and that excitement is over for that evening.

Altogether it is a most agreeable way of spending an evening; the fine music, the uniforms of the troops, the beautiful women, their carriages that crowd around the square, the brilliant lights reflected from the rich green of the tropical vegetation, taken in connection with the balmy air and the delicious fragrance of the *Londres superfine*, make up one of the most enjoyable cases of *dolce far niente* imaginable,—if one is fortunate enough to have moonlight nights, it is just as enjoyable, only—more so. Then, if you have acquaintance with any of the pretty women that are seated in those elegant quitrins, your pleasure will be much added to, for it is now that you will see the Cuban beauty to the best advantage, seated in her easy, comfortable gig, in full evening attire.

At the café of the Louvre, one can get as fine ices and sherbets as

Quitrin

are to be found in the United States,—and here is probably the best place in Havana to see fashionable social life of an evening; for, after the *retreta*, or the opera, every one resorts to some café or other, the *refresca*, whether drank or eaten, making up for our tea.

Ladies, with gentlemen, visit these places without the slightest hesitation; but if unaccompanied, they remain seated in their volantes at the door, where their refreshments are served to them, and they hold a levee of their male friends. The ice-creams (*mantecados*) are more French than American, but their ices or sherbets (*helados*) are superb, being flavored, many of them, with the luscious fruits of the country,—those of the sapote, guanabana, and guava being an entirely "new experience" to a foreigner.

When there is an opera troupe in Havana, representations are given generally four times a week; and, as all the best troupes generally go there sometime during the winter, one is always sure of hearing some good music during the season,—particularly is this the case in the holiday season, and usually, Sunday nights, the house is crowded. Off-nights, they have sometimes excellent dramatic performances by native or Spanish troupes.

To enter the house, gentlemen simply buy their *boleta de entrada* (entrance ticket), and if they wish a seat, they need also to buy a *boleta de luneta* (a seat in the pit), which is that part of the house frequented almost exclusively by gentlemen in full dress.

If it is desired to be economical, a seat in the *tertulia*, which answers to our second tier, is quite comfortable, respectable, and much cheaper. The seats called *butacos* are armchairs. The part of the house containing these is divided into two portions, one of which is reserved exclusively for ladies unaccompanied by gentlemen, the other for ladies and gentlemen.

The *palcos* (boxes) are the fashionable parts of the house, and these are known as *primer, segunda*, and *tercer pisos* (first, second and third stories), all of which are good, though preference is usually given to the first or second.

These boxes have no fixed seats, simply four or six chairs, and are all open, being divided from the lobbies by a simple movable blind, partition, and door, and in front, a light and graceful railing, surmounted by a velvet-covered balustrade.

At night, when there is a full house, it is a really beautiful sight to see the elegantly dressed women, *en grande toilette*, as they sit in the boxes in the different tiers, the light railing in front not preventing the full length figures of elegant material showing, which, with the bright and cheerful colors in which the house is painted, give a very brilliant appearance to the scene, the sombre-coated men in the *luneta* only serving to make an effective background or setting.

Now (supposing it is a moonlight night) let us stroll out on the neighboring Paseo de Valdez, which at this hour is likely to be very quiet, and see the bay by moonlight, and get a sniff of the evening breezes from old ocean. What is more beautiful than that? Gaze at the quiet sea beyond there, looking as smooth as glass, on this tranquil night; and the giant walls of the Morro and the Cabañas, in their depths of light and shade. And see, far upon the waters of the bay, the sheen of the silver moon, as it plays upon the waves. Happy the man indeed, who, with some fair one at his side, drinks in the beauty of this scene.

A favorite amusement with us, after *retreta*, was to get a party of ladies and gentlemen, and take one of the small boats for a sail of an hour in the bay. It is charming by moonlight, but a cloudy, dark night is best for seeing the peculiar phosphorescent effect of the movement of the oars in the water, while the track of the boat seems sparkling fire. Ah! shall I ever forget those romantic sails?—when, to use Byron's words—

"All is gentle; naught
Stirs rudely; but, congenial with the night,
Whatever walks is gliding like a spirit.
The tinklings of some vigilant guitars
Of sleepless lovers to a wakeful mistress;
*   *   *   The dash phosphoric of the oar;
Some glimmering palace roof, or tapering spire,
Are all the sights and sounds which
Here pervade
The ocean-born and earth-commanding city."

Eh bien, let us leave this quiet scene; and, calling a passing volante, we will go out to "El Louvre." This is the best and largest café in Havana, and may be said to be "the club;" for here you see all the world (without his wife). It is a fine, large saloon, opposite the Tacon theatre, at the corner of the streets, and is a very cool and pleasant place in which to get your *refrescos*, or smoke your cigar with a friend.

The Tacon is a large, substantially-built theatre, capable of holding about three thousand persons, and was, until within the last few years, considered, with the exception of the Grand theatre at Milan, to be the largest and handsomest of the world. There is a colonnade in front that in bad weather the carriages are allowed to drive under, and discharge their occupants; also a fine, large hall, with refreshment-rooms on each side, into which open the entrances to the lobbies of the theatre. The interior of the theatre is very handsome and capacious, is five stories in height, and possesses a very large stage, to the right of which, looking from the auditorium, is the box of the Captain-General, with its state decorations, by whom of an opera night it is generally occupied.

There is always present, also, an official representative of the government, whose business it is to see that the performance goes on properly; and if anything happens by which it appears the public are being trifled with, the manager or the singers at fault are arrested, and compelled to perform, under penalty of a heavy fine.

The Cubans, like all natives of warm climates, are very fond of

Inside of the Tacon Theatre

music, and have exceedingly fine taste and a correct ear; and as a consequence they will stand no nonsense from the performers, condemning them with the noise of their feet, which they move in measured time. It is proper to applaud only with the hands.

Between the acts there is a good deal of visiting by the gentlemen upon the ladies, who usually remain in their boxes to receive their friends, seldom or never going into the lobbies. The gentlemen, on the contrary, fill the main lobby during the acts, to chat together, smoke their cigarettes or the heavier "entre opera" cigar.

Some oddities will strike the stranger, even in the opera house, particularly that of the dandified, showily dressed little negro pages, most of them bright-eyed, sharp little fellows, who, in most "gorgeous array," stand outside the boxes of their beautiful mistresses, ready to obey any mandate or execute any commission they may entrust to them,—such as carrying messages from one box to another, or slipping a card or note into the hand of some gentleman admirer. The government, too, takes particular care to keep everything in order and propriety, to secure which there is a special force detailed from the Guardia Civil to keep order. Outside they even station the

Negro page

military on opera nights to prevent the carriages from going through the streets alongside of the theatre, since, as they are entirely open, the noise from them would drown out the performance. These

Mounted guard

sentries are perfect pictures, being mounted *gens d'armes*, on superb gray horses, and uniformed in white cloth coats, large boots, white tights and black chapeaux; looking altogether, as they sit immovable on their well packed saddles, the very models of *chasseurs à cheval*.

The Parque de Isabel, which has lately been put in fine order, is a charming resort in the evening whenever one has nothing else to do; for it has in a great measure robbed the old-time Plaza de Armas of its glory, as the bands play here now every evening, as well as there, from eight to nine o'clock.

Ah! this easy going, aimless life of the Cubans! Is it to be all changed some day by the infusion of the energy, the restlessness, and the bustle of a people from another land? Perhaps it will be as with the writer, that the influences of the tropics will change, for the time, the nature of the newcomers, and they will fall into the easy, courteous ways of El Cubano, whose whole of life, apparently, is the present, which he takes easily enough. *Ay, de mi.*

But here we are strolling up the Paseo, and again we pass by the Fountain of India, even more beautiful by moonlight than in daytime. Now, as we reach the Paseo opposite the Tacon, look at the quiet beauty of that scene towards the sea: here, in the foreground, the Parque of Isabel, with its velvety grass-plots surrounded by neat wire borders, dusky figures in contrast to the more fairy-like ones beside them; the fine façade of white buildings to the left, over which the moon casts a beautiful, mild tint; the long perspective of the colonnaded buildings, with the shadowy avenue of trees, broken here and there by silvery light; while in the distance is the calm sea, whose gentle murmurings against the rocks of La Punta we faintly catch. It seems like fairy-land, indeed, or something to dream of; and so, *amigos, "buenas noches."*

A

DOUBTFUL CHAPTER OR TWO,

NOT PARTICULARLY INTENDED FOR

LADIES' READING

SUNDAY AMUSEMENTS

"Well may the earth, astonished, shake,
And nature sympathize;
The sun, as darkest night, be black."
—HYMN

If the traveler reaches Cuba with the idea, which education, habit, or principle has imposed upon his mind, that the Lord's day is, or should be, kept in every civilized land, he will be somewhat, and perhaps disagreeably, disappointed. Like the "old salt," who always contended there were no Sundays in four fathoms of water, I must likewise confess that in Cuba there is no Sunday; at least, such as we know and revere as a sacred day. That there is such a day in the almanacs of Cuba is beyond dispute, and that there is supposed to be a Sunday at the churches, is also true; but I am willing to wager that if any American were dropped suddenly down in Havana on Sunday, without being told what day it was, he would, likely as not, pronounce it Fourth of July.

With your mind prepared for it, then, don't be shocked when I tell you that Sunday is the great day for cock-fights, bull-fights, and masquerade balls. Of course you won't go! No more would I (early training has been too much for me); but then, when one sets out to write a book, it must be complete, you know. So, on the principle of the disguised Chicago clergyman, who went to the theatre as a matter of duty, I also must confess, being of an inquisitive turn of mind, to seeing all these things, as in duty bound.

Imagine not, then, O innocent reader! that cock-fighting or bull-fighting is, like dog-fighting with us, confined to the "roughs." On the contrary, they are both under the government patronage; and at the bull-fights will be seen the best people, innocent little children, and, on special occasions, refined women; while at the cock-pit, though there are no women, the audience is pretty well mixed with men of every grade; and in the country, I have met gentlemen as much interested in the breed of "cocks" as we would be in a fine horse or dog. After all, it is perhaps not "only a difference of education," but simply *una cosa de Cuba*.

Tell any driver, therefore, of a Sunday morning, that you want to go to the "Valla de Gallos," which is situated in the outskirts of the city, beyond the walls. You arrive outside of a lot with a board fence, and a small, wooden office, where you purchase your ticket for twenty-five cents, which puts you with the crowd in any part of the house; and it is a pretty hard crowd, too, to tell the truth. For one dollar more, however, you can get a seat in the judge's box (*palco*), which is supposed to be kept entirely for the umpire, and which will hold half-a-dozen persons comfortably, in chairs, seated away from the confusion, though not the noise, of the crowd. It is the little compartment immediately over the door of the pit, as you see it in the picture.

Having now provided ourselves with the necessary tickets, we pass through an open lot to the "Pit," which proves to be a circular frame building, two stories in height, and constructed in the plainest manner, capable of accommodating one thousand persons, I should think. It has two galleries, an arena in the centre, is furnished with hard, wooden seats, and makes no pretense whatever to elegance or comfort.

The "play" commences in the morning, and is kept up as long as there are any parties to present chickens for battle or audience to bet. And think not, O novice! that there is no science, blood, or points in cock-fighting; on the contrary, it would appear there is much of the former and many of the latter.

The best breeds are those called fine, or English, and are distinguished by their breeding being more or less fine, taking their name from that of the breeder or master of the place (*patio*) where they are raised. They bring, sometimes, exorbitant prices, according to their own merit or the stock from which they spring. I was surprised to find how small they all were; it being invariably the case that the smallest were the pluckiest and best fighters.

There are various modes of fighting: *Al cotejo*—that is, in measuring, at sight, the size or spurs of both chickens. *Al peso*—or by weight, and seeing if the spurs are equal. *Tapa-dos*—where they settle the match without seeing the chickens, or, in fact, "go it blind." *De cuchilla*—when they put on the artificial spurs, in order to make the fight sharper, quicker, and more fatal. *Al pico*—when they fight without any spurs.

The prevailing mode, however, is to produce the chickens, compare them, and make up the match, weighing the birds to see that they are equal in weight, and trimming the natural spurs to make them sharper and more effective; while in the centre of the arena, where they fight, they sprinkle sawdust. The weighing business is a comical proceeding; there is an old spectacle-fellow who, with much gravity, takes the chicken and draws over its claws and around its body a kind of sling, which he attaches to one arm of the scales that are pendant in the center of the ring, and in the pan of the other he carefully puts the weights.

While this is going on, and the fight being arranged, the arena is filled with chickens to look at, and people to hear and to adjust the match, the bystanders and those in their seats shouting, bawling, vociferating, and motioning to each other in the making of their bets, until the place is a very Babel. Then, at the cry, "clear the pit," every one takes a seat without any distinction, the arena remaining to the umpire and the backers, with their birds still in hand.

Good heavens, what a racket! While this is going on, from up stairs to down stairs, and *vice versa*, from one side to the other, from back to front, they are all bellowing and calling, like mad, gesticulating their fingers, slapping their hands,—all signs having their peculiar meanings,—accompanied with cries of "four to two on the black," "take you six to eight on the white," "an ounce to an ounce on the little one," and so on,—the *gentleman* with the driver, the planter with the *mozo*, without regard to previous rank.

The arena is now cleared. At a sign, the chickens in the hands of their owners, with their superfluous feathers stripped off of such parts as would be likely to interfere with their good fighting, are given a preliminary pass or two at each other, and then freed from restraints.

Valla de Gallos

They spring at each other with the utmost fury, and the battle begins in good earnest. Now mark the little fellow, how wary he is; he makes a feint, and then, by a well-directed nip, takes the big one by the comb, who frees himself by ducking under his adversary. "Twelve to eight on the little one," is now the cry from the excited crowd. Down goes the little one, with the big one on top, who manages to give a poke or two with his spur; and thus they keep it up, fighting away, while the crowd scream and yell and bet at every new change.

At last the combatants are both seriously hurt, and perhaps blinded, by the blood and dust; and then there is a lull in the fighting, while the backers doctor up their birds, wiping the blood from their heads, blow through a quill a little alum to heal their eyes, or squirt a mouthful of *aguardiente* over their heads; the audience, meanwhile, keeping up the racket until the chickens commence at it again, with just the same fury, clawing, nipping, and dodging, until one or the other is either dead or so disabled he can no longer fight, when the play is up, and a roaring cheer breaks from the lucky betters. Then they all settle up, as calmly and coolly as if, the moment before, they had not been getting themselves hoarse, or looking like so many fiends; and the only wonder is how they manage to recollect with whom they have bet, or to what amount. The whole thing is arranged, however, peaceably.

Thus it keeps on; pair after pair are fought, amid the same scenes, the same noise and confusion; and, reader, if you want to see the workings of all the evil passions in the human face, just pay one visit to a cock-fight, and I guarantee you'll not go again, but will come away intensely disgusted.

Every stranger in Havana notices the variety in the appearance, as well as the numbers of the negro population, many of whom are very fine looking men; some being of such light mulatto color that they are nearly white, while others, again, are just the opposite,—being jet black, and having all the characteristics of the pure African. Many of them are the imported slaves of Africa, who have bought their freedom, while others, again, belong to owners who let them their time, allowing them to pursue any vocation they choose, only requiring them to pay so much per day out of their earnings.

The regular Africans all seem to retain their clanship, just as our negroes in the south used to do,—preserving their customs and habits in some degree amongst themselves, and following such pursuits as suit them best. Some go into houses as servants; others drive volantes or carts; others, again, carry water about for sale.

As Sunday is for them as well as their more civilized neighbors a *dia de fiesta*, they have their merry-makings and meetings together. And as all secret assemblies are against the law, these people meet in rooms together, which they call *cabildos*, or assembly rooms,—council chambers, in fact.

Once or twice, just for the novelty of the thing, it pays to visit these places, many of which one sees in walking through the street, just inside the walls, known as "Los Egidos." The visitor need not have the slightest hesitation in entering, for he will always be treated with great respect by those present, including the dancers, who are only too happy to have a white audience. A *peseta* or two will quicken their movements, and probably add to the number of the dancers, for whom the banjo, or a sort of tum-tum, is constantly played; the latter always looking to me like the half of a big pumpkin, with cords over it. The visitor sees on the plantations the same characteristics, and I

Negro dancers

don't know that the Cuban negroes differ much in their appearance from those of the south.

It is night,—the first Sunday night of Carnival, and a good time to see the masked balls, not only at the Escauriza, but the more *recherché* ones at the Tacon theatre. We will go first to the former (as it is convenient to the Tacon), tickets for which cost an *escudo*. It is only ten o'clock, the fun has hardly yet begun, and yet we can see enough. It is the same old story of masks and mummery, the dance and the music; the monk cheek-by-jowl with the devil; the apparently innocent shepherdess and the gay Lothario; the graceful and pretty *débardeuse*, and Mr. Bruin,—there they are, all masked, in all manner of costumes—the rich, the poor, the high, and the low, but all equal on the score of morals.

They are dancing their favorite Cuban dance, the *lanza* (a sort of shuffling waltz), pretty enough and proper enough when danced with fair women and proper men; but as danced here, one of the most indecent spectacles I have ever seen at any public ball.

This is the favorite ball of the *demi-monde*,—the lorettes, and other low beings; for here they are allowed more liberty than at the more select affairs over at the Tacon, and the ball will have hardly begun in earnest until the "wee sma' hours" of the night.

Let us go from here now. We have had quite enough to satisfy our curiosity, and so we enter the Tacon, paying a dollar for our ticket. Here are pretty much the same scenes, only a better class of people, and the ball on a larger scale. The large parquette, or pit, has all been floored over even with the stage, making a splendid ball-room; a band of music is on each side of the house, posted in the gallery, and alternating in their performances. The boxes are filled with curious and elegantly dressed women, unmasked, who come here with their male friends to witness the revel of the maskers, and as mere lookers-on; while the floor of the house is covered with the dancers, in all varieties of costumes. It is the same thing here. There is nothing new to any one who has ever been to a masked ball, and it suffers in comparison with the elegant affairs of the New York and Philadelphia German societies, where taste and expenditure are displayed to some purpose. If you want to dance, walk up to any of the female costumes, and ask them to dance. There is only one that they do, and that is the universal *dansza criolla*, before mentioned, but which is here danced with some degree of propriety to the music of the band, one or two of the pieces of which sound exactly like the scraping of shuffling feet upon a sanded floor, the only recommendation being that they keep excellent time.

Enough of this, too. We sally out into the open air (for all these ball-rooms are insufferably warm), to see what is going on in the streets; and there we find, also, numerous mummeries, and maskers strolling the Paseo, or dashing around in carriages, and raising a racket. Some of them have a curious way of joining hands and forming a circle, which keeps moving round and round, while the maskers chant a slow, monotonous strain, of some Spanish or Cuban origin. In the daytime, too, in this season of Carnival license, there is this driving round of masqueraders, in carriages or in processions, preceded by bands of music. I must confess that this show, if a fair sample of the usual season, is a very poor one indeed; and these festivities are gradually dying out, much to the delight of the better class of people, I believe.

I recollect reading in some description of Havana, written years ago by a clergyman, his account of the beautiful women that he saw, and of the *sociable*, friendly disposition manifested towards him by numbers of ladies whom he saw at the windows. He, struck with the view presented to him in passing by some houses where the *family* consisted *only* of beautifully dressed young ladies, remarked upon the beauty of the sight, regretting his inability, through ignorance of the language, to converse with them. Bless his dear, innocent heart! I wonder if he never found out his mistake in thus endowing those frail *filles de joie* with the charms and attractions of pure women?

The sensitive stranger will be frequently shocked, as, passing through some even of the principal streets, after dark, he has his attention called by some dark-eyed syren,—frequently very handsome, too,—who winningly invites him to enter her domicile, and pay his respects to some one of the many richly-dressed women he finds seated in the *sala*, and who can be easily and sufficiently seen through the bars of the open window in passing.

The authorities permit no street-walkers such as disgrace our cities; and yet, in some portions of fine streets, like Havana, Teniente Rey, and others, these women are allowed to "ply their vocation" from the windows of the houses, in which they are only compelled to keep the peace.

It is sad to relate that many of our own countrywomen, lured out here in hopes of gaining large sums from the wealthy Spaniards, come only to find themselves a more despised and unfortunate class than they were in their own country; while it is the Cubans' boast, that their women, illiterate and peculiar as they are, add nothing to the *materiel* of this class of people.

> "One more unfortunate.
> Weary of breath,
> Rashly importunate,
> Gone to her death."

chapter fourteen

THE PLAZA DE TOROS

Nota.—Todos los domingos que hay funcion se compran caballos hasta las dos de la tarde.*
                                    —Play Bill.

Every traveler who visits old Spain has something to say of the bull-fights in that country; and almost every writer gives rather a glowing description of that popular amusement, while he professes to look upon it as disgraceful to the nation that retains it among its customs.

Even our own Washington Irving has not been ashamed to confess that, at first seeing them, he was quite fascinated by their attractions, while I acknowledge that many high-minded *foreigners* whom I have met in Havana avowed having the same weakness; and one distinguished gentleman, a foreign representative, informed me that when first he saw a bull-fight he was intensely disgusted; but that with every succeeding one, he became more and more fascinated. It can matter little what my own feelings were; but honesty compels me to confess that at the first one I saw, a very exciting contest, in which one of the wretched *picadores* came near losing his life, I became very much excited, and whooped and howled with the rest of them, the only difference being that I was cheering for the gallant old bull, while the audience were yelling for the hounds of tormenters. Since then, although I have visited several, to accompany friends, I have never been able to sit another one out.

I know not if the bull-fights of Cuba differ from those of old Spain—I am led to believe they do not; but such as are seen in Havana and other parts of the island have filled me with disgust at the performance, and with contempt for the people who continually patronize such an ignoble amusement, maintained at the expense of so much suffering to poor dumb creatures, and carried on in such a

---

* Note.—Every Sunday that there is a performance, horses will be bought until two o'clock in the afternoon.

ridiculous manner, and by means of such cruel expedients. It is something in the praise of Cuban ladies that they never patronize them except when gotten up for some charitable (?) purpose. For my part, of the two amusements, I have more respect for the vulgar cock-fights; for in these, at least, one sees pluck and courage, and some degree of equality between the combatants, insignificant as they are.

However, our business is now to describe and give a detailed account of a bull-fight as carried on at the present day in the civilized capital of the island, and such as they have every clear Sunday in Havana.

These take place at the Plaza de Toros, or Bull-ring, in the street Belascoin, near the sea, some distance outside the walls of the city. Upon the posters stuck all over the city is a most glowing and attractive account of the inducements and fascinations to be offered at this particular bull-fight, which, of course, is better than any other that ever was, something as follows:

PLAZA DE TOROS DE LA HABANA.

Great running of
BULLS,
For Sunday, the 29th April, 1866,
(If the weather permit).
THE CELEBRATED SWORDSMAN
JOSE PONCE,
Will have charge of the ring,
* * &c. * * * * &c.
There will be fought
SIX BULLS
† † To the Death!   † †
There will be firework darts for the bulls that don't
show much fight.
[Then follows a list of the heroes, under the names of swordsmen, lancers,
and dart men (*banderilleros*).]
Doors open at 3 o'clock; performance to commence at 4½.

It must be understood that the afternoon fight is the only one that is fashionable, there being one early in the morning for the *canaille*, called the *Toro del Aguardiente*, or the Rum Bull,—from the fact, I suppose, that many of the audience get "set up" a little before they enter the ring, which they are at that time allowed to do, and have a fight on their own account.

Well, then, half an hour before the time of commencing, we drive out to the Plaza de Toros, which we find to be a large frame building, occupying a good portion of a block, with great numbers of people gathered around, and a detachment of lancers on guard outside to prevent disturbance. At the office, we purchase our tickets, marked "shady side" (*entrada de sombra*), for which we pay a dollar, and which entitle us to a seat anywhere in the house.

In order to understand why the shady side is the choice place, one must comprehend that the bull-ring is simply an uncovered circus, the seats of which recede from the ring, rising up in regular ascent from the ground to the upper range of boxes, which are covered by a narrow roof. As a consequence, then, that portion of the house exposed to the rays of the sun is very hot, and is called *a sol*, while the other portions are in shade, cool and comfortable.

Entering the building, the best position is that on either side, to the right or left of the music stand, which is over the door by which the bulls enter the arena. You will find, now, the audience composed entirely of men; if there are any females in the boxes, they are "of a kind."

Look, now, beneath your seats, and you will most probably find you are directly over the bull-pens. The bulls are kept in separate stalls, which have doors that can be opened from above, and where, just before an animal is required, he is stirred up with a long, sharp pole, to make him come out "in style."

Now the band, consisting of, perhaps, two brass horns, a big drum, and a little one, begins its performances, when suddenly a signal is given, and the doors are thrown open,—the key having been first obtained in a formal manner by the key-bearer, from the presiding authority, without whose presence the performance would not be allowed to go on. Then commences the grand entrance of all

The Bull-ring

the performers; at the head of whom comes the same key-bearer, mounted on a thing which has evidently been, at one time or other, a horse,—himself most gorgeously arrayed in velvet, trimmed with gold and silver lace, and a short, jaunty little Spanish cloak over his shoulders. Then come the *picadores*, or lancers, also mounted on the same kind of cattle, a long pole pointed with iron in their right hands, their legs wadded and encased in

Key-bearer

leather, their bodies enclothed in stunning jackets and vests of velvet, trimmed with gorgeous lace, on their heads a hat that I can compare

El Picador

to nothing except a large inverted soup-plate, the decorations of which are all rosettes. Then *los banderilleros*, or the dartmen follow on foot, clad in velvet and gold, with knee-breeches, white stockings, pumps, and their hair carried behind their heads and tied in a knot, like a woman's, with ribands; on their heads, a velvet "bonnet," decorated with feathers.

But the men on whom all eyes rest are the swordsmen (*matadores* or *espadas*), generally Spaniards, from Castile, and famed in the annals of bull-fights there as men of prowess and skill.

Note the natty swing they have as they march around the ring, with their gorgeous dresses of green velvet, trimmed with gold bullion, enough to set a pretty woman crazy to have a jacket, *à la zouave*, just like it.

The procession is closed by the three mules, harnessed together, that are used to drag off the dead carcass of the bull when the fight is over. These are richly caparisoned with cloths, bells, and any quantity of fringe, in the Spanish muleteer style, while guiding them are two bandit-looking fellows, in short jackets, white pants, and with silk handkerchiefs round their heads. After marching round the ring, the mules are taken out, a signal is given, and Mr. Bull comes jumping and tearing into the arena, with probably a dart or two sticking in his side, to which are attached gay ribbons, just to make him "playful." His entrance is greeted with shouts and jeers by the audience, and by the performers with a very rapid "making themselves scarce."

The bull now takes a stand, and looks around the ring. The *banderillo* men, attired in the same manner as the *matadores*, then begin the game by making a flirt at the bull with their gaudy colored cloaks, at which the bull gives chase, and double-quick becomes the

El Banderillero

order of the day with *los banderilleros*. The bull being by this time somewhat excited, the *picador*, mounted on his wretched and blindfolded horse, in a saddle that would do for a cradle, makes a dash at him, poking him with his sharp-pointed pole. Mr. Bull, not liking this, makes a dash in return at the *picador*, and if he is not stopped by the horseman bracing himself in his saddle, and keeping his lance at him, he is apt to put his horns pretty roughly against the innocent horse, the cowardly rider being out of his reach. Again and again this play goes on, sometimes with more success on the part of the bull, who upsets horse and rider, or, more frequently, plunges his horns into the breast or bowels of the horse, until the latter protrude, or the blood spurts out in streams.

Then commences the racket. The audience, hitherto quiet, now break forth in yells. If they think the horse has done well, they scream "*musica, musica,*" at which the *band* begins a tune of rejoicing; if the horse is badly hurt in one of these charges, and they think there ought to be a fresh animal, they yell out "*caballo, caballo, otro caballo,*" (horse, horse, another horse), at which the poor bleeding equine is led out, to be replaced by another. And it is now that the reader will understand the note at the head of this chapter; for he will see that all the broken down, worthless, diseased horses must have been purchased to produce such wretched stock as is seen in the ring, the price never being over twenty dollars, but generally from eight to ten.

At last the bull refuses to attack the horse any longer, and amid cries and yells of "*banderillas, banderillas*" (darts), the bugle sounds, and the *picadores* retire. The field is now open to the *banderilleros* and *espadas*, who, failing to excite the bull any longer with their colors, resort to the use of darts to effect their purpose.

These are short pieces of wood about a foot and a half long, and pointed with an arrow-headed piece of steel, which, when once in the flesh, cannot be drawn out; the whole encircled by fancy-colored paper, cut something in the style of the fly-paper that one sees upon the ceiling of country taverns. One of the dartmen now takes one of these darts in each hand, while another man attracts the attention of the gazing bull, who makes a dash. While the bull is in

El banderilla

full charge, the man with the darts (facing him) skillfully plunges them into his body, one on each side, and then nimbly jumps aside, the bull in his speed passing by him.

Infuriated now by the pain, the bull stops a minute or two in the ring, lashing himself with his tail, pawing the ground, and giving vent to a deep roar; and with head down, warily watches his adversaries, who are now pretty careful to keep out of his way. Suddenly one of them picks up courage to approach him with a cloak; the bull makes a quick dash, and catches the cloak on his horns, while Mr. Banderillero takes to his heels, and by great agility jumps the barrier just as the bull charges against it.

Again, maybe, the bull is not plucky enough to fight with *even* all this provocation; and then commence cries from the audience of "*fuego, fuego*" (fire-works); or, perhaps, they are disgusted with the

"Fuego"

bull altogether, and yell out "*fuera, fuera*" (take him out). If the fire-works are brought, however, they are pretty certain to wake up the bull, for they are something similar to the *banderillas*, only having a species of cannon-rocket attached to them, which, the moment they enter the bull, explode with a loud report, amid flame and smoke,— burning the poor beast till he roars with pain, and dashes madly around the ring, sometimes in his fury even attempting to attack the audience behind the barriers.

At last, if the presiding officer thinks it has lasted long enough with this bull, he directs the bugle to sound, and the *matador*, or *espada* (killer, or swordsman), prepares himself to put an end to the bull with the rapier.

As a preliminary, he makes his bow to the official, puts his hand on his heart, nodding triumphantly to the audience, and then, with a *pirouette* on one foot, gives his hat a shy to one side, in token that he is going to spread himself.

He takes now in his left hand a gay red cloak, kept spread open by means of the small stick over which it is thrown; a long, thin piece of bright steel, resembling a rapier or sharp foil, in his right hand; he makes a speech to the audience, the sum and substance of which, done into English, is, that he is going to kill the bull at the first pass,— "If I don't, you may shoot me."

El Matador

The bull, meanwhile, has been quietly looking on from his corner on the other side, until the *matador* approaches, and, with the assistance of the *banderilleros*, draws him into the centre of the ring, where the *matador* begins flirting his red cloak before the bull's eyes. This insult the bull resents by making a charge, the *matador* simply raising the cloak over the bull, and jumping aside as he rushes by. At last the bull, tired with this sort of disappointment, stands warily watching only, or butts his head without advancing, gradually lowering his horns. This is the opportunity the skillful matador seeks to dispatch the bull, for the whole of the body of the bull is exposed by the lowering of his head. Amid cries of "*ahora, ahora*" (now, now), from the audience, which has hitherto remained in almost breathless silence, the *matador* raises his sword-arm, makes a pass, and the bull being too quick for him, after all his bravado, simply runs the sword through the fleshy part of the body, causing the blood to spurt out in torrents. Then there is a row. The bull roars, runs, and kicks; the audience yell, howl, and jeer the *matador*; and, to add to the confusion, the band pounds away, at the satirical cries of "*musica, musica.*" The *matador* then gets another sword, and goes through the same performance; but the bull being now weakened by the torrents of blood pouring from him, stands a little more quietly, and then a flash, a straight pass of the sword, and it is buried up to the hilt in the body of the bull, who staggers, sways to-and-fro, giving a deep, dying roar, turns round once or twice, and then, falling over on his side, is easily dispatched by the knife of the negro attendant, who thrusts it into the brain.

But there was one *matador*, Jose Ponce, from Cadiz, who was a really skillful swordsman. If there could be anything pleasant in such an exhibition, it was to see him, without any fuss or parade, gracefully take up his position in front of the bull, and quick as light make the thrust, up to the hilt, directly to the heart of the bull, who, dropping upon his knees in his very tracks, bellowing and vomiting forth blood, fell over on his side, stone-dead.

Amid the roar of the *bravas* and the *bravissimas*, the mules come in; a rope is placed around the neck of the defunct bull, and he is dragged out to give place to another; and thus half a dozen bulls are slaughtered at one of these exhibitions; while these people, supposed to belong to a civilized community, laugh and cheer, praise or condemn the torturers and butchers of the poor dumb beasts.

The bulls being dead, are carried out to the slaughter-house in the court-yard, outside the building, which can be seen from the windows back of the boxes. The meat is all disposed of in charity to the public hospitals, so that eventually, "good results from evil doings flow."

Entrance of mules

If disgusted with this sight, look through the same window at the scene far beyond, in the now quiet hour of evening sunset. See the beautiful blue sea in the distance, the white walled houses gilded by the setting sun, and the pretty green garden of the Casa de Beneficia in the foreground. A contrast, indeed, to the scene below. *Vamos! caballeros.*

"Sublime tobacco! which, from east to west,
  Cheers the tar's labors or the Turkman's rest;
Divine in hookahs, glorious in a pipe,
  When tipped with amber, mellow, rich, and ripe.
Yet thy true lovers more admire, by far,
  Thy naked beauties;—give me a cigar."

— BYRON

Sitting on the warm side of the hearth, this bitter winter's night, "owling" as they say in the army, in the "wee sma' hours," one is apt to become, under the influence of a fragrant Cabañas, something of a dreamer, or builder of mansions in the air.

In every cloud of aromatic smoke breathed forth, fancy seems nothing loth to picture scenes from memories of the sunny land where grows the "*puro tabaco*," which, had it voice, might truly, in the words of Moore's "Hyperborean," sing —

"I come from a land in the sun-bright deep,
  Where golden gardens grow;
Where the winds of the north, becalmed in sleep,
  Their conch shells never blow."

But a truce to fancy, and so to fact. Never do smokers of Cuban cigars begin a discussion upon the "weed" but what some new theory is adduced about the plant, its history, culture, or brand. How often and how variously even have those mystic words, seen so frequently on the ends of cigar-boxes, been explained!—how truly we shall see.

"Vuelta Abajo" and "Vuelta Arriba" are words well understood by every Cuban,—the first signifying "lower valley," the other, "upper valley." In the Vuelta Arriba, which is that portion of the

Vuelta Abajo

island generally to the eastward of Havana, there is some tobacco cultivated, though not much, and not of superior quality; while in the Vuelta Abajo, which is the country lying to the west of Havana, is raised all the good tobacco, that section being celebrated as the tobacco growing country of the island; the words, therefore, on the cigar-boxes signify that the cigars are made of the best tobacco from that section.

The first account we have of the cigar is found in the works of Navarrete and Las Casas, and is quoted by Irving. In describing the first voyage of Columbus, he says: "They beheld several of the natives going about with fire-brands in their hands, and certain dried herbs which they rolled up in a leaf, and lighting one end, put the other in their mouths, and continued exhaling and puffing out the smoke. A roll of this kind they called a '*tabaco*', a name since transferred to the plant of which the rolls were made," though that is the name by which the cigar is to day known in Cuba.

Oviedo speaks of it (Historia General de las Indias) as among "the evil customs of the Indians of Cuba, very pernicious, and producing insensibility." Their mode of smoking was by inhalation through the nostrils by means of a hollow forked cane, of which we give an engraving, the forked ends being inserted in the nostrils, the other end applied to the burning leaves of the plant.

Smoking tube

It would appear from various authorities that soon after the conquest of the island, some attention was paid to the cultivation of the plant, which in after years grew to such an extent that the government claimed the monopoly of the trade of cigar-making. As early as 1716, it is stated that the planters, having become tired of the restrictions imposed upon its cultivation as regards the price allowed by government, mutinied against the inspector who came around to fix the price for their crops, and again in 1721; and yet again, in 1723,

Military Hospital

when the government inspector visited the *vegas* to fix the price for the coming year, the planters, to the number of five hundred, rose up, refusing to accept the terms, and destroyed the fields of those who did accept. This was so serious an affair, that it was only put down by a company of horse being ordered against the insurgents, and after numbers were killed. In 1761, the government constructed the edifice now known as the Military Hospital, situated on the bay south of the arsenal, outside the walls, and then known as the "Real Fabrica de Tabacos." In 1815, the restrictions and monopoly were removed, the trade opened to the public, and from that time it may be said, commenced the cigar business which has grown to be the second business in extent in the Island of Cuba.

Although the Vuelta Abajo is the district *par excellence* for the finest tobacco produced in the world, yet there are other portions of the island where it is grown; the brands, however, of the "Yara," "Mayari," and the "Guisa" being perhaps the only ones worthy of mention. Of the "Yara," which has some considerable reputation, particularly in the London market, I confess I cannot speak favorably. Cigars that I smoked made from this leaf, and which are much smoked in the vicinity of Santiago de Cuba, I found had a peculiar

Cheap cigar factory

saline taste which was very unpleasant, as also a slight degree of bitterness; many smokers, however, become very fond of this flavor.

When I state that in Havana alone there are over one hundred and twenty-five manufacturers of cigars, it will readily be understood there must be a great many inferior cigars made, even in Cuba. The tobacco on the farms, when duly prepared and dried, is packed in bales, and shipped to Havana, which is the distributing market of Cuban tobacco for the world. In fact, Havana might be called the "city of cigars," from its reputation and the immense number of factories there are in it for the manufacture of cigars,—from the smallest shop opening on the street, employing three or four hands, to the immense *fabricas* erected expressly for this purpose, and employing five or six hundred.

Let not any one imagine, then, that because he is in Havana he will get no poor cigars, for a greater mistake can not be made, for just as vile trash can there be purchased as anywhere; and it appeared to me that in buying, from time to time, in different *fabricas* a few cigars, it was rarely I found a really good one. It behooves, then, every lover of a good cigar to make himself familiar with the best makers and brands, and to purchase those, and those only, that suit his taste. To the traveler in Havana, this is easy enough, as he can there buy sample boxes from any of the factories, and of any of the brands. There are, in addition to the hundreds of other cigar factories, some of which—such as Cabargas, Figaros, Luetanas, Victorias, etc.—are first class, three or four at least in whose cigars every smoker may have *perfect confidence*, the brands of which are known all over the world. These are: Cabañas, Uppmann, and Partagas; for whose brands, perhaps, one pays something more, but has always the satisfaction of finding them good. To the kindness of the gentlemen connected with some of these factories I am indebted for most of the information in this article, and particularly to Señor Don Anselmo G. del Valle, the present proprietor of the Cabañas Factory, who was good enough to show me through his establishment, carefully explaining to me its peculiarities. As the process of manufacture and description of grades and qualities are the same with all the best makers, I give here a detailed history of this factory and its products.

The factory for Cabañas cigars has been established seventy-two years, the founder of it being Don Francisco Cabañas; his son Don M^a de P Cabañas succeeding him, to whom has succeeded *his* son-in-law, Señor del Valle, the present proprietor and director of the factory.

When it was founded, the cigars were sold to the public in bundles of twenty only, amounting to a total number, per year, of four or five hundred thousand cigars, the sales of which kept constantly increasing until 1826, when there were sold two millions. At this period the demand for exportation commenced, increasing each year until 1848, when the number sold amounted to three and a-half millions. At this time, the present director came in charge, and increased the sale to eight millions per year, until, in 1866, the total sales by this one house only amounted to the enormous number of sixteen million cigars, which went to different parts of the world in about the following proportions:

Cuba,	2,000,000	England,	3,000,000
Spain,	2,500,000	Germany,	2,500,000
France,	1,000,000	United States,	3,000,000
		Spanish America,	2,000,000

The tobacco manipulated in this factory is, with some few exceptions, that grown upon plantations in the Vuelta Abajo, with the proprietors of which Señor del Valle has a special contract for their products. The most noted of these places are known as "La Leña," "San Juan y Martin," "Los Pilotos," "Rio Hondo." The firm also own three *vegas*, as do also Partagas, Uppmann, and others, in greater or less degree. The amount raised upon those *vegas*, in connection with the Cabañas Factory, amounts to five thousand bales, of from first to eighth quality, leaving the *most inferior* qualities, which amount to about one thousand bales, for exportation,—the *factory not using such common grades*.

It is computed that each bale will yield about four thousand cigars, and it is a custom of the manufacturers to keep a supply of the best qualities always on hand, from year to year, in order that, should the tobacco crop, in any one year, be bad, the reputation of the house can be maintained by using the good tobacco in store.

The factory is a large stone building, opposite the Campo de Marte, in which all the operations connected with cigar making are carried on (excepting the manufacture of boxes) by over five hundred operatives, all males. It is the custom of the factory to permit the operatives to smoke as many cigars as they wish during the day's labor, and on going home, they are allowed to carry off with them five cigars each per man. This, at first sight, looks like a trifling matter; but when it is figured up, it is found that the number disposed of in the course of the year in this way is over one million eight hundred thousand, which, taken at a value of twenty dollars per thousand, amount to the enormous sum of thirty-six thousand dollars.

The following is the process of manufacture: Arrived at the factory, the tobacco bales, carefully packed and wrapped in palm leaves, are kept in a cool, dark place on the first floor, being divided off into classes according to quality and value, which latter varies from twenty to four hundred dollars per bale of two hundred pounds. When wanted, the bales are opened, the *manojas* and *gabillas* are separated, and the latter carried in their dry state to the moistening room. Here are a number of men whose business it is to place the leaves, for the purpose of moistening and softening them, into large barrels in which is a solution of saltpetre in water; this done, the water is poured off, and other workmen spread out the leaves with their hands upon the edges of the barrels, ridding them, as much as possible, of any surplus water; after which, the leaves, from being moistened, unfold very easily, and, with care, without tearing. The stem is then taken out,—the process being known as *disbalillar*. These stems, with the refuse of other tobacco, are sometimes used as filling for the commonest kind of

Leaf washing

cigars. The filling is known as *tripa*, the very best being selected, like the leaf, for the best cigars.

Now comes the maker, and supplying himself with a hand-full of leaf (*capa*) for wrappers, and a lot of the *tripa* for filling or really making the body of the cigar itself, he carries it to a little table, and spreading the wrapper upon the table, cuts with a sharp knife the different portions of the leaf. This is a very nice operation, requiring skill, knowledge, and experience; for it is in this operation that the different qualities of tobacco are separated, the outside of the leaf being generally the best; next that, another quality; and that portion adjoining the stem, the worst. The general sorting of the tobacco is done by hands of great experience and judgment, who are the highest in consideration in the factories, some of them receiving large pay;

thus, for instance, the official *escojedor*, or chooser, gets from five to seven dollars (gold) per day, and the *torcedores*, or twisters, from two to four,—the workmen being paid so much per thousand cigars, generally from two to four dollars.

To show how very careful the maker must be in cutting out the leaf to make the most of it: Mr. del Valle was explaining to me the process of manufacture, and directed the maker to

Leaf cutter

cut the leaf. This the man did, drawing his knife in the manner denoted by the dotted lines in the engraving. This it appears was not making the most of the fine part of the leaf, for Mr. del Valle, annoyed, took the knife himself, and after rating the maker soundly for his carelessness, showed him how to cut it properly, as defined by the black line,—the difference being, as far as I could judge, a slight inequality of color between the two parts.

The manufacture of the cigar is very simple. The cigar-maker, being seated before a low work-table, which has raised ledges on every side except that nearest him, takes a leaf of tobacco, spreads it out smoothly before him, and cuts it as in the drawing. He then lays a few fragments of tobacco (*tripa*) in the centre of a leaf-strip, and rolls the whole into the shape of a cigar, and taking then a wrapper, rolls it spirally around the cigar. If the workman is skillful, he makes it of just the right length and size, without any trimming of the knife. The cigars are assorted, counted, and done up in bundles of generally twenty-five each, and then packed in the boxes, ready for market, under their different names of "*Londres*," "*Regalias*" etc. These names are generally understood to have the same meaning throughout the trade, the "*Vegueros*," for instance, being the plantation cigars, made, at the *vegas*, of the best leaves, roughly twisted into shape, and much esteemed by smokers, though they are rarely to be met with for sale, or, if so, at an exorbitant price. The "*Regalia Imperial*," the finest and best, is nearly seven inches long, the price varying from one hundred and fifty to three hundred dollars per thousand (gold). The "*Regalia*" is not so large, but fine; the "*Trabuco*" short and thick; the "*Londres*," the most convenient in shape, and most smoked in this country and England; the "*Dama*," the small-sized one used by ladies (?) or by men between acts of the opera (*entr' operas*).

There are also other names which each factory has for some particular kinds. Artificial flavors are given to cigars, when some particular taste is to be satisfied, by the use of flavoring extracts. Each of the above names has different *qualities*, as—

Londres *"superfine,"* the very best of that size (delicious.)
"   *"fino,"* not quite so fine.
"   *"flor,"* finest, or firsts.
"   *"superior,"* next, or seconds.
"   *"buenos,"* next, or thirds.

Again, these different qualities have different colors, known as: *"madura,"* strongest; *"oscuro,"* strong (dark); *"colorado,"* medium; *"claro,"* mild. *"Brevas"* means pressed. Thus, supposing one wanted a good cigar to suit his taste, he would perhaps order: *"Partagas"* (maker), *"Londres"* (size), *"flor"* (quality), *"Colorado"* or *"oscuro"* (strength), and he would get a good cigar, nice size, best quality, not too strong, or too mild. Cabañas' *"Londres"* *thirds*, are worth in Havana thirty-two dollars, gold; packing, thirty cents per thousand; drayage, one dollar; consul's certificate, two dollars and sixty-two cents; freight to New York, regular rates, five dollars and twenty-five cents. Their net weight per thousand is fourteen pounds. The duties are two dollars and fifty cents per pound, and twenty-five per cent *ad valorerm*; to all of which add the premium on gold. For small lots, it is just as cheap to buy from any respectable importer here. I must confess to a weakness for the Uppmann cigars, which I have found, without exception, to be good, and which have a fine reputation throughout the West Indies. A millionaire need not want a better cigar to smoke than their *"Londres superfine,"* at sixty dollars (gold) per thousand, in Havana, or their *"Cazadores,"* at fifty dollars.

Partaga's cigars, of course, every one knows are good; and he keeps generally pretty well sold up, but fills orders as they come in. For a new experience, one of his *"Regalia Reyna, flor,"* is something to try, even if they do cost out there eighty-five dollars, gold. In all the factories they make about the following rates: For every order of ten thousand, costing fifty dollars per thousand, five per cent, discount is allowed. Less than five thousand will pay five dollars per thousand extra. I should, perhaps, mention that no distinction is made to dealers, the only advantage they have over the private buyer is, that they are enabled to get the discount for large lots.

To convey an idea of some of the prices for the best cigars in Havana, I give a list of choice brands and weights of the Cabaña cigar; the weights will give an idea of the sizes.

						WEIGHTS	
					PRICE	LBS. GROSS	LBS. NET
Napoleons de Lujo (gold tipped),					$300	64	22
Regalia Imperial, *flor fina*,					120	32½	20
"	de la Reyna,	*flor fina*,			100	28	16
"	Britannica,	"	"		70	28	16
Conchas,		"	"		70	22½	15
Cazadores, pressed,		"	"	(superb),	60	24½	16
"	small,	"	"		40	21	14
Londres		"	brown,		45	21½	14
"		"	superior,		40	21½	14
"		"	bueno,		32	21½	14
Damas,		"	fina,		40	16½	11
"		"	superior,		30	16½	11

The absurd notion, so prevalent with us, that the Cubans only smoke their cigars *green*, is an error, since the leaf is entirely dried in the sun before being touched by the manufacturer. The Cubans are very particular indeed to preserve the aroma and fragrance of the cigars, by keeping them in wrappers of oiled and soft silk; it is, in fact, quite a sight to see with what ceremony some of these are produced at gentlemen's tables, with much unction, like the ushering in of old wine.

My chapter on cigars would be incomplete did I fail to note the beautiful and courteous way in which all Cubans, no matter of what position, whether the exquisite at the club, or the *portero* at the door, ask you for a light. "Do me the favor, Señor?"—and you present your cigar, the lighted end towards the speaker. He takes the cigar delicately between his thumb and fore-finger, lights his own, and then, with a quick, graceful motion, turns yours in his fingers, presenting you, with another wave, the mouth end, makes you a hand salute, utters his *gracias*, and leaves you studying out the "motions," and thinking what a charming thing is national politeness.

In this connection there are several little points of etiquette we Americans might profit by. When a light is requested, the *smoker*, before handing his cigar, takes care, by a puff or two, to see that it burns well, as also to take off the ashes. In a party of gentlemen, the one who furnishes his cigar for a light, extends this courtesy to but one of the number, who in his turn is expected to pass his new-lighted cigar to another. Cubans always, in taking out their cigar-cases (*petacas*), offer them to every one in the party.

The "*Candela*" is a Cuban institution in connection with smoking. This is generally some gracefully shaped silver or plated dish or vase, filled with wood ashes, in which lies buried a live coal or two, served at each meal as regularly as any other "*plat*," generally just after fruits, and which offers a much more pleasing and convenient way of lighting one's cigar than the odorous match.

Candela

Fabrica La Victoria

"Noble weed! that comfortest life,
And art with calmest pleasures rife;
Heaven grant thee sunshine and warm rain,
And to thy planter health and gain.
When love grows cool, thy fire still warms me,
When friends are fled, thy presence charms me;
If thou are sure, though purse be bare,
I smoke, and cast away all care!"

Notwithstanding that Nature has been so liberal to the Habaneros, in supplying them with water of all kinds, whether dashing in salt spray at the very foot of the city, or flowing, pure and fresh, through the many beautiful—sometimes odd-looking—fountains that are erected throughout the city, yet, either from the nature of the climate or from mere love of that which is novel or uncommon, great ingenuity has been displayed in inventing many new and refreshing beverages to satisfy either the thirst or the bibitory predilections of the Cubans.

We Americans have a greater reputation than any other nation for being able to make numbers of mixed drinks almost unknown outside our own boundaries, or if known in other climes, the knowledge of making them has been carried by some wandering "Yank," desirous of drinking his "cocktail" at the North Pole, or of sucking his "cobbler" 'neath the suns of India. Be this as it may, the Cubans have quite a formidable list of drinks which are really worth knowing about, and some of which might be introduced in our own cafés as summer drinks, in lieu of those heating, stimulating ones now in vogue, made of ardent spirits. Every one in Cuba indulges, at some hour of the day or evening, in a "*refresco*" of some kind, and the ladies are just as habituated to the practice as the men, sipping their "*limonadas*" or "*naranjadas*" with quite as much gusto. Most of the drinks used are perfectly *safe*, suggested, I suppose, by the experience of life passed in a country always more or less warm, and in which some sort of cooling refreshment of this kind seems necessary, even foreigners acquiring the taste and habit of indulging in drinks of which eventually they become very fond.

And first, that which stands upon every table, whether of the merchant or mechanic, though of perhaps different qualities; which is given to you on all the steamboats on which you travel; is the *vin ordinaire* of the café, where it is used in lieu of water almost, and may, in fact, be called a true *cosa de Cuba*,—the "*Vino Catalan*," or wine of the country, though it is a wine brought from old Spain in large quantities, and sold in Cuba at very cheap rates. It is a dark claret-colored wine, of great body, very strong, and used generally diluted with water, though some of the better grades, not so much adulterated by foreign matter as are the lower qualities, are quite as good drunk pure as many of the Burgundies. It is used at both breakfast and dinner, and is considered better than the French clarets from the fact that it is not so acid upon the stomach (a consideration in this perpetually warm climate), though the French wines are much used, and can be had at reasonable prices.

No matter where you go upon the island,—in the mountains, through the valleys, wherever you can find an inn (*fonda y posada*), no matter how small or mean-looking, and where, perhaps, you can hardly get a decent mouthful to eat,—you will always be able to find, of the very best, a bottle of the Britisher's "beah, you know,"—for ale may be said to be as much the drink of the island as *vino Catalan*.

Often, after a long, hot ride, I have been able, at some filthy-

looking *posada*, to make, with the assistance of some bread and cheese,—which is always sure to be good,—an excellent lunch, washed down with good English ale, when, perhaps, tired hungry human nature even would have revolted at the sight of the messes of meat, oil, and garlic set before one at an interior *fonda y posada*.

Fonda y posada

Coffee is, also, one of the great drinks of the country. It is the first thing you have in your bed in the morning, and the last thing after you have disposed of your dinner. Taken either with or without milk, it is generally sure to be very excellent. Many drink nearly a cup full of boiling milk into which has been poured a small amount of coffee to color it; this is good for the stomach. Coffee with milk (*café con leche*), on an empty stomach; coffee without (*café solo*), after eating, is the Cuban general practice.

First upon the list of strictly artificial drinks are the "*Panales*," being exactly what their name denotes,—honey-combs, made of the whites of eggs and sugar, and about the shape and size of a small ear of corn, which they resemble somewhat. These are placed in a glass of water, one or two at a time, where they gradually dissolve, making a very delicious and cooling drink, something like *eau sucrée*, and said to be very wholesome. If it is desired to improve it, a few drops of lime-juice give it a delightful flavor, particularly as a drink for ladies.

Panales

The national and favorite drink of the island, and of a warm day the most agreeable to take, is the "*Naranjada*" or orangeade. It is made from the orange in lieu of the lemon, and is at the same time a wholesome and pleasant drink, rather sweet in its taste, but, if nice and cold, very pleasant to the palate—a favorite beverage with the Señoras. Made with bitter oranges, it is even better; but this is only done amongst people in the country.

"*Limonada*," or lemonade, is similar to that made by us, though limes are more frequently used than lemons, and the Cubans have fallen into the habit, lately, of keeping the syrup already made, which is not so good. A lemonade is vastly improved by pouring gently over the ice floating at the top some good Jamaica rum, which gathers at the surface, and which, when sucked through a straw, is not hard to take. It is known as *limonada con ron*, and is good in any country in warm weather.

The above all come under the generic name of *refrescos*, which it is the custom in every Cuban family to drink during the heated hours of the day. "*Orchata*" is something looking exactly like milk punch, being made of the milk of almonds, sweetened with sugar, and diluted with water; it is much drank, and is very refreshing and very nourishing. "*Cebada*" is nothing more or less than barley-water, and is served at all the cafés. Although with us it is generally considered a sick-room beverage, it is very good in mid-day if nice and cold.

"*Agraz*" is a slightly acid, pleasant drink, made from the juice of the unripe grape. It is very refreshing and pleasant to the taste, but I am unable to answer for its medicinal qualities, although it is much drank. The usual charge for any of the above drinks or *refrescos* at the best cafés is a *real* (ten cents), or a *medio* at those "down town."

But the beverage that can be had *par excellence* in Havana is a cup of chocolate, for the making of which, I believe, all Spanish countries

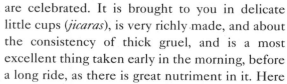

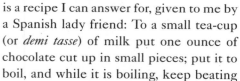

are celebrated. It is brought to you in delicate little cups (*jicaras*), is very richly made, and about the consistency of thick gruel, and is a most excellent thing taken early in the morning, before a long ride, as there is great nutriment in it. Here is a recipe I can answer for, given to me by a Spanish lady friend: To a small tea-cup (or *demi tasse*) of milk put one ounce of chocolate cut up in small pieces; put it to boil, and while it is boiling, keep beating

Molinillo

it with an egg beater until it becomes quite thick and frothy, when it is ready to *eat*. For every cup of chocolate you wish, you must have one of milk; thus for six cups of chocolate you take six ounces of chocolate and six cups of milk; if this be not rich enough, add half an ounce more of chocolate; if too rich, make it with half milk and half water, or all water. The Spaniards use what is known as a *molinillo*, or chocolate mill, which is nothing more than a chocolate pot made of metal, with a mouth on one side, and a beater or paddle inside, worked by a rod running up through the top upon which the palms of the hands are placed, and the rotary motion kept up while the chocolate is boiling. With one of these that has a small spirit lamp under it any one can make delicious chocolate at his own table, or in his own room. It is the fashion in the island, on taking it in the morning on rising, to eat with it a light, thin cake, or what is better, a small piece of well-toasted bread; after which a glass of water is drank.

There are also other drinks peculiar to the island, though in the cities the above modern-invented beverages have pretty much taken their place; but occasionally one meets with them in the *pueblos*, or villages.

"*La Chicha*" is water with sugar broken up in it, and toasted corn, which makes it ferment. The "*Zambumbia*" is made with water and cane honey or molasses, and the "*Gara piña*" is also a fermented infusion of pine-apple rind, sweetened with sugar.

Life, it would be supposed, would be almost insupportable in a climate like that of Cuba without plenty of ice; and, fortunately, in Havana and the principal towns of the island there is no lack of it, costing from two to three cents per pound according to the supply; but it was only in 1806 that ice was introduced into the island.

At the Louvre café they have a most ingenious way of making it, which must be much more economical than buying it and wasting it, as is done with us. The decanters are filled with water, which by some process is then frozen in the bottle, forming a solid lozenge-shaped lump of ice, the which, when you ask for ice-water, is brought to you partially melted. You use what is wanted, and it is then taken away, refilled, and refrozen.

In the interior of the island they are not so fortunate as to have ice, and they, therefore, resort to the porous jars for cooling the water, which answer the purpose admirably, the water reaching a temperature not so cold as that of ice-water, but still sufficiently cool for drinking purposes.

Estelladora

The article of furniture used for that purpose is a household institution in all Cuban houses, some of them, made of fine woods, and of tasteful designs in carving, being very handsome, looking, as they stand in a corner of the hall or dining-room more like an *étagère* than anything else. In addition to the large stone jars seen within the closet, as in the accompanying sketch, there are generally two or three pretty, odd looking jars standing on the top, of a convenient size, and with handles on the sides, used for drinking purposes in lieu of pitchers or glasses.

The "*estelladora*" is the name of the piece of furniture above described, and it might be introduced, with advantage, into the

Water jar

interior of some of our Southern States, where it is often difficult to get a glass of cool water.

The supply of water for drinking purposes in Havana seems to be very good and quite a sufficient one, it being brought some distance by means of a fine aqueduct, through the Canal Isabel II, the water coming from the streams of Vento and Almendares, in the neighborhood of Puentes Grandes, and conducted throughout the city to the many fountains of different design and material with which the city abounds, though the supply of water having been somewhat limited lately, the fountains do not all of them flow, but still remain as oddities or ornaments to the city.

An essay might, I think, be written upon the "customs of the tropics as results of climate;" for in a country where there is perpetual summer, habits of life seem to be specially arranged to suit; and I do not question for a moment but that we of the north would gain greatly by following in our hot summers the example set us in Cuba, if, with our habits and hours of business, it were possible so to do.

There no one eats until he is hungry; thus, in lieu of turning out of bed of a warm morning and going immediately to the breakfast table, these people take a simple cup of coffee or chocolate, and then go to their places of business, and get, with clear heads, three or four hours of good hard work. Then, when the heat of the sun is pretty well felt, they go for an hour or two, with sharpened appetites, to their cool dining-halls or airy cafés, to enjoy a substantial breakfast.

For this reason, one finds in Havana, in almost every square, restaurants, cafés, confectioners, and other places known as "*lecherias,*" where all sorts of milky drinks are made and sold, with, perhaps, a bit of toast or light cake.

Again, in the evening, when the business of the day is done, these same cafés become the resort of the people. As their dinner at home, at five or six, is usually the last meal they have, the evening is most generally passed—by the men, anyhow—at these places, where they get a cool drink for a *real*, smoke their cigars, and meet their friends.

Of course the Habaneros have their clubs and private social

organizations just as much as any other people; and those known as the "*Liceos*" are worthy of all emulation. These are really lyceums, as they are intended to combine pleasure and instruction, affording to their members opportunities for social intercourse, as well as instruction in music, painting, the languages, etc., giving exhibitions, lectures, balls, etc., being in fine, large buildings, many of them possessing good collections of paintings, books, and works of art.

During the winter season, their receptions, balls, and masquerades are frequented by the best people of the city, and the stranger is always well received when properly introduced. One thing I must confess is, that during my entire stay on the island, I never saw, in town or county, a person whom we should call drunk. It may be these people deserve no credit for this, for the climate is such that cooling drinks are what one wants; and yet we have hot days, and drunken men too.

While the law there, as it does in other lands, prohibits gambling, it does not prevent it; and any one inclined to lose his money has plenty of opportunities of doing so at the games of "*lotto*," "*burro*," "*monte*," "*faro*," etc.

Havana may, undoubtedly, be called a military city; for
at every corner you meet a soldier, before nearly every
public office there is a guard, and at various hours of the day and
evening, and in various parts of the city, one's ear is greeted by the
notes of the bugle, or the rattling of the drum; while many of the
barracks and a fort or two are right in the midst of the city.

At night, sometimes, these sentries are troublesome with their
challenging, in an open city; and if one approaches too near their
posts, he hears the words, quickly rung out, "Who goes there?" (*Quien
vive*)? As a reply has to be made, the Habaneros say "*España*," the
regular pass-word. I found always no trouble in replying "*Forastero*"
(foreigner), or "*Americano.*" But now-a-days, the latter might be
dangerous, as the name does not seem to be popular with either the
catalan or the *voluntario.*

A great deal of good sense has been displayed in uniforming the
troops for this climate; an example which, I must confess, might be
followed to great advantage in our army uniforms.
In lieu of the heavy cloth in which our poor fellows
have been required to swelter during the warm
days of summer, or of service in the South, the
Cuban soldiers are clad in simple linen, of various
colors,—white, blue and brown,—than which
nothing can look more soldierly. Take, for instance,
the infantry soldier, in full uniform. He wears a sort
of dark blue dungaree blouse, gathered at the waist
to give it a natty shape, a pair of neat brown-drilling
pantaloons, and a low-crowned cap of leather, with
visor enough to be of some use. In lieu of the stiff,
uncomfortable coat collar, and the still more
uncomfortable and unhealthy leather stock, he

Infantry

Cavalry-man

wears a neatly rolled collar, of red cloth, which, with his cuffs of the same, can be taken off when he sends his kit to the wash.

Others, again, are uniformed in pure white, with pretty "shoulder knockers," and collars and cuffs of red; while the cavalry and artillerymen wear loose short jackets, pants of blue linen, and broad palm leaf hats. This uniform, far from being uncomfortable or unsoldierly, is just the opposite; and Spanish troops have the appearance of clean and well instructed soldiers. I have seen them at drill, on different occasions, and I must confess that some of their officers lack "vim." Slowness of movement on the part of the men follows as a natural result. This is particularly noticeable in the infantry; while I have also seen some very bad drilling in the artillery, which I was informed was an old organization, and, therefore, had no excuse for drilling like recruits. There was on duty in Havana a battalion of "mountain" artillery, in which everything was on horseback,—caissons, carriages, and cannon, all strapped on the backs of horses. It was out exercising frequently, and seemed to be well organized and instructed.

The Captain-General is the superior military chief of the island, and commander-in-chief of its armies; while next to him in rank is the second chief, who has the rank of brigadier-general, and pay of ten thousand dollars per annum, and who is also the sub-inspector of infantry and cavalry. The corps of artillery and engineers have special sub-inspectors, with the title of *mariscales de campo*.

The fortresses of the island, in which are nearly always the prisons and the barracks of the troops, have their own governors or commanders, with special staffs.

The army consists generally of twenty-five or thirty-thousand men, with its proportion of infantry, artillery, cavalry, engineers, and marines. The organization, as regards company formation, is about the same as with us; there being about two thousand men in a regiment, consisting of two battalions, each one thousand strong, divided into eight companies. Each regiment has a colonel and lieutenant-colonel, a drum-major, and six contract musicians. The battalion has a first and second commander, an adjutant (lieutenant), an ensign, a chaplain, and a surgeon, a chief bugler, and a master armorer. These regiments are all known by names (not numbers), such as the King's, the Queen's, Isabel II, of Naples, of Spain, etc., which does much towards increasing the *esprit du corps* so necessary to make good soldiers.

There is also a battalion known as the "Guardia Civil," a fine body of men, who are scattered in small detachments throughout the island, mostly as watchmen and police, or, perhaps, as spies. They are generally an intelligent set, handsomely uniformed in well-fitting dark-blue coats, white pants, and broad-brimmed felt hats, neatly bound with white. One sees them on the wharves, in the opera-house, at the theatre, patrolling the paseo,— in fact, everywhere in Havana.

I was informed by the officers that a large per-centage of the troops die every year when they first come from Spain, and therefore a large supply of recruits is necessary to keep the regiments up to their maximum. The pay of field, staff, and line is

Guardia Civil

about the same as in our army, being double that which is received in Spain; though, as some of the officers told me, "half pay" was more at home (Spain) than double pay in Cuba, everything costs so much more on the island.

In addition to the above regular troops, there are also volunteer organizations, composed of Spaniards only, no creoles being allowed to belong to the army. In Havana, there is a company of negro firemen, with officers assigned to it, which forms a quasi-military organization for the extinguishing of fires.

Havana is said to be impregnable. If it is not, it ought to be, judging from the number of its stone walls, its frowning fortresses, and its ships of war; and yet it has struck me that it is not so strong as it looks. The day is past for the simple, old-fashioned ways of attack by buccaneers, and new modes of war make sad inroads upon the protection afforded by some of these old-time forts.

The Morro and La Punta command the entrance. Across the bay is the Cabañas, with its guns pointing in every direction, and at the end of the bay the Fortress of Santo Domingo de Atares, which commands the bay and holds the city itself under surveillance. East and west, La Punta, El Morro, Cabañas, Number Four, Principe, San Lazaro, Pastora, and the Tower of Chorrera give notice to the adventurous fillibuster to "keep off."

The Castillo de los tres Santos Reyes del Morro, and the Fortress of San Carlos de la Cabaña are the ones which every traveler desires to see, and which every one, if it is possible, should visit, as they are world-renowned, in addition to being well worth seeing, not only on account of their structure, but on account of the magnificent views of sea and land from their battlements.

In former years, it was a matter of some difficulty to gain entrance to these forts, and it is not now accomplished very easily. Of course, our consul is the person to secure for us passes to the forts, and doubtless he will oblige such parties of Americans as desire to visit them, unless in war times. The authorities have a regular printed form of passes, and when mine was given me by the courteous aide-de-camp, he informed me they were always willing to oblige *los forasteros*. I made the visit after four o'clock in the afternoon, starting from the landing just outside the Puerta de la Punta, from which it is only a short pull directly across to the landing of El Morro.

Strolling up the slope from the landing, one begins to realize immediately the apparently great strength of the work. The slope itself which conducts up to the main gate of the castle is very strong, with solid stone parapets on each side, and a road laid in mortar with small regular sized cobble-stones. To the left, almost on a line with the water, is the water battery known as the "Twelve Apostles,"— twelve iron guns, mounted on siege carriages, carrying twenty-four pound shot, and worked *en barbette*, which would give them great effect at short range on any vessel attempting to pass. Passing a sentry or two, in whose faces it was only necessary to flirt my pass, I reached the main gate, which is an arched opening protected by a covered

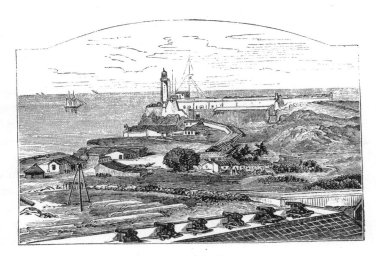

Land view of the Morro

way, at whose entrance a sentry demanded my pass, which being shown him, the sergeant of the guard came and examined it. I now gave the sergeant my card, and told him to hand it, with the pass (signed by the military governor-general of Havana), to the commanding officer, in order that he might detail for me a guide. Although the soldiers of whom you ask questions in the fort either dare not or *will* not tell anything, yet they are useful guides. The walls here at the entrance are very thick, you notice, and form casemates, the one to the right being the guard-room, which is also occupied by the officer of the day, who sometimes strolls through the fort with foreigners.

In front of the entrance are the barracks and the store-houses, which seem to occupy the hollow square formed by the walls of this portion of the fort. They are of solid stone, with their rooms arched, ceiled, and paved in stone, the bunks of the men being simply cots. Looking towards the harbor is the casemate battery, mounting about eight guns, I should think, judging from what I could see, as, for some reason, my guide would not take me through, and refused to allow me to enter. The whole of this first fort, which seems to be separated from the citadel by drawbridges, is very cramped and very dismal, and

I should hate hugely to be stationed there any length of time. On the extreme corner of the fort, at the very mouth of the entrance to the bay, stands the O'Donnell light-house, a cylindrical tower of stone, seventy-eight feet in height from the wall of the castle, and fifteen feet in diameter, being altogether one hundred and fifty-eight feet above the level of the sea. The light is of the first order of Fresnel, fixed, but alternated with large reflectors that shine, every half minute, for about five or six seconds. It is ordinarily seen at a distance of eighteen miles, though in fine weather at a greater distance.

Near the light-house, but upon the terreplain of the portion above, is a small frame house, used as the signal-station, where are kept the signal-flags, which are displayed from the masts close by; there are so many flags and signals of all nations, that the interior of the house looks quite like a dry goods store. This portion of the fort is reached by a stone slope leading up between the quarters, or by a narrow spiral stone stairway inside the walls, coming out upon a concrete terreplain protected by stone parapets, pierced with embrasures for cannon.

I was very much astonished to find that there was hardly a gun mounted on these upper walls, and the few that were mounted were all old-fashioned, bronze pieces, of hardly twenty-four pounds calibre, on wooden casemate carriages, which were worked in and out of battery by a *windlass and chain* at the rear end of the *chasis*. The walls in this portion, judging from the parapet, are about twelve feet thick, and in many places seem to be the worse for age, as I noticed a good deal of crumbling, or honey-combing.

From here, there is a fine view of the sea, the city, and the surrounding country. Here, also, can be seen the full lines of the land-face of the fort and the position of the others.

The moat is a dry and very deep one, the scarp walls of which, I should say, were fully one hundred feet high, and the width full fifty feet. The guide was so "touchy," that he would permit me neither to measure nor to sketch, saying it was not allowed; so I had to trust to my memory and one or two memoranda I made. From the battlements, one can see how much nature did for this fort in the beginning; for from the sea-side directly up to the counter-scarp, there is a natural *glacis*, commanded completely from every part by the guns *en barbette* in this part of the fort. The strongest battery that I saw, and the only one that really looked as though it were ready for work, was the one to the extreme right of the fort, entered by a covered way, and forming the sea-coast battery. It mounts about twenty-four iron guns, of thirty-two pounds calibre, on siege carriages, and appeared to be a very strong battery. Just after entering the fort, by the stone slope, in side the exterior wall, there is to the right hand a long stone-covered gallery, connecting the southern face of the fort with the covered way that leads to the sea-coast battery, as also to the road leading over to the Cabañas on the brow of the hill. This is a strong affair, arched, and lighted by long, narrow apertures. It is about one hundred yards long, according to my pacing.

This gallery, with the road beyond, is the best way to reach the Cabañas, the road being nearly level, and leading to the principal entrance of that fort, which faces the sea. This route saves the labor of mounting up the long and tedious slope on the other side of the fort, which is easy enough to go down, after having inspected that work.

The principal facts in the history of La Punta and Morro Castle have been given in the chapter entitled "Havana Past and Present." It will be remembered that the Morro Castle was mined and captured by the English in 1762, but was restored to the Spanish in 1763. In this latter year, the Governor-General, Conde de Ricla, with Marshal O'Reilly as sub-inspector, commenced the reconstruction of the Morro Castle, and the erection of the Castle of Atares, at the depth of the bay; the engineers being Abarca and Crame.

In 1766-1771, during the reign of Bucarely, the forts were completed, as well as the Fort of Principe, near the Botanical Gardens. It is stated that, during the command of Ricla, six millions of dollars were spent upon these works; the money for which was drawn from Mexico. In 1771, the Marquis de Torre made some few improvements, and the forts have, from time to time, been repaired or extended, until now, with the Casa Blanca, they form a complete chain on the eastern side of the bay.

The Cabañas fortifications are the largest on the island, and are said to be among the best in the world. In some respects, they remind

La Cabañas

me of the forts at Quebec; being upon a high, precipitous bank, that rises directly from the bay-side, completely overlooking the town, and commanding most of the bay.

Like the Morro, they are built of solid stone and concrete; are about eight hundred English yards long, and have accommodations for more than four thousand men, the capacity for cannon being almost unlimited. The bay-side appears to be intended only for guns *en barbette*, as I noticed only one casemate in the extreme western salient. There is a fine water-battery at a small elevation above the water-level, called, I think, "La Pastora," which bears directly upon the entrance,—the guns being not over twenty-four pounds calibre, and mounted on wooden casemate carriages. The visitor, on entering the fort, should ask immediately for the officer of the guard; for the sentries are so stupid that they permitted me to enter on showing my pass, without informing me that, even with that protection, it was necessary to have one of the guard to accompany me, if I wished to go all over the fort. In fact, the best way at all these places is just to send your card, with the pass, to the commanding officer. It is a compliment to him, and if he is at all courteous, and finds you are a stranger, he will see that you are properly taken around.

At the time of my visit to the forts, during the Chilian troubles, they were very particular about visitors (fearing spies, perhaps), who were only allowed to enter upon passes signed by the military governor of Havana. The sentries at the gate allowed me to go through without even showing my paper, and I went wandering about, thinking what a loose way that was of doing. In attempting, however, to mount upon the ramparts, Mr. Sentinel over the guns stopped me instanter, and flatly declined to allow me to go on, even with my pass, unless one of the guard was with me; whereupon I posted off after one of these individuals, who was kindly furnished me by the officer of the day, with instructions to take me all around; and off we started. My troubles, however, did not cease here; for, on passing the quarters of the commandant, who happened to be sitting on the porch, he sent his adjutant to inquire by what authority I was there. I told him my pass had been left at the guard-room; so he directed me to wait there until he went for it, and showed it to the commandant. This was rather annoying; so, turning to a knot of officers near by, leaning over the parapet, I entered into conversation with them, and found them very pleasant fellows, who pithily informed me that the aforesaid commandant was *una vieja* (an old woman); and that the biggest gun they had in the fort carried a twenty-four pound ball.

They were much interested in the American war, and were considerably astonished when I told them of our fifteen-inch guns at Fortress Monroe; but when I told them of the twenty-inch that had lately been mounted in New York harbor, they burst into laughter,— telling me that I was chaffing them. And I think they may be under that impression to the present day.

My pass being pronounced all right, with many apologies for detaining me, I went on with my explorations, in charge of my military cicerone, who gave me much information about the manners and habits of the Spanish soldiery. Upon the ramparts of the fort, facing the city, there is a fine, large battery of twenty-four pound iron guns, mounted on siege carriages, the only battery I saw in order; for face after face of the fort was without a single gun, and not one, either gun or carriage, did I see that had any of the modern improvements.

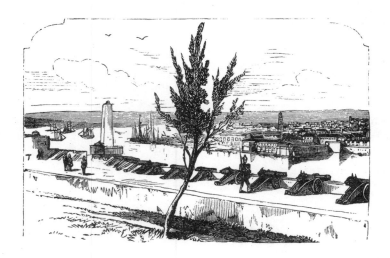

Part of the Cabañas fortifications and Bay of Havana

In some of the bastions there were one or two old-fashioned bronze mortars, but none did I see that were serviceable.

The buildings, quarters, and barracks are all substantial stone edifices. The interior of the fort is extremely capacious, there being a fine, large parade or drill-ground.

In the centre of the face of the fort, facing the city, there is erected a marble monument, surrounded by an iron railing, upon a small bastion jutting out upon the bay, in memory of a number of Spanish soldiers who were killed in the fights with the men of Lopez's expedition, and over which the government was so terribly scared. This monument is erected by their comrades, subscriptions being raised in old Spain as well as in Cuba to provide for the families of those who suffered in this affair, which it must be said were very liberal.

The views from all parts of the fort are very fine and commanding. The officers, as a general thing, do not strike me as being either so well bred or so intelligent as ours; and as to their housekeeping, if it is all of the order that I saw *en passant*, deliver me from being "one of their mess," even in garrison. I have met in Havana and other portions of the island some fine fellows,—regular thorough-breds,—and I am therefore inclined to believe they are pretty well mixed throughout this army.

On leaving the fortress, the visitor will have occasion to notice the long descent of solid stone down to the landing, and to thank his good fortune he has not to mount up it every day. The boat will land him at the *Caballeria*, foot of Obispo street.

chapter eighteen

GOVERNMENT AND ADMINISTRATION OF CUBA AND HAVANA

Division of the island into departments; Jurisdiction; The Church and State; Varieties of officials; How appointed; Severe laws; Freedom of the press; Orders of nobility; The lack of freedom.

Politically, the Island of Cuba is portioned off into four territorial divisions, known as natural, topographical, vulgar, and administrative. The natural division is that of the "Continent," which is understood as meaning the island itself, with all the adjacent small islands and "*cayos*" or keys.

The topographical divisions are the cities, towns, villages, and rural populations.

The vulgar divisions are those known as the "Vuelta Abajo," and "Arriba." The Vuelta Abajo extends from Cape San Antonio to the baths of San Diego, or even to Havana; and that portion lying between Havana and San Cristobal is called "*Partida de Fuera*" or "*Los Partidos.*" There is also the name "*Tierra Adentro*" (middle ground), which comprises the meridians of Cienfuegos and Puerto Principe, and even as far as to Bayamo and Holguin.

The above being, in fact, the whole island, are regularly divided into what are known as administrative territorial divisions, six in number, known as Judicial, Political, Military, Ecclesiastical, Maritime, and Economical or "*Real Hacienda.*"

The division Judicial comprises the whole island, or the territory of the "Real Audencia Pretorial," or General Courts. In each one of the twenty-six judicial districts into which the island is subdivided exists an "alcalde mayor," ordinary judge of the part, having for auxiliary delegates the ordinary "alcaldes," or local judges, in whose charge are the judgments of conciliation and councils. The Real Audencia is the superior tribunal of the island, holding sessions in Havana, to which any one can appeal from the inferior authorities in their unrighteous decisions, and whose Royal Body is a species of Council of State, which the Captain-General consults upon all the difficult matters of the government and administration, as well as upon the laws, concessions, and general favors.

The Political division is the whole island, which composes one single province, subject to the command of a Superior Governor, who is at the same time Captain-General. The island is again subdivided into four political governments (*Gobiernos Politicos*),—the special one of the "Plaza de la Habana," that of Matanzas, that of the Eastern department of Cuba, at which town are its head-quarters, and that of the rest of the Western department, all of which are "Lieutenantcies" of the Governor, subdivided again into "*Gobiernos*" and Captaincies. The political districts number thirty-one, each one having an "*Ayuntamiento*" or town council, at its head.

The Military division is the whole island, constituting a Captaincy-General, and is divided into two departments,—that of the west, with Havana for its capital, and that of the east, with Santiago de Cuba as its capital. The former, in charge of the Captain-General; the latter, under the Governor of Cuba, each department being divided into *gobiernos*, military districts, and districts of arms. The boundary-line between the two departments starts from the mouth of the brook Yana, in front of the eastern part of the island of Yuriguano, and terminates in the eastern vicinity of the landing at Sabanalamar, dividing the island in half. This line is also the dividing line of the two dioceses and the political government of the island.

The Ecclesiastical government is divided into two dioceses,— the arch-bishopric of Cuba and the bishopric of Havana, the dividing line being as above.

The Maritime division is subject to a Commander-General, and is divided into five provinces,—Havana, Trinidad, San Juan de los Remedios, Nuevitas, and Cuba.

In the branch of Economy or Royal Property, the whole island constitutes a Superintendency General, delegated and annexed to the office of the Captain-General, and there is also an Intendencia of the army, whose chief resides in Havana, having in Cuba a subordinate Intendencia annexed to the political government of the eastern part of the island.

The Island of Cuba, a province of Spain, is governed directly by a Governor Captain-General of the class of Lieutenant-General in the Spanish army, whose authority, for the time being at least, is almost despotic. He is appointed by the crown, and with the consent of the council of ministers. The term of office is generally from three to five years, and the salary about fifty thousand dollars per annum, though some of those who have held this office have made millions of dollars out of it. A romantic story is told of the appointment of General Dulce. During a conspiracy to overthrow the government under Queen Isabella, it was the desire of the conspirators to possess themselves of the person of the queen, and in order to effect this, every one of importance about her palace was bribed except Dulce, who was a simple lieutenant, and considered of no value. Everything was arranged, and the night came upon which the attempt was to be made; but, much to the horror of the conspirators, they found, when too late, that Dulce was in command of the guard that night. It is stated that Dulce had discovered what was going on, and, piqued at not being thought worthy of notice, had determined to defeat the enterprise; so that when the would-be conspirators attempted to carry their plans into execution, they were met by Dulce and a few picked men, who made a most desperate defense, thereby saving the queen, who was so delighted with Dulce's honesty (?) and courage that she promoted him from one position to another until he became Captain-General of Cuba.

The Captain-General disposes of the military forces, the marine as well as the army, taking counsel in matters that refer to the marine with its chief, the commander of the marine, who is not alone commander of the forces of Cuba, but of Porto Rico also. The Captain-General is in fact a viceroy, and as such has extraordinary powers given to him in certain cases, being able to suspend even the officials from their functions, giving account thereof only to the Spanish government.

When there are extraordinary occasions occurring, he convokes a council of superior authority, consisting of the Commanding Officer of the Navy, the Regent of the Audencia, and the Bishop of Havana, and the result of their deliberations constitutes a provisional law until sanctioned or revoked by the home government.

On appropriate days, and at stated hours, he gives public audience in order to attend to the complaints and petitions of all classes of persons, taking care, however, not to grant petitions signed by more than three neighbors at a time, an occurrence which is looked upon and punished as sedition.

In case of vacancy, the Captain-General is succeeded by the second in command, or second chief, in whose charge is the army. In case of further vacancy, the next in rank takes command.

The nobility do not constitute here an element of power, but are represented in the court by some of their number, elevated to the dignity of senators of the kingdom, which are divided into two classes: the dignities and titles of Castile; the former being such as the Gentlemen of the Grand Cross of Charles III, of Isabel, etc., etc.; and the latter, marquises and counts, with and without grandeeship, a merely complimentary title.

The law of printing, promulgated in Spain when the Royal Statute was in force, in 1834, is the one still in force to-day, I believe, on the island, modified somewhat by some concessions on the part of the Captain-General, especially in regard to the freedom of the press. According to the above law, it is permitted to publish without censorship the technical works of any society or faculty, not in periodicals,—which are understood to be all publications of from one up to five sheets,—with the exception of works purely economic. The censorship rests in charge of the civil government (*gobierno politico*).

The Municipal power, though circumscribed to the economic administration of the towns, is subordinate to the civil authority; and the municipalities of the island are, in fact, consulting bodies of the government, presided over by the Captain-General, and in his name by the local governors. They represent the residents of their districts, and as such representatives they must be sworn before taking possession of their office, or being invested with authority. The councilmen or aldermen (*regidors*) are perpetual, and their office hereditary and transferable; but there are annually elected two justices of the peace (*alcaldes*), and one recorder or collector of fines (*sindico*), from among persons not aldermen.

The Sindic is the one who hears the complaints of the townspeople, and to him are also given the care and protection of the slaves and of the contract laborers. There is an alderman, with the name and character of general father of the poor class and of the absentees, to watch over *their* rights. The vacancies that occur in these town corporations (*ayuntamientos*) are provided for by the Captain-General, the members of which are honored by the title of "very illustrious," and those of Havana by that of "more than excellency" (*excellentissima*). They meet weekly for ordinary affairs, but, when circumstances require it, they have special meetings.

The municipal taxes, called "*propios*" and "*arbitrios*," consist of a poll-tax, of taxes upon property, industry, and commerce; upon all venders, markets, stores, and traveling traders; upon weights and measures; on public and private carriages, and upon performances, etc. With these revenues, the towns are lighted and cleaned (?), watchmen paid, dungeons maintained, and prisoners supported, and ecclesiastical and civil holidays, and other objects sustained.

In all the towns and cities there are *ayuntamientos*, and in the villages, which are heads of jurisdiction, there are municipal councils named by the superior authority, and composed of five or six voices, under the presidency of the Lieutenant-Governor, with powers similar to those of the *ayuntamientos*. There is, besides, a "Directory of Public Works," entirely independent of any general office, and at its head a director, with pay of five thousand dollars, employing numbers of subordinates, clerks, engineers, etc. It has in its charge the care and construction of public works, of the light-houses, telegraphs, walls, gates, and streets.

The *ayuntamientos* have a central administration which constitutes the third actual element of the government interior. There is a principal chief of the whole island, who resides in Havana, subject to the orders of the Captain-General; there are also principal chiefs in Cuba, Matanzas, Puerto Principe, Trinidad, etc. For the security of the country, there is a battalion of the soldiers known as the "*guardia civil*" before alluded to.

Infractions of the law are punished by fines and imprisonments,—the latter in case of insolvency,—and by hard labor upon the public works, in chains even. In every town are to be seen large gangs of prisoners, clad in the roughest material, their numbers marked upon their backs, led out in charge of the military guard, early in the morning, all attempts at escape being prevented by chains and manacles. Private gambling, a sort of national plague, confined to no class, is strictly forbidden, and is rigorously punished. It is allowed, I suppose, on the boats; for I never was on one yet where plenty of money did not change hands at *monte, burro,* etc., nevertheless a fine of fifty dollars is the penalty established by law,—first offence, ten days' imprisonment in the dungeon; twenty days' imprisonment, or one hundred dollars, for the second offence, if it is a nobleman or master of the house; and for a third offence, the culprit's name is recorded in a book kept for that purpose, and is published to the world in the newspaper.

Gambling is, notwithstanding, carried on to a great extent; and I heard of a marquesa, who, wishing to pass time at her country place, invited her guests—a public official, and her young nephew, then staying at her house—to play with her. She lost some eight thousand dollars to the officer before he went away, and in settling up, her nephew claimed some three thousand dollars that he, also, had won of her. "Pooh, pooh!" said she, "that's all in the family; I shan't pay you;" but the young scamp was too smart for her, and threatened to report her to the Captain-General for having gambling in her house; whereupon she settled.

Families are obliged to give notice to the *celador,* or alderman of their locality, of the increase or diminution of the family, of the admission of a new inmate, or of a guest, of a change of living, and of whatever reunion or party they may celebrate in their house, thus subjecting the whole country to a complete system of espionage.

It is necessary to have a license beforehand for the construction, alteration, or repair of houses; and, in doing this, it is required that only a third part of the public highway shall be occupied with the material, which, if left over night in the street, must be lighted by a lantern, to advise the public of any obstacle. Permission from the authorities is required to open any class of amusement or spectacle where entrance money is charged; to open any store of any kind, or to enter a profession.

The slave, living away from the house of his master, needs to have a written license, signed and stamped by the *commissionaire*, without which he is liable to capture and fine. The inhabitants cannot go from one part of the island to another without a pass or license, or leave the island without a passport; neither can a man's residence be changed from one place to another without permission of the authorities. Free negroes are required to take out a certificate for protection.

The public health is in charge of a sanitary commission, known as the *"Junta Superior de Sanidad,"* of which the Captain-General is president. This body has its ramifications throughout the island, looking more particularly after the health of the ports and harbors. There are a number of public charities in connection with the government throughout the island, such as military hospitals, houses of charity, and *beneficios*. The principal public institution likely to interest the stranger is the library of the Royal Economical Society of Havana, which is situated in the street Dragones, between Rayo and San Nicholas, outside the walls. The rooms of this society are open to the stranger from twelve to three each day, and in them he will find a large and most excellent library, many of the books being very rare, and not usually met with, particularly those relating to Cuba. There are books in all languages, though the library is principally Spanish; but candor compels me to confess that I do not think they are much used by the public, judging from the dust which I found settled upon them.

This society is divided into three sections, that of agriculture and statistics, that of industry and commerce, and that of history, science, and fine arts. Each one of these sections has a president and vice-president, a secretary and vice-secretary, elected by the corporation, and approved by the government. These sections prepare the information that the government asks, and create reforms and improvements in the branches of instruction and protection.

The corporation has in its charge a fine drawing-school, with good instructors, and a most excellent collection of casts from the antique; it has also charge of the botanical gardens, and has lectures, etc., delivered before it on various subjects connected with the improvement of the island.

THE SUBURBS OF HAVANA

Accustomed as we Americans are to the beautiful surroundings of most of our principal cities, the pretty villages, and neat little towns to which we resort for summer recreation or change of air, it is natural that we should wish to see how the suburbs of such a place as Havana will compare with those of our own homes.

In visiting different localities, it is best to start very early in the morning, when it is cool and pleasant in the country, and by this means we can spend the hours from six to ten o'clock very delightfully in these excursions.

From the Plaza de Armas an omnibus starts about twenty minutes before the beginning of each hour, and for ten cents, will carry the traveler to the "Paradero de Marianao" depot; but a much more easy way is to call a volante at the door of one's hotel, and ride directly out there, at the usual cost of twenty cents. The train starts for Marianao punctually at the hour, and the fare to that place is twenty-five cents.

On getting into the cars, one is struck with the peculiarly cool and airy appearance of the carriages. There are no glass windows, but simply blinds, the frames to which are very lightly made, so as to afford as much air as possible; the seats are cane, with backs of the same material. The way of giving notice to start is ridiculously odd: not the quick, sharp notes of a big bell, and the prompt "all aboard" of the conductor, but a blue-shirted, slippered, half Cubanized "Chinois," who walks up and down the platform, ringing the "alarm" as though he had muffins to sell, and not trains to start.

Train-starter

Arrived at Marianao, hacks will be found at the depot, that for a trifling sum will drive one all over the village and down to the sea. Unless there are ladies in the party, it is more enjoyable strolling through a foreign country village like this on foot, the distance being trifling, and the opportunity for sight-seeing much better.

Marianao is simply a pretty little Cuban village, rather newer and neater than most such villages, owing, I suppose, to its being a place of summer resort for the wealthy from Havana, who come out to this cool and airy situation to avoid the long, heated term of the tropical summer. Strolling down the main street of the town, you will see the usual amount of rustic architecture, of country stores, small *posadas*,

A country garden

and lounging idlers; while if you are tempted to try an investment in the fruits of the country, you will have the opportunity of purchasing an early mango, a ripe orange, or perhaps the odd-looking *mamey* or *zapote*, at any of the numerous fruit stores on the street. At the end of the street and crossing the brook is a long and well-built stone bridge, composed of a high single arch, which, seen from the bank of the stream below, has a somewhat picturesque effect.

To the left of the bridge, keeping on up the bank of the little brook, you will perhaps notice one or two rather pretty oddities in the shape of balconied windows or quaint roofs, of which one can always find some in a place like this, noticeable either from their novel and peculiar shape, graceful form, or oddities of color. At the very foot of the hill upon which stands the village, are found the bathhouses, which were in a very dilapidated state when I saw them. The fountain from whence the supply of mineral-water comes was surrounded, at that early morning hour, by a motley crowd of water-carriers, of

Balconied windows

different ages, who drove mules or horses, carrying upon their backs, after a most primitive fashion, water casks. A jolly lot they were; and seating myself on a stone near by, I entered into a conversation with a "*Viejo*" (old man). You always find these Cuban peasants ready for a

Water carrier

chat, and willing to give information, if they can; and if they can't, they lead you to believe they know a great deal more than they tell. I was informed by this venerable that the people in the village had become so lazy that they wouldn't come to bathe, or drink the water any more, and so these water-carriers took it around to supply the indolent public.

"What kind of water is it?"

"*Bueno, Señor*" (good, sir)!

"Yes, I know; but what are its qualities?"

"*Ojala! Señor*" (with a shrug), "*muchos*" (O heavens! why, many).

"Well, what are they?—do they make you drunk, or strong, or hungry, or what?"

Here the old dog, struck with the novelty, perhaps, of the water making anybody drunk, removed his hat, and, breaking into laughter, replied, as he scratched his head,—

"*Hace buen apetito, Señor, y otras cosas,*" which I found, after drinking a glass or two, to be partially true, at all events; and Nicholas, my attendant at the café, must have thought my breakfast was to last for all day.

On the top of the hill are several really pretty lanes, with some very handsome houses and country seats, which have an indescribably charming appearance, presenting their pillared piazzas and imposing white fronts through a vista of luxuriant tropical vegetation, with brilliant colored flower-beds; while in the distance are the graceful palms and cocoa-trees, and overhead the wonderfully pure blue sky.

Having strolled sufficiently through the village, if you want a dip in old ocean before going back to town, get one of the volantes to drive you down to the sea-shore, and then you will have a delightful, refreshing surf-bath, that will invigorate you for all day, and start you on your way back, vastly refreshed, and with the "*buen apetito*" before mentioned.

Puentes Grandes is a pretty little village, about half way back from Marianao to Havana, and is also a place of *recreo* in the summer months, though it is not so large as Marianao; and unless the traveler is fond of manufactures, it will not pay him to stop; but if he *is*, then he will find there the only nail-factory on the island, prettily situated in a ravine below the village, and having fine water-power from the neighboring stream, which is here dammed up by a solidly-built stone dam. The factory gives employment to about sixty hands, all of them Chinese, under the superintendence of an Englishman, and runs about thirty machines, turning out daily one hundred barrels of nails, which are sold as fast as made at six dollars per barrel, and are used, principally upon the island, for nailing up the sugar-boxes,—immense quantities being consumed in this way.

Taking another morning, we visit Guanabacoa, an old town a short distance from Havana, on the eastern side of the bay, which is reached by crossing over in the ferry-boats, running every five minutes from the foot of Calle Luz to Regla, on the opposite side. From there the cars run every fifteen minutes direct to Guanabacoa, starting from the same depot as those for Matanzas, though on a different road. This short road, commenced to develop a supposed coal mine near Guanabacoa, was finally completed for purposes of travel between this town and Regla.

On getting out at the station in Guanabacoa, you will find two-horse volantes, which, for four *pesetas* (eighty cents), will drive you all over the town. This is a quaint, antiquated old place, celebrated for its age,—being one of the oldest towns on the island,—and for its fine mineral baths and waters. It was originally a village of Indians. In 1554, all the wandering natives were collected from its neighborhood, and organized into a village, which, in 1743, was thought worthy of being called a town.

The principal objects to see are the mineral baths of Santa Rita, celebrated for their wonderful cures. There is no hotel in the town; but opposite the depot is a very neat, clean *fonda* where one can get a very good cup of coffee, or a *refresco*. Boarding, I was informed, could be had in private families. The best plan, however, for any one desiring to take the waters regularly is to stay in Havana at the hotel, get up early every morning, come out here, drink the water, take his bath, and return to his breakfast in town; after which, refreshed by the pure air, the short ride, and the medicinal waters, it will go hard if he does not have a fine appetite. By this means the pleasures of Havana life can be enjoyed the rest of the day and evening. This can be varied by driving out from Regla in a carriage, of which there are always some at the ferry; the road is good, the scenery pretty, and the distance short.

The baths of Santa Rita are well built of stone, under cover of roof, and the rooms are kept tolerably clean. There are separate rooms for ladies and gentlemen, and private rooms for those who desire them. The mineral spring pours out of a rocky basin, which is also walled and roofed in, the waters of which are cool and very pleasant to take. They are very strongly impregnated with *chapapote* (a species of bitumen), iron, potash, and magnesia,—so much so, that the mineral substances may be seen floating very thickly upon the surface of the water. The charge for the public baths is ten cents; for the private ones, twenty.

The stranger in Cuba is always particularly struck by the

Bath room

appearances of the mineral baths, many of them being arranged with a good deal of taste, while they all have a substantial look, with their stone basins and solid tiled floors. Some, as at Santa Rita, have highly decorated shrines, at which the devout or faithful make their offerings.

There is a public square, in the town, known as the Plaza, in which the *retreta* is played, every Thursday night, by a band from Havana, the last train for which city leaves Guanabacoa at half-past eleven o'clock at night.

There is also a church, which is honored with the name of cathedral, a convent or two, and two market-houses, which have nothing to recommend them except their filthiness.

Some distance from the village is the old church and cemetery of Potosi, which is worth seeing from its antique appearance and peculiarity of structure, though as workmen were painting and repairing it when I was there, it may not now look so venerable. The arrangement of the tombs and vaults is to us a novel one. They are arranged like so many baker's ovens, one over the other, in the walls around the cemetery; each one is numbered, and on the slab that closes it up are the particulars and history of its occupant. It does not make much difference, I suppose, where one lies after death; but if I did have a choice, I should prefer not to bake away in one of those white-washed, sealed up ovens, with a hot, tropical sun doing me brown by degrees, especially as here the sun has only a chance at one side; and it would be a situation like that of a priest, told of by Ingoldsby, "who, being a great gourmand, was punished in purgatory by being set before the fire to roast. The old fellow, though, having an eye to the proper way of doing things, remarked that he didn't mind the roasting so much, as that he was being done too much on one side, and quaintly requested the head devil to turn him, in order that the roast might not be spoiled." Beyond the walls of the

Cemetery of Potosi

cemetery is the church, a small, odd affair, and not much used for purposes of worship, I believe.

Having finished Guanabacoa, the traveler can, on his way back, stop at Regla, and see what are generally interesting to every one who comes to Havana, and those are the *"Depositos Mercantil"*—large buildings for storing sugar that comes to Havana from the interior.

These are the most substantial warehouses it has ever been my lot to see, and I am told rival anything of the kind, in capacity and system, to be seen in Europe. They are the property of a stock company, who are also owners of a bank in Havana, are built, in a most substantial way, of stone, iron, and corrugated metal, and are situated directly upon the shore of the bay at Regla, where are erected fine substantial wharves, affording the vessels an opportunity of coming directly up almost to the very doors of the buildings. These warehouses consist of a long series of one-storied buildings, of great height, with solid stone walls and stone floors, and numerous iron pillars, upon which rest great iron beams, from which rises a roof of corrugated metal. Along these iron beams there are tracks, upon which small iron truck-carriages run, long iron bars extending from one to the other, over which are hung the falls and tackle for moving the boxes of sugar from one place to another, and for hoisting them upon the higher piles. All the labor is done by Chinese coolies, who

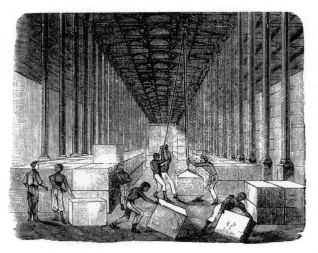

Warehouse

work there on contract. They have, generally, no clothing on them except a pair of pants. In front of the eastern range of buildings, which extends several squares, there is a fine, long shed, roofed in the same manner as the buildings, with plates of corrugated metal, which makes, at the same time, a neat, serviceable, and fire-proof roof. A few years ago, a fire destroyed a portion of the former sheds, which were also strongly built, but not fire-proof.

It used to be the custom for the sugar-planters to send their sugars to their merchants, who stored them in their warehouses, and then advanced money upon them. Now, it is said, the planters are so rich they can afford to send their sugar to these store-houses, draw what amounts they may want, and bide their time until they get their price, the merchants simply acting as commission men between the buyer and seller. This is brought about by the high prices received for sugar during our war, by which so many planters became rich. The company that owns these buildings is a very rich and profitable one, paying generally twelve or fifteen per cent, charging insurance on every thing stored there for a whole year, whether it remains so long or not. This is almost clear gain, for it would seem there is no possible chance for fire to make headway in the midst of iron and stone. These store-houses are well worth a visit by every stranger at Havana, and if he does not care to go to Guanabacoa, he can come over, in the ferry mentioned, directly to these warehouses; or, if there is a good breeze, he can go to the quay Caballeria, and take a sail-boat, and sail over the beautiful bay directly there in a short time.

Of course such store-houses as these facilitate business very much, and it is quite a sight to go into such a house as Morales & Co., and see the sort of sugar exchange held there every day,—long tables with small papers of sugars ranged along, as samples of perhaps thousands of boxes stored away in the warehouses, or on their way from the plantations.

Matanzas

In going from Havana to Matanzas, the traveler has the choice of two roads,—the longer and more beautiful one, starting from the depot at Villa Nueva, outside the walls; the shorter and more traveled one, starting from the station at Regla, which is reached by the ferry from the foot of Luz street, Havana. The fare on these roads varies inversely as the time,—being four dollars for the two hours' ride on the shorter road, and two dollars for the four hours' ride on the longer one.

If the traveler is not pressed for time, and desires to see as much of the country as possible, my advice would be to go to Matanzas by the short route, and return by the other, and he will then have the opportunity of seeing fully the beautiful country between the two places; and he may, perhaps, wish to stop at the watering-place of Madruga, and the pretty village of Guines—a place of *recreo*—on his way back.

The train leaves Regla three times a day: at 6 o'clock, and at 10.40, in the morning; and in the afternoon at 3.25, arriving at Matanzas in time for dinner.

In traveling in the cars in Cuba there are some peculiarities it is well to observe in reference to one's baggage. Any valise, carpet-bag, or portmanteau that can be carried conveniently in the hand should be taken in the cars, as for every piece of baggage that one has checked there is an extra charge, no baggage being allowed except what is carried in the hand. In fact, the notice to travelers by some of the railroad companies is very definite on that subject, as: "NOTICE.—The Señores passengers are notified that there will only be allowed as baggage on this road, one valise (*maleta*), one hat, and one game-cock." In lieu of a check, a regular ticket is given by the baggage-man, for which the charge is generally, from Havana to Matanzas, about sixty cents per trunk. The cars are first, second, and third-class. First-class cars are generally cane-seated, cool, and airy, with but very few passengers in them, and those mostly ladies, as nearly every one who travels takes second-class cars, which have cushioned or wooden seats, as it may be, and in which the fare is one-third less; the third-class taking all the roughs, laborers, and colored people, at about half the price of first-class.

The trains are prompt at starting at the hours advertised, and are run with rapidity and regularity, and, on some of the roads, with great speed,—the roads being well built, and kept in good order, the engineers being mostly Americans. The trains by the long route, from Villa Nueva, run through, twice a day, to Matanzas, leaving at 5.30 o'clock in the morning, and at 2.40 in the afternoon. On leaving the hotel with one's baggage (if a trunk, it has to go in a cart), it is well to take plenty of time, there being no such things as baggage expresses or wagons, or hotel coaches, and every one having to look out for his own conveyance and baggage-cart. On reaching Matanzas, the cars of the short route stop at the new town, those of the long one at San Luis, one of the suburbs,—the former, only a few minutes' walk from the hotel; the latter, some distance. Outside the depot will be found volantes, and also a baggage-wagon, into which the traveler can put his baggage, taking care to get the driver's number, which he is obliged to have marked in a conspicuous place. Opposite to the depot (new town), is the French hotel "Ferro Carril," whose proprietor will doubtless accost you, as he did us, at the door of the depot, and most probably, discovering that you are a foreigner, will tell you in English that his is the only place in the town to stop at,—that the other hotels "are all Spanish garlic and oil." Don't be humbugged, *amigo mio*, by this talking Gascon, by whom I may confess to having been "sold" myself, when, having such faith in French restaurants, I was induced to patronize the fellow. The Endsor House is a new house, lately opened, and spoken well of; but the hotel to stop at, by all means, if you can get rooms, is in the centre of the town, kept in a very excellent, comfortable way indeed, with good cooking and good wines, and the service of the table very proper, while some of the rooms are quite large, and cleanly enough kept. Traveling with ladies, I should invariably telegraph from Havana for rooms, or engage them by letter, a day or two before coming to Matanzas,—the proprietor's address is Antonio Gutienes, Hotel Leon de Oro, No. 6 Calle Govellanos. What propriety there is in "Golden Lion" as a name for a hotel I have not been able to discover, even with the assistance of the good-humored waiter José, who is always ready to explain things, learn a little English, or teach one a little Spanish. I can only imagine it must have been given by some wag, who was struck with the idea that he could "feed" like a lion, at a hotel, if he were as solid in gold.

I believe travelers unite in saying that this hotel is the best on the island; and my own experience is the same, with, perhaps, a little prejudice in favor of Madame Adela's, in Santiago de Cuba,—on the score of economy, anyhow. The charges at the Golden Lion are three dollars and fifty cents per day, including *vino catalan*, if you drink that. If, however, you drink other of the wines which are upon the table, and which, as a matter of course, the waiter asks if you will have, you are charged extra, though the price is very reasonable, considering some of their clarets—such as the *Bonnafon*, *Haut Brion*, and a Spanish wine, like a light Burgundy, known as *Vino de Vicenza*—are excellent; while for those who like the pure Burgundy, there are some excellent qualities of Beaune.

There are in Matanzas no other chamber-*maids* but *males*, who take care of the rooms and attend to the duties usually attended to by females. My particular friend and attendant was a highly intellectual and intelligent *Chinois* boy, as you may perceive from his portrait, whom I addressed always by that title, and who, seeing my desire to acquire languages, took great pains to instruct me in "chow-chow" dialect, in which, candor compels me to confess, I made no progress; nevertheless, we were fast friends, owing to sundry *medios* that passed between us, and which resulted in my boots being always "done" to a shine, while I was always sure of a lump of ice

Chinois

in the late night, to cool my *aguardiente*. (*Verbum sat*). For those who do not speak Spanish, there is a very decent man who acts as interpreter, speaking English quite well, and who, in fact, transacts most of the business with the travelers, while the waiters pick up enough English to understand what is wanted.

"El Ciervo de Oro" (the golden stag), on the street Ricla, next above the Leon, is also a most excellent Spanish hotel, with a fine table, and tolerably clean rooms; but it is not very large, and, I think, not so pleasantly situated as the others; and from its limited accommodations, there is no certainty of getting rooms. The charges are the same as at the Leon de Oro.

As a *dernier resort*, if it is not possible to get into either of the above, then the French hotel, "Ferro Carril," must be patronized. The house is good enough in its rooms and table, but it is in a bad situation, in the dusty street opposite the railroad depot, and within a door or two of a machine-shop, in which they keep up a "din infernal" at all hours of the day; add to which, this hotel is in the new or lower town, away from the Plaza, the Paseo, the theatre, etc. If, however, the traveler does go there, he must have it distinctly understood what he is to have, and what he has to pay, as mine host has an easy way of saying, "Oh, my charges are reasonable, and you can have anything you like;" and the result will be that your bill will astonish you in its amount, and there will be "war in the camp."

And now, *amigo mio*, being comfortably established at the Leon, let us take a view of the situation. We have now to begin our first *real* experience of Cuban life; for that in Havana is more or less tinctured with foreign innovations. First, if we are lucky, our room is a high-ceiled, airy one, with immense windows opening onto the balcony, from which we have a view all over the city; the walls are gay in most gorgeously-painted frescoes, representing Flora, Venus, and other charming nymphs, evidently, from the scarcity of their clothing, trying principally to keep cool; the beds are neat little iron bedsteads, with simple sacking bottom, covered with clean linen, and the whole affair neatly trimmed in with a pretty mosquito-bar. From the window of our room, if it is in front, we look directly into our neighbor's sitting-room, where we can study Cuban "inner life," if so we are inclined; if that don't interest us, then we have a glimpse of the beauties of the hills surrounding the town, with the soft twilight and gorgeous sun-set effects thereon; while, maybe, if we are gallant, we shall have the opportunity of raising our *sombreros* to the *bonita Señorita*, in the balcony opposite, wishing her, at the same time, a courteous "*buenas tarde.*" If our room is in the rear, and we are fond of practical study, we can just lean over the railing, and, looking down into the *patio*, take our first view of a Cuban kitchen, and our first lesson in Spanish cookery; but I would not advise you to do so unless your stomach has been through the ordeal of army living, in the shape of "hard-tack and commissary beef."

On your arrival at this or any other Cuban hotel, don't be scared by the appearance of the lower story, which, in this case, is used as a cafe for "the people," while for *los caballeros*, the upper stories of the building are used. The dining-room and *sala* are immediately at the head of the stairs. In the former, the table is always "laid" for use, with a profusion of colored glass, silver, crockery, etc., while the *sala* looks inviting, with

A Cuban kitchen

its cool marble floor, and its stand of flowers, with pictures round the walls; and the ubiquitous rocking-chairs, in which one so naturally indulges in his siesta.

But now, as we are upon the subject of Cuban dining-rooms and kitchens, it may be as well that you take a lesson in what to eat, and what to let alone, and by what names the different articles are called. And first, the breakfast, which the traveler will find out is no small matter, is begun with eggs (*huevos*), in some shape or other; if boiled, *pasados por agua*; if poached, *estrellados*; if fried, *fritos*; if in omelette, then *una tortilla*; ham and eggs, *huevos con jamon*; if a compound omelette, then *una tortilla con riñones* (kidney), *con jamon* (ham).

The Cubans have many ways of cooking eggs new to us, which are exceedingly agreeable to take. With poached eggs they serve stewed tomatoes, a spoonful of which over your eggs, improves them much. Boiled rice is served with eggs at every meal, and is eaten with the eggs alone, or with eggs and tomatoes, as above, called *huevos con tomato y arroz*.

Huevos rellenos (stuffed eggs) are delightful, particularly with a dash of lemon-juice over them, as also are *huevos guisados*, (stewed or fricasseed). Their *chef d'oeuvre*, however, in eggs, is the omelette, with green peas (*una tortilla con petits pois*), or with tomatoes, or *champiñones* (mushrooms).

Of fish there are numerous kinds, cooked in various ways; but it is safest to order it fried (*pescado frito*), being fried generally in good olive oil, which is considered better than lard or butter. It comes to table dry, and of a beautiful brown color, resembling, to use the Spanish expression, *color de oro*. A dash of lemon-juice over every kind of fried fish improves it vastly. Of fish boiled, it is safe to order *pescado cocido*, simply specifying the kind of sauce, whether white (*salsa blanca, picante*), or of tomatoes.

A dish of which all Americans become very fond, is the shrimps (*camarones*), which are found in great profusion in nearly all parts of the island; they are perfectly delicious, very wholesome, and make a most delicate salad, or are eaten with a little salt. The Leon de Oro is celebrated for a dish which is exceedingly fine, very delicate, and very pleasant for invalids or ladies of delicate appetites. It is known as *sesos* (sheep's brains), and is served either *fritos* (fried), or *guisados* (fricasseed).

Having disposed of the above courses, you are now ready to discuss the *substantials*, which are generally, for breakfast, the following: *Higado guisado, barillado* (liver, stewed or broiled); *chuletas de carnero* (mutton chops); *ternera* (veal); *riñones guisados* (stewed kidneys).

The ubiquitous "bifsteck," generally speaking, is very poor, as is nearly all the beef in the island. They give you, however, the "fillet," at El Leon, when you ask for steak, which of course no *gourmet* will grumble at. Of *salchicas* (sausages), I must say my experience has not been favorable, except of the Bologna, which we are accustomed to. Of *picadillos* (hashes) there are always one or two served, and the only way to do is to experiment with them, as some times they are very nice,—when made, for instance, of rabbits and tomatoes. I may say here that the traveler has been needlessly alarmed if he expects to be attacked with garlic and oil at every place; my experience has taught me these are only objectionable where used in profusion and without judgment, which is only done among the negroes and lower classes. At none of the hotels in the principal places, or in private families, are they used to excess, if at all.

With the meats at breakfast one is generally served with potatoes (*papas*) *fritas*, and the standard Cuban vegetable *platanos* (plantains or bananas), *fritos* or *asados* (fried or roasted).

In the *buniato*, or sweet potato, the traveler will recognize an old friend, though of much better quality than ours. Now you are ready for your *ensalada de lechuga* (lettuce salad), or of tomatoes, or—what can be had in great perfection all over the island—*berros*, delicious water-cresses, crisp, fresh, and pungent, from some cool, running stream.

A new "wrinkle" which you will see in due course, and which, however much the novice may turn up his nose at it, I advise you, my friend, to try, is *dulce con queso, pasta de guayaba,* (jelly with cheese, jelly of guava). There is no accounting for tastes, and maybe you won't like it; but it is in general use with *los Cubanos*, and I must say, according to my taste, is very pleasant, the piquancy of the cheese adding to the delicious, fruity flavor of the jelly. At all breakfasts there is generally a profusion of fruits of some kind, mostly the orange and the banana, which latter is of different kinds,—all of which are eaten by most persons after the breakfast, but by others before; and I confess that if one wishes to enjoy the delicious, fresh, juicy taste of the orange, or the delicate, fragrant *platano de Guinea*, he should eat it before his palate has become demoralized by the taste of the more necessary but coarser foods. Now, leaning back in your chair, if *satisfied* with breakfast, a cigarette is produced, and the waiter having furnished you with *candela* (light), you direct him to look up your *café solo*, while you proceed with your little paper digestor. Coffee having been brought and disposed of, you are then ready for your more serious smoke of a Partagas or Cabañas.

Expect not, O reader! that such an article as butter—butter, golden, fragrant, and sweet as we know it—is to be found in all Cuba; no! *that* is not a *cosa de Cuba*; for all that the inhabitants of this prolific isle know of that article is from some wide-mouthed bottle, that contains a yellowish-looking material, which, from its strength or odor, you would say was wagon-grease, but which is nevertheless sold and received as *mantequilla* (butter). No one ever uses it,—certainly no foreigner would; and it is astonishing how little one misses it, after all. As for pepper,—good, red hot cayenne,—were you to ask for it, the authorities would be called in, under the idea that you wanted to commit suicide, so entirely unused is that article amongst the condiments of the island.

For the dinner, which is really not so important a meal as the breakfast, and is always taken in the cool of evening, after the labors (?) of the day are over, the soups are first, which, as a general thing, are not very good, according to our ideas of things, and are certainly not according to "Soyer."

Foremost upon the list stands the *caldo*, which being the pure juice of the meat, is more like the French *consommé*, or our own beef broth; it can be varied, too, by asking for *caldo gallina* (chicken broth), *caldo con pan tostada* (with toast), or *caldo compuesto* (a thick soup made of onions, carrots, etc.). *Sopa de pan* (bread soup) is a good deal like a bread-and-milk poultice. *Sopa de fideos* (soup of vermicelli); *sopa de arroz* (of rice); of maccarones; *de leche* (of milk); *de tortuga* (of turtle); and also the soup Julienne (of vegetables) can be had.

Fish is the same as at breakfast. And now it is well to impress upon the mind the words *asado* (roasted), and *cocido* (boiled), which once gained, simplify matters wonderfully,—for then you have *carne de vaca* (literally cow meat, but known when roasted as beef); *ternera asada* (roast veal); *carnero asado* (roast mutton); *pollos asados* (roast chickens). *Lenguas* (tongues) are invariably fresh, and cooked well,—

with some appetizing sauce of tomatoes, olives, or pickles,—and one is always safe if they are on the table for an *entrée*.

The national dish, *bacallao* (codfish), I have never been able to manage in my own country, and can hardly, therefore, be considered a fair judge; but on one or two occasions, at private houses, I found myself taking to it very kindly, as it is there prepared with some skill and many condiments; but on the public table, *"para me, no, Señor! "* Still, as a curiosity, I give it you, and if you want a new sensation, try it.

They put with the fish small pieces of lemon, onions sliced, laurel leaves, potatoes, a piece of *lard*, or, perhaps, some oil, some Holland sauce, a dash of flour, salt, pepper, yolks of eggs, a little vinegar, and, when it is ready to serve, a few crisp, brown slices of bread, fried in oil, with some green peppers on the top. Try it, *amigo mio*, *pre*-haps you will like it, and *pre*-haps not.

The number of vegetables is limited throughout the island to *buniatos* (sweet potatoes); tomatoes, not very good; *platanos*; *habichuelas*, or frijoles beans; and green peas, known by the name of *petits pois*, rarely by their own name of *guisantes*. *Coles* (cabbage), also, forms a standard dish, while lettuce appears at every meal, together with rice, which latter may be called the principal vegetable. Then come the *pollos* (chickens), with the salads, varied occasionally by *pichones* (squabs), or some small birds of various kinds. The dinner is wound up by canned fruits or some light custard, pastry being almost unknown, except on grand occasions, or in private houses of great wealth, where there is talent in the *cuisine*. Coffee finishes every meal, with the universally used cigar, the lighting of which is as much provided for as any other want.

A peculiarity of the table service amongst the Cubans in their homes, and in all the Spanish hotels, is that the entire meal, except the dessert, is served upon the table at once; so that the gourmand can feast his eyes while tickling his palate. Perhaps the more refined *gourmet* will regret that he is not left to enjoy the pleasures of anticipation as well as of satisfaction, in looking forward to the next course, instead of having his dinner paraded before him at once.

José, the waiter, was quite a character in his way at El Leon,—he either knew or wanted to know everything, and his assiduity in studying English in exchange for Spanish, at the table, deserved encouragement. He was a wag, too, in his way; for while in Havana, I met some acquaintances who were coming to Matanzas, and were at a loss what to ask for to eat, as they knew no Spanish; so I made out a little list for them, recommending them to José's particular care.

Three months afterwards, happening in Matanzas, I asked José if he treated the party well. "I think so," was his reply; "the gentleman drank the Bonnafon wine all day, and the lady did nothing but eat *tortillas con tomate*," both these articles being on the list, and particularly good.

The force of habit

We had while here a very amusing illustration of the force of habit. Myself and friend, having a spare bed in our room, generously allowed a newly arrived acquaintance, who was exceedingly fond of the "essence of rye," to occupy it. Heavens and earth! Such profound noises as his nostrils emitted, it is impossible to describe. Suffice it to say, we were not able to charm the soporific god, and, therefore, did our best, with pillows, boots, shoes, etc., to make our friend cease his noise, but with no effect. We tried sulphur matches under his nose,—the same result; when,—oh, happy moment!—my friend seized an empty whiskey bottle on the shelf, and placed it to the nostrils of the sleeping thunderer; when, magical to relate, a beatific smile spread itself over the face of the sleeper; one hand was gently extended, the horrid noises ceased, and those well-known words of such great import were breathed upon the midnight air, "Give me a drink."

MATANZAS SIGHT-SEEING

Of all the towns in the Island of Cuba visited by travelers, Matanzas is the one, to my knowledge, that gives entire satisfaction to the generality of visitors. Built with regularity and in good style, it lies prettily at the foot of surrounding hills, on the shore of the beautiful bay of Matanzas, while through its limits run two small rivers, which empty into the bay, and serve to give additional character and beauty to the place. Away from the grand rush of travel that fills up Havana in the winter, Matanzas gets a smaller share of the attention which, from its many attractions, it more richly merits than almost any place upon the island. The inhabitants are polished and hospitable, and there is great wealth amongst them, while the women are remarkably pretty (naturally). These things, with the natural beauties of the city, make it the pleasantest place for an invalid, or any one desiring to pass several months on the island without traveling.

Matanzas, now the second city of the island in riches and commerce, is situated at the depth of the bay of the same name, formed by an arm of the sea, into which empty the waters of the rivers San Juan and Yumurri. The city proper is bounded on the north by the river Yumurri and on the south by that of San Juan, while on the east side are the brilliant waters of the noble bay.

It is said that the town is built upon the site of a former Indian village, known by the early discoverers by its original appellation of "Yucayo." Some thirty families, having emigrated from the Canary Isles, located themselves upon the spot, or in the neighborhood; for Manzaneda, to effect a settlement, had purchased from Charles II about one hundred and fifty acres of land, with the adjoining *corral* (a cattle-field), known as Matanzas, which signifies "slaughter-pen." The same name is retained today, with the addition of those of its patron saints, San Severino, and San Carlos.

The above regular settlement took place the 10th day of October, 1693, which was on a Saturday, and on Sunday, Bishop Compostello arrived. On Monday, the ground having been previously marked out, he laid the first stone for the future church or cathedral, with the celebration of a grand mass; at the same time were traced the lines of the castle, known as San Carlos, still standing as a fort upon the Punta Gordo. Like many of the towns of the island, Matanzas was threatened at various times by attack from buccaneers and enemies, and has even had naval engagements off its harbor; but its most serious loss was in 1845, when there took place, in the month of June, a great conflagration, which destroyed over two million dollars' worth of property.

It is now, however, a pretty, well-built city, with a really fine public square,—the Plaza de Armas,—which is prettily laid out with walks, shrubbery, and flowers, with a fine statue of Ferdinand VII in the centre. On the east side are the residence and offices of the *commandante*, while on the other three sides are well-built, handsome houses and stores, with one or two cafés, the whole having a very fine appearance. There is only one church, a large antique looking old building, remarkable for nothing except the rough architectural

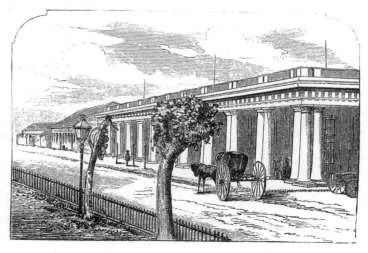

Casa de Commandante

beauties of its towers, particularly the taller one of the two, which has some considerable height. There is a fine new theatre, only lately completed, the handsomest on the island; also, a number of public buildings, none of which are remarkable in any way.

That portion of the town lying to the south of the river San Juan is known as "Pueblo Nuevo," in which is situated the railroad depot, and in its outskirts several beautiful country places, the river being crossed by well-built bridges of solid stone. On the other side of the river Yumurri, this portion of the town is known as Versailles, reaching to the very foot of the hill, known as the "Cumbre," from the summit of which is seen the beautiful valley of the Yumurri; while on the hills facing the bay stand the military hospital and the barracks of Santa Isabel, capable of containing over fifteen hundred men. Close to it, on the extreme edge of the bay, is the beautiful paseo of Versailles, the favorite drive of the inhabitants, of an evening. At the end of the paseo is the small castle and fort of San Severino.

The object of greatest attraction, however, to the passing traveler is the "Caves of Bellamar," situated to the south-east of the city, about two and a half miles, and reached by a very pleasant hour's drive, a portion of the way being by the sea-side. This trip is usually made in the early morning, though it is a pretty drive at any hour, and the caves are worth going to see several times.

Having ordered your volante (if only gentlemen are in the party, go on horseback) the night previous, you will find, at six o'clock in the morning, waiting your coming, a two-horse volante and driver; for which you will be charged about six dollars and thirty-seven cents for the excursion. On the way out, you cross the stone bridge over the San Juan, known as the "Belen Bridge," and pass through the town beyond, known as "New Town." These rivers running through the city in this way give it a particularly Venetian appearance, and views taken from one or two blocks upon the river bank might be readily mistaken for scenes in Venice.

In the new town, there is a handsome street that the traveler should direct his driver to go through *en route* to the cave; it is called the "Calzada de Esteban," and contains together, in one block, a collection of private dwelling-houses, the newest, most tasteful, and

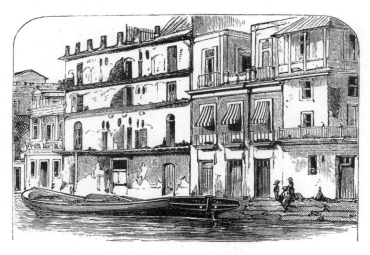

Scene on the river at New Town

beautiful I have seen in Cuba. The houses are large, beautifully built, with very imposing and handsome pillared fronts and porticoes, generally with large and luxuriantly flowering gardens, while the combination of iron-railing of pretty designs, with stone pillars and bases, gives a most charming effect.

There will, also, be noticed here the happy use made of prettily-colored tiles in the formation of terraces (if I may so call them) to the fronts of the piazzas. I have often endeavored to study out the pleasing effect of this style of architecture in Cuba; when, if the same style were adopted with us, it would be pronounced too gaudy, or ginger-bread looking; while here, I suppose from the peculiar climate, where the sky is always so beautifully blue, and the sun brightly hot, the high colors used in architecture seem in harmony with those of nature.

Leaving now the town behind us, and passing by some straggling houses, we come out by the side of the bay, whose emerald-green waters wash gently the sandy shore, and from whose blue distance come the cooling ocean breezes of early morning; while across the bay are the verdure-clad hills that over-top the valley of lovely Yumurri; the picture being completed on our right hand by green banks and

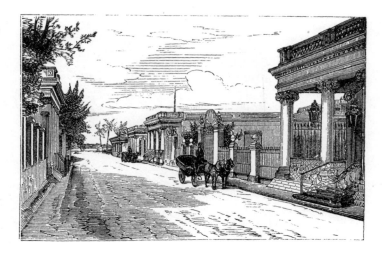

Calzada de Esteban

hills, overshadowed by the tall and graceful palm, or the fan-like branches of the cocoanut tree. Turning off from the sea-side, and winding up a rugged and stony road, some distance up the hills, upon the top of the plateau, we come to the "Cave House," a large frame building, erected over the entrance to the cave, and containing the visitors' register, as also numerous specimens of the crystal formations of the cave. In the centre of the building is the stairway leading into the entrance of the cave.

I would advise all visitors to the cave to divest themselves of any superfluous clothing in the way of coats, shawls, vests, etc., which they can leave in charge of the attendant at the bar; for the atmosphere inside is quite warm, and with the exercise, gets to be, before coming out, quite oppressive. I would, also, advise the traveler to insist upon a more liberal allowance of lights than those that are furnished, the supply being limited to one large beeswax taper, with double wicks, carried by the guide, and which does not serve to light up the cave as brightly as its most wonderful beauties deserve. There ought to be, at least, a light apiece allowed to visitors (I hope this will reach the eye of the proprietors), in order that their combined effect may serve to illuminate the cave in a larger expanse at a time than a

Gothic temple

simple cluster, or some one part of a column. I was awfully desirous to set off some blue lights in the cave, as they allowed us to do in the Kentucky Mammoth Cave, which have such weird, wonderful effect; but the guide would not permit it, on the plea that the smoke of too many lights would spoil the crystals.

Well, we pay our dollar each; the *muchacho* takes his one candle, and following him, we descend the stairs into the cave. After a few paces, we cross a small wooden bridge, and find ourselves in the "Gothic Temple," the accompanying view of which is taken from the bridge, looking towards the entrance. Even in the obscure light (though in this particular place one or two lanterns are hung up) one can see that it is very, very beautiful, with its millions of crystals, its thousand weird forms, and gloomy corners. When the candle is placed behind some of the columns or projecting crystals, their transparency produces a most lovely effect, their colors varying from the purest white to amber and the most tender of rose tints.

This temple, I should think, is quite two hundred feet long, and about seventy wide, and is about one hundred and fifty feet from the entrance of the cave; and while it far surpasses in richness and splendor the temple of the same name in the Mammoth Cave, it does

Fountain of snow

not equal it in size or solemn grandeur, though as far as the ease and comfort with which the cave is seen, it is far ahead of the Kentucky cave, as the proprietor has had enterprise enough to make strong bridges, plank walks, and, when necessary, strong iron-railings for protection from slipping.

The Mammoth Cave leaves upon the mind an impression of solemn, gloomy grandeur, and one peoples it with gnomes and demons. This cave is a dream of fairy-land, with its sprites and lovely fairies keeping gay revel to soft music; and one almost expects to see shooting from the crystal shadows some lovely Undine or beauteous naïad. I am becoming thus dreamy under the influences of the names of some of the most striking places, many of which, the *muchacho* says, "some call one thing and some another;" for every pillar has its great name—as "Columbus' Mantle," and every mass is likened unto the "Guardian Spirit," or more sacred "Altar," while without the "Cloak of the Virgin" it would not be a Cuban cave.

This *"Fuente de Nieve"* (fountain of snow), was to me one of the loveliest portions and most striking objects in the cave; but it contains attractions enough to bring one here again and again, when he can get the chance. The cave is thus far opened about three miles in extent, and its greatest depth below the surface of the earth, as far as I can ascertain, is five hundred feet. It has been opened about ten years, having been first discovered, in an accidental way, by one of the workmen of Señor Don Manuel Santos Parga, who, while working near by, saw his lever sink through the hole which proved to be the entrance to the cave. We occupied about three hours in the cave the first time we went in, coming out by a different passage, which, however, opens into the same Gothic temple, and which is as yet the only part of the cave lit by gas, though the boy said it all would be. "Who has not seen the Caves of Bellamar has not seen Cuba."

The views of the valley of the Yumurri should by all means be seen both at sunrise and sunset, though I give the preference to the *caida del sol*, particularly as seen from the *cumbre*, or top of the mountain, which lies far beyond the city. This excursion should be made on horseback, by young people, as it is a beautiful road of an afternoon, winding up the hill to the *ingenio*, or sugar estate of Mr. Jencks, the town being left behind until it becomes only a confused mass of buildings in the distance; while to the right hand is the bay with its shipping and forts, and beyond, the hazy landscape; and after a short ride, a full and splendid view of the ocean breaks upon you. The ascent is a steep one, though over a very fair road, particularly for horses, and the change in the atmosphere can be noticed almost immediately after the first turn on the hill, while before the return at night it is quite cold, so that a shawl will not be amiss for lady travelers.

After about an hour and a half continuous ascent, the road suddenly winds around the brink of a grassy precipice, and there, spread out at one's feet, lies the far famed, poetically described, beautiful valley of the Yumurri, with its patches of green and gold, and its groups in twos and threes of graceful waving palm-trees, while meandering through its grassy banks is the little stream of Yumurri, looking like a silver riband, except where, here and there, its waters are golden-hued from the setting sun; and over all these hangs that air of perfect stillness—that grand, quiet solitude—which one often realizes amid such noble expanses of nature as this.

When I was there, the air was so exhilarating from its freshness

Valley of Yumurri

and purity that I felt "jolly happy," to use the words of the great Webster, "that I still lived;" and I am sure that if I had had "the wings of a dove," I would have taken a delightful "fly" over the lovely valley, just to bathe myself, or at least attempt it, in that wonderful blue that almost touched the hills.

At the estate of Mr. Jencks (I think that is his name), where all travelers are in the habit of stopping to see a sugar-house, and get a view from the top of the dwelling, one can get a general idea of sugar-making, though on a very small scale; or he can taste the boiling *guarapo* (sugar-juice) from the trough, and if he is consumptive, "sniff" the odors of the boiling sugar, said to be so beneficial to weak lungs.

Our interview with the little black *niños* was highly amusing. On entering the court-yard of the negro quarters, a dozen little black imps, of all ages and sexes and sizes, perfectly naked, rushed towards

"Master, thy blessing."

us, and crossing their arms upon their breasts, fell upon their knees before us, and jabbered and muttered, out of which could be distinguished "Master, master, give us thy blessing," which we interpreted to mean "tin;" whereupon we scattered sundry *medios* amongst them. Hey! presto! what a change! The little black devils fell over one another, fought, tugged, and scrambled to secure a prize; while any one who had been lucky enough to obtain a coin, marched off in a state of dignified delight, his distended little stomach going before him like a small beer-barrel, while the owner of it kept shouting out "*Medio, yo tengo medio*" (five cents, I have five cents).

There is another view of this charming valley of the Yumurri to the west of the town, out over the hills, known as the "Abra de Yumurri," or "Boca," as it is sometimes called. The view is of the whole valley, from the left bank of the river, with the grand, majestic opening in the rocks, as though they had been sundered expressly to let the river through.

From the top of the hill can be seen the picturesque towers of the city, and the waters of the bay, with all its shipping displayed therein; while in the background, towards the south, are seen the distant hills that extend from the hill of San Juan to those of Camarioca, looking like blue clouds against the roseate sky.

A delightful and popular excursion is to take a small boat, with a pleasant party, and ascend the river San Juan about four miles, to the place called "Los Molinos," where is a sugar estate, the power used upon which is water, and the grounds of which are quite pretty.

The livery stables of Matanzas furnish very fair teams, and the saddle-horses are also very good; they can be had by ordering them at your hotel. Ladies who are not accustomed to riding much will find riding the Cuban ponies a very easy affair indeed; for their gait is a species of amble,—what we call racking,—and our fair novices in equestrianism pronounced it "divine."

Securing a stylish turn-out, about six o'clock in the evening, we will drive down to El Paseo, which is on the extreme edge of that portion of the city known as Versailles, and immediately on the shore of the bay, from whence come, morning and evening, the delightful sea-breezes which everybody comes down here to get.

This paseo is a pretty drive, about half a mile long, and beyond it a road of about the same length to the castle. It is laid out with gravel-walks, rows of trees, and a stone parapet, with iron-gates at each end of the drive; and if the stranger wants to see the beauty and fashion of Matanzas, it is here that he can do so, particularly Sunday afternoon—that being the great day. Quite as many elegant equipages can here be seen, in proportion to the population and size of the place, as in Havana. Starting from the front gate, they drive the whole length of the paseo, turning at the other end and retracing their course; and this they do for an hour or more at a time, until there is a perfect string of carriages following one another around and around. Towards eight o'clock, if it is the night of the *retreta* (always Sunday), when the band plays at the Plaza, most of the carriages file off to that square; and the scene already described at a similar occasion in Havana is presented here on a smaller scale.

Los Molinos

Abra de Yumurri

One of the most delightful pleasures we had while in Matanzas, was that of the bath at the *Ojo de Agua* (eye of water), where, on the bank of the Yumurri River, some springs of pure, cool water burst forth, and many of the young men walk out in the fresh mornings, and get a dip. We were advised to drink fresh cocoa-milk after our bath, but for what purpose I did not learn. It seems to be a "*cosa de Matanzas.*"

CARNIVAL IN MATANZAS

It was our good fortune to be in Matanzas during the last three days of the Carnival; and while the whole time was occupied by noisy processions and grotesque street masqueraders, the crowning ceremonies were on the last Sunday night; then the whole town used every effort to wind up the season in a *feu de joie* of pleasure and amusement.

In almost every town of any importance there is an association of the young men, generally known as "El Liceo," organized for artistic and literary purposes, and for social recreation. A fine large building is generally occupied by the association, with ample space for theatrical representations, balls, etc.; in addition to which there are billiard-rooms, and reading-rooms, adorned, probably, with fine paintings. In Matanzas, this association is known as "El Liceo Artistico y Literario de Matanzas," and is a particularly fine one, being composed of the *élite* of the city, with a fine large house, to which they have lately made addition by purchasing the "Club," beautifully situated upon the Plaza.

Thanks to our letter of introduction, we were, through the kind offices of members, permitted to enjoy the pleasures of their grand ball, called the "Piñata," which was indeed a very fine affair, and came off on the aforesaid Sunday night, attended by the beauty and fashion of Matanzas.

The ball commenced at the sensible hour of eight o'clock in the evening; and at entering, each one was required to give up his ticket to a committee of managers, who thus had a kind of general inspection of all those admitted.

Passing through the main hall, which was ablaze with light reflected from the highly colored walls and polished marble floor, we entered a *salle de réception*,—which, even at this early hour, was quite

Ball-room scene

full,—and which opened into the ball-room. Dear me, what a sight it was! Such crowds of beautiful women, such pretty dresses, such elegant *coiffures*, in which, from the abundance of the raven tresses of the Señoras, no "*rats*" or "*mice*" were necessary,—at least, I don't think there were; but then we men are *so innocent!* I do not think I ever saw so many beautiful women together. The ball-room was a long, large hall, at the other end of which was a pretty stage, for theatrical representations; on each side of the room was an arched colonnade, over which were the galleries, where the bands were posted. Ranged in double rows of chairs the full length of the room, in front of the colonnade, sat hundreds of dark-eyed angels,—calm, dignified, and appearing, most of them, to be mere lookers-on; not a black coat among them. All of these, with the exception of a few courageous ones that were facing all this beauty, were huddled together at the other end of the room, wanting the courage (it could not be the inclination) to pay their respects to *las Señoritas.*

What is exactly the trouble in Cuba between the gentlemen and the ladies I have never been able quite to understand. The men are polished and gentlemanly, as a general thing,—sufficiently intelligent, apparently; while the ladies are dignified and pretty. And yet I have never seen that appearance of easy and pleasant intercourse between the sexes which makes our society so charming.

I am inclined to believe that it is the fault of custom, in a great degree, which surrounds women in Cuba with etiquette, iron bars, and formality. This would seem to apply to the natives only; for nothing can be kinder, more friendly, and courteous than the manners of the Cuban ladies to strangers, at least, judging from what is seen. It may be as a lady with whom I was arguing the point said: "It is very different with strangers, Señor, and particularly with the Americans, who are celebrated for their chivalric gallantry to ladies." Now, I call that a very pretty national compliment.

Taking the arm of my friend, we walk up and down to see, as he expresses it, "who there is to be presented to;" and faith, if beauty is to be the test, it would seem to be a hard matter to make up one's mind, there is so much of it; but after a turn or two around the room, this form is gone through with, and one begins to feel at home and ready to enjoy one's self.

The Cuban women as a class have not the reputation of being educated. I can say that in all my travels I rarely ever saw a lady sitting quietly reading a book, or even having the semblance of doing so; nor have I ever been able in conversation to find that, with some few exceptions, they know anything about books or authors. Yet I must confess that in some way or another they make themselves very agreeable when they choose. They have an abundance of small talk, a profusion of compliments, and a pretty way of expressing themselves, making happy use of their large, expressive black eyes and gracefully managed fans.

When, however, one finds ladies (and there are numbers) who have been educated abroad, either in the United States or Europe, he finds them highly accomplished and entertaining. Several that I had the pleasure of meeting on this and other occasions spoke French perfectly, some English, and one or two both of these in addition to their native tongue.

There is one general peculiarity, and even defect, I must say, against which, had I any influence over these beauties, I should enter my solemn protest,—and that is the lavish and perfectly palpable use made of chalk. This is a cosmetic made from powdered egg-shells, known as *cascarilla*, and put upon the face, neck, and shoulders after they have been moistened by a little rum, and wiped with a towel. Imagine, O reader! the feelings of an ardent admirer of the sex, who, seeing at a distance an apparently lovely young creature of, perhaps, not more than fifteen or eighteen summers, on going up to her to be presented, finds her a mass of powder; and in lieu of a maiden with beautiful pearly or peachy skin, finds her made up like an old "guy" of a dowager of fifty years. Encircle her beautiful, slender waist in the graceful movements of the waltz, and, ten chances to one, your "immaculate black" shoulder, over which has been swaying her graceful head, is a mass of white chalk; in fact, even portions of those dangling, decorating ribbons (dear only knows what they call them!) whose ends touch her neck at intervals, become entirely transformed in color.

But let us return to the ball, which is all this time going on with great *éclat*. It opens with the advent upon the stage of a dozen or more young men, under the direction of a leader, in some fancy costume very handsomely made, who, after making their bow to the audience, go through some novel kind of dance. The performers are all members of the *Liceo*, and known as *comparzas*, and take this means of filling up the intervals of the general dance, and amusing the audience.

Galops, quadrilles, and waltzes are on the programme; but the prevailing dance is here, as everywhere on the island, the creole dance or waltz called *"La Lansza,"*—a quiet, graceful dance, and the only one which, owing to the heat of the climate, can be enjoyed with any degree of comfort. The following description of the dance, written by a Cuban author, gives the best idea of it:

> "Though there are known and executed in the island all the modern dances, yet preponderating over them and eclipsing them all is the irresistible *Danza Criolla*,—true Cuban specialty. It is nothing else than the old-fashioned Spanish contra dance, modified by the warm and voluptuous character of the tropical climate. Its music is of a peculiar style,—so much so, that any one who has not heard it

played by one already initiated in its mysteries, will attempt in vain to play it, though he may have it perfectly written before him.

"It consists of two parts; each one with eight bars, of two-four time, forming by their repetition the number thirty-two. To each eight bars corresponds a figure in the dance; the four being called *paseo* (promenade), *cadena* (chain), *sostenido* (sustained waltz), *cedago* (turning partners, etc.)

"In the first two, music and dancing have less expression and movement, as if the soul and body should show themselves obstinate against pleasure; but in the *sostenido* and *cedago*, that correspond to the second part of the music, are playful and piquant,—now sorrowful, now joyful, and always passionate. The couples then move with enchanting coquetry, and dance with the heart as well as the feet. Finally, the Cuban dance one can feel, but not describe. He that hath once danced it, gives it the preference over all others."

But here has my graceful, masked companion, whose brilliant eyes have been fascinating me, for the past half hour, through the openings of her "domino," while treading the lively paces of the galop, been puzzling me as to her identity.

However, on the score of heat, I finally persuade my fair unknown to seek with me the refreshing influences of an *helado*, in hopes that during the disposal of that edible, I may discover something by which to identify her. Prayers, protestations, and requests are of no avail, however; and I content myself with seeing the snowy and refreshing spoonfuls conveyed to what I distinguished to be a lovely mouth, even under the sombre hues of the slightly raised mask. Confound these masked balls! What humbugs they are! particularly when you can't find out who is the *inamorata* by your side.

Thanks, however, to the generous impulses of lovely woman, who likes not, even in her fun, to prolong one's torments, the domino is sufficiently raised to permit of my discovering the charming features of the Señora * * * * *, appearing in truth, *como una angel de cielo*.

It is now getting late, and the rooms are terribly warm; the fans of the long rows of lovely sitters, who have not moved out of their places

A Cuban belle

the whole evening, keep up a constant flutter, and one begins to sigh for a breath of fresh air, and relief from the discomforts of a full-dress suit; but the grand affair of the evening is yet to come off, we are told, and so we linger on, and are finally rewarded by the grand ceremony of the *Piñata*, from which the ball takes its name. This word I can hardly give the meaning of as applied to this ceremony, which consists in having pendant from the ceiling a form of ribands and flowers, the ribands numbered and hanging from the flowers, the rights to pull which are drawn like prizes in a lottery. Of these ribands, one is fastened to a beautiful crown of flowers, which, when the riband to which it is attached is pulled, falls into the hands of the lucky person, who has then the privilege of crowning any lady he may deem worthy of the honor, "Queen of the Ball," to whom every one is obliged to yield obedience, homage, and admiration. There is, also, the same opportunity afforded to the ladies to crown a king. The whole ceremony is pretty, and creates much merriment and amusement.

This ceremony over, at midnight we sally out into the open air. But, good heavens, what a sight greets us there! Lights blaze in such profusion that it seems more than day; music and dancing are everywhere; songs, deviltry, and mirth have taken complete

A carnival scene

possession of the place; while people of all ages, sexes, and colors are mixed up together, in what seems inextricable confusion, intent upon having a good time in the open air, while their masters and betters are doing the same thing under cover. This is a Carnival sight indeed, and only to be seen in a tropical climate.

Some one suggests that we go down to the theatre, as the fun only commences there after midnight; and so we go there, passing a soldier or two on guard, to see a new phase of life in the form of a *mascara*, or ball of the lower class, known as the "*Cuña*" where people of all colors and sexes go who are not required to show certificates of character (and could not do it if they were) other than a golden dollar, which is taken at the door.

Truly it is a mob indeed,—a dancing, noisy, masked mob, who, amidst shouts, the din of music, and the shuffling of feet, are going through *all* the figures of the *danza criolla*, most of which are entirely unknown to its more refined female admirers. Keep your hand on your pocket-book, my friend, and cover up your watch-chain with your coat, as you go through the crowd; and more than all, don't tread on any one's toes, unless you are prepared to "hit out" more quickly than steel flashes; for these *canaille* have an unpleasant way of using the knife *que no es bueno para la salud* (which is not good for the health).

chapter twenty-three

THE VICINITY OF MATANZAS, MADRUGA, ETC.

Cuban saddles; Visiting sugar estates near Matanzas; Kindness of the managers; Ingenio Concepcion; Steam ploughing; Confiscation of property; The Cuban Saratoga; Madruga Springs; Routes there, and appearance; Beautiful views; The Plaza; A country funeral; Funerals of the wealthy; Lovely ride, via Guines, to Havana; View from the hill of Paradise; Limonar.

The traveler at Matanzas, in addition to the charms of the place itself, finds a great deal to interest him in the surrounding country, possessing as it does some of the most productive and beautiful sugar estates on the island. For instance, he can take the cars on the railroad from Matanzas to Baro, and stop at the little *pueblo* of "Union," around which place are any number of fine estates, which can easily be seen by simply going to the sugar-house and asking for the *maquinista* (engineer), who is generally English or American, and will be very glad to see strangers. There is a train that leaves at about 8.20 o'clock, reaches Union at 9.40, in the morning, and leaves there again for Matanzas at 12 o'clock, noon, affording ample time to look through a sugar estate.

Or, a shorter and just as pleasant a way is to go from Matanzas on horseback in almost any direction, and, stopping at any place that attracts one's fancy, ask for the *administrador*, or engineer. Many pleasant rides can in this way be had on horseback, and even one who is not a horseman need have no fear; for, with the small, easy-going horses, and the wondrous huge saddles, a child can ride with ease and safety.

Cuban saddle

As an instance of the hospitable courtesy of these planters, the following occurred to my friend and myself while we were at Matanzas. We met a gentleman at dinner, and entering into conversation with him, happened to inform him, in the course of it, that we had forwarded letters of introduction to a gentleman in the neighborhood, and were waiting the result, as we were very anxious to visit a sugar estate. He informed us that he was on his way to visit one of his estates in the vicinity, and he would be pleased to have us accompany him for the few days that he was going to spend there. I explained to him our situation,—that I had sent my card with my letters, and expected to hear that day or the next. He then said : "Well, if you will go with me this evening, good; if not, I will send my carriage for you tomorrow morning; and if you find you can come down and spend only a day, come, *francamente* I shall be glad to see you. If you cannot, my carriage will be there all the same, and no harm done." With which we exchanged cards, and next morning we went down, and spent a most pleasant day and evening with our hospitable acquaintance.

He was a resident of Havana, owning his place here in the country, upon which was a fine large house, with abundance of piazza, cool halls, a billiard-room, and a *cuisine* with which to sustain the arduous (?) life of Cuba.

Thanks, also, to our letters of introduction, we had the opportunity of visiting one of the model estates of the island,—the "Concepcion," one of a number owned by the Aldama family, and of which Mr. C—— is the able administrator. Nothing could be handsomer than the way in which we were entertained by this accomplished and courteous gentleman. Mr. C—— is a fair representative, I imagine, of the progressive man of the age. He took the estate, of which he is now in charge, when it was given up by others as unproductive, and only retained in the family as a matter of pride; and by scientific knowledge practically applied, has made it one of the model ones of the island, and the finest one in its system, arrangements, and productions, that I saw while in Cuba. Even the Yankee invention of the steam-plough, has been brought to bear upon the obstinate difficulties of the soil, and we saw it frequently and successfully in operation during our visit. Some of our Southern planters, with their loose and shiftless way of managing their cotton estates, might easily take profitable instruction from the systematic and advantageous way in which the Concepcion is managed. There are quarters for the negroes, built in the form of a quadrangle, a fountain in the centre, at which bathing can be done, a neat, and well organized hospital, in which the sick are skilfully and kindly taken care of, and an interesting and amusing nursery, where the "picaninnies," in

Casa de vivienda del yngenio

charge of two or three old crones, are looked after and kept out of mis-chief while the parents are at work. The tasteful manner, too, in which the lovely garden was laid out, with its orange groves, and fra-grant walks, and the scientific way in which the sugar-making was carried on, attracted our attention; and, if I may speak of it without any breach of the laws of hospitality, the genial table at which were had so many pleasant hours of conversational enjoyment aided in stamping upon our memories those few days of our stay at the Concepcion as amongst the most enjoyable of our trip.

Alas for the changes of this world! Since this was written, the wealthy and polished owners of this beautiful place have been com-pelled to flee their country on account of the interest they took in the "new cause," and those fine estates of which they were the liberal and worthy owners have been confiscated by the government.

If, while at Matanzas, the traveler wishes to visit a Cuban water-ing-place,—the Cuban Saratoga, in fact,—it can be easily done, any day, by taking a ticket for Madruga. Now *entre nous, o viajero,* unless indeed thou art an invalid, troubled with partial paralysis, stiffened with rheumatism, or suffering from some other unfortunate malady, think not of going there, even if thou feelest for a moment the glowing influence of a Cuban's description of the waters and place— "*Son magníficos; está un lugar muy bueno.*"

Madruga is a small village, to the south-west of Matanzas, about two hours' ride by railroad, and can be easily reached twice a day, being on the direct road to Havana, by way of the long route. Trains leave Matanzas, from the station on the other side of the river known as San Luis, at 5.45 in the morning, and at 2.30 in the afternoon, connecting at Sabana de Robles with the branch for Madruga, for which place travelers should be careful to get through tickets.

Madruga is simply a watering-place, and as such is celebrated for its mineral springs, which are certainly very beneficial,—and wonderful, if all the accounts be true that are given of them. The season begins for the fashionable world about the middle of April, though the baths are taken all the year round by the villagers and strangers.

The hotels are not by any means first class, and are entirely different from anything we are accustomed to; but any one desiring particularly to try the waters, can make himself pretty comfortable in the hotel known as the "Deposito de Don Cidra."

Though there are some inducements on the score of health that might tempt one to make a prolonged visit, yet I advise all those who have any thoughts of staying there to run down from Matanzas before moving their baggage, just to "look before they leap."

Dr. Wurdiman, considered good authority in matters of health, in his "Notes on Cuba," says of Madruga, that its high situation renders its air much more cool and pleasant than that of the plains during the spring, when the south-west winds are so annoying; and for invalids, it would form a desirable residence at that time.

The village itself is an ordinary country village, the principal part of it being around the Plaza, and is situated on high ground, in a beautiful rolling country, celebrated for being remarkably healthy. Its public buildings are confined to one small, neat church, in addition to the baths, which are all public. These are the property of the town, having been presented to it by Don José O'Farrell, Governor-General in 1820, on condition that the town should keep them in order and have them in charge. They are in direct charge of the Captain of the district, and are kept in repair by the contributions of the people of the village, who find it to their interest to attract strangers to their town.

The baths are all more or less impregnated with sulphur, some iron and magnesia, and some potassa, and are said to be sovereign cures for rheumatism, paralysis, weakness of the stomach, scrofula, and some other complaints.

The bath "La Paila" is most strongly impregnated, and its waters are very powerful. The "Templado" is the one that is most used in first going there, followed by the use of La Paila; but it is as well to consult one of the resident physicians, in order to know in what manner the baths are to be used, as the same treatment is not advisable for all persons or diseases.

The baths are very pleasant to take, the water being rather cold. They are taken early in the morning, and then, after the *siesta*, in the middle of the day, a glass or two of the water being drank after each bath. Invalids from all parts of the island come here, and it is not a very pleasant sight to go into the bath-room, sometimes, and have the eye displeased and the mind shocked by the cases of paralysis, rheumatism, etc., that are there presented.

With a jolly party, one can have a pretty good time at Madruga,— bathing, riding on horseback, and walking to the tops of the neighboring hills, from which fine views may be had. The view of the "Valley of Glory," from the top of the hill "Cupey," is very fine, as are also some of the other views, and the change of temperature from the country below is very agreeable.

Far as the eye can reach are seen the waving fields of sugar-cane, darkened here and there by patches of woods or clumps of palms; while in the foreground are the tall, white chimneys of the sugar-mills belching forth their black smoke. In the distance there is just the faintest glimpse of the hazy sea, the distant mountains and hills seeming to fade quite away into it.

One sees a good deal of primitive life in a village like this, off of the main route of travel, and away from the "grand world" influences. There were two funerals while I was there, which gave me a different

Loma de Gloria

idea of the "last sad scene of all" from that which I had received from similar ceremonies witnessed in Havana. First came the small boys, with white linen gowns over their clothes, short enough to display their ragged pants and dirty boots, the boy in the centre bearing a tall pole, upon the top of which was a silver cross partially draped, while each of the other boys carried a tall candlestick. Behind them came the priest, in shabby attire, in one hand his prayer-book, from which he was chanting from time to time, while in the other hand, the sun being hot, he held an open umbrella; behind him, again, came tottering along a venerable old man, personating whilom the acolyth, the bell-ringer, the sacristan, or other church functionary, as might be necessary, and now croning out in his dreary voice, as he went swinging the burning censer, the *second* to the chants of the priest. The coffin then made its appearance, formed of rough boards, but covered with black paper-muslin, and borne upon the shoulders of four of the villagers, a crowd of whom, all uncovered, brought up the rear. Here, as in all other Catholic countries, the spectators uncover their heads at the passing of the funeral cortège. I followed the procession into the church, where the further ceremonies of reading prayers, burning candles, and sprinkling the coffin with holy-water were duly

Funeral procession

observed; after which the priest went his way, and the procession took up the line of march for the new-made grave in the dilapidated and neglected cemetery, where the coffin was deposited without further ceremony. No females were present during the whole affair.

This humble funeral was a very different affair from what one could see in the larger cities, and particularly Havana, with its ostentatious display of the corpse upon a sumptuous catafalque or under a crystal urn, its crying and screaming women, its long line of carriages, and its various ceremonies, arranged and provided for by a "funeral agency."

A family in mourning in Cuba not only dress in dark clothes upon which there is no lustre, but they keep the windows of the house shut for six months; in fact, by an ordinance of the government, it is now prohibited to display the corpse to the public through the open windows, as was formerly done, both they and the doors being now required to be shut.

The traveler can leave Madruga for Havana or Matanzas twice a day,—morning and afternoon,—passing on his way to Havana the beautiful little village of Guines, where many people stay during the hot season. There is no particular attraction here, except that the village is pretty, and the country around attractive, there being some pretty rides and drives, and the horses being very good. The road to Havana runs through a very beautiful country, amid lovely scenery, and is a very pleasant ride.

Near to Matanzas, on the road to Bemba, is a very pretty little town, known as Limonar, one of the pleasantest places on the island, and most desirable for the invalid, as the air is fresh and very invigorating. From there, one can drive over to the baths of sulphur, at San Miguel, which, in the early spring months, are well patronized by the people of the district.

From Matanzas, there are a great many pretty drives to neighboring places, where lovely views can always be had; and it is as much owing to this fact as to the pleasant society of the town that Matanzas is so popular a place with the stranger.

After Yumurri, one of the most extended and pleasing views is that from the Hill of Paradise (*Loma del Paraiso*), looking down into the Valley of the Magdalen (*Valle de la Magdelena*). A picture, vast and interesting, is offered to the eye of the spectator by this magnificent panorama.

Valley of the Magdalen

Imagine a space of some fifteen miles long, surrounded by hazy mountains, in a country slightly rolling with verdure-clad hills, which serve as points for the eye to rest on; graceful groups of palms and other trees, and the picturesque edifices of an immense number of *ingenios*; the whole limited in the distance by the city of Matanzas,— the bay with its shipping; beyond which is seen the almost atmospheric sea uniting with the azure sky.

If the traveler, being at Matanzas, desires to visit Cardenas or Sagua la Grande (and he will do neither, if he takes my advice, unless business compels him) he has the choice of two routes,—by cars or by steamboats. This latter, however, I will not take into consideration,— the boats being small and dirty, and irregular in their trips.

Mrs. Woodbury's hotel is the only place in Cardenas it is possible to stop at; that, though with rather a plain table, is a comfortable house, with good beds, and clean rooms.

Cardenas

The traveler in Cuba will notice in almost every church a poor-box, similar to that at the head of this chapter, with its accompanying inscription, appealing for "alms for the souls of those in Purgatory;" and if he is about to visit Cardenas, Sagua la Grande, or Villa Clara, he would better deposit a small contribution on his own account.

Cardenas, called the American city, is situated directly upon the sea, though protected by a neck of land that stretches out to the north-west of it, forming in some degree a bay, in whose waters there is always more or less shipping. The town has about thirteen thousand inhabitants, and is, as far as business is concerned, a thriving place enough, being the depot and shipping point of the fine sugar-growing district lying adjacent. It is regularly laid out, with broad streets, and makes some pretensions to display, having a fine, large plaza in the centre of the town, in which stands a bronze statue of Columbus. In was only settled in 1828, but is now one of the most flourishing towns on the island, owing, it is said, to the large number of Americans who are engaged in business there, and who form a large proportion of the mercantile community.

The town boasts of one church, several cafés, and a number of fine, well-built wharves, some of which extend a long distance from the shore in order to facilitate the loading of vessels, the water of the bay being quite shallow in most parts of what may be called the harbor. It is also the head-quarters of the military district, and is connected with Havana by the railroad to Matanzas, and by steamers twice a week. It is said that the town is generally a cool place, having the benefit of the breezes blowing directly off the ocean; but that is not my experience, nor that of any one of my acquaintances; while for persistently attentive mosquitoes it takes the first rank in my estimation.

I can not, at this moment, recollect any one inducement to the traveler to visit it, unless he is in the sugar and molasses line, though there is in the vicinity what is said to be the finest sugar estate on the whole island, known as the "Flor de Cuba."

This superb place is easily reached on the Cardenas and Jucaro railroad, by getting off at the station of Pijuan, from which the estate lies one and a half miles off.

It contains about three thousand acres of land, and possesses a fine lime-stone quarry. The ground rolls in the most beautiful and favorable manner, affording to the fine dwelling house (*casa de vivienda*) a most beautiful site upon the hill. A substantial factory makes all the tiles used on the place, a supply of water, equal to five hundred pipes daily, being obtained from streams on the premises by means of a steam-pump.

The entire range of buildings, in which the cane is ground, is of the handsomest and most substantial kind; while the dwellings of the officers and the work-people are all of the best.

This estate was begun in 1838, with only about six hundred acres of land, and the production has grown to over ten thousand boxes of sugar of the best kind, and about one thousand five hundred hogsheads of *morcobado*.

There are daily trains on the Coliseo road from Cardenas for Matanzas, connecting at that place with the afternoon trains for Havana. There is also what is called a special train, I believe, leaving at six o'clock in the morning, and going through to Matanzas in time to take the 10.30 train for Havana.

There are also several lines of steamers from here to various points. For Havana, they leave Wednesdays and Saturdays at 7 o'clock in the evening, and arrive in Havana at daybreak the next morning; fare four dollars and twenty-five cents. The boats are small and filthy, with no state-room accommodations.

For Sagua la Grande, the boats leave Wednesdays and Sundays at 8 o'clock in the evening; and as it is the only means of reaching that place, there is, of course, no choice to any one desiring to go there.

Sagua la Grande is what we call a large village, numbering about seven thousand inhabitants, situated some distance from the sea, and

Ingenio Flor de Cuba

Sagua la Grande

about seven leagues from the mouth of the river of the same name; being also about seventy-six leagues from Havana. It is a most wretched place, with a very bad hotel indeed; but is connected with Villa Clara and Cienfuegos by railroad, while steamers of several lines touch there at irregular intervals.

The hotel "Las Cuatras Naciones," is in itself very badly kept; but there is a sort of club of merchants and business men who keep a table there, and have their own cook, and they live very well indeed; and if the stranger is fortunate enough to claim acquaintance with any of the members, and to be permitted to join their mess, he will be very well taken care of. I can only say, however, to the traveler who is so unfortunate as to have arrived within the limits of the town, to get out of it as soon as possible; which he can do by the first steamer back to Havana, or by crossing the island to Cienfuegos, if he is desirous of going to that side of the island. Trains leave daily for Cienfuegos, starting at mid-day, and arriving there towards six o'clock in the evening. It is best to inquire particularly about the hours of trains on this route, as they are sometimes uncertain.

Santa Clara, or Villa Clara, as it is now more commonly called, is in the interior of the island, seventy-two leagues from Havana, on the

Villa Clara

line of railroad to Cienfuegos. It is a very old town, having been founded in the year 1689, and now numbers about eleven thousand inhabitants, many of whom are persons of great wealth; the female portion being celebrated for their great beauty. It is an uninteresting town to strangers, who accidentally reach there in their wanderings. The country in its neighborhood is somewhat flat, and the *ingenios* are not so large as in other parts of the island. There are no accommodations for the traveler except the usual village inns, or *fondas*, of which the best is "El Leon de Oro."

From Villa Clara to Cienfuegos there are two daily trains; the morning train leaving at 6 o'clock, and the afternoon train at 3.30.

If the traveler has reached Villa Clara, and desires to visit Cienfuegos or the south coast at all, during his sojourn on the island, it is better to take the railroad across than to return to Havana; for, in the first place, he will save time, and in the second, he will not have to retrace his steps over the unpleasant route *via* Sagua and Cardenas. Once arrived at Cienfuegos, he can get back easily and pleasantly enough to Havana, every few days, by means of the fine steamers that ply on the south coast to Batabano, and from thence by railroad to Havana in a few hours.

The road from Villa Clara to Cienfuegos runs through a fine section of country, most of the estates being those of large producers of sugar and molasses, which find their market generally by way of Cienfuegos.

That town is in some respects like Cardenas, having a number of American merchants, and being celebrated for the zeal and enterprise of its business men. It is situated on the beautiful bay of Jagua, a large sheet of water with fine entrance and anchorage for vessels of every size, while the ranges of majestic hills that surround it add to its beauty.

Laid out in a regular way, with streets generally at right-angles to each other, and with well-built houses extending from the bay-shore, the town presents quite a pretty appearance from the deck of the steamer. Numbering about eleven thousand inhabitants, it possesses an old church, a fine building, occupied as the palace of the Commandante of the district, some handsome dwellings, and the largest public square or plaza, I should think, in Cuba. At each end of the main avenue of this square there are fine statues, upon the bases of each one of which are inscriptions, informing the passer-by of their purport; the one at the west end informing the inquirer that this is the *salon* (promenade) of the Captain-General Serrano; the other, inscribed to the Señor Brigadier-General D. Luis de Clouet, founder of the town of Cienfuegos, who, it appears, was an *emigré* colonel from Louisiana.

In strolling through the square, I met some little children, with school-books under their arms, of whom, as it was only seven o'clock in the morning, I asked where they were going at that early hour. A bright, dark-eyed little girl replied to me: "We are going to school; we have school from seven to nine in the morning, and four to six in the evening, because we cannot study when it is hot."

"What do you learn?" I asked; "do you learn anything about the United States?"

"O, yes, sir; I know all about them, and I can speak English too!" Whereupon she opened on me in English, asking me if I was an American. One can hardly realize the pleasure of thus hearing his native tongue spoken in a foreign land by an innocent like that, until he has experienced it. There is comparatively little to interest the

Cienfuegos

stranger in Cienfuegos, and the hotel accomodations are very
limited.*

I have never been more forcibly impressed by the peculiarity of
the Spanish character than I was at the hotel "La Union" in this town;
for it must be understood by all travelers in Cuba, that if you want
anything or any information, ten chances to one *you* will have to teach
the man that he has what you want. Here is a specimen: My friend
and myself had come into town very early in the morning, and not
wishing to wait from seven o'clock until our regular breakfast hour of
eleven o'clock, we concluded we would stroll into La Union and have
a bite of something to sustain our hungry stomachs. At the door stood
the *mozo* (waiter), who ushered us into the saloon, with dignified
grace, and—

"Good morning, *caballeros*."

"The same to you, *mozo*."

"What will you be pleased to have, sirs—coffee or chocolate?"

"Neither; some breakfast."

(Waiter, with a look of horror on his face), "Breakfast, sir? it is
only seven o'clock!"

"That makes no difference; what have you?"

"Nothing, sir; it is too early."

"Why, hang it, man! you can give us something, can't you? we are
starving!"

"No, Señor, it is *impossible!* we have nothing."

"What! have you no bread?"

Waiter here breaks into a laugh at the idea of no bread, and
replies,—

"Bread, sir? oh, yes,—plenty."

"No eggs?"

"Of course, sir! (a little piqued) we always have eggs."

"Well, then, I suppose they couldn't be beaten into an omelette,
could they?"

"Oh, yes, sir; the cook makes fine omelettes."

"Well, my man, (I was beginning to feel hopeful, and getting
courageous), I shouldn't be surprised if you could make it with green
peas."

"Certainly, sir, if you wish it."

Whereupon, off he goes to give the order, leaving us both amused at this corkscrew process of getting something to eat, and determined to persevere in our researches.

(Enter waiter.)

"I say, waiter, the oysters around here are very good, aren't they, in the shell?"

"Oh! yes, sir; we have some fine ones, fresh from the sea this morning; on ice now, sir."

"It is too early to have anything though, now, is it not?"

Oh! no, sir,—not oysters; you can *always* have those, if you want them."

"Well, we would like to have some, if we could get a bottle of Sauterne; but, *of course*, you do not have wine *so early* in the morning, do you?"

The waiter, now entirely out of his mind, but rather enjoying the joke,—

"You shall have anything you want, sir."

And, by Jove, we were in a few minutes seated at as comfortable a little *déjeuner* as could be desired by two famished young fellows.

There was just one little drawback; for as I was seated with my back to the window, my friend punched me, and said,—

"You didn't order chicken, too, did you?" (He understood no Spanish).

"No, I did not; why?"

"Well, just look behind you; I thought maybe *that* was for us."

O, madre de Dios! there was a negro boy, with a fine, large chicken, from which he was coolly picking the feathers, and the poor thing was perfectly alive and kicking *Cosa de Cuba!*

The water in the bay is here noticeable, from the fact that it is of the most beautiful transparent green color,

Cosa de Cuba!

through which can be seen the pure, white sandy bottom, at a great depth. A good arrangement they have here, also, for unloading or loading vessels, by means of a circular railway on the wharf. The vessel comes up to the dock, the truck-car is run alongside, the goods are hoisted on to it, and off it goes under a large shed or warehouse, where, thus protected from the intense heat, the car is unloaded by the half-naked laborers.

Trains leave Cienfuegos to cross the island for Villa Clara and Sagua la Grande twice a day; the best is the one that leaves in the morning, at 6.20, and arrives at Las Cruces at 7.28. From there the same train goes up to Villa Clara and returns to Las Cruces before the passengers have an opportunity of getting away to Sagua, making a delay of some three hours at that place.

There are several lines of steamers that stop at Cienfuegos, running in connection with trains from Havana, to Batabano, Trinadad, Santiago de Cuba, Isle of Pines, etc. They are all fine boats, very comfortable, large, and fast.

---

* Since this was written, I learn there is now a very fine hotel, called "La Union," kept in a building erected expressly for the purpose.

Cuba is divided, rather indefinitely, into two unequal portions,—the "Vuelta Arriba," or higher valley, and the "Vuelta Abajo," or lower valley. General usage seems to settle the point, that the Vuelto Abajo is all that fertile low country lying to the west of Havana; at all events, it is only from that section that the true "Vuelta Abajo" tobacco comes, and it is also there that one finds not only sugar but coffee-growing estates.

For the traveler desirous of seeing some portion of the far-famed valley, the best points are "Pinar del Rio," near the baths of San Diego, or Rio Honda, in the same locality, being the only points easily accessible by steamboat.

The same idea of the country, and the productions of the particular localities can be as well, and more pleasantly obtained, by taking the cars from Havana, to the rather pretty little village of Guanajay, which will put one in a neighborhood where, with the assistance of a good horse, he can, any day, in the surrounding country, gain a fair idea of tobacco culture, coffee-growing, or sugar-making.

Trains leave Havana, from the station of Villa Nueva, outside the walls, every morning at 6.45, for Guanajay, arriving there at 8.45, in ample time for breakfast; the afternoon train leaves Havana at 3.40, and arrives at Guanajay at 5.45.

There being no choice, we will put up at the Hotel of Carrera & Co., the exterior of which is rather calculated to inspire respect, a feeling which quickly vanishes when we are ushered into the *salle à manger*. Don't be dismayed, though, my worthy friend; "not so bad as we seem" is a very good motto in Cuba; and thus, after making your host understand that you want a good room, a good table, and everything nice, he will take you up from where the common people (*gente*) live below, to the aerial regions above, passing in the ascent through a portion of the stable, and by the kitchen, into a capacious hall on the second floor, where you will be agreeably surprised to find a neat and clean table, a cool portico looking down into the pretty plaza, and a tolerably fair bed-room; for all of which, having your meals private, when you want them, and with a bottle of fair French wine at each, you will be charged two dollars and fifty cents per day.

Guanajay is a small and prettily situated village on the grand mail route, that runs through the Vuelta Abajo. It has a population of about four thousand inhabitants, possesses a very pretty public square, around which are built some very imposing houses. The town lies in the heart of a beautiful section of country, some twelve miles from the sea. To the north of it, between it and the sea, are any number of fine, large sugar estates, beautifully situated in a rolling country, which extends to the very borders of the ocean, upon which, and within a short drive, are the towns Mariel and Cabañas, upon bays of the same names, containing a population of some thousand inhabitants each.

Explain to your worthy host that you want to see an *ingenio* (sugar estate), *cafetal* (coffee place), and a *vega* (tobacco farm), and that you want a good volante, and a driver who knows the road. Stipulate, also, in order to save dispute, *cuanto* (how much).

Tobacco farm

The best properties known as *vegas*, or tobacco farms, are comprised in a narrow area in the south-west part of the island, about twenty-seven leagues long by about seven broad, shut in on the north by mountains, and on the south-west by the ocean, Pinar del Rio being the principal point in the district.

These vegas are found generally on the margins of rivers, or in low, moist localities, their ordinary size being not more than a *caballeria*, which amounts to about thirty-three acres of our measurement. The half of this is also most frequently devoted to the raising of the vegetable known as the *platano* (banana), which may be said to be the bread of the lower classes. A few other small vegetables are raised.

The usual buildings upon such places are a dwelling-house, a drying-house, a few sheds for cattle, and, perhaps, a small *bohio* (hut) or two, made in the rudest manner, for the shelter of the hands, who, upon some of the very largest places, number twenty or thirty, though not always negroes,— for this portion of the labor of the island seems to be performed by the lower classes of whites. Some of the places that are large have a *mayoral*, as he is called, a man whose business it is to look after the negroes, and direct the agricultural labors; but, as a general thing, the planter, who is not always the owner of the property, but simply the lessee, lives upon, directs, and governs the place.

Platano

Guided by the results of a long experience, transmitted from his ancestors (says a Spanish author), the farmer knows, without being able to explain himself, the means of augmenting or diminishing the strength or the mildness of the tobacco. His right hand, as if guided by an instinct, foresees what buds it is necessary to take off in order to put a limit to the increase or height, and what amount of trimming is necessary to give a chance to the proper quantity of leaves. But the principal care, and that which occupies him in his waking hours, is the extermination of the voracious insects that persecute the plant. One called *cachaga* domesticates itself at the foot of the leaves; the *verde*, on the under side of the leaves; the *rosquilla*, in the heart of the plant; all of them doing more or less damage.

The planter passes entire nights, provided with lights, cleaning the buds just opening, of these destructive insects. He has even to carry on a war with still worse enemies,—the *vivijaguas*, a species of large, native ants, that are to the tobacco what the locust is to the wheat. This plague is so great, at times, that prayers and special adoration are offered up to San Marcial to intercede against the plague of ants.

Cohiba

The plant, whose original name was *cohiba*, grows to a height of from six to nine feet, as allowed, with oblong, spear-shaped leaves; the tobacco being stronger when few leaves are permitted to grow. The leaves when young are of a dark-green color and have rather a smooth appearance, changing at maturity into yellowish green.

Among the Cubans, the leaves are divided into four classes; first, *desecho*, or *desecho limpio*, which are those immediately at the top of the plant, and which constitute the best quality, from the fact that they get more equally the benefit of the sun's rays by day, and the dew by night; second, *desechito*, which are the next to the above; third, the *libra*, the *inferior*, or *small* leaves about the top of the plant; and fourth, the *injuriado*, or those nearest the root.

Tobacco of the best quality, such as is produced in the choice vegas of the Vuelta Abajo, is known by its even tint of rich dark-brown and freedom from stains, burning freely, when made into cigars, with a brown or white ash, which will remain as such on the cigar, sometimes, till it is half smoked, without falling off.

Of the *injuriado* there are three qualities; the best is called *injuriado de reposo*, or "the picked over," and the other two, firsts and seconds (*primeros y segundos*). Tobacco of the classes *desechito* and *libra*, of which the leaves are not perfect, is called *injuriado bueno*, while all the rest, of whatever quality, that is broken in such a manner as to be unfit for wrappers is called *injuriado malo*. Amongst the trade, in place of the above names, the different qualities are simply designated by numbers.

After the harvesting and curing of the tobacco, it is formed into bundles (*gavillas*) of thirty or forty leaves of the *injuriado*, and about twenty-five of *libra* tied together; these are then gathered into the *manojas*, which consist of four *gavillas* tied with strips of the *guano* (palm-leaf); the union of from fifty to eighty of these composes the *tercio* (bale), in which form the

| Manoja | Gavilla | Tercio |

tobacco is transported to the railroad upon the backs of mules, each mule carrying two bales, the average weight of which is about two hundred pounds per bale.

The vicinity of Havana has the honor of being the first place in which tobacco was grown. Its culture commenced in 1580, there being nothing heard of the now famed Vuelta Abajo until 1790. This culture is one that has increased very rapidly in the island; it being stated upon good authority that, in 1827, there were only five thousand five hundred and thirty-four tobacco farms, while in 1846, there were more than nine thousand, and in 1859, some ten thousand, which shows a very rapid increase indeed; and it is now estimated that the tobacco crop alone of the small portion of the island under cultivation is worth from eighteen to twenty millions of dollars annually.

Bales *en route*

A *caballeria* of thirty-three acres of ground produces about nine thousand pounds of tobacco, made up in about the following proportions: four hundred and fifty pounds of *desecho*, or best; one thousand eight hundred pounds *desechito*, or seconds; two thousand two hundred and fifty pounds of *libra*, or thirds; and four thousand five hundred pounds of *injuriado*. From these figures, taking the bale at one hundred pounds, and the average price of the tobacco at twenty dollars per bale (though this is a low estimate, for the crops of some of the vegas are sold as high, sometimes, as four hundred dollars per bale), an approximate idea may be formed of the profit of a large plantation, in a good year, when the crops are satisfactory.

San Antonio de los Baños is a small and pretty town, with well-built houses, and about five thousand inhabitants, situated

Cafetal

twenty-three miles from Havana, on the railroad to Guanajay. It has mineral springs and baths, and is frequented as a summer resort by the people of Havana. Near to it is the district of Alquizar, celebrated for its beautiful coffee estates, which the stranger can see by hiring a volante in San Antonio, and telling the driver to go to the *cafetal mas proxima* (nearest).

The accompanying drawing will give an idea of the general appearance of one of these coffee places, with its superb entrance and avenue of *palmas reales*, and, at regular intervals, rows of orange, banana, and other trees, whose golden fruit forms a strong and striking contrast to the green, wax-like coffee leaves.

The volante with three horses shows a peculiarity of fashionable volante-riding in the country; the *calisero* riding one horse and guiding the other two, the three being harnessed abreast; the Señoras, meanwhile, reclining at their ease, escorted by their mounted and ever-attendant *caballero*.

The palm-tree is probably the most useful if not the most beautiful tree in the island of Cuba, and is found in every portion of it, giving at once character and beauty to the scenery; and that known as the *palma real* (royal) is only one of the twenty-two varieties which are enumerated in this majestic family of the tropics. Its feathers or branches fall airily and gracefully from the top of a cylindrical trunk of fifteen or twenty yards in height; in the centre of the branches is the heart (*cogollo*, or bud of the plant), elevating itself perpendicularly, with its needle

Cogollo

point like a lightning-rod. This heart, enveloped in wrappers of

Expliation

tender white leaves, is called *palmito*, and makes a most nourishing and delicious salad; it is also boiled like cauliflower, and served with a delicate white sauce. In either way it is a very agreeable esculent for the table. The branches, numbering from twenty to twenty-two, are secured to the trunk by a large exfoliated capping called *yagua*, and between each scale there starts out one of the feathers or branches. At the foot of these burst little buds, which open into delicate bunches of small flowers, followed by the fruit or seed, which is used as nourishment for the herds of hogs on the breeding-farms; it is also used as a substitute for coffee amongst the poor people of some portions of the island.

The trunk of the palm is a cylinder or tube, filled with milky fibres, which, torn off in long strips from top to bottom, are dried, and make a narrow, thin kind of board, with which the peasants form the walls of their rustic habitations; while the branches serve as roofs or covering to their lightly constructed houses; though for this latter purpose are also used the leaves of the *guano*, the generic name of all the palms, if we except the *palma real*, the *corojo*, and the *coco*.

The *yaguas* serve for roofs and for lining the walls of the huts, and for general purposes of shelter for the country people of Cuba; while they are used also as wrappers for bales of tobacco and other materials. Torn into narrow shreds, they answer for tying packages in lieu of twine.

El yasey is another one of the palms that merits especial mention, for from it they make the excellent palm-leaf hats that are commonly worn on the island amongst the country people and the villagers, the manufacture of which constitutes one branch of industry amongst the women, and for which they get from one to two dollars per hat.

Still another palm, known as the *miraguano*, is very useful; as from it is obtained a kind of moss, which, in the country, is used to stuff pillows and mattresses,—where they are used.

LIFE ON A SUGAR ESTATE

Being armed with letters from the owner of a fine estate to his *administrador* in charge, as also with a private note to the chief engineer, we made up our minds, one beautiful evening, to present the same in person for a few days' visit; and, making our preparations accordingly we notified our host to procure for us a conveyance or horses from Guanajay.

"To-night, Señor?" said he; "it is impossible,—wait until morning."

"No, to-night, in the cool of the evening, we will go, and start at six o'clock."

"But, good heavens, *caballeros!* it is five leagues, the road is bad, and it will be a bad night."

"It makes no difference,—we can ride ten leagues, if necessary; there will be a moon, and a little rain won't hurt us;" and finding that we were not going to increase his bill by a prolonged stay, he added, with a sigh, "it will cost you very dear for a volante, gentlemen."

"Never mind; send us the man, and we will make our bargain with him;" and in the course of half an hour there rattled up a two-horse affair, that swung and swayed about in such a manner that we began to have doubts about arriving at our destination in such a rickety affair.

"Does the man know the road?" we ask.

"Oh, yes! in the day time."

"Not at night, then?"

"He can find it; but it is very bad indeed, Señor,—*mucho* mud, *mucho* creeks, etc.,—better try it on horseback."

"What's the price of this broken-down old conveyance?"

"*Una onza*" (seventeen dollars, and double the usual price).

"*Picaro!* you know that's too much."

"Well, what would you have, Señor? People don't travel here in the night; it will be dark, and the road is bad, and my volante will possibly get stuck in some creek."

"And where will we be then?"

"*Dios sabe!* " (God knows), with an irresistible shrug of his shoulders.

"Well, we won't go in that way, then; we will have horses."

"Ah, Señor! (very humbly), I have fine horses at your service."

"What will you charge?—be careful, now; there is that other stable we have not yet tried."

(Calling all the saints to witness the truth of his statement). "You shall have them for a song;—*splendid* horses, and a fine guide, at half an ounce" (eight dollars and fifty cents), which striking us as reasonable enough for fifteen miles, we made the contract, settled our bill, and awaited the appearance of the equines.

Shades of Bucephalus! what a jolly lot they were, to be sure!— exactly the bull-fight style of horses. And the guide especially!—an old, weather-beaten fellow, of about seventy years, as he afterwards told us, who came mounted on a little bit of a horse about half as big as himself, a straw pack for a saddle, and over that two great panniers of straw-matting, upon the top of which he sat perched, his slippered feet projecting on each side, in front of the horse's head, the heels being armed with tremendous spurs.

With a hearty laugh at the outfit, but still determined to go on, we accepted the owner's offer of spurs, and mounted our *Rosinantes* amid an interested crowd of small boys, negro wenches, and a soldier or two, who were muttering over and discussing the folly of *los Americanos.*

Leaving the town and following our guide, who was elevated yet a little higher with the aid of our valises that he had put in the panniers, as also by a "snifter" of *aguardiente* put inside himself, we struck the open country, taking a bridle-path, as he said, for a short cut.

He was a guide indeed, full of song and story, well posted in the people and country, and knowing the roads, which he had lived among all his life, as well as his hand. Various were the topics we discussed, and in which he seemed *au fait*,—the *breed* of his horse, the making of sugar, the coal trade (i.e., running in Africans), etc.; but he rather staggered us on his history.

"Did you ever hear of Columbus?" we ask.

"Oh! (with a short laugh), knew him very well."

"Ah! (somewhat taken aback); oh, you did, eh? What manner of man was he?"

"Oh, a first-rate man!—plenty of money,—knew him very well."

"Lived around here, perhaps?"

"Oh, yes; we are right near where he lived, now."

"He doesn't live about here now, then?"

"Well, I guess not; he died ever so many years ago."

"Left a family, of course?"

"Well, no,—I don't think he did; he was rather a hard case."

"Oh! I guess you are mistaken; it is not the man we are talking of. What was his first name?"

"Same man; same man! I knew him well. He was called Cristobal."

And so, entertained by startling facts in the life of the great discoverer; lighted on our way by the fitful gleams of the moon from behind the clouds, or by the blazing chimney of some mill; driven by frequent showers to seek the shelter of convenient sheds, whose piles of cane-stalks furnished us with temporary beds or with the means of enjoying sugar *à lo Cubano*; amused by the occasional disappearance of our guide over his horse's head into the mud; delayed by swollen streams and treacherous marshes, we were not sorry to hear the announcement of our guide, that we had reached the "Ingenio Asuncion," our point of destination. We soon discovered that we were at a large mill, not in operation; the dwellings were dark, with no sign of habitation, if we except the barking of the dogs. Not caring to disturb the family at such an hour, we roused up the watchman, who informed us that every one had retired except the engineer, to whom I had a letter, and who was just about retiring when I knocked at the door of his bachelor apartments in the mill.

"Who is there?" he asked.

"An American."

"Well, that's pretty general; but I guess I'll let you in, seeing I am of that kind myself." Whereupon the door was opened unto us; and, on making ourselves known, we were most hospitably received and kindly treated by him, finding, luckily, a spare bed in his quarters.

We found our host to be a young Philadelphian, an intelligent, capital fellow, in charge of one of the finest mills on the island, the machinery of which, we were interested to learn, had been erected by the well-known house of Merrick & Sons, of Philadelphia.

What a jewel is hospitality! what a pleasure is given by the reception of a stranger without formality or stiffness, so much more appreciated by a traveler in a foreign land! On awakening in the morning, we found our letters had been presented by the engineer to the administrator, who had read them, and was prepared to make our personal acquaintance, and act as our host. We were immediately made comfortable in his spacious mansion, and in a short time, by his cordial manner and glad welcome, were made to feel perfectly at home; and as we sat chatting over our *café con leche*, we could afford to laugh over our delays, discomforts, and adventures of the previous night.

Our daily life upon this estate was as follows: About six o'clock in the morning the servants entered our bed-room with coffee, whereupon we arose and dressed ourselves. We then strolled around the grounds until our horses were saddled, when, in the delicious morning air, we galloped down to the sea-shore, and in some quiet cove or sheltering bay took our morning bath in the foaming, dashing, and invigorating surf.

Fancy a narrow strip of golden sand, fringed on one side by the luxuriant vegetation of the tropics, and washed on the other by the foaming surf; picture to yourself the emerald water near at hand and the dark-blue distance which meets the wonderfully clear and transparent sky; breathe with us the delightful air, at the same time balmy and invigorating, and you will form some faint conception of this glorious morning bath.

Scattered along the shore are thousands of beautiful shells, pieces of coral, and strangely formed sponges and weeds, many of the shells making exceedingly beautiful ornaments in the form of ear-rings,

The morning bath

breast-pins etc., so rich are they in delicacy of color and polish, and graceful shape.

Mounting our horses after our bath, distance by the sea-side, and then turning off through the woods, took our way by varying routes, over rolling hills or beautiful valleys, homeward, stopping once in a while at some neighboring mill for a chat with the engineer, or possibly at a rural *bohio*, to study negro character. Reaching our homes with a fine appetite, we proceeded to make our toilets for the day, and were then ready for breakfast, which is usually served between ten and eleven o'clock, and occupies some two hours in its disposal.

A Cuban breakfast is no small affair, I assure you, at this hour of the day. One's appetite is sharpened, rather, by an early cup of coffee and long fast; and he must be a very sick man indeed who does not do justice to his meal, which consists almost always of eggs and rice, fish, meats, and vegetables, poultry and salad, cheese and jelly, a cigarette, and then the ever present *café* with your cigar.

Field laborer

The country-houses of Cuba are, as a general thing, on the sugar estates, very large and roomy mansions, built of stone, floored with tiles of either clay or marble, according to the wealth or taste of the owner; the doors and windows like those already described in city houses, are immense, and the latter entirely without glass, while no provision is made for fire, and, from my experience of one or two northers, it is never needed, though it is said that in some seasons, when *los nortes* are particularly cold, a fire would be very comfortable indeed for a day or two, as long as these winds last.

The houses have generally piazzas front and back, which are very spacious, and frequently used as dining and sitting rooms, being enclosed by canvas curtains lowered from the edge of the roof. These houses are rarely more than one story high, built with the closest eye to a certain kind of lazy comfort and coolness; they have a large hall or room, generally as large as one of our public parlors, from which open on each side one or two suites of rooms, used by the family as bed-chambers and sitting-rooms. Beyond the hall there is, perhaps, a dining-room or the aforementioned piazza, curtained or closed in by blinds, and looking out upon one side of the court-yard, or *patio*; on

Country house

each side of this extends back a wing, used on one side for offices, servants' quarters, etc., and, perhaps, on the other for stables,—the whole with a wall at the other side, forming an enclosed quadrangle, in which horses are fed, negro children play, and servants chatter.

This court-yard is varied in some of the more tasteful ingenios by beautiful gardens, laid out with orange, lemon, pomegranate, and other fruit trees, while the jessamine and heliotrope, and other bushes, add fragrance and beauty to the scene. The mention of these flowers reminds me that I was surprised to find so few on the island. Although some of them were intensely brilliant in color, yet it did not strike me that there was nearly such a variety of beautiful roses and smaller plants as there is in America. Even in the luxuriant vegetation of the Coffee Mountains of Guantanamo, there is a scarcity of handsome flowers; and I have upon my memorandum book several commissions to send seeds from the United States to Cuban ladies.

Breakfast over, and our cigar disposed of, we sought some cool spot about the house, and lazily reclining in the comfortable chairs found in every dwelling, slipped off, in spite of ourselves into a *siesta*,—a pleasant little pilgrimage of an hour or two, to the land of dreams. This finished, we took a stroll through the mill, tried a game of billiards, enjoyed the more quiet pleasure of a book, or found a more agreeable occupation in conversing with the ladies. The fair sex, however, do not like the plantations much, and therefore stay there very little, visiting them at rare intervals,—generally at Christmas, when there is a regular frolic, or for a few weeks in summer. On some of the plantations whose proprietors are very wealthy, when the ladies are present there is great style,—servants in livery at table, service very elegant, and both ladies and gentlemen *en grande toilette*. This is particularly the case with those planters and their families who have been abroad. Generally, however, every one seems desirous of taking life in the most quiet, easy, and agreeable way, with as little trouble as possible.

The afternoons, before dinner, we generally devoted to a ride on horseback. One morning's ride through some most beautiful scenes in the most charming portion of western Cuba, beyond Cabañas, a neat little village on the sea-coast, I shall never forget. We started just after

El mayoral

daybreak, as we had a long ride before us, with the *mayoral*, in his holiday garb, for our guide. His get-up was a most stunning affair indeed. Imagine a swarthy Cuban, clothed in a pretty suit of clean, blue-striped linen, an immaculately clean, white straw hat, with its broad brim acting as a perfect shelter from the sun, his feet clothed in clean, white stockings, pushed into low pumps of shining patent-leather, upon the front of which glistened polished silver buckles, while from his heels hung jingling a most gorgeous pair of silver-mounted Mexican spurs; around his waist a scarlet silken scarf, from which protruded the haft of a handsome dirk-knife, universally carried by every Cuban about some portion of his person. And then his horse, in fine trappings, with his tail plaited in most careful and curious plaits, the end of which was fastened to the crupper of the saddle, while his mane, cut apparently by line and measurement, was a model of neatness.

Off we started, at full gallop, and rapidly we passed by mill after mill, in full operation even at that early hour; now riding over rolling hills of waving cane, now through some red, clayey, but hard road, with hedges of the beautiful *Piña Raton*, while, ever and anon, some new and beautiful view was displayed before our fascinated vision. This plant, the *Piña Raton*, by-the-by, is about the only generally used fence there is in Cuba, if we except an occasional hedge of the regular Mexican *maguey*, which one sees now and then, with its broad sword and saw-like leaves. The botanical name of this plant is the *Bromelia Pinguin*, but it is known more generally by its vulgar name of *Piña de Raton* or *maya*. It grows to a great height, very thick and strong, and has somewhat the appearance of the above-named *maguey*; the leaves are dentated, ending in sharp needle-like briers at their points; the

Piña Raton

outside leaves are generally of a beautiful green, but some of the interior ones are of an intense vermilion color, looking exactly like long, thin strips of coral; while the flower, which appears as a kind of core to the plant, is very beautifully formed, of delicate tints, and looks like the most exquisite wax-work. To see this curiously shaped and brightly colored hedge, stretching as it does for

Flower of Piña Raton

miles and miles on both sides of the road, has a strange and pleasing effect upon the eye.

On our way, we were joined by two or three officers and men of the Guardia Civil,—a jolly set of fellows, one of whom, an immense fellow, with a Falstaffian corporation, and a round bullet head, reminded me of some of the pictures I have seen in Don Quixote of honest, stout, and trusty Sancho Panza; and who, on the score of my having been a *soldado*, fraternized with me, and informed me that he had been a Carlista, in Spain, which he considered, he said, as bad as being a rebel. A roystering, swaggering, fat officer he was, and being splendidly mounted myself, I could afford to hear his praises of the thin, wiry horse he was riding, and which was so badly broken that he came near breaking his rider's skull several times. Gradually increasing my pace, I at last got the fat man into a terrible state; his face became red, his eyes glared, and his body swayed to-and-fro in his saddle in such a way that he was compelled to pull up, with curses loud and deep upon his now *maldito caballo*, and I have no doubt smothered ones upon his "wild Yankee" companion.

But the object of our ride was principally accomplished when we arrived at the "Valle de las Delicias," or Valley of Delight. If the one mentioned by Bunyan, in his "Progress," was as beautiful as this, I do not wonder at the "Pilgrim" wanting to stay, particularly if he found such a host as we did in the neighborhood.

This view was the most beautiful I had seen. Though, perhaps, not so extensive as the Yumurri, it was even more beautiful, to my eye, from its not being so tame, the scenery partaking of something

Valley of Delight

of the savage grandeur of American landscapes, combined with the peculiarities of the tropics.

Continuing our journey, our party, which now amounted to a dozen persons, arrived at the Ingenio San Claudio, celebrated for making the finest sugar on this end of the island, and, from the specimens that I saw, equal to some of the refined loaf sugars in the States. Rum, sugar, and molasses are all made at this estate, which is an exceedingly profitable one, so I understood, being situated in a most fertile country.

Night found us home again to dinner; after which, we gathered together upon the piazza to enjoy the evening breeze and our fragrant Havanas with the pleasure of conversation. A game of cards in the evening, or a stroll through the mill to inhale the fragrant odor of the boiling sugar, or watch the hands as they piled the cane into the crusher, served to pass the hours pleasantly till bed-time. As a preliminary to retiring, it was our custom, being invalids (for all of whom it is prescribed), to drink a hot *guarapo* punch, which is said to be very beneficial for diseases of the chest and lungs, and which I found very palatable indeed. This punch is made by taking an egg, and beating it up with a "sufficient quantity" of rum, whiskey, or brandy; the boiling cane-juice, fresh from the boilers, and known as *guarapo*, is then poured into it, and this mixture, after being poured backwards and forwards until there is a fine frothy bead on it, is drank; and I can assure my reader, from frequent experience of it, it is *muy bueno*, indeed.

With the daily life herein described and the frequent visits to the sugar-mills as detailed in the next chapter, time passes more quickly than one would think; and if one is an invalid suffering from any diseases of the chest or lungs, this kind of life is more calculated to benefit him than any I know of, working as it has done, in many cases, a sovereign cure. It is advisable, in such cases, when staying on the sugar estates, to be as much in the atmosphere of boiling sugar as possible, and it is even pleasant to sit within its fragrance, and read one's book for hours at a time.

On every estate, I noticed that the negroes who worked over or near the boiling sugar were universally muscular men, with most extraordinarily large chests,—the result, as I was invariably informed, of the good effect of the fragrant vapor I have even envied an old man of eighty years his splendid development of muscle and expanse of chest, for he seemed, notwithstanding his great age, quite as young and active as most of the others working with him at the boilers.

* The experiences contained in this and the succeeding chapter are those gained by visits to several of the finest estates in different parts of the island.

SUGAR-MAKING

A book on the Island of Cuba without a chapter on sugar-making would hardly be complete. As the following facts were given to me at different times while staying on sugar estates, I have thought a simple account of the process of sugar-making, devoid of any technical peculiarities, would interest my readers, as it interested me in seeing it as here described.

To the cultivation of the cane is also added, on the same place where the cane is raised, and by the same proprietor, the manufacture of sugar, such places being called in the Cuban dialect "*ingenios*," or sugar estates, the carrying on of which requires a large amount of capital, a great degree of intelligence, and much mechanical skill.

These *ingenios* vary in size from five hundred to ten thousand acres, though the results of their crops are not always in proportion to the number of their acres, that depending more particularly upon the nature of the soil of the particular locality in which they are situated, and the degree of intelligence and amount of labor with which they are worked. Each one of the *ingenios* is, in some degree, like a small village, or, as with the larger ones, quite a town, in which are substantial edifices, numerous dwellings, and expensive machinery, together with a large number of inhabitants, the different officials necessary for their government and management representing the civil officers, except with, perhaps, greater power.

The buildings upon a first-class sugar estate are generally a dwelling-house (*casa de vivienda*), which, from its size, style, and cost, might sometimes be called a palace, some of them having, in addition to numerous other conveniences, small chapels in which to celebrate the religious services of the estate, the dwelling being occupied by the owner and his family, if living on the estate; if not, by the *administrador*, who is charged with the care and management of the

El Mayoral

estate in the absence of the owner, and who, in fact, may be said to be the man of the place. There is also the house occupied by the "*mayoral*" as he is called, the chief of the negro laborers, whose business it is to follow the laborers to the field to see that they do their work properly, and that sufficient amount of cane is cut to keep the mill constantly supplied with material to grind; in fact, he has a general supervision of all the agricultural duties of the estate, receiving his orders only from the owner or *administrador*, as the case may be. The *mayorals* are generally very ordinary men, of no education, the intelligence they possess being simply that gained by long experience in this kind of business.

The *maquinista*, or engineer, is really the most important man upon the place, as upon him depend the grinding of the cane and the care of the mill and its machinery—that it is kept in good and running order, so that no delay may take place in the grinding season. His quarters are generally in some part of the mill, where he manages to be pretty comfortable. These engineers are mostly young Americans, with now and then an Englishman or a German; but the Americans, I found, were much preferred on account of their superior intelligence and assiduous attention to their business. Their pay is from one thousand two hundred to two thousand five hundred dollars for the grinding season, which begins about December and ends nearly always in or before June, most of the engineers going over to the States to pass the summer, or, as they express it, "to have a good time."

The Hospital is always an important building on these places, as it is the only place where the sick can be treated and properly taken care of. It is usually arranged with a great deal of care and neatness, the building being divided off into different wards for men and women, and also for contagious diseases; it is generally in charge of a hospital steward, who has quite an apothecary shop in his charge, and who receives his instructions from the attending physician, who also attends a number of the estates in the same locality, visiting each one generally every day, and receiving compensation at so much per year. As a matter of simple economy, to say nothing of charity, the invalids get the best of treatment, and are not sent back to work until they are completely restored, though while convalescing they are required to do light work, such as making baskets, hats, etc.

The Nursery is also quite an important place, and is highly amusing to visit, for here the future hopes of the plantation are cared for. These little black, naked sinners, running and tumbling over each other in great glee, are generally kept in a large room, with rows of cradles or cribs on each side, in which each little one is kept at night, the old women who are too feeble to work any longer being retained as nurses in charge, while the mothers of the little ones are out at work in the fields, being allowed, two or three times a day, to return and suckle such infants as need the mother's milk. It is very amusing to enter one of these nurseries when the children are being fed, and see their gambols and antics, and the expression of the little ones' eyes as they see the white master, as he is called, and with whom they keep on friendly terms, enter their quarters. They all appear to be happy and jolly, and make as much noise and have as much fun as would satisfy any "radical" in the States. Poor things, they happily know nothing of the hard lot in store for them.

But the most important of all the buildings is, of course, the Sugar-mill, which generally consists of the engine-house, where is all the machinery and power for grinding, boiling, and working the cane and juice, and the purging and drying houses. The engine-house is generally an extremely large roof, supported by pillars and posts, and entirely open on all sides,—in fact, nothing more than a very well constructed shed to keep off the sun and rain, the floor being mostly paved with brick, and the stairways leading from one portion of the building to another being of solid stone. In fact, one of these mills of the first class is a very handsome affair—everything about it, the engines and the machinery, being kept in the most scrupulously clean order, equal to a man-of-war.

On the larger places, there are generally what are called barracoons, or quarters for the slaves. They are large buildings,

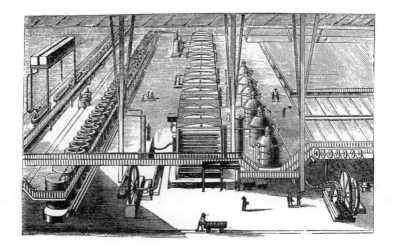

Interior of a sugar-mill

constructed of stone, in the form of a quadrangle, on the inner side of which are the rooms for the negroes, to which there is only one main entrance; this is shut at night when the hands are all in. On the outside, and much better built, there are rooms occupied by the different white men connected with the place and not otherwise provided for; probably, also, a long row of stables for the many horses usually kept upon places of this kind, and of which there is no lack, either for work or play.

On other places, again, the negroes live in *bohios*, or huts,—some few constructed of stone, but most of them simply log or cane huts, of the most ordinary description, thatched with palm-leaf or grass, and making no attempt at comfort, but simply serving as shelters from the rain. I thought, in my journeyings through the Southern States, that the miserable habitations called cabins were bad enough; but I must confess that these were worse; though, to be sure, in a climate like this, it does not matter much about shelter,—all one wants is shade.

The Purging-house (*Casa de purga*) is generally of very great extent, being two stories high, and of great length. The floor of the upper story is simply is simply a series of strong frames, with apertures for placing in them the *hormas*, funnel-shaped cylinders of

Section of purging-house

tin or sheet-iron, into which is put the molasses to drain troughs beneath. One side of this house is open, in order to permit the *gavetas*, or large boxes upon wheels, into which are put the forms of sugar, to be run in and out conveniently. In these boxes, which are immensely large, the sugar in forms is broken up and exposed to the air and sun, for the purpose of thoroughly drying it. The number of these *hormas* is something wonderful, there being in some of the houses as many as twenty thousand. Beneath the upper floor are a number of troughs, each trough having a slant to a main trough. Over the minor troughs are the mouths of the aforesaid funnels, which permit the molasses draining from the pans of sugar above to run into the troughs, which again convey it to large vats or hogsheads, called *bocoyes*, each of which holds from twelve to fifteen hundred gallons. It is in this process that they make the distinction of the different sugars,—*blanco*, or white; *quebrado*, or broken; and the common, dark-colored sugar called *cucurucho*. In making these three qualities of sugar, a layer of moist earth or clay is placed upon the top of the pans of crystallized syrup, from which the moisture, draining constantly through, carries off all the imperfections, leaving the pans full of dry sugar in the form of solid cases, and generally of three colors; that nearest the top, pure

Drying-house

white; next below that, the discolored; and at the bottom of that, the moist or dark colored. If, however, it is desired to make only a *mascabado* sugar, which is of a rich brown color, and does not require the same time or pains as the finer qualities, the syrup is simply put in the large hogsheads, before described, and allowed to drain off in

Sugar cake   Horma

the natural way without the process of "claying" it, as it is called. This, of course, makes more sugar of an average inferior grade, which weighs more, having the molasses in it; and this is the sugar generally preferred, I believe, by sugar refiners.

Besides the above, other buildings there are, of different kinds, necessary to large establishments like these, such as cooper, carpenter, and black-smith shops; while there are also, on the best estates, gas works, at which is manufactured the gas with which the mill and buildings are illuminated, it being found much cheaper and cleaner to manufacture and use gas than oil.

Cooper shop

Of the persons directly in charge of making the sugar there are one or two upon each place whose business it is to see to the boiling and refining of the sugar, and who are known as sugar-makers, receiving for their services from eight hundred to one thousand dollars each per annum.

It is calculated that to every one thousand boxes of sugar, consisting of four hundred pounds each, it is necessary to have from fifty to seventy-five hands; for, of course, the greater supply of labor there is, the better are the chances of making the sugar of superior quality. Of these laborers the larger proportion are negroes, while upon nearly every place there are more or less Chinese or Coolies, all of whom are divided into classes and divisions, according to the labor for which they are desired.

Guadieros, or guardians, are stationed in small huts at the entrances to the estates, and act as porters, though their lodges are nothing more, usually, than a simple shelter hut, of grass or palm-leaf, the occupants being generally old men unfit for hard labor. Fire-men attend to keeping up the furnace fires, which are generally placed in a cavity, or sort of cellar in the ground, upon one side of the mill, there being left a large space in front of the furnaces into which the carts,

Furnaces

Waiting rations

upon backing up to its edge, empty their loads of mashed cane, the only fuel used to generate steam. These carts are rude, rough affairs, invariably drawn by either one or two yoke of oxen.

The *contra mayorales*, or directors of the gangs into which the negroes are divided, follow them up into the field with a long strong whip, which they crack frequently, and use whenever they in their ignorance and stupidity see fit, upon the bare backs or naked legs of the laborers. It is their business, also, to see to and inflict any punishment that may be ordered by higher authority.

The bulk of the hands used in the general operations of the place, cutting cane, plowing, etc., are known as the *gente*, or "people." They are pretty well taken care of as regards food, at least in quantity if not in quality; they get *tasajo*, or dried beef, *buniatos*, or sweet potatoes, rice, and plantains which answer for bread, and of which they are very fond, eating them either roasted or fried. The clothing they wear is limited, not only in quality but quantity, the children usually going about stark naked,—the women with only a calico dress on, and the men wearing only their pants. It is rather a novel sight, at the eleven o'clock halt from work, to see these people gathering for their rations, which are served out to them once a day.

Attached to every estate is the *potrero*, or corral, where are herded the cattle used in doing the hauling on the place, and also those intended for supplying the hands with meat.

Of the cane itself there are several species known in Cuba. The *criolla*, or native cane, is the oldest known, being that brought to Spain by Columbus, on his second voyage, from the Canaries, but is thin, poor, and not very juicy; that of Otahite, which is large, thick, and preferred by the sugar-makers, being introduced into the island in 1795; that of the Cristallina, last introduced, and cultivated by many as preferable to that of Otahite, a cartful of which will give a pan and a half of dry sugar, amounting to about sixty pounds. The height attained by the canes, averaging as it does six or eight feet, and sometimes reaching twenty, the length of joint, the color, and many other particulars, vary with different species, with the character of the soil, and with the mode of culture adopted. The stems are divided by prominent annular joints into short lengths, from each joint of which there sprout long, narrow leaves, which, as

Sugar cane

the canes approach maturity, drop off from the lower joints. The outer part of the cane is hard and brittle, but the inner consists of a soft pith containing the sweet juice, which is elaborated separately in each joint. This is very nutritious, and is eaten in large quantities by the negroes, who in their leisure moments are generally supplied with a piece at which they constantly suck, having prepared it by stripping off the outer skin, which leaves in a good piece of cane almost a solid lump of sugar.

The cane is propagated by slips or cuttings, consisting of the top of the cane with two or three of the upper joints, the leaves being stripped off. These are planted, either in holes dug by hand or in trenches formed by a plough, about eight or twelve inches deep, the earth being banked up upon the margin, and well manured; two or more slips are laid longitudinally at the bottom of each hole, and covered with earth from the banks to the depth of one or two inches. In about a fortnight the sprouts appear a little above the earth, and then a little more earth from the bank is put in the hole, and as the plants continue to grow, the earth is occasionally filled in a little at a time, until, after four or five months, the holes are entirely filled up.

The planting takes place in the intervals of the rainy season, which commences regularly in June, and lasts until October or November, the cutting taking place immediately after the Christmas holidays, and continuing on up to May, even, in some cases.

The maturity of the cane is indicated by the skin becoming dry, smooth, and brittle, by the cane becoming heavy, the pith gray, approaching to brown, and the juice sweet and glutinous. It is usual to raise several crops in successive years from the same roots, the plan, I believe, being to plant about one third of the grounds every year.

Cutting the sugar-cane

When the cane is ripe for cutting, the mill is put in complete running order, and the hands, under the charge of the *mayoral*, proceed to the field of now green cane, each negro—man, woman, or child—armed with a *machete*, or knife of peculiar construction, something like a butcher's cleaver, and very strong and sharp. Spreading themselves out over the field, they begin the cutting of the cane, first by one cut at the top, which takes off the long leaves  and that part of the cane which is worthless, except as it is used for food for the cattle; a second cut is then given as near the root as possible, the cane falling carelessly to the ground, from which it is gathered as wanted. A field in the cutting season presents a lively sight, with its three or four hundred laborers superintended by the *mayoral* on horseback, its carpet of cut cane, and its long lines of slowly-moving carts, with their noisy drivers, while the sea of standing cane, sometimes extending for miles and miles, is stirred by the gentle breeze into waves of undulating green.

The carts being now piled up with the cane, and the fodder left upon the ground to be carried off another time, they drive back in a

Carts on the return

long line to the mill, where they empty the cane under a large shed, close to that portion of the mill wherein is the crusher.

This pile of cane generally becomes immense, as the carts keep continually bringing it in faster than the mill can grind during the day; and at night, work in the field, as a general thing, ceases,—a portion of the hands going in the early part of the evening to get their rest, while the others keep feeding the cane to the mill. Towards morning, when the stock on hand gets low, the negroes are called up, and sent out to the field to keep up the supply of cut cane, the engine never ceasing to run night or day, unless in case of accident, during the whole of the grinding season.

The cane being deposited under the shed at the mill in sufficient quantities, the engine is started, and the machinery put in motion. The cane is then thrown by the hands upon an endless inclined flexible conductor, formed of strips of wood and links of chain, which, being constantly in motion, and passing round a cylinder near the crushers, throws the cane into their jaws, by which the juice is completely pressed out of it, and passes in a continuous stream into the troughs beneath, while the refuse cane is carried out on the other side into a wooden trough, from which it is taken by hand, placed in

Unloading the cane

carts, and carried off to the furnaces. These crushers, or *maquinas de moler*, as they are called, consist of three immensely large, solid, iron rollers, placed horizontally, revolving, one above and two beneath, in a kind of pyramidal form, the opening between the upper and first lower one being larger than that between the upper and second lower one in order to form more of a mouth with which to draw in the cane from the feeder.

The juice as it now runs out in a liquid state is an opaque fluid, of a dull gray or olive-green color, of a sweet, pleasant taste, and is known by the name of *guarapo*. It is quite thick, and holds in suspension particles of the cane and refuse, which are separated from it by filtration. This liquid is so exceedingly fermentable that it is necessary to clarify it immediately. It runs from the mill by means of troughs or conductors, passing in its course into pans of copper, pierced with holes like a cullender, through which the liquor runs, leaving its refuse matter on the surface to be disposed of by a man constantly in attendance for the purpose. It is then forced, by means of pumps, into large tanks, from which it is conveyed by a trough to the clarifiers, which are large kettles heated by steam. In these, defecation takes place, the process being assisted by four or five

Maquinas de Moler

ounces of lime to every four hundred and fifty gallons of boiling liquid contained in each kettle. Sometimes more lime is required, this depending entirely upon the density of the juice.

In connection with these vats, which are known as clarifiers, there is generally used a test paper (*torna sol*), by which the juice is tested as it comes from the mill, to ascertain the amount of acidity in it. This is a simple chemically-prepared paper, of a blue color, which, on being put into the liquid, turns to a red color, more or less intense according to the degree of acidity in the juice.

From the clarifiers, the juice, after settling, is filtered through vats, filled nearly up to the top with bone-black, which is usually used two or three times, or until the juice changes color or does not run off well. I was told that the length of time which the bone-black was used was the real secret of the difference in some sugars; and, as proof of this, on the estates where the finest sugars are made, the bone-black is changed every eight hours; while on the estates where the poorest sugar is made, it is changed only once in two or three days.

From these clarifying vats there are three copper troughs,—one for molasses, one for cane-juice, and one for syrups. From these three troughs as many pipes lead to large tanks, which are simply receptacles for the material accumulating. From these tanks, again, the liquor is conveyed to the vacuum pans, which are mostly those of Rillieux's patent, and made by Merrick & Sons, of Philadelphia, the principle of latent heat being made use of to evaporate the cane-juice. These vacuum pans are three in number, the first of which is for juice, the second for syrup, and the third a strike-pan, as it is called. The vacuum-pan consists of a close copper vessel, perfectly air tight, the middle portion cylindrical, and from six to seven feet in diameter, the upper portion convex or dome-shaped, and the bottom also convex, but less so than the top. The bottom of the pan is double, the cavity between the inner and outer bottom forming a receptacle for steam; and there is also a coiled steam-pipe just over the upper bottom. There is one pipe of communication with the vessel of clarified syrup, one with the vessel which is to receive the crystallized sugar, and one with an air-pump, and there are numerous valves, gauges, etc. In using the pan, a quantity of liquid sugar is admitted,

Vats and vacuum-pans

and the air-pump is set to work to exhaust all the air from the pan in order that the contents may boil at a low temperature. To enable the person who superintends the process to ascertain when the syrup is sufficiently evaporated, the pan is supplied with a very ingenious appendage, called the proof stick, by which a little of the sugar can be taken out, and its state ascertained by the touch. Some of the pans have a small glass window, through which can be seen the liquid in a boiling state.

The clarified juice from the tank before mentioned is pumped into the first pan, from the first into the second, it having now become syrup of twenty-eight degrees density; thence it is pumped into syrup clarifiers, then skimmed, then run again through filters of bone-black; out of those filters it goes to the syrup-trough, and thence to the syrup-tank before mentioned. It is now ready for the third or strike-pan, being drawn up by the vacuum at the option of the sugar-maker, and when the pan is full, it is discharged by a valve into the strike-heater, a double-bottomed kettle with a sufficient amount of steam to keep the sugar warm, and create a certain degree of crystallization; from this it goes into the moulds, or *hormas*, before described. These moulds are then run on small railway trucks into the purging-house, and then through the different finishing processes before described in the *Casa de purga*. The molasses that drains off in the purging-house is afterwards re-boiled and made into a common grade of sugar, known as molasses-sugar. The best molasses comes from the *mascabado* sugar, since it has not passed through so many purifying operations, and, therefore, has more saccharine matter in it.

The sugar being thoroughly dried, sorted, and pulverized, is carried into the packing-room, where, ranged upon a slightly elevated frame, are the empty packing-boxes, capable of holding four hundred pounds each. These are filled with the loose sugar, a gang of negroes or coolies range themselves on each side of the rows, with broad, heavy packing-sticks in their hands, and thus all together they pound away, keeping time with their strokes, and making music with their voices. This seems to be a very primitive way of packing the sugar, taking as it does so much time; but no other plan, I was informed, had ever been successfully tried.

The sugar being now tightly packed in the boxes, the latter are closed up and strapped with narrow strips of raw hide, and are then shipped to market.

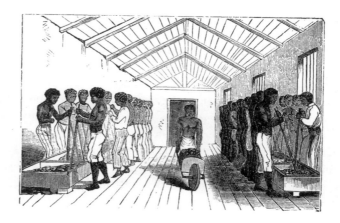

Packing sugar

The foregoing process of sugar-making differs, of course, in some respects on different estates; but the general method is the same, the differences being generally due to some variation in the kind of machinery,—some of the manufacturers, for instance, still clinging to the old-fashioned method of boiling the sugar in open pans, which of course allows a great deal of valuable matter to escape; others not going through so much of the refining process with the crop.

In concluding this chapter, it may interest the reader to know that sugar-making was first tried in Cuba as far back as 1535, when a grant of land was made for that purpose on what is now known as the Cerro, near Havana, though good authorities state that it was in Havana itself, and at Regla, on the other side of the bay, in 1598, that really paying sugar estates were established.

BATHS OF SAN DIEGO

Tell a resident of Havana you have rheumatism, and he will tell you to go to San Diego; consult a physician in Havana in reference to some obstinate malady, and he will advise you to try the water of San Diego; ask your native friend if he ever goes out of town, "O, yes! to San Diego," is his reply; and one really begins to think there must be a sovereign panacea for all the ills of the body in the mineral waters of springs so often spoken of.

Cuba is specially favored with mineral springs, one of which, that of San Diego (as well as that of Santa Fé, on the Isle of Pines) has, beyond dispute, the most wonderful curative properties. There are thousands of invalids in the United States to whom these waters would prove a sovereign cure, while either of the two places would afford an opportunity of seeing new phases of Cuban life. San Diego particularly, from its location, its hotel, and the character of the people who visit it, is the Saratoga of the tropics.

Here the stranger will have a fine opportunity of studying the manners and etiquette of the best people of Cuba and Havana, and the student of Spanish will have full opportunity of practicing the formal salutations that are seldom or never dispensed with, even amongst familiar friends; literally,

"Señora, at your feet."

"I kiss your hand, Señor."

"How do you do, Señor?"

"At your service, Señor. Thanks."

"Señor, I have the honor of presenting to you," etc.

"Sir, I celebrate the occasion of your acquaintance," etc.

The baths of San Diego are situated in the Vuelta Abajo, on the left bank of the river Caiguanabo, at the foot of the hills of La Guira, from where the river is known as San Diego, distant in a southwesterly direction from Havana, in a direct line, about ninety miles. The climate is mild and pleasant, the prevailing wind being from the south, while the waters of the baths have the reputation of performing miracles,—so much so, that a Cuban writer, becoming enthusiastic, writes almost impiously of their qualities when he says: "In this new pool, rival to that near Solomon's Temple, judging from what we see and feel, it would appear that the Angel of the Lord had descended and returned to it the waters of Bethesda, in Jerusalem, of which the Evangelist St. John speaks when he refers to the cure of the paralytic by the Son of the living God."

These baths are reached from Havana by cars to Batabano, on the south side of the island, leaving Havana at 5.45 on the morning of Thursdays; the train connecting directly with the boat at Batabano for Dayaniguas. Passengers for Batabano must be careful to change cars at San Felipe, and, on arriving, go directly on board the steamer "General Concha," which connects with the train from Havana, starting for Dayaniguas on arrival, and reaching there next morning before daybreak, at which time (Fridays) the trains of carriages leave, escorted by a detachment of the mounted Guardia Civil, and arrive at Paso Real at seven o'clock in the morning, where they stop for breakfast and rest, and to change horses. At half-past nine o'clock, the traveler arrives at San Diego.

The expenses of the trip are for each passenger: from Havana to Batabano, *via* cars, two dollars and eighty-seven cents; Batabano to Dayaniguas, *via* boat, five dollars and thirty-seven cents; Dayaniguas to San Diego, *via* volante, eight dollars and fifty cents.

Before leaving Havana, the traveler intending to go to San Diego should buy a through ticket at the office of the company, No. 2 Calle de la Cuna,—otherwise his passage from the boat to San Diego will cost him more; and if there are a number of passengers with through tickets, he may if not thus provided have to remain a day at Dayaniguas, until the carriages return again.

The best hotel in San Diego is that of Cabarrouy, which is about the largest, being also in the best locality, in the center of the town, and having gardens attached to it; it is the one patronized by the fashionable Cubans. Attached to the hotel are cottages for private

Hotel Cabarrouy

families. All the hotels make the singular charge of seventeen dollars for the bed, no matter how long one uses it, it being supposed to be thrown away when its occupant departs, from fear of contagious diseases, I presume; the other charges are from two dollars and fifty cents to four dollars per day.

In the morning after the bath they serve coffee, tea, or milk, breakfast not being served until nine, and dinner at four in the evening, after which is a light supper. Out of the regular season, which is understood to be from January to June, the charge is two dollars and fifty cents per day, which covers all expenses. The next best hotel is that of "Bardino," at the corner of Amistad and Recreo—charges the same.

The particulars of the founding of the village and the discovery of its waters, are wrapped in mystery. It is only known from some parish records that in 1793, 22nd of March, they celebrated the first mass in the town. As usual, however, tradition gives a romantic account of the discovery of the waters, which occurred, so goes the story, in the following manner: It happened, that in the neighborhood of the river, there lived a planter who, finding that one of his slaves, named Domingo, was attacked with leprosy, had built for him a hut in the mountains, prohibiting him from coming near any habitations, and ordering that no one should go near him, even to carry him provisions. The negro thus remained in his solitude until seeing himself thus left alone, and becoming disgusted at his solitary life (the people always fleeing from him for fear of contagion), he went roaming around in search of adventures. Going towards the north, in search of pure air, in his journey he came across a cave (which is shown to this day), and in which he took up his residence, subsisting on roots and wild fruits. One day, in which he suffered more than usual from his disease, he went down to the river to take a bath, and, going into a pool, it appeared to him that the water was peculiar, and came from a warm spring. He found himself so well in it,—his suffering being much alleviated,—that he continued his baths for a long time, until finally his sickness entirely disappeared, his health became good, and he returned to the house of his master. It is easy to imagine the astonishment of the master and his family at seeing the leprous negro restored to perfect health, who, upon being asked how the cure had been effected, replied with the simplicity of his race, "It is a miracle of our holy father, San Diego," whereupon his master bestowed upon him his freedom and kept him always near his person.

The news of such an unheard of cure spread throughout the country and people of all classes, colors and conditions flocked to try the miraculous waters of the new "Baños de San Diego." Simple huts of palm leaves were at first put up upon the river bank, and rich and poor vied with each other in suffering all manner of discomforts for the purpose of taking the waters.

Now, however, there is a little town with solidly built and handsome houses, with a neat little church, and numbers of hotels, while during the gay season there are over two thousand visitors there.

The government has assisted with its officers and convict laborers in building up the town, while the "Credit Mobilier" has taken hold of it as a pecuniary speculation. The baths are, therefore, in fine condition, large and quite numerous, while the *malecon*, or dyke, that has been constructed is quite a work of engineering skill, keeping off the waters of the river from the springs known as the "Tigre" and "Templado."

Baths of San Diego

The bath of the Tigre is composed of a tank, circular in form, built of a kind of concrete, known as *mamposteria*, and is about thirty feet in diameter, though not of any great depth. It is supplied from the principal spring from which the bath takes its name, and from various smaller ones that together give it a good supply of water.

The water of these springs is of an average temperature of about ninety degrees Fahrenheit, in any part of the tank, emitting a great quantity of sulphuric acid gas. A platform of wood serves as one story of the clothing-room used by the bathers, from which there is a stairway, leading down to the bath, the whole being covered by one roof, and shut in by a stone wall, the water being allowed to run through continually to the river.

The *Baño del Templado* contains the most abundant supply of water, and is the largest of the baths. It is a tank almost square, being about twenty-eight by thirty feet, about two-and-a-half feet deep, with solid stone floor, and a large dressing-room, all under the same roof. The water is of about the same composition as the Tigre, all of the springs and the water of the river containing sulphuric acid, carbonic acid, sulphate of lime, bicarbonate of magnesia, aluminum, silicic acid, carbonate of iron, oxygen, nitrogen, etc.

The *Baño de la Paila* is that formed by the waters of the river after the springs of the Tigre and Templado have emptied into it. The dressing-room of this bath is a very large one, from which are two stairways leading down into the bath, and in the bathing season there is extended over the front of the bath in the river, an awning, which makes a very delightful bathing saloon, outside of which again, there is sufficient depth for swimmers, though beyond the barrier the waters have not many medicinal qualities.

The other spring of Santa Lucia, it is said, is good for diseases of the eyes.

These waters are all excellent, taken under advice, for the following complaints: rheumatism, strains of the muscles, tumor, syphilis, gout, catarrh, bronchitis, leucorrhœa, and chronic diarrhœa and dysentery. The waters are used externally and internally in conjunction, and it is advised, in some cases, before drinking the waters, to take some preparatory medicines. The patient, with the advice of the physician, can be the best judge of that for himself, for in some cases it does not seem to make any difference.

The hours reserved for gentlemen are from half-past six to half-past eight o'clock in the morning, and twelve to two in the afternoon, each bath costing twenty cents, tickets for which can be procured at the hotels, no money being received at the entrance.

If there happens to be a party of friends together they can make the trip to San Diego, and pass some weeks there agreeably enough, taking care, however, to carry with them some light reading, of which none can be had, either in Spanish or English, in the town. The country around is quite picturesque, and, like almost all parts of Cuba, beautiful in the novel character of its scenery and vegetation, while there are numerous objects of interest to visit in the neighborhood. Of course, in a place like this, if the traveler can speak no Spanish, he is thrown entirely upon his own resources, unless, indeed, he makes, as he is likely to do, the acquaintance of persons who can speak English.

One of the excursions which can be made in the neighborhood, is that to the "Arcos de Caiguanabo," which is the official name given to the "doors" or caves formed by the river San Diego, passing through a peculiar natural formation of rocks, a magnificent and imposing arch divided by a grand pillar, the arch being about one hundred feet wide, one hundred feet long, and sixty feet high, the river running quietly beneath it.

Beneath this portal, and on a level with the river, upon its right bank, is the first cave, the entrance to which is straight and stony, and suddenly opens into a large chamber filled with quantities of stalactites, or specimens of concrete petrifactions; columns large and small, and, in fact, a thousand figures of fantastic and capricious shapes, which a fertile imagination can liken to a number of things. This saloon receives the light by two apertures that permit also of exit on both sides of the hill.

Beyond the arch, and reached by a narrow path made at the foot of the range of hills, for a short distance, is the second cave, which presents the same characteristics as the first. From this cave there is a descent, when, following the base of the hills for the distance of about one hundred and eighty feet, another ascent is made by a path to the third cave, called the "Cathedral," to enter which it is necessary to have torches, as the light penetrates no farther than the entrance. The dimensions of this chamber are larger than those of the others. The world-wide custom of inscribing names is here noticed.

The journey to these caves is made mostly on horseback, and it is quite the fashion to come out on breakfast picnics here, amid these wild and picturesque scenes. Those who have been fortunate enough to visit the caves of Bellamar, near Matanzas, will not appreciate these so much.

The cave of "Taita Domingo," said to be the identical cave inhabited by that hardly-treated but diseased negro who discovered the baths, is to the north-east of the town, and is a large gloomy cavern not yet explored. With a good guide and much labor the traveler can also make the ascent to the top of the "Loma de la Guira," from which can be had a fine view of the surrounding country, and the north and south seas; the former about eighteen miles distant and the latter about twenty-five.

A walk or ride up to the "Casita de la Loma," or as it is more properly called, "Hermosa Vista" (beautiful view), which is the hill seen to the north from the Plaza of Isabel II, is good exercise and pleasant occupation.

Tobacco growing and culture can be seen at the houses of Hato, a place not quite a mile distant, and at which there is a very courteous *administrador*, who is very kind in showing attention to strangers.

In addition to the shooting, which can be had in the mountains, there are the usual diversions in the way of balls and dancing, at which there are frequently present very pretty girls, whilst for those whose taste runs that way there are occasional "cock-fights."

In returning from San Diego, it is more convenient, if the traveler has gone there by the route described in the beginning of this chapter, to return *via* the western railroad. This can be very pleasantly and quickly accomplished by taking a horse or volante to San Cristobal and the cars from that place.

A TRIP TO THE ISLE OF PINES

Lounging around Havana with a severe bronchial affection, I was informed, "officially," that I would have to do one of two things for a cure, either give up smoking or go to the Island of Pines and take the miraculous waters of its mineral baths. Considering the latter the least of two evils, I made my preparations, and in company of my *compagnon de voyage*, spent sufficient time there to completely effect a cure of the above complaint and having much and varied experience in that desert isle, I give it for the benefit of future travelers.

The Island of Pines, or, as it is also called, *Reina Amalia*, is an island containing about five hundred and forty square miles, lying directly south of the western end of the Island of Cuba; its length from east to west is sixty-five miles, and its greatest width from north to south is forty miles. From Havana it is a little more than ninety miles, and from the landing at Batabano, where the traveler takes the steamer to cross over to it, is about fifty-four miles, in a straight line. On account, however, of the numerous keys or islets that surround the island, the channel is a very intricate one for vessels, and it takes longer for the steamer to run over there than it otherwise would.

It is this island upon which Columbus bestowed the name of *La Evangelista*, having arrived there on the 24th of June, 1494. It is now in nearly as unsettled a state as when discovered, for, though there are two towns upon the island, the number of its inhabitants is very small,—only two thousand and seven. It was off this island that Drake's expedition, on returning from Costa Rica, was attacked by the Spanish Admiral Avellaneda, who succeeded in capturing one of his vessels.

It is in its form the exact representation of a volante body seen in profile, and has one or two considerable ranges of mountains, known as the *Sierra de la Cañada*, fifteen hundred feet high, and the *Sierra de la Daguilla*, sixteen hundred and fifty feet high. In addition to its medical reputation, it is celebrated for its quarries of marble and fine specimens of rock crystals.

The island has, however, a great reputation as possessing the most wonderful mineral springs in the world, which have, without doubt, effected some very astonishing, not to say miraculous cures, of which there are large numbers on record, people flocking from all parts of the Island of Cuba, the United States, and even from the Old World, to try the efficacy of the waters.

The island is reached from Havana once a week, by taking the cars at 5.45 on each Thursday morning, from the depot Villa Nueva, outside the walls, to Batabano, the traveler taking care to change cars at San Felipe. At Batabano, which is a small straggling village, with no accommodations for travelers, there is, on the arrival of this train, the fine little steamer "Cubano Nuevo," waiting to take passengers over to the Isle of Pines. The boat goes directly to the landing for Santa Fé, which is the place where travelers are advised to go.

Nueva Gerona

There are two points to which these steamers run, Santa Fé and Nueva Gerona. The latter place is a very small town at the foot of the hills, with plains of palm trees in its neighborhood, the town itself being on the "Rio de Serra de Casa," some distance from its mouth. It is the seat of such government as there is upon the island, and has a number of troops stationed there, for whom there have been erected barracks.

It can be easily visited from Santa Fé on horseback or *en volante*; the hotel, if one does go there, is "Hotel de Fargas," a tolerable one only.

Santa Fé, which is the prominent place of resort for travelers, is of itself a miserable congregation of houses, on the bank of the river of the same name, some distance from its mouth, and also some distance from the steamboat landing. This landing is a rough wooden wharf, from which carriages and stages ply to Santa Fé.

And now we are going through the town of Santa Fé, as we are told, and the plaza is pointed out to us, which, in fact, seems to be the town, as around it are built the houses that serve to make up the principal part of the village, while the square itself is occupied with

Plaza

dust heaps, piles of shavings, wandering donkeys, and hungry-looking dogs.

With strange forebodings of what our fate is to be until the next boat leaves, we drive on across a little wooden bridge, underneath which, we are told, are some of the springs; and ascending a slight hill on the other side of the town, are agreeably surprised to find before us two or three quite imposing-looking stone buildings, which are said to be the hotels. We drive up to the one said to be the best, and known as the "Hotel de Santa Rita."

We find the rooms large and the beds clean, the proprietors courteous and kind. The house is kept by a Cuban, Doctor Diaz, who, with his wife and children, lives in the house.

Our first experience in our room was not all that could be wished; for on proceeding to make use of a washstand in the corner, I stepped

Only a spider

back horror-struck at the apparition that met my view,—nothing more or less than a tremendous insect, with a sort of humped body and great long flat legs, armed at different distances with peculiar filmy points, altogether a horrible-looking object stuck on the wall. Not succeeding in persuading my friend to dispose of him,—he declining, as I thought in an unnecessarily decided manner, to "touch" him,—and desirous of increasing my knowledge of natural history, I called mine host and asked him in what name and by what right there was an occupant in our quarters. "*No vale nada*" (it is of no account), "it is only a spider," was his response; whereupon he brushed it down with his hand, and finished its existence with his boot.

"I am going to appropriate this table drawer," selfishly remarked my friend, as he reached to pull it out with a jerk; but, in so doing, he found he had disturbed a family-nest of roaches, of which there must have been at least fifty of the largest size in the drawer, which he immediately let drop upon the floor, the roaches scattering in every direction, while my poor friend sought madly to stop their flight.

As from such experience we judged there might have been a zoological garden at some previous time in our room, we took the precaution to make close examination of the interior of our beds and the corners of our room, but, fortunately, without further result.

A surprise party

The climate of the Isle of Pines is perfectly delicious, the air is pure, dry, and balmy, and the winds coming from the sea and passing over pine forests are gentle and invigorating.

At present only one of the springs is used as a bath, and that is the "Templado," over which are bath houses erected in two compartments for the sexes. Each of these baths is about twelve feet by six, with solid stone floor, and depth of water about three and a half feet. The water is about eighty-two degrees Fahrenheit in temperature, and is impregnated with oxygen and carbonic acid gases, chloride of sodium, sulphate of lime, carbonate of lime, iron, magnesia, chloride of calcium, nitrate of lime, silex, and extractic organic matter.

I am prepared to testify from actual observation and experience to the benefits derived from both bathing in this water and drinking it.

I had been suffering for some time with a bronchial affection, which necessitated the interior of my throat being touched frequently with caustic and salts of copper, without producing any material or permanent benefit. On coming here to the Isle of Pines, I in no respect changed my way of living, being only careful to take my two baths and drink about four glasses of the water per diem; yet, at the expiration of ten days, when I left the island, I was completely cured, and have never since had a return of the complaints; probably the fine air and exercise assisted materially in the result.

The general routine is to go to the bath before breakfast, drink a glass of the water, and then take the bath, remaining therein about a quarter of an hour; then another glass of the water, and return to the house. In the afternoon the same course. There were quite a number of Americans there during my stay, some of whom had been there a long time, and almost all of whom derived great benefit from the use of the water. One old gentleman, over sixty years of age, was so low on leaving the United States that he required to be carried on a litter to the steamer at New York. When I saw him he was riding on horseback.

Santa Fé is not a place that can be recommended for the mere pleasure-seeker, but of course when health is at stake, and perhaps life itself, many inconveniences will be submitted to patiently in hopes of a cure. A pleasant party going to these baths, taking with them books, and some few condiments and luxuries, which can be readily purchased in Havana, can have a very agreeable time. If these springs and this delightful climate were anywhere within the United States, Santa Fé would become a great place for invalids, to which even Saratoga and Sharon would have to give way.

At present the expense of living there is quite reasonable, the charge being two dollars and twelve cents per day, and there are few extra expenses. Horses can be had at a very reasonable rate—a dollar or a dollar and a-half the afternoon. There are also some very good two-horse carriages, which can be had any time except steamer days.

Immediately in the neighborhood of Santa Fé, and in fact nearly all over the island, the country is quite flat, but there are beautiful drives and walks some distance back, where the country is more rolling and even hilly. Only here and there does one encounter a *hacienda* (or farm), used for raising cattle and a few vegetables, so sparsely is the island as yet inhabited. I saw upon this island the only regular pine-apple plantation that fell under my notice while abroad, though there are some, I believe, in the neighborhood, and back of Baracoa. This fruit is cultivated in a different way from what we are accustomed to see it treated, as an exotic in our hot-houses. Here it is

Pine-apple plantation

cultivated as cabbages are with us, and at a little distance has somewhat their appearance. Each plant bears but one apple at a time, and when that is ripened it is broken off and the plant trimmed to its one stalk. It then springs out again from three or four shoots, and again bears fruit, for which, as far as I could learn, there is no particular season of ripening.

The inhabitants of the island are a very simple, kind-hearted set of people, and very fond of a chat with strangers. They have a natural dignity of manner, a courteously hospitable way, as also a degree of freshness and innocence of the ways of the world which is charming and refreshing from its great rarity, while some of their customs strike one as slightly peculiar,—especially that of permitting young children to go entirely nude. This practice, however, is not confined to the Isle of Pines, but will meet the traveler all over the island of Cuba. The simple-hearted people never seem to regard it as sometimes inconvenient, if not indecent.

At one of the hotels in Santa Fé, patronized mostly by Cubans, was a billiard-room, containing a table rather the worse for wear, where my friend and myself spent our leisure hours after the bath, and for which the proprietor thought himself well paid when he received for four-ball American games, ten cents per game. We were his only customers, if we except, now and then, a party of noisy farmers, who would get up an exciting game of pin-pool, for a *medio* (five cents) a chance. This, by-the-by, is about the principal game of billiards played by the Cubans.

The traveler will probably here make his first acquaintance, in any number, with those annoying pests, the fleas (*pulgas*), the mosquitoes troubling him very little. Fortunately for me, my friend was a thin-skinned youth, and, as a consequence, he "took" exceedingly well with these voracious gentry. I have frequently roared with laughter at seeing him forced, by their "attentions," to take off his "next of skin" garment, and, with moistened fingers, grasp wickedly at one of these nimble-footed insects. One, however, gets accustomed even to them, in time.

The Isle of Pines is generally a plain, slightly inclined to roll, with here and there ranges of hills hardly high enough to be called mountains. On its southern boundary is an immense swamp, known as the "Cienaga;" a vast extent of marsh, water, and rocks, totally uninhabited, except by a few half-savage fishermen, and without any means of access, except by a dangerous and uncertain foot-path on the land side, or by a two days' journey from Nueva Gerona, in a sail-boat. I was told by the inhabitants, that to the curious or scientific traveler this swamp offered several inducements; for, on the point known as Cape Frances—which is a rocky point, stretching out into the ocean, and forming, with the main land, a large bay—there is a small key or island connected, which is the constant home of large numbers of the hugest specimens of the crocodile family, after whom the key has been named. Upon the shore of the point, also, is to be found an innumerable quantity of beautiful shells of rare species, as also coral formations. Time did not permit of our going there, but a guide and boat can be had by any traveler who is desirous of visiting the place.

From the description given us of these huge leviathans, they must be the species spoken of by Bibron as the *crocodilus rhombifer*, since they are so much larger than those known with us as the simple alligator. In Cuba the common name for them is *caiman*.

A place that every traveler to the Isle of Pines should visit is the *Cerro de los Cristales*, or Crystal Hills, a high point of land situated nearly in the centre of the island, and about twelve miles from Santa Fé. A party of us, ladies and gentlemen, got up a picnic, one lovely morning in March, to breakfast at the foot of the hills. We started at about six o'clock in the morning,—a party of eight, mounted on horseback.

Our road lay amid wild and beautiful scenery—now winding through pine forests,

A little bit

now crossing some gurgling silvery brook, and now leading us to the top of some high ground, where we obtained extended views of the country around. Even in these lovely scenes we were amused by various *cosas de Cuba*, such as the *trepador de palmas* (palm-tree climber), a perfectly nude negro boy, who, with hands and knees, climbed the smooth trunk of the palm-tree like a young monkey; or such as the green parrot, which deafened us with its hideous noises. A pleasant ride of three hours brought us to the foot of the Crystal Hills, and as our appetites were vigorous, we proceeded, before attempting the ascent, to breakfast beside a babbling brook, with the soft grass beneath us and the graceful palms waving above our heads. This being finished, we remounted our horses to make the ascent of *los Cristales*.

Cerro de los Cristales

Though not of itself very high, the Crystal Hill, being situated upon an elevated plateau of ground, commands, it is said, the finest views on the island. It takes its name from the large quantity of rock crystals found around its base and on its steep sides, and is quite barren and rocky, with no vegetation but a scraggy bush or two, or a stunted tree growing here and there. The view from its summit is surpassingly beautiful in every direction. You see, laid out at your feet, the whole island, as though you were in the centre of a map. To the north, the hills of Nueva Gerona distinctly visible; to the south the ranges of hills known as the *Sierra de la Cañada*, nearly fifteen hundred feet high, hiding the great swamp from view; while east and west are extended views of hill and valley,—the hazy distant waters of the sea hardly distinguishable from the sky above.

What a peculiar stillness! not a sound; hardly a breath of air; and far over the landscape not a sign of life. What a feeling of sad solemnity comes over one gazing at such a scene as this, so wild, so tropical in its aspect—unchanged, perhaps, since the days of the great Colon, who first landed upon these shores, or still later of the bold buccaneers, who, laden with their booty, returned from their seafaring raids to hide their plunder, and enjoy the delights of their bacchanalian revels in this quiet island.

The pirates, it is said, had a great deal to do with this island, having their depot and head quarters upon it, and starting out from it on their different expeditions. Whether it is this or not that has given the isle such a bad reputation with the authorities, I do not know; but they do, even at this day, use the island as a place of banishment for such individuals as will drink and will not work, for political prisoners, etc., who, without any provision or allowance from the government are turned loose upon the people of the villages.

On our way home, we stopped at a farm-house for a short time, to avoid the heat of the mid-day sun, as well as to have a chat with the *guajira* (country woman), and while there we were all very much amused, and some of the ladies a good deal scared by the arrival of a stalwart negro, clad in a ragged pair of trowsers, leading and pulling by a rope a fine specimen of the *iguana*, one of the most hideous animals, I think, I have ever seen. The negro wanted one of the party to buy it.

A nice pet

"What shall I do with it?"

"Eat him."

"Couldn't do that, if I was starving."

"Make 'a nice pet' then, for your Señora?"

At which, as there was strong dissent from the Señora, no trade was made.

En passant, O, reader! a word of friendly advice: don't trust any of your wardrobe to the washerwoman at the hotel, unless the proprietor agrees to be responsible, for a more disgraceful, annoying result you can hardly imagine. Twenty-five and fifty cents for each article, and when they are brought to you, you will probably do as we did,— "chuck" them on the floor and perform a war-dance over them, much to the surprise and horror of the piece of six-foot sable humanity whom we graciously informed that we wished she was a man just for the pleasure of making a "spread eagle" of her, for having torn, lost, and soiled our clothes under the plea of washing them.

Our leaving the island was a rich piece of experience. The boat leaves at about eleven o'clock; our baggage was ordered to be put upon the cart, to be sent as it was called "by express" at eight o'clock, while we were permitted to get our breakfast, which, notwithstanding repeated calls that the carriage was going, we finished to our satisfaction.

We had proposed to take our baggage in the carriage and drive down at our leisure, but that was not permitted, since it was a two-horse barouche, of the capabilities of which they had not the faintest idea, and they were also going to start nearly three hours before the boat time, to travel six miles. By dint of taking it coolly, and telling the landlord to get another carriage,—there was not another one to be had for love or money,—we managed to delay our departure to suit us. Even then, on arriving at the landing, we had nearly an hour to spare, for, of course, the boat was not going, while our baggage "by express" was just making its appearance around a turn in the road; four great oxen pulling slowly along a large unwieldy cart, upon which were placed our three small valises.

Baggage by express

A poor young fellow from Maine, who was dying of consumption, and who had come out here in hopes of being benefited, was with us, on his way home to die, the physicians here having told him he was too far gone to be cured or even benefited by the waters. I could not help pitying the poor fellow as we parted from him on the wharf at Batabano, sitting on his trunk, in a foreign land, amongst strangers to whom he could not speak an intelligible word. I explained to the people about what he wanted, bade him good-bye, and wished him a safe return to his friends, whom, however, he did not live to see. He died on board the American steamer.

If the reader is not favorably impressed with my description of the Isle of Pines, I cannot help it. I write just what I experienced— much pleasure and some few discomforts, with lasting benefit in health. Tastes differ; perhaps the reader would enjoy it more, and if he is an invalid I would advise a trial, for one can leave Havana Thursday morning, and if not agreeably impressed with the island can return again Monday night, or if going along the south coast, can take the steamer at Batabano on that morning for Trinidad, etc.

"Quand on voyage on apprend."

THE SOUTH COAST TO TRINIDAD

Reader, we have now together wandered amidst scenes of Cuban city and country life, where civilization and nature presented to our view pictures that afforded us much pleasure mingled with some annoyance; where so long as we were in the habit of meeting travelers from the north, we did not feel that we were so very far away from home and friends; but sail now with me along the beautiful south coast, away from the usual route of the foreigner, where, gliding gently along, we hang over the vessel's side and see far beneath us, through the pure green water, the white sandy bottom of the sea, that looks smooth enough and pretty enough to be the veritable play-ground of the mermaid, although not even a fish is in sight; or stretch ourselves upon the upper deck and drink in the delicious balminess of the soft southern air, while our eyes are feasting upon the mountainous beauties of the verdure-clad shore.

If the traveler in Cuba desires to see its most beautiful portions, and also some of its prettiest, quietest towns, he will do well to make this trip along the south coast, from Batabano to Santiago de Cuba, stopping at Trinidad, and, if he likes, taking the steamer at Santiago home to the States. Or if he desires to visit the British West Indies, he can do so by means of the French steamers running from that place.

The trip is a very enjoyable one, even for ladies, the boats are large and fine, and the accommodations on board them excellent; the voyage is as pleasant and beautiful as a summer trip on the Hudson, or as a sail on Lake George, the sea being generally as calm as a lake. With a good party and plenty of light reading it is as agreeable a trip as can be taken. All the information necessary in reference to the time of sailing of the steamers can be obtained at the office of the company, No. 16 Armagura street, Havana.

The price of tickets to Cienfuegos, by these steamers, from Batabano, is twelve dollars, and to Trinidad, the first place the traveler will want to stop at, is sixteen dollars. Leaving Havana at 5.45 in the morning, the traveler reaches Batabano at 8 o'clock, and goes immediately on board one of the above steamers lying at the wharf; and he should immediately see the cabin-boy and make his choice of a stateroom, which should always be taken in the upper cabin, if one can get it there. An eye after one's baggage will not be amiss now, for they do sometimes make mistakes, notwithstanding the baggage man's *"bueno, muy bueno."*

And now we are afloat and have time to look about us, and we already feel quite at home from finding the boat and machinery are "Yankee notions," being made either in New York or Philadelphia, while the cheerful looks and courteous manners of the passengers demonstrate that we are in good company. A *"buenas dias"* or *"que tiene"* will soon establish an acquaintance if the traveler is able to speak any Spanish; if not, all he has to do is to look pleasant, like the rest of the people, and watch his chance of finding some one who speaks English, and who will be delighted to explain to the *forastero* (stranger), in his own tongue the beauties of the Cuban shore.

Ten o'clock, and there goes the breakfast bell. No hurry, gentlemen, every body is provided for and there is none of that scrambling and struggling for a seat at the table, so disgraceful to us Americans on our boats; no, everything here is quiet and orderly, the ladies go leisurably to their table in the upper cabin, and the men to theirs arranged in a cool place on the main deck.

Now you will want your Spanish bill of fare, *amigo*, and if you have studied that given you in the early part of this book you will get along very well indeed, for the table is bountifully supplied with the best of food cooked in the best Spanish fashion, while there is an ample supply of ice and *vino catalan* to wash it down with; don't hurry, either, my friend, these people don't propose to make a labor of what should always be a pleasure.

The coast for some distance after leaving Batabano is quite low, and generally marshy; but, on nearing Cienfuegos, it gets higher and even mountainous. To the right, some distance from the coast, and inside of which the steamer always keeps on her passage, are low keys or rocky islets, known as *Los Jardines*, and likely to prove very dangerous to the navigator, if not acquainted with their locality.

Many of the passengers, after breakfast, seated themselves at a table with the game called "Loto," at which they all gamble more or less. Even the chambermaid is a party to the gambling speculation, for she goes about the boat offering you a *boleta* (ticket) in a raffle for a gold watch, or something else, and finding as many purchasers among the ladies as among the men. And so the day slips round, and we have the beauties of a moonlight night in a tropic sea, which add vastly to our pleasure before turning in for the night into our cane-bottomed berth, over which is simply thrown a sheet—a capital idea for boats in warm weather, for such beds, being cool and quite elastic, are most comfortable.

We arrive off the harbor of Cienfuegos some time during the night, but as vessels are not allowed to enter any of the ports of the island at night, particularly during war times, we have to wait until daybreak, when we get under weigh and enter that beautiful port by the light of the rising sun. The bay is a very extensive one, known by the name of Jagua, the entrance itself being quite narrow, with a lighthouse on the extreme point, and stone forts upon the adjacent hills at the mouth, none of which appeared to me to be very strong.

The bay has anchorage for vessels of the largest class, while the high hills that surround it afford ample shelter from any stormy winds that may blow. It was this bay that Columbus visited on his first voyage, and Padre las Casas in speaking of it, calls it the most magnificent port in the world, comprising within its shores six square leagues. Herrera also, describing the port and bay of Cienfuegos, as seen by Ocampo in a voyage round the island, says: "There was Ocampo very much at his ease, well served by the Indians with an infinite number of partridges, like those of Castile, except somewhat smaller. He had also abundance of fish (*lizas*, skate). They took them from this natural fish-pond, where there were millions of them just as safe as if they were in a tank attached to one's home." Whether the same abundance still prevails I did not learn.

The steamer reaches the wharf about six o'clock, and, as she remains until eleven, the traveler has ample time to go ashore and see the town or try the excellent oysters, of which they have large quantities at "La Paz" or "La Union."

Probably no place on the island offers greater advantages for seeing sugar-making in its most favorable aspects than Cienfuegos, as it is surrounded by an immense cane-growing district, with some of the best estates on the island.

It is flattering to an American to know that one of the handsomest and best-managed of these estates belongs to one of his own countrymen, and any one that has been to Cienfuegos will be familiar with the name of the "Ingenio Carolina."

This is a most superb estate, the property of William H. Stewart, Esq., of Philadelphia, situated about twelve miles from the town, on the bay.

It contains about five thousand acres of land of the best quality, the buildings and mill grounds of which are located most picturesquely—a fine freshwater brook running through the place— and are all constructed in the most solid manner, of *mamposteria.*

The mascabado sugar produced on this estate, by the improved means of defecation, has the reputation of being amongst the cleanest and best on the island.

There are about five hundred hands upon the place, who live in small houses of stone, each one with a porch in front, and all ranged in streets in regular order, presenting a neat and an attractive appearance.

For the supply of the hands, the owner has established a store for the sale of clothing, groceries, and edibles, with the view to prevent the negroes from going off the place, and to induce them to spend their money where they will get its equivalent. The sale of liquors is not permitted on the premises.

Says a Cuban author of this place: "The degree of prosperity with which this estate is blessed, is due solely to the happy administration of its owner, whose example it is to be desired all in the island will imitate."

The production is about 4,000,000 lbs. of sugar, mascabado, and 200,000 gallons of molasses.

Of the town itself, the reader has already had a full description in

Ingenio Carolina

another chapter; and so, returning to the steamer, we have another fine opportunity of seeing the beautiful bay, as we go out.

Still, keeping close to the coast, we begin to see some of its mountainous beauties; for, sailing within a mile or two of the shore, we have a constantly changing panorama of green hills, that come down to the very water's edge, while, in the distance, they stretch away until some of their tops appear to be holding up the heavens.

I know not if Tennyson has ever been in the tropics in person, but he must have been there in mind when he wrote, as though filled with their ardor:

> "Oh, hundred shores of happy climes,
> How swiftly streamed ye by the bark!
> At times the whole sea burn'd; at times,
> With wakes of fire we tore the dark;
> At times a craven craft would shoot
> From heavens hid in fairy bowers,
> With naked limbs and flowers and fruit,
> But we nor paused for fruits nor flowers."

Breaking in upon our romantic musings comes the sound of the hand-bell, and we wonder what it can be for. Our late breakfast was over only an hour or so ago. It cannot be anything to eat; no, innocents, it is only something to drink, in the shape of *frescos*, which may be made either of lemons or oranges, placed nice and cold, in large pitchers, for you to help yourself to at discretion.

It is an attractive sight to see these pretty Cuban women sipping their *frescos*, holding the glasses to their ruby lips with the smallest hands imaginable; while, perhaps, peeping out from beneath their dresses, are the tiny feet for which they are celebrated, evidently never intended by nature to walk on. "To be sure" (I think I hear some uncharitable lady reader say), "if I made as little use of my hands and feet as they do, I could have such trifling appendages." *Quien sabe?* Nevertheless, they are very pretty, and I think most of the Señoritas are positively aware of the fact, from the way they display them.

The dainty way in which they smoke their cigarettes, after their *frescos*, the graceful way in which they hold their little apologies for cigars, between their pearly teeth, is truly bewitching; and it certainly does add to the pleasure (for the time being), of one's smoking, to be able to present to one of his fair companions a delicate cigarette.

About four o'clock in the afternoon, we arrive in sight of those high and beautiful mountains of Trinidad, a continuation and part of the range which we have been seeing all day, known as the "Guanahuya"; and, at last, we see Trinidad,—beautiful Trinidad—on this balmy south coast, which, seen from some distance out at sea, looks, as it lies far up the mountain side, its white walls glistening in the golden light, like a babe nestling on its mother's breast.

It takes some time to get up to its port, for in front of the bay there is a large narrow point of land, known as the Punta de los Negros, which, with the main land, forms the bay and port of Casilda.

Reaching this, we steam around the point, and then, retracing our course in the direction from which we have come, we see, upon the shore of this beautiful bay, the little village of Casilda, which is the port of entrance for Trinidad. There are two other ports of entrance, though not in use—that of "La Boca," to the south-west, where empties the river Táyabo, and that of the river Musé, to the south-east. The anchorage in the bay is not a very good one, as the water is so shallow that it necessitates the loading of vessels by lighters, unless they happen to be quite small. The town has quite an extensive series of wharves and warehouses, the principal portion of the shipping business being done down here, though the town itself is a straggling village, with a few large warehouses, and the depot of the railroad, which connects it with Trinidad.

If the traveler can find a volante, I would advise him to take that and ride up, unless the cars are ready to start, for sometimes there is a delay of several hours after the arrival of the boat, before the train gets off, and as the distance is only three miles, over a good road, with beautiful views, it is quite as pleasant to go in a volante as in the cars, though somewhat more expensive, the charge being about two dollars, while the fare in the cars is only twenty cents. It is an ascent all the way.

One is not very greatly struck with the appearance of the town of Trinidad upon getting out at the depot, for the streets lying immediately

Street in Trinidad

in its neighborhood are anything but attractive, though they are rather antique and rugged, looking as if you had come to some third-rate village.

One has to look out now for his own baggage, engaging a *carreta* (cart) to carry it, and seeing himself that it is put upon the cart, which is then driven to the designated hotel, there being no carriages at the depot, usually.

Generally there is not much choice of hotels in Trinidad, and the best way is to examine all of them that are tolerable enough to go to, before deciding.

Madame Caroline keeps a large boarding-house, where a good many people go, and where they can be tolerably well accommodated, and, perhaps, as there are female attendants there, it would be more comfortable for ladies, if they can get a room to suit them. It did not suit us, being too much like an ordinary boarding-house, and the only vacant room not being an agreeable one. We therefore went back to the hotel Niagara, in the street Rosario, No. 46, and I advise all to call there before they take rooms elsewhere. The house is quiet, centrally located, and if you can get rooms upon the first floor, you will be tolerably comfortable. It has a fine large *sala*, airy, and with cool marble floor, where it is pleasant to eat and sit. Mine host is, as far as he knows how to be, as obliging a landlord as I ever saw, and a jolly old fellow too, who likes his little chat and quiet smoke. If you are careful to "kick up a row" when you go there, and explain to him that you want everything good, you will get along finely. The charges are about two to three dollars per day.

Our first experience there was, however, very amusing. After securing our room, we ordered the waiter to provide us a dinner, hot, good, and as quickly as possible, which instructions were received with a frequent "Si, Señor, warm and quickly, Señor." A few minutes finds us seated at table and prepared to enjoy the said dinner.

"Serve the soup, waiter."

"There is none, Señor; there is theatre to-night, sir."

We try the fish. "Why, confound it, this fish is cold as a stone."

"Yes, Señor, do you go to the theatre to-night?"

"Hang the theatre, we want dinner! What else have you?"

"Salad and meat, Señor."

We try the oil; it is bad. The meat turns out to be pork. We are hungrily, furiously angry by this time, and jumping up from the table we ask if we can have a dinner or not.

"But, Señor, I am going to the theatre to-night; are you not going?"

"Hang the theatre!" we roared, thinking the man was crazy, "bring out our baggage and (in a theatrical manner) we will go hence."

Waiter (humbly but sullenly): "If the gentlemen will wait I will warm the fish, and give them some good oil. I have some most splendid boiled ham, with some fine fruit; and if the gentlemen will have patience till to-morrow they shall live like lords."

We relent, having no other place to go to, and make a tolerably fair meal, but the climax was reached next morning, when having had an elegant breakfast, at which mine host was present, I remarked to him "We are glad to see that you do have good meals here sometimes; our dinner of yesterday was a disgrace to your house, sir."

"Yes," he replied very coolly, "I know it was, it was that boy's fault (pointing to the waiter); he wanted to go to the theatre on a 'free ticket.'"

The waiter makes some deprecatory remark.

"You lie, scoundrel," said the old man with much vim, "I heard you."

"Why, where were you?" I asked, rather astonished that as he had heard the row he had not made his appearance.

"In the room there, lying down."

"Well, why did you not come out and attend to your guests?"

"*No valia la pena,*" (it wasn't worth while) in a perfectly innocent manner; "the boy wanted to go to the theatre." *Asi, asi,* o reader, you have another *cosa de Cuba.*

Trinidad

Trinidad de Cuba is a pretty, rambling, hilly town, of about fifteen thousand inhabitants, situated on the side of the mountain of the *Vijia* (watch tower), and elevated about four hundred feet above the level of the sea, from which it is distant some six miles, and from Havana, by land, about two hundred and seventy miles.

Exposed to the combined breezes of sea and mountain, with a most delicious climate, it is reputed to be the healthiest town upon the island, while from its beautiful situation in a rich and fertile country, its exquisitely grand and extended views, the beauty of its lovely maidens and the general hospitality of its inhabitants, it would be, were there only a good hotel, the most attractive town upon the island for the sojourn of the invalid traveler. Here one can find quiet, kindness, and every inducement for taking pleasant exercise in the way of walks, rides and drives.

Historically, I don't know that it has much to interest the general traveler, and yet it was here that that "gay Lothario," gallant adventurer, and sagacious but cruel conqueror, Hernando Cortés, came after parting with his uncertain employer and governor, Velasquez, of whom he took "French leave," with all the vessels and men fitted out for the conquest of Mexico; here it was, too, that he added means and men to that same expedition, the history of which seems at the present reading like some wondrous fairy tale.

Trinidad is also one of the oldest towns on the island, having been settled by Diego Velasquez, in 1513, and suffered in its earlier days, like many other Cuban towns, from various attacks of pirates and enemies, one of which was made, in 1702, by the English corsair Grant, who, with three hundred men, invaded the town and made good his retreat without suffering for his intrepidity. The bay of

Casilda is also famous as being the battle ground of three British men-of-war with the Spaniards, under Don Luis Bassecourt, whose command consisted of militia and a few veteran pickets, but the English were compelled, notwithstanding, to withdraw after three days' fighting.

The streets of the city are, with some exceptions, narrow and tortuous, and many of those upon the edge of the town entirely unpaved, while the houses in the best streets are generally comfortable, well built, stone houses, some of which are really magnificent private edifices, as for instance, that of the Cantero family, or the residence of Señor Bequer, nearly opposite the Plaza de Serrano, which latter is a pretty square in the upper portion of the city, very neatly laid out.

The building, as seen in the accompanying engraving, on the hill, is the military hospital, a fine large building in a high and airy situation, some distance above the town, where are sent the invalid soldiers of the district.

The house with the arcade front is that of Señor Buenet, and was the one that before our war was occupied as a hotel, kept by an American, who did extremely well, I am told. The building on the

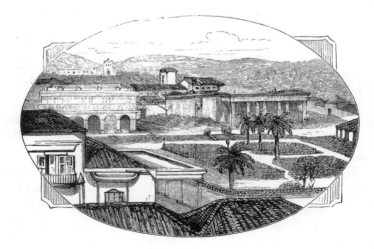

Plaza de Serrano

other side is the *Yglesia Vieja* (old church), intended to be, I suppose, at one time a fine church, but now a mass of ruins, except the few massive pillars still standing.

The houses of Trinidad differ from those in Havana in not having dividing walls to separate the dining room and the saloon, but in their place they have, generally, open stone arches, which, while separating the apartments in some degree, yet add to their beauty and comfort by permitting a free circulation of air and affording a charming prospective of marble floors, mirrored arches, and richly furnished rooms.

Some of the streets are quite odd in their appearance, with their rough tiled houses, their narrow pavements, and the funny names which are seen, just as in Havana, stuck up over the store doors. The house seen at the upper end with the tower is one well known in Trinidad as that of Señor Bequer, which means in English Mr. Baker; an American citizen who resided there, his house being considered one of the finest in the island.

The "Campo del Marte" is a fine large place at the south-east end of the town, with barracks and drill-grounds for the troops. But the plaza, *par excellence*, of Trinidad, and in fact of all Cuba, for I think

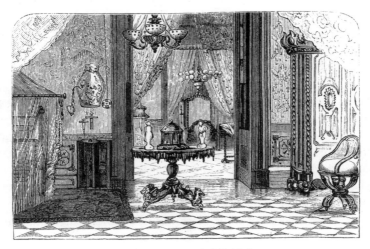

Interior of a house in Trinidad

Street scene

it is certainly the most gracefully beautiful square that I saw during my visit, is known as the "Plaza de Carillo," situated nearly in the centre of the town, and opposite which is the governor's house.

The square is most beautifully laid out, with vines and shrubbery shading the stone walks, on either side of which is a profusion of flowers, while in the centre of the square there is erected a graceful dome-like arbor, completely covered with flowering vines. Extending around the square is a broad stone paseo, which is separated from the main garden by a tasty iron railing, and from the street by a stone base. A profusion of gas lights are ranged at intervals around the square, which at night, when illuminated, have a most beautiful effect.

The square is always open, but the *retreta* is only about three times a week, one of those times being Sunday. On such occasions the plaza is brilliantly lighted, and the music, the soft breezes, and the delicious fragrance of the flowers, are enjoyed by throngs of "fair women and brave men."

O dolor! since these lines were written, how changed has been the fate of many of those same promenaders. To some—fathers, mothers, and sisters—have come sorrow and mourning; to others—

Plaza de Carillo

men, brothers, fathers, and husbands—wounds, exile, or death. Alas! and alas! is it all for naught that those brave hearts have laid their hands upon the staff that bore the banner of liberty, only to give another illustration of the motto, *"dulce est pro patria mori?"* Truthfully can we say in their own expression, *"Dios sabe."*

The *Vijia* is probably the greatest attraction to the town proper, for no matter how often we go up, there is always some new beauty discovered, either in land, or sea, or sky. It is very easily reached on horseback, to its very top; it is a pleasant walk before breakfast, or can be easily gained by elderly people in a volante, which can go nearly to the top. No one, however, can be said to have seen *La Vijia* who has not visited it both at sunrise and sunset; let us try it.

It is a fine bracing morning, and, having had our bath and coffee, we sally out at the door of our hotel, and find in the dusky morning (it is not yet daybreak) our horses, ordered the previous evening, awaiting our coming; they are not "much," but they will do to carry us up the hill. So, mounting, we wind through various streets of the upper town, and come out at last by the rustic road leading past the *Ermita de la Popa* and the military hospital, which are about half-way up the mountain. Leaving these below us, we strike a rough steep road, ascending which we get far above the town, and begin to take in something of the vast scene, which at this early hour of the morning is somewhat indistinct. Higher and higher we go at a slow pace, until at last we reach the top, where is a small house or hut in which lives the signal-man, and in front of which is the mast where signals are made to the town below, of any approaching vessels. Here we leave our horses, and on foot proceed by a path leading beyond the house, that takes us to the very summit.

What a scene bursts upon us here! We seem to be on a high point, around which are vast seas of mist and vapor, that, floating far below us, look like grand lakes, while some, not so distant, are yet more opaque, resembling solid fields of cotton; but now, over the distant eastern hills, the first rays of the rising sun begin to shed their light, and, gradually getting higher and higher, the orb of day rises, in all its magnificence of blazing golden glory, over the top of the neighboring mountain.

The scene now rapidly changes, the vast bodies of vapor that hung like a pall over the whole face of the lower valley, are now rapidly dissolved by the warm rays of the risen sun, and then we have unfolded to our astonished vision, piece by piece, the loveliest bits of hill and dale, of fields of waving cane, as bright and green as the emerald water of the ocean itself. The neighboring hills, too, in their glittering and verdure-clad robes, deign to appear, one by one, gorgeously gilded by the morning sun.

Turning to the south we have the town, and the country between it and the sea clearly defined, while beyond is the sea itself extending its blue waters until lost in the hazy clouds of the distant heavens; and this scene is not the same with every morning, for there is always some difference of light and atmosphere that gives a changing beauty to the views. Our consul, General Cabada, a warm lover of nature, an artist in feeling and practice, told me he generally walked up here every morning, and he always found some new beauty to admire.

The scene is changed; it is now the evening hour of sunset, and seated upon the rocks we gaze at the same scenes in a different light. Everything is now quiet and peaceful,—not a sound is heard from the great world below. We see the people moving like mere specks in the streets of the town,—even the trains of cars, winding swiftly over the long black trail, look like small boxes endowed with some supernatural power of motion, for we hear no noise of engines. We look up the valley, and from clumps of green foliage, shoot up here and there the tall white chimneys of the sugar mills puffing out their black smoke, which rises in clouds, higher and higher until it vanishes away into air; the little stream that wanders between its wooded banks looks, as we catch a glimpse of it here and there, like a silver riband. And then the sea, too, as blue as blue can be, with not a perceptible ripple on its surface, but quiet as a lake, while a white sail here and there seems to make a boundary between sea and sky, which latter is assuming all those beautiful golden crimson tints peculiar to a tropical sunset, and yet so beautifully graduated one into the other that it is hard to say where the blue leaves off and the gold and grander tints begin.

But hark, even now there is a sound—a quiet soft musical sound—that comes stealing up the valley as the sun is slowly going down, and which truly harmonizes with the scene,—the vesper bell. How apropos the lines of Byron to such a scene, and such an hour as this:

> "Sweet hour of twilight!
> Soft hour which wakes the wish and melts the heart
> Of those who sail the seas, on the first day
> When they from their sweet friends are torn apart;
> Or, fills with love the pilgrim on his way,
> As the far bell of vesper makes him start,
> Seeming to weep the dying day's decay.
> Is this a fancy which our reason scorns?
> Ah! surely nothing dies but something mourns."

There, far down in these peaceful valleys, that looked so calm and still when I saw them, and which even then seemed to fill one's breast with prophetic sadness, have taken place some sharp, fierce struggles—where a little band of patriots badly armed and equipped, but with stout hearts, in a good cause, have essayed to plant firmly the flag of freedom. Now forward, now backward, sometimes in good success up to the very foot of the hill of Trinidad they have pressed, and yet again been forced back amidst the shades of these palmy groves, or the shelter of the waving cane. These grand old hills have witnessed horrid deeds of cruelty in the beautiful plains below, which rival in brutality and bloodthirstiness any that the page of history yet can show. Earnestly will we pray, *Dios guarda las almas de los muertos.*

On the other side of the valley, the highest peak which the traveler is able to see, and one whose top is frequently hidden in fleecy clouds, is the "Pico del Potrerillo," one of the highest mountains in Cuba, being some three thousand odd feet above the level of the sea. It is said that the view from there is even more grand and extensive than that from the Vijia, but it is a long ride, and involves the necessity of staying in its neighborhood over night. I did not go there, but the traveler who wishes to do so can get information and horses at the hotel, and what is actually necessary, a guide.

The drive to the "Loma del Puerto" is a very beautiful one that should be taken by every traveler at Trinidad, presenting, as it does, grand and beautiful views of the hill "Del Puerto" and a portion of the valley.

This valley is said to be the most beautiful of the island seen from this side, as there one sees the beautiful perspective of mountains, that rise to good height at the depth of the valley, and towering above which is seen the "Pico de Potrerillo." Within the boundaries of the valley there are no less than fifty *ingenios*, some of them of the finest class. It is watered by a number of beautiful streams, two of which, the Ay and the Agabama, unite and form the river Manati, which empties into the sea to the east of Casilda, and which is navigable some seven miles, and by which the planters send their sugar and molasses to the shipping points. In this same river of Ay there are sulphurous mineral springs, the water being delicious to drink; and in the centre of the valley, and on its banks, is a village of the same name as the river, prettily situated in a grove of trees—in fact, the whole of the valley is one scene of beauty. The railroad from the Casilda runs through the valley some distance, and if the time-table is so arranged that the traveler can go from Trinidad in the morning and return in the evening, he will be delighted with his trip. At present, the road not being completed, they have no regular time of going or coming.

On the way back from the Loma del Puerto, the tourist can visit the magnificent place of Recreo, "Quinta," or country house of the Cantero family, which is situated a short distance from the town, at the head of the beautiful valley, and at the foot of the mountains, which rise up behind it forming a majestic background to the lovely beauties of the place.

The Quinta—rivaling in beauty even Los Molinos, of the Captain-General, at Havana,—is occupied by the family, who have also a handsome town residence during the summer months, though they come out frequently during the winter, as do most families who own plantations, spending their Christmas holidays in merry-making, bestowing presents to the hands, and in general festivity.

It is a lovely walk to this estate of an early morning from Trinidad, and one can go in and walk around these beautiful grounds with constant and renewed pleasure, the owner being exceedingly kind to strangers in admitting them.

In the north of the town is the *barranca*, as it is called, a place of very rapid descent, leading from the town down into the valley, the road being dug out of the side of the hill and paved with stone as far down as the bank of the river Tayabo, which flows by the town at this point. Here the washerwomen have established their city laundry, as it may be called, and a ridiculous and not very decent sight it is of a wash-day to see men and women, many entirely naked, seated upon the rocks or half immersed in the water, washing, slashing and pounding the clothes with pieces of stone, and if the traveler has been unfortunate enough to trust any of them with his wardrobe, he will learn to his cost with what effect.

En passant, I would advise the traveler invariably to inquire for French washerwomen, as although their charge is much greater, one is sure to have his clothes returned to him in good order, and well done.

This *barranca* is also a lovely stroll of an evening, when the shadows of night are stealing over the quiet hills and valley below, giving them a peculiarly quiet and sombre hue.

There are several public buildings and churches in the town of Trinidad, which offer nothing in particular to the traveler, except it may be the extreme filthiness of the hospital for women and children, and the dreary jail-like appearance of the *carcel* or dungeon; while of the churches, the only one of any size is that of San Francisco. The church of Santa Anna is small and old, and Paula, at the Plaza de Carillo, not much better.

On Palm Sunday, doors and windows are decorated with the graceful branches of the *real* palm, and it is a great day with church and state, the morning mass being celebrated with great pomp at the church of San Francisco. The governor and staff, in full uniform, the town council in sombre full dress, the officers of the troops stationed in the town, "pipe-clayed and mustache waxed," are all there to assist; but all these sink into insignificance for me, when I enter the church and see the crowds of pretty girls devoutly kneeling on their elegant rugs and slyly peeping over the tops of their fans at their *enamorados*, standing in the shadow of the arches. Nothing can be more charming than these *women* of *fifteen* or *sixteen*, (now laugh not, o reader), for most Spanish girls are as much women and as fully developed in body, if not in mind, at fifteen or sixteen as our own at twenty; and even now I think of the beauteous, graceful, bright-eyed *Carmela*, who, with a prayerful movement of her tiny hands, was bemoaning to me, at *fifteen* years of age, her sorrow at *getting so old*.

Trinidad, in the winter or gay season, is a very hospitable, pleasant place for the stranger. Almost every night there is a ball or party, and in the daytime there are frequent excursions made up the before mentioned lovely valley, to the *yngenios* for a day or two's frolic, and to drink the punches of *guarapo*. From all that I have seen, I want no pleasanter place to spend my winter in than Trinidad de Cuba, and to any traveler not caring to travel over the island, but who wants quiet, rest, and pleasant enjoyment, my advice would be to winter there.

And now the boat is in, and will start in a few hours. We order our volante, make our preparations and bidding adieu to our kind friends after giving a knuckle-breaking shake of the hand to the jolly old landlord, we turn our backs upon the varied attractions of this city, carrying away with us a lively memory of its beautiful scenes, lovely women and hospitable people, the delightful ride down the mountain forming a fitting close to our exceedingly pleasant stay in Trinidad.

FROM TRINIDAD TO SANTIAGO
DE CUBA

The traveler, before leaving Trinidad, should purchase his ticket of the agents of whatever boat is in, taking it direct for Santiago de Cuba. The steamer leaves Trinidad in the afternoon, at three or four o'clock, and the fare is about forty dollars.

Here, for the first time, I felt the loneliness of the traveler in a foreign land. I was leaving behind me pleasant scenes, which I had enjoyed much in the good fellowship of my *compagnon de voyage*, who had just left me the day before for home, while I was to continue on my travels alone; and nothing has a sadder effect, for a time, upon the traveler than this breaking up of those pleasant ties of *camaraderie* that have lasted for several months. Nevertheless, one is more fortunate, sometimes, than he anticipates or deserves, perhaps; for I found a very pleasant party of Cubans on board the steamer, and among them some agreeable Señoras, whose acquaintance I was fortunate enough to make. I also made the acquaintance of two capital traveling companions, in the shape of two members of the "Canadian Commission," sent out by the home government to open trade communications with the West Indies; and I have to laugh, even now, as I think how our acquaintance was first begun.

I was seated alone at the table, in the evening, and not feeling very well, had been supplied with a cup of tea, in which I was sulkily soaking bits of toast, my hat over my eyes to escape the glare of the lamp, when a gentleman, drawing a chair beside me, began abruptly, in broad Gaelic, with,—

"Ye're a Scotchman?"

"No, I am not," I rather shortly answered.

"Ye looked to be Scotch."

Entrance to the Port of Santiago de Cuba

Not quite knowing whether this was intended to be a compliment or not, I made no reply.

"Well, ye're English, then,—that's something."

"No, I am not," (with emphasis on the word); "I am a 'Yankee.'"

"Well, I mean you speak English, and that's something in a strange land. My name is S——, sir."

"Thank you."

"And my friend and myself are the commissioners from Canada."

"The deuce you are!" (with life). "Why, then you must be the jolly fellow Doctor—— (a mutual friend), traveled with?"

"Why, certainly; do you know him,—and how is he?"

And thus in a few moments we were friends, and I was presented to his companion, Mr. De L——, an elegant, polished French gentleman, and member of the Canadian Parliament; and a very pleasant time we had together for several days. Mr. S——himself turned out to be the Comptroller of St. John, New Brunswick, and on comparing notes, we found we each had letters to the same people in Cuba, and we therefore fraternized at once.

After a sixteen hours' sail from Trinidad, we steamed through the Archipelago, known as the "Jardines de la Reina" (Gardens of the Queen), a cluster of small *cayos*, or keys. Columbus on his first voyage named these islands as above, and disembarked there after suffering many hardships. He supposed them to be the islands spoken of by Marco Polo, as existing on the coast of Asia. These islands, the greater part of which are deserted, vary in length from one to four leagues; some are low and barren, others covered with grass, others wooded with high and graceful trees. The sight of these at sea, clothed with such a variety of colors, fired the imagination of the admiral, disposed always to receive favorable impressions of the Cuban scenery, and from the impossibility of giving a name to each one of them, he called them all by the poetical name "gardens."

Arriving at Santa Cruz, which is a very small place, a number of our passengers leave us to take horse or volante for Puerto Principe, situated in the interior of the island,—a very tedious and uncertain journey, but the only means of reaching that place from this side of the island.

Six hours more, and entering the Gulf of Guacanayabo we reach Manzanillo, in the afternoon, where the steamer remains long enough to see quite as much of the town as one wants. It is a small place, of about six thousand inhabitants, and has the appearance of having been built up rapidly, and then left by the inhabitants in disgust. It has, of course, the eternal "Plaza," in name only, a stone church, whose bells make just as much racket as any other bells, and the always-to-be-found commandant's *palacio*.

Fonda y posada it hath also, but no respectable place for the weary traveler to lay his head, or to satisfy his inner man in a Christian manner; and I have not been able to see why there is a town there at all, unless on account of the sponge and turtle fisheries which are carried on in the waters lying between it and Santa Cruz.

It is an old town, being founded in the reign of Las Casas, in 1790; and it was here that Giron, a pirate, landed, in 1604, passed on into the village of Yara, and possessed himself of the person of the Bishop, Fray Juan de las Cabezas, who was paying that town a holy visit. The bishop was ransomed by the payment of two hundred ducats, some hides, and other things to the wanderer of the seas, who, however, came to grief himself, being ambuscaded by some of the islanders on his way back, who quietly put him to death, and "fobbed" his booty.

It is from here that a large portion of the celebrated brand of "Yara" tobacco finds its way to market; and, having heard so much of it, I was induced to purchase a few hundred cigars made of it, which, however, I presented to the first dusky Hebe that waited on me in the town of Cuba, that being a more acceptable gift to these inveterate smokers than a golden *peso* would be. The cigars were bitter and strong, and not to my taste at all.

Leaving Manzanillo, we in some degree retrace our route, in order to pass around the extreme southern point of the island, the Cape of the Cross (*Cabo de Cruz*); and now we begin to see some of the grandest and wildest coast scenery of Cuba.

Immediately after leaving the cape, there begins the range of mountains known as the "Macaca," or "Sierra Maestra," which extends from Cape Cross to the river Bocanao, in the east of Cuba, and in which range there are some of the highest peaks on the island, with their bases washed at some points by the sea itself, and their tops hidden in the clouds. This range of hills affords some superb views of grand mountain scenery as we have in the United States.

The first mountain after passing the cape is the *Ojo del Toro*, or Bull's Eye, a sharp-pointed peak, rising up to the height of thirty-five hundred feet above the level of the sea. Still farther on, we come to the Sierra Maestra, which, as a range, has an average height of forty-five hundred feet; while standing boldly out and towering far above even that range of high mountains is the peak Turquino, which is set down by most authorities as being about eight thousand feet high, and which is the highest point in the whole island of Cuba. In fine weather, it is distinctly seen at a great distance out at sea, serving for a conspicuous landmark to the mariner making the port of Cuba. Now as we look, it is enveloped in clouds, that hang in sombre masses around its very peak.

Here, amid these scenes, so changing yet so beautiful, there come naturally to the mind these lines of Tennyson: —

"By peaks that flamed, or, all in shade,
Gloomed the low coast and quivering brine
With ashy rains, that spreading made
Fantastic plume or sable pine;
By sands, and steaming flats, and floods
Of mighty mouths, we scudded fast,
And hills and scarlet-mingled woods
Glowed for a moment as we passed."

Some one now remarks that we are near to Cuba; but, looking landward, nothing is seen but the same continuous mountains which we have had for the past twelve hours, except where, low down on the shore, there seems to be a slight opening in the rocky coast, above which stands, apparently, some dwelling-house. However, time tells, and in a half-hour more we discover the small opening to be the entrance to a valley, and the dwelling-house to be the fort of the Cabañas. Still, no town and no harbor; and yet ahead we see, high upon a rocky cliff, a queer-looking old castle, with guns frowning from its embrasures, and its variegated walls looking as if they were ready to fall into the waves dashing at their base. That is the Morro Castle, which, with the battery of Aguadores, the battery of the Estrella, and the above-named Cabañas, commands the approaches to the harbor and town of Cuba. The rocky shore above and below the castle has scattered along it the remains of several vessels, whose captains, in trying to escape from the dangers of the storm, have vainly sought to enter the difficult harbor, and the bleaching timbers are sad warnings to the mariner not to enter there except in the proper kind of weather. And now we are up to the castle, and a sharp turn to the left takes us into a narrow channel and past the Morro and the battery adjoining, whose sentry, with a trumpet as big as himself, hails our vessel as she goes by; and soon we find ourselves in a gradually enlarging bay, around which the mountains are seen in every direction,—a beautiful, beautiful bay, reminding one very much of some places in our own romantic Hudson, where one at times seems to be sailing on a beautiful lake encompassed by green mountains. As yet we have seen no town, and no place where there is likely to be one; but now a turn to the right, and there, rising from the water's side almost to the top of the mountain, is seen Santiago de Cuba, with its red roofs, tall cathedral towers, and the green trees of its pretty Paseo, lighted up by the evening sun, forming a beautiful foreground to the hazy blue mountains that lie behind the city. Being told that "La Suss" is the best hotel, kept by a Frenchman, and in the best style, we have our baggage placed upon a *carreta* (cart), and, forming round it as an escort, we begin the ascent to the upper portion of the town. We arrive at the hotel only to find it full, and therefore seek the shelter of the "Hotel del Comercio," and consider ourselves fortunate in being allowed to occupy two miserable rooms, the house being quite full.

It is Holy Week, and as a consequence there is no theatre in operation, though there has been an opera company performing during the past few weeks, but the authorities commanded its performances to cease until after the solemnities of the week were over; so, for amusement, we strolled up to the Plaza de Armas, or "of the Queen," as its tablet informs us; and a pretty little square it is, with its broad walks, beautiful wide-spreading trees, and pretty shrubbery. On the western side is the residence of the Governor-General of the district, of which this is the head-quarters, with the offices of the *Ayuntamiento* or Town Council adjoining. On its northern and southern sides are the handsome residences of two marquises, while facing it, on the east, is the imposing cathedral said to be the largest in Cuba.

It is Holy Thursday, and certainly, whether we be Protestants or Catholics, we shall most devoutly pray to be delivered from such another night as the past; for, in truth, we have made the acquaintance of "near relations" of that same family of "wicked fleas" so happily depicted in "Cuban Pictures."

As the places of business are all closed from ten o'clock today until the same hour on Saturday, I hurry down to present my letters of introduction and credit; and very pleasant it is to find myself received with cordial kindness, in strong contrast to the usual mode of Cuban business men. I found we had been misinformed as to the hotels, and that the hotel of Madame Adele Lescailles is considered the best. Fortified with a short note from my friend, I immediately sought out the landlady, and found her to be a jolly, immensely stout old French creole, keeping a comfortable, and what is more remarkable in Cuba, a scrupulously clean hotel. Thanks to my note, we succeeded in getting very comfortable rooms, and so were prepared to see the town in the best manner. We were glad to find quite a number of Americans in our hotel, and among the rest our *compagnons de voyage*, the Canadian Commissioners. After dinner, in the evening, we strolled up to the square opposite the Cathedral, to see the grand procession of the Virgin sally out from the church and parade through the city. First came a band of music, and then, upon one side of the street, in single file, citizens and negroes together; on the other, military officers, of all grades, in full uniform, all of them uncovered, and with long wax tapers, lighted, in their hands; then another band of music, and there appeared the Governor-General, with his riband of office, in a splendid uniform covered with decorations,—a grizzled soldierly-looking man of about fifty, smiling in spite of the solemnity of the occasion; around him his staff in brilliant uniforms, and the members of the Town Council in their full dress suits,—many of them, I must confess, were not overcome with the piety of their office, for they were constantly breaking into laughter. Now, borne upon the shoulders of eight stalwart negroes, and preceded by a few priests, comes the catafalque, gorgeous in paper flowers, lighted candles, glass shades, gold and silver foil, velvet and ribbons, surmounted by a large figure of the Virgin, under a velvet and gold canopy, and guarded at each corner by miniature cherubim, with spread wings. It is hard to say why the natural impulse of a stranger should be to do as he sees the multitude around do, and uncover his head to something, which, if he was inclined to be impious, he might appropriately call the "What-is-it." Nevertheless, the procession moves on, the Bishop and his clergy, in their gorgeous robes, following in the wake of the Virgin, the military band plays a solemn march, and with a battalion of soldiers, with their arms reversed, and stepping short in measured tread to bring up the rear, the cortege goes elsewhere, to pass before the eyes of the silent, credulous, and uncovered multitude, who turn out in such vast numbers to see the pageant thus made up of "church and state."

Good Friday comes, and still the services are going on, the churches being filled all day with worshippers, the streets with people as though for a holiday, and yet there is no merry-making. Everything has still that horrid dolefulness, and we are beginning, all of us, to vote the holy season as kept up here a nuisance. We visit the churches, too, call at all the shrines, and do our best to sympathize with the feelings of these people. In some respects we succeed, for we are always found willing to act on the suggestions of our native friends, when they say "*refrescos*," as we find so many pilgrimages in the hot sun conducive to inclining us for visits to some of those cool, pleasant-looking shrines near the square, where are dealt out rewards to the faithful, in the shape of orangeades or *limonadas con ron*.

At the shrine of beauty, too, we are heartfelt in our devotions, as at every church we visit we find crowds of pretty girls, many of them most exquisitely dressed for the very purpose of being admired, I should judge, from the little attention they pay to the services in the church.

And here, while I am on the subject of pretty women, I will allude to what this town of Cuba is celebrated for, and what every stranger that comes to the place immediately notices,—I mean the beautiful mulatto girls, as they are called, though many are quite white, mostly descendants of French or Spanish Creoles, serving as domestics in many families, or getting their living, if they happen to be free, by sewing or washing, and many, I fear, by not quite so honest a vocation.

Bang, bang, boom! "What on *airth* is the matter," asks one of our friends; but all hearing the noise of pistol-shots, yells, and shouts, rush to the door, early Saturday morning, to see for themselves the meaning of the row.

We find that it is the ceremony of the "persecution of Judas, the betrayer of Christ,"—the winding-up of the sacred season of Lent. The ceremony consists in parading for two or three hours after sunrise, the effigy of Judas the Betrayer. As he passes by in the street, pistol shots, fire-crackers, and squibs are let off at the apathetic figure,

Hanging Judas

whose fate is probably ended by dragging through the streets, and hanging to the most convenient lamp-post. This is the closing ceremony of the solemnities of Holy Week, to be followed on the morrow (Sunday) by a cock-fight in the morning, two bull-fights in the afternoon, and the opera in the evening.

Santiago de Cuba

chapter thirty-three

THE TOWN OF CUBA

Its situation; The grand cathedral; The St. Domingo gun; The markets; The mango and other fruits; Street sights and architecture; Drives around Cuba; Trip on the Sabanilla railroad; Mahogany and other woods; The San Carlos and Philharmonic Clubs; Our landlady; Shopping in Cuba; An earthquake; History of the town.

"From whence these direful omens round,
Which heaven and earth amaze?
Wherefore do earthquakes cleave the ground?
Why hides the sun his rays?"

—Hymn

The town of Cuba offers to the stranger many inducements to pass a few weeks within its limits, or in the beautiful country around it. Rising gradually from the bay, upon the mountain side, to the high plain called the Campo del Marte, it reaches in its highest point one hundred and sixty feet above the level of the sea, and commands from almost any portion superb views of the bay at its feet and of the majestic ranges of mountains that surround it. With a population of about fifty thousand inhabitants, it has regularly laid out streets, and well-built houses of stone in most portions of the city; though being built as it is upon the side of a hill, many of the streets are very steep in their ascent, and from the constant washing of the rains and the absence of sidewalks, are anything but an agreeable promenade. The most beautiful square, and, in fact, the only one of importance, is the "Plaza de la Reina" (Square of the Queen), situated in the centre of the city.

The market-house presents, of an early morning, not only an amusing but a very instructive sight to the traveler. Almost all the venders are negroes, mostly women, who bring all manner of fruits peculiar to the country for sale; and one can spend some time very profitably in wandering through the market. Here in this is market we succeeded in getting an opportunity of trying the much-vaunted fruit, the mango. The trees I had seen growing in many parts of the island (and noble ones they were) resembling very much some of our larger

Mango

pear-trees. The fruit as it grows looks exactly like a large, green pear, but from the fact that it does not ripen until late in the spring, we had no chance of trying it before. It is very luscious, and when perfectly ripe is said to be too rich. I prefer our peaches.

On the water side of the town, the only buildings of any importance, aside from the business houses, are the custom-house, and the depot of the Sabanilla railroad.

Some of the older streets offer many curiosities in the way of architectural oddities, which are at the same time antique and romantic looking, particularly some of the window-frames, made of carved wood, and projecting out from the fronts of the houses in the form of a balcony, thereby affording the female inmates an opportunity of peeping out from behind a corner of the curtains, and seeing what little life there is astir in the streets.

The grand Cathedral, the largest in Cuba, is situated on the eastern side of the square, and from its position, being elevated upon a plateau,

Street in Santiago

commands a fine view of the city and its surroundings. It is a very handsome structure, built of stone, with the walls painted to represent blocks of that material, and it has lately undergone considerable improvement and repair. The numerous earthquakes that visit this portion of the island have at different times done great damage to the church, and it was almost reconstructed at the beginning of the present century. The main aisle of the church, giving a view of the altar and the grand choir, is very imposing, from the height of its arches and the massive pillars which support them. The cathedral has a number of chapels very elegantly decorated, and the

The grand Cathedral

usual number of confessionals. It is also worthy of a visit in the evening, when the effects of the fading day are very fine. This is the only church worthy of attention, unless we except the church of San Francisco, where those fond of military music may hear mass every morning about half-past six o'clock, at which the principal participators are the soldiers.

In the base of the plateau, upon which the cathedral is situated, is a niche, in which is placed a large iron cannon, supported on props, and protected from the passer-by by an iron railing. Rather curious to know what a cannon had to do with a religious edifice like the cathedral, I inquired why it was placed there, and was informed that it was the cannon (I am not prepared to say it was the only one) captured during the war in Santo Domingo; and so proud were the officials of it, that it was sent to the city of Cuba by one of its sons, then a Spanish officer, as a *memento gloriae* of their success.

There are many beautiful drives in the neighborhood of the city, and for those fond of horseback exercise, a ride up to the barracks of the troops, in the highest portion of the city, will give not only a good view of the large structures, not yet completed, for quartering three thousand men, but also the finest view of the city and the surrounding country. The "Paseo de Concha" is also a pleasant and fashionable drive, particularly on Sunday afternoons. A charming ride, and not a very long one, is that to the Castle of the Morro, at the entrance to the harbor, admittance to which can generally be obtained by permission of the officer of the guard at the gate, on representations being made that one is a stranger.

A pleasant and beautiful trip in the cars can be made, any morning or evening, on the Sabanilla railroad to the end of the road, taking your ticket at the station on the edge of the bay for "Dos Caminos" (two roads) and return. The road runs through a portion of wild and beautiful country, passes by some sugar estates, and, to a person not desirous of going farther into the interior, gives a good idea of the mountainous and varied aspect of this portion of the island.

This trip to Dos Caminos gives one an opportunity, too, of seeing something of the lumber trade of the island, as a great deal of mahogany and other hard woods is cut in this vicinity and hauled down to the railroad, and thence, via Santiago de Cuba, exported abroad.

Mahogany cart

Some of these logs of mahogany that we saw were enormous, and required six or eight yoke of oxen to haul them,—a difficult matter at the best of times over some of these muddy roads.

Cuba is very prolific in woods of various kinds, and the more valuable classes form an important item in the aggregate exports of the island. It is estimated that of nearly twenty millions of acres of land still remaining perfectly wild and uncultivated on the island, nearly thirteen millions are of forest land, uncleared as yet, the timber upon most of which is valuable for many kinds of manufactures, such as fine cabinet furniture, buildings, carriages, etc. The Cuban ebony is celebrated for making beautiful household furniture, canes, etc., and the *caoba*, cedar, *sabicei*, and *granadilla* are all exported largely.

There are two very good clubs in the town—the "San Carlos" and the "Philharmonic." The first is composed, in a great degree, of

French members, and their rooms are a very comfortable, pleasant place to while away a leisure hour or so. Most of the members speak English, and they have a very good library of French, English, and Spanish books, as well as most of the principal periodicals and papers of the day. The rooms are also furnished with a piano and billiard tables, and to strangers, to whom the members are very hospitable when properly introduced, a card of invitation is given for thirty days.

The best hotel in the town, particularly for ladies, is that of Madame Adele Lescailles, at the corner of Jaguey and Juela de Escudero streets. This is one of the cleanest and pleasantest houses I saw in Cuba, and seemed more like a home to me than an hotel, owing largely to the kindness of the good landlady. I used to wonder how she got about with her mountain of flesh. I never shall forget her expression when, one day, I was twitting her with not having given me a

Our landlady

mattress, on the ground, as I told her jokingly, that she did not like Americans.

"Ah, *Monsieur*," she said, putting her hand on her heart (or where it ought to have been, since it must have been covered with fat a yard deep), "I have a large, good heart, and I love all the world, but *particularly* the Americans." Her manner and words were irresistible; and, as well as my laughter would permit, I told her she should be presented to the American public in my book, for the which she smilingly thanked me, in the gravest, most polite manner possible, with her inimitable *"Merci, Monsieur."*

The next best hotel, considered, perhaps, by gentlemen better than Madame Adele's, is "La Suss," kept by a Frenchman of that name, on the street Las Enramadas, above Gallo.

The theatre building is very good in Cuba, and the opera is produced in good style, and patronized, to a great extent, by the beauty and fashion of the town during the opera season.

In this town I had a new sensation, one day, in the form of an earthquake. Mr. De L. and myself were in one of the principal stores, at the corner of a street, on a shopping expedition, and were

An earthquake

examining a lot of articles, when suddenly there was a sound as of artillery caissons passing over the stony street, immediately followed by a tremendous shaking of the earth. Instantly the salesman dropped his goods, and, followed by every other clerk, leaped the counters, and went out of the doors "like mad," much to our astonishment. Mr. De L. and I looked at each other, not quite understanding the state of affairs, and then hearing loud wailing and screaming in the street, walked out to the door, where the matter was explained by loud cries of "*terremoto, terremoto*" (earthquake). The street was, by this time, filled with kneeling people, praying women, and screaming children, while from the houses came pouring out the inhabitants. A space of some five minutes elapsed, and then the hubbub subsided, people went into their houses again, and matters were restored to a state of tranquility. I inquired if there were always such a row about a trifling shake like that. "Oh, sir," replied the trembling clerk, "it is not the first shock we mind, it is always the second one that does the mischief, and which always comes a minute or two after the first, which serves as a warning, at which we all run to the middle of the street for safety."

I inquired then if that was considered a good strong "shake," and was answered that it was; and I must confess it wasn't my idea of a tropical earthquake at all, as, had it not been for the actions and noise of the people, we should not have noticed it.

Cuba is a favorite place with ladies for shopping, as they have here some articles direct from France, made only for this market, and which seemed to us to be most beautiful articles, at extraordinarily low prices. Most exquisitely made fans, for instance, at fifteen dollars, which could not be bought for thirty dollars in the States; beautifully embroidered handkerchiefs, of piña cloth, I think they called it, at from three dollars and fifty cents to twenty dollars, that were extremely delicate and beautiful; dresses of a most peculiar and delicate fabric, as well as skirts of novel and graceful design, of which I had never seen the like, and which my Canadian married friends told me could not be bought at any price in New York or Canada. *"Quien sabe?"*

The town is supplied with an abundance of water, brought by an aqueduct from "El Paso de la Virgen," and has also gas works.

There is a large amount of business done in Cuba, in the way of shipping coffee, sugar, and molasses, mostly to European ports, I believe; and there is also connection here with Jamaica and Santo Domingo, by a line of steamers running about twice a month; there is also an occasional steamer to New York direct.

There is a line of tolerably good steamers, also, running regularly around the eastern end of the island and by the north coast to Havana, two or three times a month, stopping at Baracoa, Jibara, and Nuevitas.

As Santiago de Cuba is almost the oldest town upon the island, a few historical facts may not be uninteresting to the reader.

The town was founded in 1515, by Diego Velasquez, considered the conquerer of the island, who landed here in that year, on his first voyage; and it was from here that Juan de Grijalva, in 1518, started on his expedition for the conquest of Yucatan, being followed by Hernando Cortes, who, however, was compelled to stop at Havana (as it was called then), now Batabano. In 1522, the distinctions of "City" and "Bishopric" were bestowed upon the town, having been taken from the older town of Baracoa, where they had been bestowed in honor of that place being the first European settlement; and in 1527, Fr. Miguel Ramirez de Salamanca, first Bishop of the island, arrived and established here his head-quarters.

In 1528, Panfilo de Narvaez set sail from here on his expedition for the conquest of Florida, where he met his fate, and found a tomb.

It is related that in the waters of the bay, in 1537, a curious affair took place between the vessel of one Diego Perez, a native of Seville, in Spain, which was well manned and armed, and the vessel of a French pirate, which arrived in the bay, a combat immediately ensuing, which continued until night, when the stars appearing, it ceased, and the commanders of the two vessels exchanged courtesies, having had, say the authorities, a good time. At sunrise, they began the fight again, which lasted two days; but the third night the Frenchman availed himself of the opportunity to leave, according to the custom of his country.

In 1528, Hernando de Soto arrived here with nearly one thousand men, having been authorised, in addition to the command of his Florida expedition, to assume that of the whole Island of Cuba.

In 1553, the city was captured by four hundred French arquebussiers, who took possession of it until a ransom of eighty thousand dollars was paid, the invaders remaining nearly a month in the city; and as late as 1592, so frequent were the attacks of pirates on this town, that it is related the place was almost depopulated by the inhabitants taking refuge at Bayamo, some distance in the interior.

In 1608, the cathedral having been ruined by an earthquake, the Bishop Lalcedo removed his residence to Havana, and almost all the diocesans, as well as the ecclesiastical chapter, did the same, which action created great excitement, the Superior Governor and Chief of the island opposing it.

The Parroquial Church of Havana was about to be made into a cathedral, through the efforts of the prelate Armendariz, but these were opposed by the Captain-General Pereda. The bishop, then excommunicated said chief and all in his vicinity, all the clergy even going in procession to curse and stone his house.

In 1662, there was a serious attack made upon the place by a squadron of fifteen vessels, under Lord Winsor, whose people landed at the place now known as the "Aguadores," and to the number of eight hundred men, marched without opposition on the city, of which they took possession, after repulsing a small force sent out to meet them. The invaders, it appears, partook freely of the church-bells, carried off the guns from the forts, took charge of the slaves, and not finding the valuables they anticipated, which had been carried off by the retreating inhabitants, they in their disappointment blew up the Morro Castle, and destroyed the cathedral, remaining nearly a month in possession of the city.

It was not until 1663, therefore, that the castle now known as the Morro was rebuilt, by order of Phillip I, and at the same time the fortresses of Santa Catalina, La Punta, and La Estrella.

In July and August, 1766, a large portion of the city was ruined by earthquakes, more than one hundred persons being killed.

The town has the honor of having for its first mayor or "alcalde" Hernando Cortes; and it is said that the remains of Diego Velasquez, the first explorer and conqueror, were buried there in the old cathedral. It is related in corroboration of this fact, that on the 26th November, 1810, on digging in the cemetery of the new cathedral, the broken slab of his tomb was found, seven and a half feet under ground, the inscription upon which was illegible, with the exception of a few Latin words giving name and date.

Before going in

No stranger should visit Santiago de Cuba without going out to the Cobre Copper Mines, said to be the largest in the world. While paying them a visit, he can also see the Shrine of the Virgin (of which more anon), in the same village.

The village of the Cobre, one of the most ancient in Cuba, containing about two thousand souls, is situated in a valley, about twelve miles from Santiago, and can be reached either by boat and cars or by horse and volante. For myself, I would advise every one to go either on horseback or in volante,—probably the latter, as it is necessary to have a guide if you go on horseback, while the *caliseros* all know the road. The cars run only three or four times a week, connecting with the boat from the city, and starting from the station on the other side of the bay. The most comfortable method is to do as we did,—order a volante at six o'clock in the morning, have coffee before starting, and then, in the cool of the morning, set out. The ride is a very romantic and beautiful one, though in some places somewhat rough, and occupies, with good horses, about two hours. Arrived in the village of the Cobre, we put up our horses at the "Fonda de Molla," near the Plaza, ordered our breakfast, and, while this was preparing, availed ourselves of the opportunity to visit the "Shrine of the Virgin," described in the next chapter.

Breakfast over, we went to the office of the Mining Company, where every courtesy was shown us, and all necessary information given about visiting the mines.

Arriving at the mines, and presenting our letter of introduction to the affable and gentlemanly manager, Mr. Dumas, we were put in charge of two captains who were going in, and proceeded to the robing-rooms, which were situated in a long wooden building,

Cobre Copper Mines

furnished with bath-tubs, and containing suits of mining clothes for the use of the officers of the company and such visitors as desire to enter the mines from time to time. These suits consist of coarse flannel shirts, stout linen-duck coats and trousers, heavy leather shoes, and a species of night-cap for the head, over which is placed a peculiar kind of mining hat, to which, I think, judging from its weight, Don Quixote's lavatory head-covering would have been as a feather. These hats are made in England, and are a composition of felt-cloth and rosin, as solid as iron, preventing injury to the miners from falling stones when in the mines.

The Consolidated Copper Mines are the property of an English stock company, most of whose shareholders reside in England. The mines were originally owned and worked by various companies, but the present company has succeeded in buying up all the different interests, with the exception of one mine belonging to, and worked by, a Spanish company.

Don Pedro Ferrero is the general manager of the company, residing most of the time in Santiago de Cuba. The number of men employed is about two hundred and fifty, with six captains and five assistants. Most of the captains are from England, and are practical miners, who have learned their business in the mines of Cornwall and Wales; the assistants are generally also miners from the "old country," and the laborers are negroes and Chinese. These mines are situated in a wild and mountainous locality, in a valley formed by the Cobre Mountains, and form, with their buildings, machine shops, furnaces, and the houses of the workmen, quite a large village. The bottom of the mine is reached by two perpendicular shafts; the first one nearly seven hundred feet deep, connecting with a level, or "drift," which leads to another shaft of about three hundred feet in depth, which connects with another level leading to the main avenue or mine.

As much as fifty tons of ore are taken out per day, the richest portion of which, being broken up, is shipped to Europe, while the poorer part is smelted at the works, giving about fourteen per cent of metal. There is a railroad extending from the mine to the shipping point (Punta de Sal), on the bay.

Everything being now in readiness for our entrance into the mine, we were supplied with long, thick tapers, of bees-wax, and, escorted by two of the captains and a negro carrying a jug of fresh water, we proceeded to the entrance of the mine, at the mouth of the shaft, which we found to be a rectangular opening, about eight feet by six, over which hung a sort of two-storied octagonal box, attached by wire rope to a windlass worked by steam power, the sides of the shaft being

Descent

protected by narrow strips of wood. We lighted our tapers, and two of the party getting into the lower compartment of the box, it was lowered until the rest of us could step into the upper story; and then slowly we went down, down the "dark and narrow way," into unfathomable blackness and quiet, the light of our tapers only serving to show us how gloomy and intensely dark it was.

At last we came to a stop, and were told to step out carefully into the "level," or gallery, that connected with the shaft. Our guides led the way, and we followed carefully in their path, which was through a narrow opening, or "gallery," as it is called, about six feet in height and three or four feet in width, the upper portion somewhat smaller than the lower. As we went along, we found our feet splashing in the rather warm water that ran over the rocky floor. Again we arrived at another shaft, that we had to descend by means of wooden ladders, set up nearly perpendicularly from point to point.

At last, after much descending, we reached another gallery, along which we found a railroad laid, upon which the cars, filled with ore, were conducted out of the mine.

What a strange sight it was, in our subterranean wanderings in this dark cave, to meet a group of begrimmed men coming from out

In the mine

the gloom! First we heard in the distance the rumbling of wheels and the smothered sound of human voices; then in the deep obscurity we saw a little speck of light, then another, and another, gradually growing brighter and brighter, until, coming up to us, they proved to be the lights in the hats of the men with the car,—half naked, begrimmed looking subjects, whom it would not be hard for the imagination to picture as demon inhabitants of this rocky purgatory. We were informed that the narrow passageway where we stood was the old lead or vein, of which the direction had been lost.

We still advanced along the passage, and then, turning off, came to a place where they were digging out the rock, in hopes of again striking the lost vein. Three or four perfectly naked Chinese were at this work, the perspiration pouring off them as they used their picks and gads in prying out the pieces of somewhat soft rock. The pick resembles that in common use, but is smaller and more convenient, the iron head being very sharp and pointed at one end, and at the other, broad and hammer-shaped. The gad is simply a wrought iron wedge used in conjunction with the pick.

Resuming our steps, we followed up the main gallery which led to the main mine, noting as we went the roof over-head supported by immense braces of timber, some of which were cracked and wedged in by the excessive weight of the earth and rock above them.

The value of experience in even trifling things was here exemplified; for on inquiring if these braces were made of the hard woods of the country, I was informed that they had learned that the strongest wood was not the best for such braces, from the fact that it did not bend, but broke quickly, without giving any notice, causing much damage, and being very dangerous; whereas the weaker woods, like the pine, always bent before breaking, showing exactly where other and stronger braces were required in time to prevent accidents.

Finally, we came out into an immense cavern, some sixty feet in height, twenty in width, and some hundreds in length. Here was where the largest quantities of the ore were being taken out by means of blasting.

In this cavern we were one thousand feet down below the surface of the earth, and there was still another mine below us, filled with water, which rises sometimes to the depth of twenty-five fathoms. It was almost as though one were in a hot-air bath, with the thermometer at one hundred and forty degrees. Just think of that, ye who grumble when the thermometer is at ninety degrees!—one hundred and forty, and the water running off us like rain!

Think of it, O ye who live in the light of day, in the midst of God's pure air, where, even in the hottest summer day, there is some gentle breeze to cool your burning cheek!—think of these human beings who spend their lives laboring in this heated obscurity, and for a very pittance, too.

"Look out! they are going to blast," was the cry. So negroes and Chinese, visitors and workmen, all ran for shelter to one of the galleries, some short distance off.

I expected to have heard a tremendous noise, as though the whole earth was caving in; but there was simply a series of loud reports, like those of small cannon, followed by a sound as of a cartload of coal being emptied, while the reverberation sounded throughout the cavern near us, and then grew fainter and fainter as it was lost in the distant galleries.

The average charge used in these blasts is four ounces of mining powder to each drill, which blasts blocks of rock into pieces of very large size. Of course, the drainage and ventilation of a mine like this, one would imagine to be a very serious matter; but as they have no fire-damps in copper mines, the different shafts that are sunk throughout the mine, in connection with the galleries, serve to keep the air purer, though it remains very much heated.

The drainage, however, is a very difficult matter, for there are immense quantities of water coming in at times; and in the last year or two, we understood that the company lost over one hundred thousand dollars by not being able to pump the water out fast enough.

Having "done" the mine pretty thoroughly, bumped our heads sufficiently, stepped into muddy pools from off planks that wouldn't be steady, and, more than all, "sweated" off the extra flesh on our bones, we concluded we would adjourn outside, and so started back.

Good heavens! what labor that was—labor that I shall never forget. Hitherto, our troubles had only commenced; for, *lector mio*, you know that in this world, either practically or theoretically, it is easy enough to go down, but to go up,—ay, that is the rub indeed, as we found to our cost; for the whole series of steep ladders had to be gone over again, only this time in continuous ascent, and it did seem to me sometimes as though they never would end. Personally, I suffered more than any

Hill of difficulty

of the party, though I noticed the two stout, burly-looking men we had with us did their share of puffing. I am not ashamed to confess, that, with a somewhat dilapidated lung, I had to give up several times, and stop to rest on the landings.

At last, O happy moment! we reached the foot of the main shaft, and, giving the signal, the boat or box was lowered to us, into which we stepped with alacrity, at the idea of once more seeing the face of the earth, and not having to work our passage up any farther. Slowly we mounted, and, when about half-way up the shaft, were surprised to hear a voice beside us, proceeding from the darkness, inquiring as to the state of our health. This was rather startling; but it appeared that a solitary workman was repairing some portion of the planking in a side gallery. This led to the *apropos* relation of how about the same number of persons, in about the same place, were precipitated, by the breaking of the rope, to the bottom of the shaft, where they were found afterwards "knocked to smash," to use the homely but forcible language of the relator.

Reader, are you an early riser, or do you ever make it a point to get up early enough to see the sun rise? Well, take my advice, stay in your bed, and when you want to have a sensation, just bury yourself for a day, and then let in a little sunlight through a small aperture. You will be astonished; for though I have seen sunrises in all manner of places and ways, never did the most glowing one seem to me so bright, so brilliant, as did God's own magnificent light of day that afternoon when we came up out of that pit, after being half a day in total darkness. Ah, well, thank God, we were at the top, and like those who have read "Paradise Lost," we were glad to have "done it." A beautiful pair were my fellow voyager and myself; at all events, *he* was a perfect "guy," and if he is to be believed, I was, too; but I had the advantage of my friend,—I could "take" him.

After

The bath

But now, reeking with perspiration, we were hurried to our dressing-rooms, immersed in a warm bath, and being taken possession of by negro women, were pounded, and scrubbed, and sponged, and washed, until we began to have those heavenly feelings, said to be the exquisite result of the Turkish bath.

This bathing is gone through with by everybody that goes into the mines—workmen or visitors—the moment they come out, as the temperature is so much higher in the mine that it would be dangerous to come to the surface and remain without some preparation to avoid the evil effects of the change of temperature.

Our hospitable friend, Mr. D., took charge of us as soon as our toilettes were complete, and sent us to a most capital dinner, at which we did ourselves the pleasure of drinking his health in some most unexceptionable Sauterne of his own importation. *Vaya con Dios*, Señor D., may thy shadow never be less!

I was fortunate enough to get some very beautiful specimens of the pyrites, which are of very odd shapes, varied and brilliant colors, and made very curious articles of *bijouterie*.

Aside from the practical interest that these mines have for the traveler, there is a good deal of romance clustering around their history, as it is believed they were the first mines ever worked by Europeans on the American Continent; for it is related that, upon the death of Diego Velasquez, who was the conqueror of the island, his followers, in 1524, began to get out copper from them; and, in 1544, an enterprising person, Hernando Miñez Lobo, endeavored to benefit the neighborhood of Cuba by interesting the authorities in the working of the mines; but there was nothing of importance done for want of intelligent laborers.*

In 1550, the German founder, Tezel, contracted with the municipality, and gave origin to the village of Cobre, though even he did not have great success; and after his death the matter remained neglected for a long time. It was again thought of when, at the end of the sixteenth century, the earthquakes and attacks of pirates drove the inhabitants of Santiago de Cuba to take refuge in the village of the Cobre; and a contract was placed in the hands of Juan de Equilez, by the terms of which he was to explore the mines, and deliver to the foundry established in Havana for the manufacture of cannon, on account of the government, two thousand quintals of copper; but the attacks of filibusters prevented the completion of it. Since then the mines have been worked irregularly, until now, in the hands of a company they are regularly made to produce large quantities of ore, though not so much in present as in former years, when the quantity exported added much to the total value of shipments from Santiago.

* It is even stated that Hernando Cortes worked these mines, and gained large wealth thereby, though he succeeded in killing off numbers of the Indians in their mining labors, unused as they were to any hard work.

chapter thirty-five

NUESTRA SEÑORA DE LA CARIDAD DEL COBRE

The Cuban Mecca; Devotions of Cubans; The shrine; Wonderful history of the discovery of the image; Description of; The church, buildings, and town; Enthusiastic account of a Cuban author; Trip to Guantanamo; The village of Santa Catalina; Easy way of treating strangers; Preparing for the Coffee Mountains.

What Rome is to the devout Italian, and Mecca to the faithful Turk, the town of Cobre is to the pious Cuban, containing as it does, the shrine of "Our Most Holy Mother of the Cobre, the sanctified Virgin of Charity," which, from time immemorial, has been visited, at certain seasons of the year, by pilgrims anxious to pay vows or make offerings promised in some season of great peril, sickness, or sorrow.

The village of the Cobre, located four leagues from the city of Santiago de Cuba, is a small, quiet place, prettily situated at the base of the Cobre Mountains, containing about three hundred houses, an inn or two, several houses for pilgrims, and a church in front of its neglected public square.

Up to within a year or two, the miraculous image of the Virgin has rested within the sacred precincts of the old church, far up the side of

Cobre village

the mountain, around which were gathered the houses occupied by the poorer classes of pilgrims when making their visit to the Virgin.

Such has been the success of her wonderful miracles and so great the accumulation of wealth from the grateful offerings of devotees (the income from this source now reaching, under the administration of the society of priests who have it in charge, thirty thousand dollars per annum), that it has been decided to erect such a temple as shall be a worthy resting place for the form of *la sanctissima Virgen*.

The old church has, therefore, been torn down to give place to the new one, and the Virgin has been removed into the small church in the town.

Fearing to undertake the task with my own unsanctified hands, I present to the reader, in the words of a pious son of the church, a reverent and truthful (?) account of the history and mystery of the most sanctified Virgin of Charity and the Cobre.

"Without fear of the image-breakers, though they are today as numerous as ever, I wish to give an idea of the veneration of this sacred image, and of its marvellous appearance in the island.

"The tradition of the finding of the image, whose representation I offer here, together with the history of its veneration, was set forth in a manuscript of the priest, Don Onofre de Farseca, chaplain of the sanctuary of the Cobre, who wrote it in 1703, basing it upon those declarations, which, in 1688, were made before competent authority, and executed in the archives of said church. The manuscript was afterwards commentated by the priest, Don Bernardino Ramar Ramirez, and published, in 1829, by Don Alexandro de Paz y Ascanir.

"It is related in this work that, in the year 1627 or 1628, there went out from the corral (cattle-pen) in the recently founded village of the Cobre, two Indians, called Rodrigo and Juan de Joyos, brothers, accompanied by a boy of the village, of nine or ten years of age, being a creole negro of the name of Juan Moreno, who was the same person who afterwards gave testimony as *eye witness* on the judicial investigations of the case.

"These three, directing themselves by land to the Bay of Nisse, in search of salt, and having embarked in a canoe, saw, at daybreak, near Cape Frances in said bay, a white body floating in the water. Pulling their little bark to it, they found upon a board an image of the "Sainted Virgin Mary," fifteen inches in height, with her precious child, of proportionate size, on her left arm, and a golden cross in her right hand. On the board was an inscription, in large letters, which Rodrigo read, and which said: 'I am the Virgin of Charity.'

"These good men arranged on a shelf this precious prize, and took it with great care and great reverence, so soon as they had provided themselves with salt, to the fold of Verajagua, where, by order of the administrator of the mines, they constructed a shelter of palm-leaves, where the miraculous image received the proper veneration. Simple people in their faith believed that it was the same that a certain Indian chief had had bestowed upon him by Ojeda when he visited the province of Cuba, and which the chief in his devotion fearing that he would be robbed of so precious a relic, had committed to the waters of a river.

"Judge ye with how much fervor they would venerate now their ancient protector and advocate. Afterwards, the image was transported to the grand altar of the parochial church of Cobre, where they took it in grand procession, and where it was received with ringing of bells, firing of guns, and amid the great rejoicings of the inhabitants. There it remained three years, at the end of which time this most holy image appeared to a certain young girl, called Apolonia, on an eminence near to the village, where also were seen mysterious lights for three consecutive nights. It was then determined to construct for the image on that hill a special temple."

And thus, reader, you have the origin of the famous sanctuary of Nuestra Señora de la Caridad del Cobre, to which so many pious pilgrims resort that it is now a very celebrated *cosa de Cuba* indeed. This old church was situated, at four hundred paces from the village, on the top of the hill, to which the ascent was made by means of stone stairs, with landings at intervals. The church consisted of a single nave, twenty-seven yards long and nine wide, the roof of painted cedar, and the pavement laid with blue and white painted tiles. A terrace wall encircled the temple that serves

as porch, and formed before it a little plaza, of twenty-seven yards square. The façade was adorned by a portico of stone, of good architecture, from which rose gradually the bell-tower. But this old church was ruined by an earthquake in June, 1766, and in its place there was constructed afterwards a little temporary tower, the same which now contains the bells.

This church again is being now torn down, and the image is temporarily placed in the little village church until the new and magnificent temple intended for it is built.

The shrine

For the principal *fiesta*, which is consecrated to the "Most Holy Virgin," and which begins about the 8th of September, lasting, some years, all October, they arrange the image on a portable throne, towards the centre of the church. This tabernacle has various handsome ornaments of tortoise shell, ivory, gold, and silver, and is enclosed in a case, with four glass sides. Around it they arrange some twelve angels, with burning tapers in their hands. Upon this precious throne descends from the roof, in order to cover it after the ceremonies, a cloud of blue taffeta, and from this mysterious veil

The image

hang the innumerable offerings and *ex votos*,—each one of these objects being a testimony of the counsel that some unfortunate mortal has received.

Having passed one day in visiting the mines and offering our devotions at the shrine of the Virgin, we started for Cuba, in the cool of the evening; and a very lovely ride we had of it,—with the setting sun lighting up some of the beautiful views that one sees along the road, and particularly on nearing Cuba, where there are one or two views commanding the city and its surroundings worth in themselves a day's journey.

Our pleasant little party in Cuba was now, in some degree, to be broken up,—my friends, the commissioners, both most excellent company, taking their way to Jamaica; my friend, W——, *en route* for home, and I about to seek the celebrated attractions of the Coffee Mountains of the Yateras. *Bien caballeros, adios, y buen viaje.*

Fortunately for me, since I desired to visit the Coffee Mountains, I had a letter of introduction to a member of the large and well-known firm of Brooks & Co., who treated me in the most cordial manner, giving me all the information I required in reference to that journey, and so far smoothing my way as to ship me to the care of their house in Guantanamo or Catalina. Had it not been for this, I do not know that I should have had the great pleasure which I so much enjoyed of passing some time among the most beautiful mountains and scenes in Cuba.

If the reader will examine a map of Cuba, and look at that portion lying upon the extreme south-eastern coast, he will there see, some distance east of Santiago de Cuba, a bay marked Guantanamo, but known by foreigners as Cumberland Bay. This is an exceedingly large and beautiful sheet of water, with a narrow entrance, guarded by high hills. A portion of the shore of this bay is low, flat, and marshy; but beyond this is some of the finest land in Cuba, lying at the foot of the range of hills known as the Yateras.

Fifteen miles from the landing at Guantanamo is situated in these plains the little village of Santa Catalina de Guaso, also known as the "Saltadero" from there being a fall in the waters of the neighboring stream. From this little village to the landing at Guantanamo is an excellent railroad, which is constantly busied in carrying the immense quantities of sugar, coffee, rum, and molasses raised and made in this section of the country, and for which Catalina is the depot, the other terminus of the road being the point from which it is shipped to all quarters of the world.

Connecting Cuba with Guantanamo is a line of small steamers, running two or three times a week, leaving Cuba in the night, and arriving at Guantanamo at daybreak.

Bidding good-by, then, to my friends in Cuba, I took the boat, at ten o'clock at night, and started anew on my journey; and, being tired, slept soundly through the night, to find myself, on awakening in the morning, at Guantanamo, accosted by the apparently irrepressible inquiry of the steamboat waiter, *"Café solo ó con leche, Señor?"*

The cars were soon ready, and taking my seat in the first-class carriage, I found I was to be the only passenger, the balance all going second-class, as is generally the custom. A clerk of the house to whom I was consigned, however, joined me afterwards, and my ride was, therefore, an agreeable one, though there is nothing in the scenery of the low, marshy grounds through which we passed to interest one. A thick, scrubby forest covers the ground, in which are abundance of deer, that afford ample sport to the gentlemen of the village.

On arriving at the village of Santa Catalina, I found Mr. McKinley, the resident partner of the house of Brooks & Co., to whom I handed my letter, being also presented by my fellow-traveler, the clerk. Without any ceremony, I was just taken possession of, my baggage ordered out of my care, and myself marched off up to the dwelling-house, where I was immediately directed to make myself at home, being put in possession of my room, with the remark that "this is bachelor's hall, and the breakfast hour eleven o'clock." Acting upon these friendly hints of my hospitable host, I made myself comfortable, and, with the assistance of a refreshing bath, perfected my toilette; and then for breakfast.

Fortunately for me, the very morning I arrived, the gentleman whose place I was to visit up in the mountains came down himself to the village, reaching the house as we sat down to breakfast, and we soon made each other's acquaintance, as also arrangements to go up the next day.

Santa Catalina, is a rather small place, situated about nine miles to the north of the depth of the bay of Guantanamo, and is about seventy-five miles by land from Santiago de Cuba. It possesses one church, some few well-built houses, and has generally a battalion of soldiers stationed there.

There is no hotel there now, and the stranger who visits the place has to be entirely indebted to the kindness and hospitality of the inhabitants for shelter.

Mr. McK., with whom I stopped, told me when he first went there, eighteen years ago, the place was a very small one indeed.

Establishing himself there as the representative of Brooks & Co., the town began rapidly to grow; the produce of the back country sought this place as the most convenient outlet; other houses were established, dwellings were built, and finally, the railroad also, which made the town a fixed fact, and a permanent depot for the coffee and sugar of the district, until now the business done there is quite enormous for so small a place. It has now about two thousand inhabitants, and is increasing all the time. [Since the above was written, all of this district of the Cobre has been the scene of many encounters between the Spaniards and the patriots, the latter having, for a time, according to report, actual possession of all this country almost up to the city of Cuba itself.]

My arrangements were made to start at daybreak, and such articles as I needed were sent up in a small valise in advance, on horseback, this being the only mode of progression up the rugged roads and steep ascents of the mountains.

LIFE IN THE COFFEE MOUNTAINS

"A caballo! A caballo! Señores," is the cry, as at day-break we gather upon the porch, having finished our light breakfast of *café con leche* with a morsel of bread. Our horses are all saddled and bridled, and the party, consisting of five persons, is ready to mount.

Our cigars are lighted, our *adios* made, and, mounting the sturdy beasts that have some work in prospect, we ride off in the fine bracing air fresh from the mountains.

My future host, like most of the inhabitants of this section of the country, was a descendant of the old original French settlers, refugees from the terrible massacres of St. Domingo, who, coming to the island of Cuba, settled themselves, as much as possible, in their old occupations of sugar-making and coffee-growing. French, therefore, by birth, educated in the United States from a boy, and living constantly amongst Spaniards, he had the happy faculty of being able to speak either French, English, or Spanish, as a mother-tongue, in addition to which he spoke the Creole dialect,—a compound of vile French and some little Spanish, which is the usual language of the negroes and the plantation.

A young Englishman, amusing himself and at the same time making money by traveling all over the world as a photographer, was one of our number, while two Cuban planters, one of them a nephew of our host, made up the party.

We rode through some lovely valleys, covered with sugar-cane, and then, striking the hills, began the ascent of those mountains known as the "Yateras," which appeared quite near to the village of Catalina when we started, but now seemed to recede almost as we advanced. Our journey was to be about eighteen miles in extent, continually ascending until we should reach the very summit of the mountains, where the finest coffee grows, and which is now known as the coffee district.

Gradually getting to the foot of the hills, and then ascending them for some time, we begin to take in the beauties of our road and the advantages of our position. We have left now the flat country behind us, and are coming into clumps of forests, with occasionally a *hacienda* or farm, and now and then a small coffee place, and at last we strike the steep mountain path, up which we are forced to go *poco a poco*. Now, turning in our saddles, we begin to see the magnificent beauties of the landscape. Far above us, the wild, high mountains are raising their forest-clothed crests, while around is a broken country of hills with small valleys in their midst, and far away, below us, we catch glimpses through the turnings of the road of the level green plain of the earth below. Mossy rocks, strange trees, beautiful ferns, and curious hanging vines, or graceful festoons of moss we see upon either side of the road, and here and there a wax-like looking tree pushes out to our view from the thick roadside foliage the golden but bitter fruit of the wild orange, which tempts us in vain. Occasionally we hear shouts from some of the invisible labyrinths of road, followed by the head of some coffee-laden mule emerging around the curve, and, perhaps, succeeded by twenty or thirty others, all with their loads of coffee following their leader, to whom they are attached head and tail, down to the village.

The air is pure and dry, about the temperature of that of the White Mountains in summer, with that peculiar feeling of rarity and lightness so agreeable to breathe in. Our journey is enlivened by pleasant converse and these beautiful scenes, varied by occasionally meeting some very gentlemanly French planters on their way down; and at last we begin to near the summit, when Mr. L——, my host, tells me to prepare myself for the most beautiful view I have seen. A little incredulous, after seeing Trinidad, I prepare myself to enjoy, perhaps, some wild or extensive view; when, upon turning a high, rocky point in the road, we have presented to our view nearly such a scene as Church has endeavored to depict in his "Heart of the Andes," though here, of course, there are no mountains so high. Farther than eye can pierce extends the wonderful distance in this view of the "Plain of Guantanamo," where sea and sky appear to fade

Plain of Guantanamo

A home in the coffee mountains

away into fairy mist before meeting each other. We see a vast plain of cane-fields, which at this distance appear as simple pastures, while farther away, the strong light of early morning gives the appearance of lakes of silver. Near us and above us rise the majestic hills, covered with innumerable gigantic forest trees.

Now we come in sight of our destination, which we see, as the road skirts around the mountain, to be a lovely place, nestling in the shadow of the great hills behind it, while in front is a lovely valley, teeming with the luxuriant vegetation of the tropics.

At the cross-roads we bid good-by to our planter friends, promising to pay them a visit in answer to their *"mi casa está a su disposicion;"* and putting spurs to our horses, we gallop up between the walls of the *secaderos* (coffee dryers) to the door of mine host, where, dismounting, we are cordially and pleasantly received by Madame and her two beautiful children, of whom, with my usual penchant for handsome children, horses, and dogs, I became very fond.

There is a good old custom amongst the Danes, I believe, that when the first toast is drank, it is to the "roof" of the house which covers every one in it,—meaning thereby that it is all one family, strangers included. This same custom might appropriately be kept up amongst the French coffee-planters of the mountains; for when you take your seat at the table, you are immediately installed as one of the family circle.

And how, O reader! can I adequately describe to you that most delicious life in those lofty mountains?—the pure air, the morning rides, the beautiful effects of nature, which were impressed indelibly on my memory by my ever unsatisfactory attempts to transfer their loveliness to my sketch-book. Let us try a day or two together, and see if we can form an idea of this life, so pure, so fresh, so natural.

Rising at six o'clock, we all meet around the family board, where each one takes his simple cup of coffee, with, perhaps, a biscuit, the children being supplied with milk. The gentlemen then mount their horses, the little ones go off with their governess, and we leave Madame in charge of the establishment, while we gallop off to ride over the place and see the hands at work in the coffee groves, or, perhaps, making a new road, or clearing off the timber of the forests for a new coffee-field. Try to imagine any beautiful mountains that you have ever been on, covered with woods, two or three thousand feet above the sea, with a temperature always the same the year round, the road dug out of the very mountain side, the vegetation as luxuriant as it is possible to be, with vines, ferns, wild orange trees, and shrubs, from the

The cupey

branches of which moss hangs down in graceful festoons; and more than all, the wonderful, curious parasites, which, graceful and beautiful as they are, carry certain death to any forest denizen they twine their arms around. Here is one called the "*cupey*," taken in one of the paths in the Calderones mountains. It is a parasite which entwines itself around the ceiba, or other tree, and in course of time entirely kills it. It originates on the tree itself, and throws its roots downwards, which in the course of their growth, entwine the tree in such a manner that eventually its trunk is compressed as if in a vice, and life very soon becomes extinct. The parasite, with its roots continually descending, takes strong hold in the ground. Sometimes, however, it shares the fate of the tree whose death it has caused, inasmuch as when the original tree dies, the strength of the parasite has not been sufficiently matured to support its own weight alone, and it therefore falls to the ground with its victim.

There is a great number of curious smaller plants, some of which we know, others that we never heard of before,—fit studies for the botanist. Here is the "ladies' collar," an herb with a large leaf, shaped like the old style of collars worn by ladies, from which it gets its name. There is the old familiar plant of the castor oil, of which we as children have no pleasant recollections. This grows in great quantities all over these mountains, and is prepared by the superannuated negro women, who select the beans and clean them ready for extracting the oil. I was very much amused with an old woman, perfectly blind, who seemed to pick out  the perfect and imperfect seeds with the greatest facility, while she sat croning over her task on the stone floor of the coffee dryer.

Castor-bean sorter

Still wandering along, we come out upon an opening in the woods, and, looking down, we see the new fields being prepared for coffee; which is simply done by cutting down the timber upon the side of a hill favorably situated, and burning off the brush. The seed is put in with those of the plantain, the cacao, or the palm, and left to

El jaguey

grow. One of these fields looks exactly like one of our western clearings.

Let us turn now into this grassy path that looks as if it would bury itself deep in the woods; a step or two more, and just look at that! What a curious combination of strange trees, warm sunlight, and graceful foliage.

This tree that you see in the foreground is another species of the parasite, somewhat grander and more beautiful, known as the *jaguey*; it has the same peculiarities as the *cupey*, but with the exception that after its roots take hold in the ground they unite and form one trunk of many pillars, becoming a sturdy tree, while the original tree dies out and decays, leaving a hollow space in the centre of the parasite. This one in the picture represents the *jaguey* grown quite into a large tree, and the old one entirely extinct.

It is supposed the origin of these parasites is from the ordure of the birds who carry the seed and deposit it in the tree, where it appears to take root in the branches as a simple vine, gradually assuming size and strength, until finally it causes the death of its host.

Usually, every morning, I visited with my host some neighboring estates, where we were always cordially received and welcomed, and immediately the disposition of the house was put at my service by the courtly owners.

At eleven o'clock, breakfast was served, which was the same substantial meal as in the low country, except there was a greater variety of fine vegetables,—yams, potatoes of various kinds, delicious water-cresses fresh from the cool brooks, and several that we are not acquainted with, such as the apio and the *yuca*, the latter one of the

most useful plants on the island, of which there are four classes known, but only two are indigenous to, and used on, the island. From this they make the cassava bread, and it is generally used boiled as an esculent; starch is also made from it in large quantities.

The *chayote*, which, cooked in a certain way, is as good an imitation of apple-sauce as can be made, is an odd-looking fruit, resembling

Chayote

a big, rugged pear, growing on a vine which is very tender and graceful, and when twining itself around some cacao or plantain tree, has a very pretty appearance.

The *mamey* is also a curious fruit, of a peculiar shape, like a large sweet potato, with a rusty brown skin, which, when cut in two, displays one long, milky-white seed, and surrounding it the rich reddish-brown color of the fruit, resembling a nutmeg-melon. To my taste it is too "sickish," having no juice, but being of a dead-ripe flavor.

Mamey

The *sapote* is something on the same order, only different in shape and rather more palatable.

Here in the mountains I found that siesta-taking, after breakfast, prevailed, notwithstanding the fact that, even in the middle of the day, the sun is not too hot to go out in, except in the depth of summer.

In lieu of my siesta, while the rest of the household were dozing, I would frequently stroll off on foot, somewhere in the vicinity of the house, to sketch, always being sure, when seated on some log or rock, of having the companionship of one of the many beautiful lizards that

The critic

abounded, and that were so tame that they ran all about me, being perfectly harmless, too. One little fellow, whose portrait I give you here, amused me very much. I had taken up a comfortable position, with my back against a cocoa-nut tree, when this little fellow came running down the tree, and looked over my shoulders, apparently with the greatest eye to criticism. I turned my head to watch him better, but, as he did not seem to mind me, and kept perfectly quiet, I "took" him, with his bright, knowing look. Some of these lizards are perfectly beautiful, with their exceeding brilliancy of color, those with stripes of green and black across their back, and with little jet eyes, being charmingly pretty.

The *chameleon*, that we have heard so much about, it was not my good fortune to meet the whole time I was on the island. I was struck with the entire absence, also, of venomous insects and reptiles. The worst thing they have is the scorpion, whose bite, though not considered dangerous, is very painful. The "jigger," as it is vulgarly called, is an insect that often occasions more trouble to strangers than anything else, being a small insect that gets under the toe-nails, and, if not taken out, makes its nest, inflames the foot, and causes much pain; it can then only be removed with the knife. It is the custom, which all travelers will do well to follow while they are in the country, to wash the feet every night before going to bed.

"Monte de Verde" is, probably, the finest estate in this section of the country, being a very large and well-regulated property, situated in a lovely valley, 'midst surrounding hills. The house is large and handsome, with a beautiful flower-garden in its rear. The fruit and vegetable gardens are very large and very fine; and some attempts have been made to cultivate the strawberry, this being the only portion of the island where that berry is found. Here among the mountains it grows wild, though never very large. In fact, there are no berries such as we have, upon the island, as far as my experience goes.

There are one or two fine estates belonging to the Rousseau family, who at one time resided in the United States, and their places bear the familiar names of Virginia and Alabama.

The loveliest place, however, that I saw was the one known as the "Orangeries," which, high up among the mountains, was itself built upon a plateau, from whence an ascent to the top of the still higher hills was made. It was a fine stone house, built something in the style of some of the Swiss chalets, and finished in its interior with the beautiful polished wood of the country. It commands a splendid view of the adjacent mountains and the valley beneath.

Some of the roads around these different estates were very lovely. The light fell upon them, tempered by the thick, screening branches of the fragrant orange plants, the lovely jessamine, or the delicate heliotrope; while hanging temptingly within one's reach was the large and brilliant looking pomegranate, which here grows to a size as large as the orange.

Orangeries

To the naturalist, the botanist, or the artist, this section of country offers every inducement for a visit. Rare plants, curious insects, and superb and novel views meet one at every step. At the same house with me was stopping Mr. Cleinwerche, a Prussian artist of great talent, who had passed some time in various parts of the island, painting its striking scenes, which he informed me surpassed any he had ever seen in the many lands in which he had traveled. To his kindness I am indebted for the charming frontispiece of the "Rosario Falls," in western Cuba, painted by him.

Our afternoon rides were here always as agreeable as those of the morning; in fact there was no time during the day that it was not cool enough to exercise, either on foot or on horseback; and many were the rides we had to the house of some neighbor, where, stopping to dine, perhaps, we returned in the evening over mountain paths made bright for us by the rays of the moon, which added new beauties to the scene; or, if the moon did not favor us, there was always the bright peripatetic candle-bearer, the "*cucullo*," by whose brilliant light one can not only walk, but even read.

This insect is about the size of our roach, and has somewhat its appearance, being perfectly black, with two small, bright eyes in the back of its long head, on each side of which extend two small, sharp horns, or feelers. These two eyes, in connection with another in the point of its breast, are the live orbs that give out the bright light, the three together, when the insect has its wings spread, appearing in the dark nights as one brilliant, by the light of which one can see to read a letter. They are used, it is said, by anxious lovers, at their stolen nocturnal rendezvous; and it may be for this reason they are such great favorites with the ladies, who wear them in their belts, their hair, and under their thin, gauzy dresses, which they wear of an evening; the effect, as may be imagined, is as novel as it is beautiful. In some parts of the island they also make pets of them, by keeping them in little cages called "*cucuejeras*," feeding them on sugar-cane, and bathing them!

Cucullo

A wonderful natural curiosity I saw here, also, in the form of vegetable lace, made from the bark of a tree called "*guana*." A small piece of this, not larger than one's thumb, is taken, a thin slice cut from it and moistened in water; after which the women pull it with their hands, first one way and then the other, until it opens out into, apparently, the finest threads, looking exactly like the best mull. The ladies take this, embroider it, put an edging of real lace on it, and wear it for neckerchiefs.

There is one flower I was particularly struck with, known as the "Flor de Pascua" (*gatropha sanguifolia*), as well from its profusion as its great beauty. This is the special flower of Holy Week, from which it receives its name, from the fact that about this season it comes out in all its brilliancy of color. It is a simple bush, with the leaves growing in graceful clusters, which then become of a bright vermilion color; while the flower itself is of a most delicate cup or vase-like form (something in the shape of an Etruscan vase), the colors upon which are a most delicate gradation from white to rich pink. It has also the most exquisitely formed stamens. I have seen it but once in our hot-houses.

Flor de Pascua

I must confess to being disappointed in the number of birds of Cuba, or else I was not very fortunate in seeing them during my stay. At all events, I remarked frequently, in the woods, the absence of those sweet singing birds so numerous with us; and as I have read so much and heard so much of the brilliant plumage of the birds of the tropics, I was disappointed in not seeing them. Chirping-birds abound, and the most brilliant bird I saw was the *tocorroro*, a bird belonging to the woodpecker tribe.

In the country beyond these mountains of the Yateras, which is still a wilderness, there are, I am told, a great many attractions for the scientific man, in the large numbers of strange birds, insects, and reptiles.

This is the same district where, before the present troubles, runaway negroes, deserters, and convicts had collected, and uniting together for protection, were fortified in such a way in those wild mountain passes that it would have taken a large army to dislodge them; and although detachments of Spanish troops were sent in there to reconnoitre from time to time, it never resulted in anything, from the fact that they were not able to penetrate far without meeting resistance.

If the reader will examine a map of the island, he will find that this portion is elevated and mountainous, particularly that part lying east of Bayamo and Holguin; and here it is where what remains of the patriot army of Cuba has taken up its position,—with what future results remains to be seen.

It was the last of April before I left the Coffee Mountains, and the rainy season, as they call it, had then set in. This only added to my pleasure; for the rain, as far as I saw it, consisted of a splendid shower either once or twice a day, which had the effect of making the air even more bracing than before. Sometimes, in the middle of the day, it would rain for a couple of hours as though the very flood gates of heaven had broken open, and then, having exhausted itself, it would clear up, the sun would come out in new glory, and we would have a most beautiful afternoon and evening.

For the invalid traveler I can imagine no more perfect country or life than that of the Coffee Mountains of the Yateras. Breathing the purest of air, living luxuriously upon the astonishing profusion of natural supplies, enjoying a climate that from day to day and week to week does not vary a degree, and experiencing the exhilarating and invigorating effects of the constant exercise on fine horses that becomes a daily habit, the sick man needs to despair indeed if he is not recuperated by such a life as this. Unfortunately, unless he is recommended to some of the hospitable people of that section, there is no means of living, unless, indeed, he has a taste for "camping out," which, amid such scenes and in a climate like this, would be no hardship.

If, in some happy day for the Cubans, their island shall be blessed with a more liberal government and a more tolerant religion, which will be followed by a strong tide of emigration, these hills, mountains, and valleys of the Calderones and Yateras will be the chosen spots of the island; for here, with comparatively little expense and less trouble, can be made the most beautiful homes in the world for those fond of rural life and the beauties of nature.

As for me, the benefit I derived in health and strength, and the great pleasure I experienced from a short sojourn amidst the scenes and the people of the Yateras, have given me memories never to be forgotten, and I shall ever treasure them up as we treasure the fairy visions of our youth.

COFFEE GROWING

How few of us, as we sit in our cozy dining-rooms after
dinner, of a cold winter's day, sipping our *café noir*, think
or know of the trouble, the time, and the labor that is
taken, far off under the hot sun of the tropics, to give us
that little cup-full of mahogany-looking fluid; of the
sweat and the toil of its cultivation; of the processes,
machinery, and journeys necessary before it comes to
us.

Few of us, I ween, know whether it grows like corn
on a cob, or beans in a pod; and few there are who will
not be astonished when told that it grows and looks on the tree very
much like a cherry.

Although coffee is now grown, more or less, all over the Island of
Cuba, and at one time was as largely cultivated in the valleys and
plains as is at present the sugar-cane, yet now the portion of the island
where most of the coffee-raising is done is in the district and
neighborhood of Cuba, and in the jurisdiction of Guantanamo. Land
in this portion of the island has been so cheap that planters have
found it to their interest, as their old places became worn out, to sell
them, and come with their means to these beautiful hills, where the
climate was healthy, the crop of coffee better, and the land to be had
for a song.

In addition to this, coffee culture, for various reasons, has in some
degree declined, principally owing, it is said, to the United States
placing an almost prohibitory tariff on Cuban coffee in favor of Brazil,
which empire receives our flour and grain at a nominal tariff, while in
Cuba there has been always a tax upon our exports of that kind. Be
this as it may, it is certain that many of those who formerly planted
coffee now make sugar, partly because they can use their large
number of hands to greater advantage, and partly because, owing to

the uncertainty of the coffee crop, the price has varied from three to thirty dollars per hundred pounds.

The *cafetales* most noted for their richness and for the excellency of the fruit, one finds, as I have previously stated, in the range of mountains known as the Sierra Maestra, vicinity of Cuba, in the Vuelta Abajo, and in the districts of Alquizar and San Marcos. From the fact that these latter are old places, that have been established a long time, they are possessed of all that degree of elegance and magnificence for which they were originally celebrated; nevertheless, the mountains of Guantanamo are now considered the coffee regions of Cuba, and there the cultivation is on the increase, while in other places it has decreased rapidly.

After the *ingenios*, the *cafetales* are the most extensive agricultural establishments carried on in Cuba,—the latter exceeding the former generally in their handsome appearance and care. Their size varies from one hundred to one thousand acres, or even more in the mountains. The number of hands employed in the low country is as high as one hundred, but generally averages to every one thousand acres about fifty or sixty negroes.

The first coffee plantation was established in 1748, the seeds being brought from Santo Domingo by one Don José Gelabert, of whom it is related that it was his intention when he came to make only *aguardiente*. He established himself at a short distance from Havana, but the cultivation of coffee did not really commence until the arrival of the French *emigrés* from Santo Domingo, about 1795.

In addition to the cultivation of coffee, large amounts of rice, plantains, potatoes, cacao or chocolate, and all kinds of fruit are raised; the seeds being planted in the same fields with the coffee in order that the trees may eventually afford the shade which the coffee plant requires. The *guarda rayos*, or roads that lead up to the dwellings, are generally shaded by these plants, or by long rows of palm or cocoa, and in some cases a beautiful, graceful species of poplar, all of which form very charming avenues or drives.

The cafetal has also its *batey*, or square, like the *ingenio*, formed by the different buildings, which latter are not generally so extensive as on the sugar-estates, consisting of the *casa de vivienda*, or dwelling-house, the *tendales*, or store-houses, the *secaderos*, or stone terraces for drying the coffee, the stables, the negro quarters, and the coffee-house where the fruit is prepared, this being generally the largest of the structures. The number of subordinates required is small from the small number of hands employed; and although there are sometimes administrators to the *cafetales*, in general they are managed by the proprietor with the assistance of the *mayoral*, who may be white, but who is generally the most intelligent negro on the place. It is computed by some authorities that, in good seasons, a crop is produced in about the following proportions: To every two hundred and sixty-four acres, two hundred thousand trees can be planted, which will produce, on an average, sixty-two thousand five hundred pounds of coffee, which, at the rate of twenty-five dollars per bag of one hundred pounds, will give the nice little return of fifteen thousand dollars for the cultivation of over two hundred and sixty-four acres. From that, of course, have to be deducted the expenses, which vary according to locality and circumstances, or the number of hands employed.

In the past few years, owing to the gradually increasing scarcity of negroes, many improvements have been made in the use of labor-saving machines, some of which are worked by steam-power in lieu of the old-fashioned way of working by water-power.

Coffee is an evergreen shrub, with oblong, pulpy berries, which are at first green, then bright red, and afterwards purple. That portion of it used as the coffee of commerce, and which, when ground and boiled, we drink, is a secretion formed in the interior of the seed, and enveloping the embryo plant, for whose support it is destined when it first begins to germinate. It is raised from the seed when green or dried in the air and then planted in the ground, where it is left to grow for forty days, at which time the shoot appears, if the weather is favorable. The number of seeds planted in one hole is ten or a dozen, the holes being made with a knife or pointed iron. These are made in regular rows, being carefully marked out, with a space of four inches between each plant, and four and a half inches between each row. The shoots having begun to appear and gain size, are carefully and regularly weeded, about once a month, for two years; at the end of

Coffee field

which time those plants that have attained to the height of thirty inches are cropped. At the end of the third year, they begin bearing in small quantities; at the end of the fourth year, they are in full bearing, and continue giving good crops, if the land is good, for twenty-five or thirty years; at the end of the sixth or seventh year, they require pruning; and after ten years, they only bear good crops every alternate year.

At the end of February, the bearing plants begin to blossom, and, in cold places, even as late as March and April, continuing even up to June. Now is the time to see a coffee place in its beauty. Far as the eye can reach, is one vast sea of green, wax-like looking leaves, upon bushes the branches of which are now in their luxuriant growth, mingling one with another; and scattered over this sea of green are the beautiful white blossoms, looking, at a distance, like millions of snow-drops, or, on being closely examined, resembling a most delicate Maltese cross of milky wax. In bunches, as they cluster thick around the stem, they resemble the flower of the jessamine, possibly even more delicate.

Coffee blossom

It is hard to conceive anything more beautiful, particularly, if looking over head, you see the banana tree, with its clusters of green

Bud

and red and golden fruit peeping out from their large, green leaves. At the end of each bunch there is a curiously formed, acorn-shaped, and regal purple-colored bud or blossom. Add to this sight the red, yellow, and purple fruit of the cacao, and the rosy-cheeked pomegranate, and you have an idea of this land, flowing with milk and honey,— the milk, if you desire it, being found in the clusters of green cocoanuts that hang far above your head, 'neath the branches of the slender cocoa tree.

The coffee-blossom remains in flower about two days, and then are formed the berries, the size of gun-shot, until at maturity they attain the size and appearance of very small cherries, or, to be more exact, cranberries. This maturity is attained usually by the month of September, and the picking season then begins, although it is now the rainy season. As the berries are ripening all the time, the picking season lasts as late as November sometimes. If the months of July and August are dry months, with no rain, the berries become scorched with the hot sun. Coffee is a fruit which requires a genial but even temperature, there being hardly any possibility of its having too much rain.

Coffee plant

The picking is done by the hands on the place,—men, women, and children all going through the rows, each one with two bags and a basket (according to the capability of the hand), which they are required to fill during the day with the round, rich, red berry. Each of these berries contains two seeds, side by side, as you see it in the engraving. The bags being filled, are brought to the house on the backs of mules, and there received by the overseer, who measures the fruit for the purpose of seeing how much each negro has picked, and whether he has performed his proper amount of labor.

The best trees yield half a pound but the average is a quarter of a pound per tree. The berries are now ready for the pulping-mill (*molina de pilar*), which is a large wooden wheel, set vertically in a

Pulping mill

circular canal with ribbed or clinker-built wooden sides, in which are placed the berries for the purpose of having the rind taken off, the operation being performed by the wheel, which is worked either by steam or water power, passing over them. This apparatus generally occupies the lower floor of the coffee-house, usually a large frame or stone building.

The pulp is now placed in a large, dry, stone basin, of about the form and size of a small swimming bath, and allowed to remain there and ferment for twelve hours, for the purpose of more completely separating the rind and the beans; water is then let into the basin, and all the gum, which is a sort of slimy, mucous matter that in the old process deteriorated the coffee, is washed off.

Then the coffee is taken out of the water and placed in the secaderos, where the berries are spread out to dry in the warm rays of the sun, which they do in from seven to nine days, if there is no rain. These secaderos, or drying floors, are large stone basins, quadrangular in shape, about fifty or sixty feet long by twenty or thirty feet wide, arranged in a sort of terrace, side by side, and sometimes a dozen in number, the brow of the hill on which the dwellings stand being

Secaderos

usually selected to build them upon. They are about three feet from; the ground, built of stone, with plastered floors having an inclination from the centre to the sides, to drain off the water in case of rain, they being entirely uncovered, but having a stone wall around them about a foot high. Should it come on to rain while the berries are thus exposed, they are hurriedly swept up into large heaps in the centre, and over them is placed a sort of covering similar to a small wigwam, made of thatch or palm leaves, and impervious to water, there being two handles to lift them by. The moment it ceases to rain, the berries are spread out again until thoroughly dry. They are covered in the same way at night to protect them from the dew.

Each berry now resembles a round bean, or the kernel of a small hazel nut, having its exterior pellicle quite dry and dark-colored, in which state it is placed away in the store-house until the whole crop is gathered, each batch of green fruit undergoing the same process as fast as it comes in.

Now the preparing of the fruit for market takes place, the first operation of which is placing the dry berries again in the pulping-mill, the wheel of which, being put in motion, cracks off the dry skin, and the two grains of coffee fall out, just of the shape in which we see them for sale; thence, it is put in the f a n n i n g - m i l l , identically the same as that used by our farmers to separate the grain from the chaff.

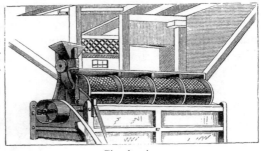

Circular sieve

Being now free from all extraneous substances, the beans are placed again in the pulping-mill for the purpose of being polished, or colored; for think not, O reader, that coffee comes to us of its natural color without a little "doctoring;" as to every thousand pounds of grain there is added half an ounce of lampblack, and the wheel now travels over and over it, until it assumes the fine green color it has when we get it. This is called the polishing process, and some planters use for the operation charcoal made of cedar wood; others, again, use soapstone and powdered white lead, according to the shade they wish to give it. For the European market, the latter is used, which gives the coffee a dark-grey color.

Now it is ready for the sorting-room, in which there is a circular sieve with several compartments of different sized wire, which, worked by machinery, revolves. From the room above, and directly over the sieve, there is a wooden box or pipe, leading down into a wooden funnel-shaped reservoir, for the purpose of conducting the grain from the room into the sieve, the quantity being governed by a wooden stopper in the side of the trough. The grain being placed in this reservoir, runs slowly into the revolving cylinder through an opening in its first compartment, and from thence into the others, being assorted in its passage through the different sized wires of the sieves into three kinds.

El caracolillo is the small round coffee, one grain of which only is found in each berry, and resembles the celebrated Arabian coffee, "Mocha," from which it also takes its name. This is the most prized, bringing usually a dollar or two extra per bag; its flavor is not really better than that of other coffee, except that the grain, being smaller and round, is more easily and thoroughly roasted; the bean also presents a much better appearance to the purchaser.

This small grain, strange to say, is supposed to be a disease in the coffee, as, generally from want of rain, or from some freak of nature, the grain appears in this stunted form. Great care is used in sorting so as to secure the best of coffee, free from dirt, pebbles, and decayed berries. This is done by the negro women picking over all the coffee. They are arranged on two sides of a long table, in a well-lighted room, used

Coffee sorters

expressly for this purpose. It is quite a novel sight to see twenty or thirty of these women in their oddities of dress, or even the scarcity of it, picking away from the great piles of beans before them, and filling huge baskets with the bright green grain, keeping up all the time a monotonous chanting, in which each one takes a part, interrupted now and then by a stranger, like myself, whose advent is an era in the lives of these out-of-the-world people, and who immediately address him with: "*Da me medio, maitre*" (give me five cents, master).

The second quality of coffee, called *el primer*, or *lavado* (first or washed), is that of which the largest quantities are made, being the coffee in its usual size, of two grains to the berry, sound and large. The third quality is the poorer or refuse coffee, the most of which is retained upon the place and used or sold at a low price for domestic consumption. The fine Caracolillo coffee is very carefully re-sifted and picked over by some specially skillful hand. One old fellow I saw at it was up in the corner of the room, with an enclosure on the floor to contain the piles of grain. Hanging from the ceiling was the sieve, a small, square box, sustained by cords, which the sharp old fellow could move backward and forward without sustaining the weight of the material himself, as in the ordinary sieve. A lively, singing old fellow he was, and it was worth a *pourboire* to hear his "*bonjour, maître.*" The coffee being now ready for market, is placed in strong canvas bags, in which we see it, and each one of which contains about one hundred and seven pounds. It is then forwarded to the commission merchant in the town, to be sold for account of the owner, or is sometimes bought outright by the merchants.

Coffee sifter

The transporting of the coffee to market is a business of itself, and is generally carried on by some native Indian, the owner of large numbers of mules, though on some of the estates where horses are plenty the proprietors send down their own trains. These consist of

Pack horse

from a dozen to thirty or forty horses or mules, which have upon their backs the most old-fashioned, useless packs that can be made, being simply huge walls of straw, sometimes covered with canvas, rarely leather, roughly put together, and retained upon the horses by girths and ropes, or canvas breeching, which sometimes are fancifully decorated with fringe, as is also the head stall, particularly of the leader, who has also a string of bells upon his neck, Spanish muleteer fashion. Upon these rude pack-saddles the coffee is strapped, a bag on each side, over which a cloth or matting of the palm is thrown, to keep it from the rain. Each train is now arranged with the head of one horse tied to the tail of the one in front of him, the guide and his assistant mount their horses, and the train is started down the mountain to the village.

It is quite a novel as well as pretty sight to see these trains taking their way down the hill-side; the long line of mules, with their curious burdens, winding in and out the romantic road, the gay appearance of the leader, the musical sound of his bells, and the shouts of the *muleteros*, all serve to make up a picture strange and interesting.

The price paid for this kind of transportation is one dollar for every two bags carried twenty miles,—an item that, with a large crop, becomes heavy in the course of the year; but there is no other way, as no wheeled vehicles can get up the mountains in the present state of their roads, the entire travel of this district being on horse or muleback.

In connection with coffee, I may as well give here a few hints about the proper disposition of coffee for domestic use, based upon the experience of these planters, who grow and use it, and therefore

Transporting coffee

understand its peculiarities thoroughly.

Much more depends upon the manner of roasting and making the coffee than upon the quality of the bean. The taste of raw coffee is somewhat sweetish, but the application of heat in the process of roasting produces important changes.

The roasting should take place in a close, revolving iron cylinder, over a clear but moderate fire, and should not be carried too far. When the beans have acquired a bright chestnut color (not black or very dark brown), the roasting should be discontinued, and the beans should then be cooled quickly by tossing in the air. The mill in which they are ground should also be closely covered.

Another important point is that the beverage should be prepared as soon as possible after the roasting, which, in private families, ought to take place at least once or twice a week; in a longer time than that the aroma is dissipated, and the liquid when made is deficient in strength and clearness. The use of the white of an egg, egg-shells, or fish-skin, to clarify it, is decidedly objectionable,—clearness being thus secured but at the expense of strength. One can always have a cup of coffee from the native Cubans in perfection, though the French, as a people, make it equally good. A cup of coffee is a courtesy that the farmer usually extends to his visitor when he enters his house.

As has been before said, the coffee plant is not the only one cultivated upon the *cafetales*, for there are several others, whose

Cacao tree

culture, in connection with coffee, is even now a very profitable one, and is becoming more so with each year's growth. First on the list is the *cacao*, or chocolate tree. Of these there are three kinds and colors,— the *caraccas*, which is red; *guayaquil*, which is purple; and the *criollo*, or Cuban, which is yellow in its rinds.

The fruit grows upon trees somewhat resembling dwarf pear-trees in size and appearance, the leaves being longer and pointed. Where the plants get a good growth, they reach as high as six or eight feet, being propagated by the dried seed.

They do not commence to bear until about the fifth year, when a few beans are produced; the quantity increasing each year, and the plant bearing all the year round, being an evergreen.

The appearance of the fruit upon the tree is most singular, as, instead of being in clusters or growing entirely upon the branches, it may be seen growing up the trunk, attached by its single stem, without leaves, and even resting upon the ground, so near does it grow to the roots. That which hangs upon the branches is isolated in the same way.

The fruit is a large capsule, something of the size and shape of the mango, though different in color, and having within it the chocolate beans, which number about twenty-five seeds to each capsule, though I brought one with me containing forty,—not an unusual number. When ripe, these capsules are broken open, and the seed taken out; the pulp surrounding them is very sweet and pleasant to the taste. In this form, it presents the curious appearance, if carefully divided in the centre of the fruit, of two cups; the one half opening like a lid, and the other, containing the beans, in a sort of

pine-apple from, the glutinous
white seeds being in regular rows,
joined together with a sort of
vegetable matter, in the interstices,
the top of which forms a delicate,
ivory-looking antler, if I may so call
it.

Fruit of cacao

The seeds are now dried, and
placed in piles,—this taking place in June and December; they are
then allowed to ferment three or four days, during which stage some
planters add to the heap red lead, others red ochre, to give the seeds
a rich, red color,—their natural one being a brown, nearly black; they
are then passed through the sieves. Dried in this state, the bean has
rather a bitter, mealy taste, and looks something like a good-sized
almond, though darker in color.

The culture of this fruit pays exceedingly well in good soil, the
best qualities selling as high as seventeen dollars per one hundred
pounds, and the common grades, twelve and thirteen,—the
cultivation of it requiring very little time or labor.

Large quantities of the chocolate are manufactured in Cuba into
bon-bons, they being the favorite confection with the ladies. Its name,
chocolate, it is said, comes from the Mexican word *chocolalt*, the name
given the tree in that country. The simplest and best form of using it
is by taking the seeds, roughly crushed, termed cocoa-nibs, and
boiling them two hours. When the chocolate is to be manufactured,
the beans, after being carefully picked so as to free them from
extraneous matter, are gently roasted over a fire, in an iron cylinder
with holes in the ends to allow the vapor to escape. When the aroma
begins to be distinctly perceptible, the process is considered
complete. After being cooled, and fanned from their husks, they are
put into a crushing-mill, made of a revolving iron roller in a copper
canal, on the same principle as the coffee-polisher, and ground to
powder; after which, the powder is made into paste and packages, or,
perfumed and flavored, into sugar-plums. This operation can be seen
in any of the *confiterias* (confectioneries) of Havana.

The beverage of chocolate as made in Cuba is very rich and

nutritious, and a *demi tasse* is quite breakfast enough to take many hours of exercise on.

But the fruit or vegetable that bears the most important relation to the agricultural labors of Cuba is the *platano*, or, as known amongst us by its French name, the banana, taking as it does the place of bread with the working people. Of this plant, some authorities say, there are as many as twenty-six varieties; others, again, only six. Be that as it may, there are a great many similar fruits with different tastes and names, though, I suspect, all belonging to the same family.

The plantain is an exotic, having been produced, it is said, from the plants brought from more temperate climes. At all events, it is at present known in various parts of the world, and is grown in great quantities in some of the East Indies. The most common, which is known by the botanical name of *musa paradisiaca*, in allusion by botanists to its being the supposed forbidden fruit, is the only one that is eaten roasted in lieu of bread, for which it is said to be an excellent substitute, more particularly in warm climates, where it is considered lighter and more digestible. This constitutes the principal food of the negroes on the sugar and coffee estates. Under its name of *platano*, it is the largest of the banana species, of a long form, green looking externally, and with a hard, white body like a turnip, growing in large clusters that weigh as much as eighty pounds. *Los chicos*, or *hembras*, are a smaller kind, and somewhat more delicate, which, about half ripe, are very delicious fried, being met with upon every Cuban table.

The platano, *par excellence*, though, is the banana, as we will insist upon calling it, of the smaller kind, which is looked upon as simply fruit much improved by cultivation and care. These bananas are small, generally of a golden, yellow color, or delicate red, with a flesh that has the appearance of the finest yellow butter, and that melts in the mouth like marmalade, the skin being easily stripped off. There are varieties known as the *Guinea, Orinoco, dato* (date), *manzana* (apple), etc.; the first being, to my taste, of the most delicate flavor, though they are all delicious, and such as we never see in this country, being too delicate for export.

The tree is planted in long rows, in fields by itself, or amongst the coffee. It often grows wild on the sides of the hills, and sprouts in various unlooked for spots, reaching to a height of nine or ten feet, and bears even when it only appears to be a bush five feet in height. It has long, broad, and curiously formed leaves that are very beautiful in their shape, the trunk and branches being quite slender, and in their appearance not calculated to bear the weight of the enormous branches one sees on some of them. It flourishes best in rich soil, for in poor, sandy places it flowers, but produces no fruit.

Still another tree, important not only as shade for the coffee, but for the thousand and one uses it is put to besides, is the cocoanut tree, known by the Cubans as *los cocos*. This is peculiar to all tropical climates, and bears a large and important share in sustaining the life of the lower-classes, negroes, etc., to whom it supplies milk, food, shade, thatch, buckets, brooms, baskets, etc. From the juice of the stem they get a species of wine, which they make into ardent spirits; from the fruit they get their cups, lamps, and oils. The meat of the green fruit made into a *dulce* or preserve, for the tables of the upper-classes, is the most delicious preserve I ever ate, and the milk, drank from the fresh cocoanut

cocoanut palm

knocked off the tree in early morning, is delicious as nectar, and said to be more wholesome.

These trees are seen everywhere on the island,—on the tops of the mountains, in the valleys, their very roots washed by the sea on the coast, or struggling for subsistence round the small patches of sandy soil on the lonely, rocky keys of the southern ocean,—always attractive, always graceful, forming a marked feature in the landscape. They grow like the palm (of which they are, in fact, a species), to the height of sixty or ninety feet, their branches shooting out from the top like beautiful plumes. Their stems are of a soft, fibrous nature, marked on the outside by rings produced by the falling off of their leaves. Two such leaves are said to drop off annually, and consequently the age of an individual tree is reckoned as equal to half the number of the annular scars on its stem.

The fruit grows high up on the stem, generally just where the branches join it, and numbers as many as eighty to one hundred nuts per tree annually.

As the cocoanut-tree gets older, it seems to get shorter, the trunk

Cocoanut tree

thickens, and has rings marked round it in the most peculiar manner, while the large pieces of brown, fibrous bark, resembling coarse canvas cloth, peel off, and hang down, one over the other, in numerous and graceful folds.

The leaves of the palm and of the cocoa differ, though having the same general appearance at a distance. On close examination, the cocoa will be found to have its leaves regularly placed in an even row on the branch, while the palm alternates,—one above and the other below.

The above sketch, in which I am not sure that I have presented the exact number of rings, is that of a very old tree, standing in its place beyond the memory of any inhabitant in the vicinity.

Ah, well, dear reader, my time is up, our pleasant sauntering days are over in the Yateras, and so I take my leave of my kind friends, and, in company with my artist-friend, ride down the mountain into the lower world, with many regrets that the happy days we have passed so near heaven are over.

It only wanted the novel departure we made from Santa Catalina to complete my romantic memories of the Coffee Mountains, and this was accomplished, after a farewell dinner with our kind host, McKinley, on a hand-car, by moonlight, to Guantanamo, being propelled by two sturdy negroes, who, for one hour and twenty minutes, never ceased to ply the crank that brought us finally the distance of sixteen miles.

Moonlight ride

We went on board the boat awaiting us, and daybreak found us once more in the heavier atmosphere of Santiago de Cuba.

chapter thirty-eight

FROM CUBA TO NUEVITAS, VIA NORTH COAST

Blockade-runner; Cumberland bay; Wild coast scenery; The Alpha and Omega of Columbus; Cape Maisi under difficulties; Baracoa the oldest town; Odd place; Pine-apples and cocoa-nuts; Peculiar manner of traveling; Curious walking-sticks; Easy life on steamboat; A Cuban swell; A devoted mother; Jibara; Holguin; Shipping platanos; "He is the Devil"; Priests; Funny baptism; Pretty children; Caspar Hauser; Devout priests; Columbus' description of the coast off Nuevitas.

As I have mentioned elsewhere, there is a line of steamers that leaves Santiago de Cuba, two or three times a month, passing around the eastern end of the island and by the north coast to Havana, making stoppages at various towns on the coast.

Arriving at Santiago, I was fortunate in finding that a steamer would leave within two hours; so, going immediately on board, I secured my stateroom, and at eight o'clock in the morning, after having said my *adios* to the kind friends in the town, I took my farewell of Santiago de Cuba.

The "Triunfo" was the name of the boat upon which I had taken passage, and which I found to be an iron-clad steamer, having been built in Scotland for a blockade-runner, during our war, and afterwards sold to the Spaniards.

The boat was good enough, with a good table and fair state-rooms, barring a roach or rat or two, but, as "Toots" would say, "it was of no consequence."

The passengers comprised a lot of young priests, on their way to Puerto Principe, a naval engineer, a Cuban "swell," who put the "aw aw" in his Spanish in true Cockney style, and a lot of women, among whom was a perfect lady, I was told, who rather staggered my ideas on that point, as well as shocked *my modesty*, by parading her *niña*, of a year old, upon the deck, every fine day, in a state of perfect nudity.

We had a fine view of the hills around the bay of Guantanamo, one of the finest harbors on the south coast; large quantities of sugar and coffee are

Cuban "swell"

shipped there from the village of Santa Catalina.

After passing here, the breeze which had been blowing already pretty strong freshened into a gale, the sea becoming rather rough, so that I soon found myself looking at the water in a very peculiar way, the mountains on shore appearing to be very unsteady, notwithstanding they were so high and majestic and grandly beautiful even, with the storm clouds gathering around them in inky masses. I held out until we reached Cape Maisi, the most easterly point of the island, as it is something to see a place that so great a man as Columbus thought, when he first saw it, was the eastern extremity of Asia, and upon which he conferred the name of Alpha and Omega,— the beginning and the end; and it certainly was the Omega of my stay on deck for some hours.

After seventeen hours sail from Cuba, we made Baracoa, a small town on the extreme north-east coast of Cuba. A very pleasant place seemed the quiet, land-locked waters of its bay to me, though the harbor is not a large one, and has a rather bad and narrow entrance.

Baracoa is a town that would interest very much an American antiquarian, from the fact of its being the first town founded on the island of Cuba; otherwise it has not much to recommend it.

Cape Maisi under difficulties

This was a favorite place with Columbus, who visited it on his first voyage, and, in writing to his sovereigns, speaks of it under the name of Puerto Santo; and in giving, in glowing words, descriptions of the surrounding scenery, makes use of the following, which will apply to-day to many other points of the island:

> "The amenity of this river through which the sand at the bottom may be seen; the multitude of palm-trees of various forms, the highest and most beautiful I have ever met with, and an infinity of other great and green trees; the birds in rich plumage, and the verdure of the fields, render this country, most Serene Princes, of such marvellous beauty, that it surpasses all others in charms and graces, as the day doth the night in lustre. I have been so overwhelmed at the sight of so much beauty that I have not known how to relate it."

The town, however, was settled in 1512 by Diego Velasquez, who gave it the name of "Nuestra Señora de la Asuncion" (Our Lady of the Assumption), made it the capital of the island, called it a city, fixed his residence there, appointed civil officers, and erected the town into a bishopric. It is said, also, that the first cathedral in the

Baracoa

island was built there in 1518, but was removed, in 1823, to Santiago de Cuba. The place now contains about three thousand inhabitants, and retains its old Indian name of Baracoa. It is surrounded by an abrupt range of mountains, known as the hills of Sagua and of Baracoa, being part of the Sierra Nisse range.

At the summit of these there is a volcanic cavity, in the form of a crater, of great depth, but of which the strata, it is said, do not appear of volcanic origin. There are, also, some strange caves in the vicinity, in which Indian relics have been found.

The town is at present famous for being a shipping point for immense quantities of pine-apples, bananas, and cocoa-nuts; and at certain seasons, the bay is alive with fast-sailing craft, seeking their cargoes.

There is only the usual *fonda y posada* here; and unless the traveler has friends in the place, or is here on business, he will find that the time allowed him between the arrival and the departure of the boat is all that he will care to spend here. If, however, he remains longer, he may be sure of seeing something novel, interesting, or laughable,—a remark which applies to every place in Cuba. Thus, by going a short distance outside of Baracoa, one can see the magnificence of the primeval tropical forests, the fragrant and shady roads, or the ludicrously odd appearance of some of their travelers.

Here, for instance, is a favorite mode of progression in this part of the island, where sometimes horses are too scarce to be had, and roads too heavy for carts or volantes: The *paisano* takes one of his cattle out of the corral, puts a saddle on its back, and running a small cord through its nostrils, has a solid and substantial, if not very fast, conveyance.

At Baracoa, also, the *connoisseur* in canes can indulge his fancy by securing a walking-stick made from the skin of the *manati*, or sea horse or lion, as it is indiscriminately called, which frequents this part of the island.

These canes are made from the dried skin of this animal, prepared in some peculiar way which makes it very tough and strong. Some of them, when properly prepared, are perfectly transparent, and, if made thin, are quite as serviceable as a rapier for protection, as

Cattle riding

well as for use as a walking-stick. Mounted in gold and silver, they cost from an *onza* upwards, according to the way in which they are finished. In Havana, if you meet with them at all, they cost as high as forty to fifty dollars.

Another very beautiful cane is that made, in some of these coast-places, from the shell of the *carey*, a species of turtle. The shell is boiled into a thin liquid, and a strong stick, of the proper length, is dipped into the material, and allowed to cool. This process is repeated several times, until the proper degree of thickness is gained, when the coating is allowed to become hard. The stick is then polished, and after being handsomely headed and ferruled, is ready for market. For the handsomest of these, having the appearance of tortoise-shell, the price is from four to five dollars.

Distant twelve hours' sail from Baracoa is the rather new and promising port of Jibara, the port of an interior town known as Holguin, with which it is connected by a *camino real* (royal road).

The steamer usually stops there a whole day, either to deliver or to receive her cargo, affording thereby a fine chance to go ashore and see the town and vicinity; though I cannot say that the place offers any very great attractions.

Jibara

The bay is very beautiful, and very capacious, though not deep enough to permit vessels to come up to the wharves; so they are compelled to anchor some distance off, and be loaded by means of lighters.

The entrance to the bay is guarded by a ridiculously small fort that keeps up a show of being armed with two or three guns; but a four hundred pound shot, I should think, would move it bodily into town from the narrow point of land on which it is situated.

Having been ashore and exhausted the wonders of the place, I took a small sail-boat and cruised about the bay, enjoying the very perfection of nature in the limpid waters, the wondrous atmosphere, and the supremely blue sky.

Gracious Heavens! what a very demoralizing climate and country this is to a lazily disposed man, with the slightest inclination to romance,—there are so many ways "not to do it," that, in spite of the best resolutions, there is no resisting the influences of an awning spread on deck, a cool *refresco*, and a fragrant cigar, even though the lovely scenes around tempt one to take up his pencil for a sketch. I think I accomplished much in the accompanying one of Jibara; particularly as I heard a country-woman (*paisana*), after looking over my shoulder, and punching her husband, exclaim, as she jerked her thumb towards me, "*Es un demonio!* " (he is the devil). Flattering, that; but she didn't know I understood her, else she wouldn't have been so polite.

The steamer was receiving a large cargo of the *platanos*, which are sent from here to Havana in great quantities, being bought for the extremely low price of from seventy-five cents to one dollar and twenty-five cents per hundred; while on the south coast at many places the people won't even take the trouble to pick them for market, the price is so low.

Most of the passengers having gone ashore, I took a stroll, too, through the town, dropping into some of the stores and chatting with the people, evidently much to their gratification, as they don't often see strangers from "beyond the seas." On my way across the plaza, which fronts the church, I found quite a party assembled at the church-door, which they seemed to have some trouble in opening, as the rusty old lock wouldn't work; so they "fixed" it by using a hammer, which did it effectually. Curious to see what was going on, I joined the party, among whom I found our fellow-voyagers, the young priests, as well as a venerable *padre*, who, bowing to me as a stranger, politely invited me in. I went, but my politeness and gravity had a severe shock, both finally succumbing. It was a baptismal party,—the mother and father, the church sexton, the three young priests, and the *padre*,—the latter of whom had evidently been persuaded by one of the young priests to let him "do it." The father took the child in his arms, while the mother went strolling off, in happy indifference, with a female friend, to examine the church, the rest of the party all gathering around the font. I was prepared for a serious ceremony, in which I was disappointed. Priest number one took the prayer-book and attempted to read the service, it being evident that this was his first effort; priest number two tried to seize the book, making an awful "jabber;" and to finish it, priest number three pushed the other two aside, and snatching the book, endeavored to find the place. Meanwhile the child had become restless in the arms of the patient father, and the business-like little sexton, becoming disgusted, pushed the priests aside, and went on with the ceremony himself.

The putting of the holy wafer in the mouth of the child, however, was too much for it, and it "broke" into noisy sounds, the climax being reached when the holy water was freely shaken on its little head from the silver rose in the sexton's hand; for the child struck out with head, feet, and hands, finishing instanter the "ceremony," to which its loud cries were a fitting anthem. *Cosa de Cuba!*

Baptism in Cuba is not always, however, such a primitive affair, as, particularly in Havana and the larger towns, it is attended with a great deal more of display and ceremony.

It is the custom for the godfather of the new-born child not only to pay the expenses of an entertainment, and himself give a ball or merry-making, but to distribute pieces of gold and silver money, appended to a silver ribbon, to all the family of the godchild, the friends, and the invited guests. These pieces of money must be silver half-dollars and gold dollars. To the mother of the baptized is given (in gold) a doubloon, ounce, or half-ounce. As it is necessary to pierce a hole in each piece through which to pass the silken cord, this custom confines to the country a certain amount in circulation of the pierced coin, since, as it will not pass current elsewhere, no one will take it away. "Pity it is," exclaims a Cuban author, "that there are not a thousand baptisms each day, and then would be circulated plenty even of ten cent pieces and quarters pierced."

It is expected that the godfather will provide a decent conveyance, if there is not one belonging to the house, since it would not be genteel to go on foot to the church, though it were very near. From this it will be seen the position of godfather is no sinecure, and, naturally, well-to-do ones are chosen.

A curious fact that scientific investigation has disclosed in reference to births on the island, made upon examination of the baptismal records (since, within fifteen days, usually, of child-birth, baptism takes place), is that the months of November and December are most prolific in births; and, arguing from that fact, the months most favorable to conception are February and March. For similar reasons, the months of September and October are least favorable, thereby showing that logical nature extends even to these latitudes the general laws of the colder north.

While the steamer was lying at Jibara, there came off to dinner a gentleman from the interior, with his two sweet little daughters. *En passant*, the children of Cuba are usually perfectly beautiful,—the girls full of grace and strange dignity, for those so young, while the boys are bright-eyed, quick little fellows, and very intelligent. This gentleman had brought his daughters to see the ocean and a steamer.

Imagine their delight; and when they saw the ice served at dinner, for the first time in their little lives, they were puzzled indeed. I prevailed upon my pretty *vis-à-vis* to take a piece in her fingers; but she quickly dropped it, with the Casper-Hauser-like remark that "it burnt" her.

They left us before we started, highly delighted with what they had seen, and much to my regret; for the oldest had been very talkative, telling me she knew all about the United States, for her geography said it was "a big world." My *"Adios, chiquitas mias,"* was met by a prettily-said *"Gracias, Señor Americano"*.

We are off at last, with our cargo of *platanos* piled even on deck in large crates, the steamer keeping well off the coast to avoid the bars which are numerous here.

The young priests had all come on board together, and amused me very much. They were, with one exception, quite a jolly lot, who smoked their cigars and took their rum as well as any of us; and they sauntered about the deck amongst the women as though they liked it.

The exception was a more steady fellow, looking up the back-sliders, and, when evening came, getting the others together for vespers, when they would all assemble, produce their prayer-books, and fall to muttering and mumbling at a most rapid gait. Sometimes they were so late getting at it that dusk would overtake them before they were through, and the steady one would propose to go below for lights. Bang would go the books of my baptismal friends, with, perhaps, the exclamation: "Enough, enough,—it is night-time now;" whereat they would all knock off, and call it "done."

Towards ten o'clock in the morning we make the bay of Nuevitas, eight hours' sail from Jibara. The entrance to this bay forms a narrow *cañon* of from four to five and a half miles long, forming two bays within its limits, one properly called Nuevitas and the other Mayanabo, into each of which empty two rivers. There are some prominent islands in it, known as *"Los Ballenatos"* (young whales).

What a glorious morning it is, as we come in sight of this superb Bay of Nuevitas!—the very perfection of a May-day; but such a May-day as few northern eyes have ever seen, with the brightness of the verdure, and the purity of the wondrous atmosphere and sky. And then the water,—it is so hard to resist the temptation of its sparkling clearness and depth, and of its seductively cool appearance, and not make a dash overboard. Irving, in describing the feelings of Columbus on arriving off this very spot, says: "Columbus was struck with its magnitude and the grandeur of its features; its high and airy mountains, which reminded him of those of Sicily; its fertile valleys, and long, sweeping plains, watered by noble rivers; its stately forests, its bold promontories, and stretching headlands, which melted away into the remotest distances." But we have entered the bay, which

Nuevitas

Puerto Principe

gradually opens out into an immense land-locked sheet of water. On its extreme southern side lies the small town of Nuevitas itself, with its few white-walled houses glaring in the morning sun. The bay is said to be the second one in size on the island, containing within its area a space of fifty-seven square miles, though its depth is not very great.

On the 14th of November, 1492, Columbus anchored in this bay, to which he gave the name of Puerto Principe, erecting a cross upon a neighboring height in token of possession, and passing a number of days in exploring the collection of beautiful islands in the vicinity, since known as "El Jardin del Rey," or the King's Garden. This, it is said, was the foundation of the town of Nuevitas, which was originally known as Santa Maria, but it was not until 1513 that a permanent settlement was made under Diego Velasquez, when the principal town was removed to the Indian village Caonao, and soon afterwards to the town of Camaguey, now known by its name of Puerto Principe. Nuevitas, a town of about six thousand inhabitants, gets its importance simply from the fact that it is the port of entry for the city of Puerto Principe, situated in the interior, at forty-five miles distance.

As a modern town, it made its commencement in 1819, under the name of San Fernando de Nuevitas. It is a growing little place, and is becoming the depot of shipment of a good deal of the sugar and molasses of the neighborhood, as well as of large quantities of hides. As the war in its vicinity has been long continued, and the port has some times been separated from Puerto Principe by the patriots, it may now have grown into greater importance as the point of supplies for that district in which the Spanish army operates.

There is also an interesting branch of commerce pursued here, though not amounting to a very large trade. This is the sponge and turtle-fishing, carried on by almost an entirely distinct set of people from those ashore. The sponges are those mostly used on the island, and a rough calculation estimates the annual production at one hundred thousand dozen, worth one dollar per dozen, which is quite a business for a people who carry it on as they do. The turtle-shell is prepared usually for export, the meat being sent to the markets of the

Sponge-fisher's houses

vicinity in which the turtles are caught. It is quite an amusing sight to see the habitations of these people, dotting some portions of the bay; and as it is almost perpetual summer, their life is not a very unpleasant one. The accompanying illustration gives a better idea of their dwellings than any description, and in these their owners live all the year round.

Puerto Principe is connected with Nuevitas by a railroad forty-five miles long, and usually there were two trains a day, between the two places; but as there has been great trouble on this road, caused by the attacks of the patriots, it is probable that their running is now very irregular.

Puerto Principe is, probably, the oldest, quaintest town on the island,—in fact, it may be said to be a finished town, as the world has gone on so fast, that the place seems a million years old, and, from its style of dress, a visitor might think he was put back almost to the days of Colon.

The road to the town runs through a fine, rolling country, affording many beautiful views; and from the hills around the place itself, not only the town, but the neighboring country, can be seen to advantage. But may heaven help you, O stranger! if you wander to

Puerto Principe without having some friends to depend on; for, city as it is of nearly seventy thousand inhabitants, it boasts not of an hotel, and even the *fondas* are wretched. It is, probably, for this reason that the Cubans, as a people, are so hospitable that they will not allow their friends to go to hotels, and even to strangers who have been presented to them they insist on showing this attention.

Lest I be misunderstood in relation to this matter, I wish to say that it is the custom in Cuba for one friend visiting the town of another friend to stay with him at his house, the kindness being returned as occasion demands; and no one having the slightest claim to a courtesy of this kind need hesitate to accept it, either on the plantations or in the interior towns. This can be done without fear of disturbing the hospitable household of the host, for he gives you what he has himself, and, as a general thing, every one in Cuba lives in a free, open-handed way, with abundance of rooms, servants, and an extremely profuse table. In many cases, too, it is as much a kindness to the giver of the invitation to accept it as for him to extend it, for the simple reason that there is not much travel or intercourse on the island, and the stranger, whether from some other part of the island or from abroad, has news to impart, a novelty to give, or business to transact with his host. The stranger may be sure the courtesy is sincere when extended with, "Frankly, Señor, I wish you to stay with me, and I shall order your baggage to my house."

Santa Maria del Puerto Principe is situated in the heart of the grazing country, from which business it derives its importance. Its streets are narrow and tortuous, many of them entirely unpaved and without sidewalks; its buildings comprise houses of *mamposteria*, several queer old churches, various convents, large quarters for the troops, a tolerable theatre, and a fine lot of public buildings for government officers. The general style of architecture, though Cuban, offers many peculiarities to the artist or antiquarian.

This town has always been looked upon with suspicion by the authorities on account of the strong proclivities its people had for insurrection; and its sons have had a greater or smaller share in almost every revolution that has taken place in the island. It has now received its baptism of blood in the cause of liberty for "free Cuba," having sustained a siege, been attacked and almost starved out,—to what effect, as yet, deponent knoweth not; but many changes in its people have doubtless taken place since he was there.

Although there is not much in the actual town to occupy the traveler, the surrounding country affords fine opportunities for studying some peculiarities of the island not so advantageously seen elsewhere as here. First among these are the *potreros*.

Potrero, in the Castilian, really means a horse-herd, a pasture-farm; but in the Cuban dialect, it has a somewhat different meaning. In the early days of Cuba, when land was plenty and the government liberal in the disposition of it, they called all grounds or properties, whether belonging to the crown or to private persons, used for the purpose of sheep-folds or cattle-herding, *haciendas* or *hatos*. These were large extents of ground, of circular form, with a radius of over nine thousand yards, the centre of which only was marked out, where the pens and buildings were usually erected. The *corral* was also a circular tract, one-quarter the above size, that is to say, with a radius of four thousand five hundred yards, intended for the care of smaller cattle, sheep, pigs, etc.; its centre being also marked by the hog-pen, or the fences of the sheep-folds.

Owing to the difficulty of always laying out the exact lines, (caused by the location of woods), the surveyors adopted the method of describing polygons, with a large number of sides, each of which was equivalent to so many yards. The spaces left between these polygons, almost circular, were considered as the property of the crown, and were known as *realengos*. But as time advanced, and the government kept on increasing these gifts, without any particular reference to the line of demarcation in the land, many centres of the new farms or folds were fixed in such a manner that, in drawing their boundary-lines according to their radii, they cut those already established, one new circle falling within an old one, creating thereby inextricable confusion, which ended in every man going to law with his neighbor about his boundary-lines; and from this came the belief that every Cuban had a farm and a lawsuit.

Many of these tracts were then, by the decision of the court, divided, and afterwards, by the will of their owners, sub-divided into small lots, appropriated for the various uses of cultivating grain, raising cattle, and fruits, while others were again cut up and laid out in town lots.

Out of these divisions came all the different rural establishments known as cattle farms, farms proper, and small truck-gardens, and which, under the names of *potrero*, *hacienda*, *hato*, *ganado*, *finca*, and *estancia*, bother the stranger or the student of Cuban life.

The largest of all the above is the *potrero*, where cattle are raised, fed, and looked after with care; while in the *corrales* they are left to run wild in every direction, getting water from the running brooks, and only attended to, from time to time, by the *sabaneros* or *monteros*.

But the *potreros* are large places, encircled by walls of stone piled up, or stone-fences. Not only the cattle of the place are taken care of, but those also belonging to neighboring *ingenios*, or farms, are fed and attended to.

The raising of cattle is a very profitable business indeed, particularly as no attention is paid to the fattening of beef, but the cattle are sold just as they are thought to be fit for market. The consequence is, that it is rarely indeed that a piece of beef fit to roast is seen,—at least as we know it.

View of a potrero

It is a great sight to see these immense herds of cattle, scattered over extensive plains, with here and there large clumps of palm or cocoa trees affording shade, while, at regular intervals, long stone walls serve to separate the herds. Many of the fiercest bulls used in the bull-ring come from this district; and when so noted upon the play-bill, an audience is sure to be attracted by the superior "sport" they offer.

As cattle-raising plays a very important part in the sum-total of the business interest of the island, it may not be amiss to give some few facts from late authorities. The prices, of course, vary in different years, but a fair average can be obtained by comparing several years' reports. Oxen, twenty-five to forty dollars. Bulls, twenty to thirty dollars. Cows, twenty to thirty dollars. Calves, ten to twelve dollars. Sheep are cheap, being sold at from one to three dollars. Hogs, eight to ten dollars.

In 1827, there were three thousand and ninety-eight *potreros*, and in 1846, four thousand three hundred and eighty-eight; which is about forty per cent increase,—equal to two per cent per annum. So that at present there must be between five and six thousand of these places.

Valuing the cattle at the lowest of the above prices, and calculating from various reports as to the number of such on the island, it is estimated there is represented, by the stock of these cattle-places and at the sugar and coffee estates and smaller farms, a capital of twenty-one millions of dollars. This is exclusive of horses and mules, too, of which there are large numbers raised upon the island, the value of which is estimated at two millions of dollars.

At one time, camels were introduced into the island, in the hope that they would answer the purposes of transportation; but they did not do well, for, strange to say, the smallest insect, the *nigua*, that buries itself in the feet and there procreates, utterly ruined all of them.

At almost all of these places, the beef is cured by putting it, salted, in the sun, and it then is known as *tasajo* (jerked beef); and prepared in this way, it will keep for two or three weeks, being used principally for home consumption, that which is prepared for market requiring more curing. This is the great article of food amongst the masses of the population, and is found sometimes even upon the table of the better class, when no strangers are present. Large quantities of the hides of the cattle are exported, while the bones are made into "bone black," of which immense quantities are required by the sugar manufacture of the island.

From Puerto Principe come, also, some of the finest horses raised on the island; for, strange to say, in the cities, the American horse is esteemed most highly, from his greater size and style.

The Cuban horse is not supposed to be a native either of the island or of these climes,—in fact, if we believe the accounts of the early discoverers, the animal was not known upon this continent; for, in every case when the natives first saw a horse, they were struck dumb with astonishment, showing that they had never seen one before.

It is, therefore, suspected that the Cuban horse of to-day, peculiar breed as it is, is simply the result of some of the Spanish stock transferred to the island and affected by the peculiarities of the climate in its breeding. At all events, it is a fine animal now, with a short, stout, well-built body, neat clear limbs, fine, intelligent eyes, and a gait for long journeys under saddle not to be surpassed. These horses have sturdy necks, heavy manes, and thick tails, and, seen on the plains, where they are raised, and before being handled and dressed they present a very rough and wild appearance. Their gait is something peculiar, it would seem, to themselves; and on a well-broken horse the greatest novice in the art of riding need not hesitate to mount.

The Cuban horse

The *marcha*, or fast walk, is simply the easiest gait in the way of a walk I have ever seen; and *el paso*, or the rapid gait of the horse is something like the movement of our pacing horses, or, as they call it in the Southern States, a single-footed rack, only it is a great deal

more easy. Some of the horses do what is known as *el paso gualtrapeo*, a movement so gentle that a rider can carry a full glass of water without spilling. It is for this reason that the Cuban horses are so much admired by lady travelers fond of horseback riding, for they can ride miles and miles without experiencing the slightest fatigue. If I were to tell all the wonderful stories about the performances of these horses, my reader would be incredulous; but this I can say, that, day after day, the Cuban horse will journey from forty-five to sixty miles without showing the slightest sign of giving out, and on forced rides, seventy to eighty miles is no unusual occurrence.

The price varies, according to circumstances, from sixty dollars to even as high as one thousand dollars for the very finest bred, and it is amusing to see with what care those owned by wealthy people are treated. Owing to the sticky nature of the mud of the country roads, it has been the custom to plait the tails of all the horses (the end being fastened to a ring in the cantle of the saddle), and to crop the manes. But in the cities, especially, is great display made in plaiting the tail with fancy ribands, and the mane is trimmed with mathematical precision.

Judging from experience, I should say that all Cuban horses were good, even-tempered animals; for, though I have backed many wild and spirited ones, both in town and country, I never found one that was really vicious, and I never saw one raise its foot for a kick at a human being. The Cubans explain this by saying that the horse is one of the family, as in town he is kept in some portion of the *patio*, usually near the kitchen, and in the country he is treated with even more familiarity.

One of the first things in a Cuban house that strikes the stranger with its novelty is the *guayaba con queso*, or guava with cheese, which may mean either guava jelly or marmalade; and from this universal custom, one wishes to know what is this guava they make so much use of; and as Puerto Principe is a place noted for its manufacture, I will give here a description of it.

In some of the towns of Cuba, such as Trinidad, Santiago de Cuba, and Puerto Principe, there is a class of women remarkable for their beauty, whose race it would be hard for the stranger to tell, with any degree of certainty,—some appearing even lighter in color than Cubans; others, again, like the far-famed octaroons of Louisiana; and still others, of the light mulatto order,—all resembling each other, however, in the wonderful blackness and brilliancy of their eyes, the jet of their hair, and a certain indescribable grace of outline and movement of figure, having in it a dash of that voluptuous languor that we believe peculiar to the Orient.

Who they are, and what their fathers and mothers have been, it would be hard to say. Some of them, however, claim to have "gentle blood" running in their veins, and, if appearances are worth anything, with good reason. Be that as it may, they are the seamstresses, very often the lady's maids, but more frequently the manufacturers of the delicious preserve known as "*Falea*" and "*Pasta de Guayaba.*"

The *dulce* or sweetmeat of guava, then, is of two kinds,—the jelly, a pure, translucent, garnet-colored substance, similar to our currant-jelly; and the marmalade, an opaque, soft substance, similar to good quince marmalade, and of about the same color, or darker.

Both of these are made from the same fruit, though prepared in a different way; and there are also two kinds of the fruit,—one known as the *guayaba de Peru*, which is very scarce, and the other, *guayaba cotorreras*, the common red apple-bearing tree, which is the one most found in Cuba; the fruit of the former being of a greenish color in the inside, while that of the latter is either red, yellow, or white.

The fruit is small and edible, having a fragrant but peculiar odor, and a sweetish taste; and the making of the jelly is an extremely simple operation, as follows: The fruit is cut

The Guava

in halves, and separated from the seeds, then gently stewed; then the sugar, thoroughly boiled to a syrup, is cleared. The guava is now strained through a bag, and the juice only being united with the syrup, it is all boiled until it reaches a proper state of consistency, when it is taken out, put into moulds of the different sized boxes required, and allowed to cool and get firm, when it is placed in long, shallow boxes of various sizes, lined with paper, then closed up, papered to keep out the air, and labeled for market.

The paste is made in the same way, except that only the seeds are taken out, and the whole fruit incorporated with the syrup is used to make the marmalade, which by many is considered the richer for that reason. To any of my readers who have ever tasted the guava jelly it needs no recommendation; but to those who have not, and who wish a "new sensation," I advise them to try it, being careful, however, to buy the small, flat boxes, which are the best, the round boxes usually being filled with very poor stuff. Large quantities of this sweetmeat are exported each year, and there are many manufactories of it in Havana; the best, however, comes from Puerto Principe and Trinidad.

From Puerto Principe there is no way of reaching Havana except by steamer, or else by hiring horses and a guide, and striking off on the *camino real* for a very long and tedious journey through the interior to some of the towns connected by railroad or steamboat. I, however, having circumnavigated the island, and crossed its interior, east and west, prefer the more easy and rapid way of the railroad to Nuevitas, and thence by steamer to Havana, which, after some three months' absence, I reach in the hot days of May. I say hot, but I think I owe the island an apology; for the hottest days that I ever experienced there were nothing in comparison with the terrible days of intense heat of the past summer; and any man who can exist through such a season, is prepared, I think, to live comfortably in any climate in the world.

Hot as it may be in Cuba, there is some way of keeping cool. You can get up in the morning, when the breeze is always fresh and strong, transact your business, and return to your breakfast, where, in some sweet-smelling, flowered courtyard *or patio*, you can, by keeping quiet, and with the aid of *refrescos*, keep cool. The afternoons bring the delicious sea breeze, that carries with it new life for the *paseo*, or the music in the evening. But my landlady cautions me, as I sit in my room, looking out upon the blue sea, where lies, far away, my northern home, "not to make any noise." I ask:

"Why?"

"Because there is a poor, sick stranger in the next room."

"Is he very sick?"

"Yes, but he will go away in a day or two."

"What's the matter with him?"

"He has a very bad case of yellow fever."

Notwithstanding I am told that I am not a fit subject for the fever,—that there is no danger, I think it just as well to anticipate my neighbor's departure, particularly as Havana is no longer the gay place it was early in the winter. The opera season is over, the circus is closed, and even the bull-fights offer no attraction. The hotels, where once during the past months it was a hard matter to get lodging-room, are now dull and deserted, and the long, gaunt faces and bearded chins of *los Americanos* are no longer seen in the cool precincts of the Louvre, sipping their cobblers or cold rum-punches.

RURAL LIFE AND CUSTOMS

"No traveler," says N. P. Willis, "except for some special or overruling reason, leaves, willingly, Havana;" but as we like contrast, and are fond of seeing the *cosas de Cuba*, both of town and country, we seek the contrast, as Baron Humboldt writes it, that "one encounters in leaving the capital (Havana), for the country, and exchanging its civilization, partial and local, for the simplicity of manners and customs that reigns in the isolated farms and little villages of the island."

Besides this, for an invalid traveler who has been passing all his winter in the tropics it is not wise, even if safe, to go north until the chill of winter days is there thoroughly thawed from the atmosphere by the genial rays of an early June sun; and as Havana has no longer attractions for us out of season, we turn to the country.

There is much pleasure, too, in wandering about among some of these little villages in the bright, hot days of the Cuban spring, when the early rains for an hour or two each day only serve to brighten up the landscape and freshen the air a little.

Making, therefore, my head-quarters in such places as Guines, where there are tolerable accommodations at the "Mansion House," and where such lovely views of the valley of Guines are afforded from the "Hill of Fire" (*Loma de Candela*), I run out to San Antonio or Marianao, where I get a sea breath, with a whiff of ocean, fresh and strong, or even to Mariel or Cabañas, twenty-five miles along the coast.

There is the *pueblo* of San Cristobal, too, in the Vuelta Abajo, in a beautiful country, easily accessible by railroad, and at a short distance from which are the romantic Falls of the Rosario, of which the frontispiece to this book is a most charming souvenir.

This, too, is the district sanctified in the cause of freedom by the struggles and final capture of Lopez, in his unsuccessful attempt at revolution, his fate being sealed almost within sight of this beautiful cascade; for, having had an engagement with the Spanish troops, he, with seven companions fled, when they fell into the power of a party of sixteen of the peasants of that section, and being sent up to Havana, were there garroted.

In another chapter there has been given an account of the manner in which the subdivisions of land in Cuba obtained their names, and it only remains now to speak specially of each one of these, first of which is the "Estancia," the most humble of the rural properties, but nevertheless the one that produces or can produce the best returns to its cultivator. Situated in the vicinity of the cities or of the large villages, its purpose is to raise for their markets garden stuff, small meats, fruits, chickens, eggs, milk, cheese, and other articles of general and necessary consumption; also forage, or fodder rather, for the horses maintained in the towns.

The size of these places varies from a dozen acres to one hundred and twenty-five, many of them being cultivated by tenants only, who pay a rent of about two hundred dollars per year for thirty or forty acres. This system of farming, so opposed to the real advancement of agriculture, and the indolence natural to the laborers accustomed to expect from the fertility of the soil what their labor ought at least to assist in bringing forth, keep these places in a state of backwardness. Only a small part is devoted to garden stuff, which requires care, while not much more is put in melons, plantains, and potatoes, more than one half usually being sown with *maloja*, a kind of corn, which grows without giving good grain, and is cut green for the fodder of animals which prefer it to any other kind of grass food.

The fruit-trees are not renewed, and the principal care of the *estanciero*, or farmer, is the raising of chickens and cows; and it is from this reason, in part, that there is a scarcity of garden stuff and fruits in the local markets,—a scarcity that is augmented when they cheapen the other products, and when the crop of beans, onions, potatoes, peas, etc., does not amount to the smallest part of the quantity consumed, although the towns are surrounded by innumerable acres of uselessly fertile land.

Estancia

In many of these *estancias* the cultivation of the soil is abandoned for the business of lime-burning and the raising of sufficient fodder for the oxen that draw the lime to market.

The dwelling-houses on these places are small and of moderate expense in construction, and the number of negroes does not exceed, on the best of these places, five negroes to every forty or fifty acres, the land being worth about sixty dollars per acre.

The sweet-potato (*buniato*), is the principal vegetable raised on these *estancias*, and is mostly of two kinds,—the white and yellow. It is similar to ours, and is eaten in the same way, and is produced all the year round. The white (or Irish) potato is not raised on the island in any quantity, being poor and small; large quantities are, therefore, imported.

"*El ñame*" is *the* tuber, solid and heavy, juicy, white or yellow, and very nutritious, being stewed with meat. This name is given it by the negroes, though its Indian name is "*aje.*" It weighs five or six pounds, and has even been known to weigh as much as twenty-five pounds. The negroes prefer it to any other vegetable, making several dishes from it by compounding it with other things. It is of somewhat the same nature as the yam.

Platanos, as described in another chapter, are raised also in large quantities. On all these places are raised lettuce, cabbage, and many nutritious seeds, most of which flourish the year round. Where the *estancia* is large, and managed with judgment, there are a great many fruits of various kinds raised; but I cannot say that I ever saw in the whole island an orchard, such as we understand one to be. And it seems to me that our system of intelligent gardening, farming, and fruit-raising would prove very profitable; for the whole island is a perfect garden naturally, and with very little attention, almost everything grows in abundance. The oranges, for some years past, do not seem to have flourished, many of the trees in private gardens having been destroyed by tornadoes, and in other places by an insect. Lemons are not now apparently as plentiful as limes, yet there are a great many raised upon the island, being sold for a mere trifle. The aguacate, the mango, and melons of various kinds, are plentiful, the first being used as a sort of salad that is served at dinner, or is mixed with the soup and with various dishes.

Gardening as a business does not seem as yet to be followed by the Cubans, and the only flower-gardens that one sees are those attached to private houses, or, occasionally, small ones near the towns. Some of these private gardens are remarkably beautiful, laid out with great taste, and presenting, when they are confined simply to flowers, a most brilliant appearance with their very highly colored plants. At Marianao, Matanzas, and around Havana, one sees these in perfection; but the most lovely gardens, combined with fruits, were those I saw attached to fine sugar-estates, if I except such as the Cantero gardens, at Trinidad, and the public gardens on the paseo Tacon. The *administrador* of the Concepcion estate, near Matanzas, being a man of cultivated tastes, had laid out a most lovely garden, attached to the dwelling; and I shall not soon forget the orange-groves, the lovely walks, shaded by the pomegranate, the mignonette, the banana and other trees, as well as many plants, curious in size and character.

Upon the *fincas*, or small country places, attention is paid more particularly to raising and keeping bees, from which large quantities of wax and honey are produced, the former being quite an important

Garden view

article of export. There are two kinds of bees used on the island, the *comun*, or exotic, brought from Florida, and the *criolla*, or native bee. The little honey produced by the latter is used by the Cubans for medicinal purposes, the dark-colored wax, under the name of *cera virgen* (virgin wax), serving as lights for the poor of the country.

The imported bee creates one of the principal sources of rural riches, as its products are exported in considerable quantities, its honey even being sent abroad, while the white and the yellow wax produced are well known articles of commerce; in addition to which, large quantities are retained for domestic use in the churches, at funerals, etc.

In a district where these rural places are of a good class, and *potreros*, already alluded to, are found, it is pleasant to mount one's horse, and ride round amongst them, as the owners, particularly of the better class, are quite intelligent about their own business, and always kind to the stranger; having, notwithstanding their rustic life, a certain air of easy politeness, peculiar, it seems to me, to the people of the Latin race. And almost the first thing you are asked, even in the humblest of these *finca* residences, is, "*Quiere café, Senor?*" (will you have coffee, sir), of which beverage these people are very fond. The houses are often very humble affairs indeed, as regards material, though they may be ample in number of rooms, with numerous outbuildings.

They are usually composed of one story affairs, roughly constructed of poles, palm-leaves, and thatch, put together in such a way as to be impervious to rain, yet light enough to admit plenty of air, especially as the doors, if there are any, always stand open.

A living-room, with a sleeping-room or two, all on the same floor, which is often of earth, make up the main building, while a simple roof connects it with an outbuilding, where is the kitchen, in which are performed the household and other duties of the women.

Many of these women, be it said to their credit, are more industrious than the men, as they attend to their domestic duties, often weave cotton cloth for home consumption from the small amount of cotton raised, and have a general superintendence over the place. Cotton, by-the-by, though it cannot be said to be one of the products of the island, does grow in sufficient quantity to manufacture out of it a rough kind of cloth, used by the country people. Every attempt to cultivate it systematically, I was told, was a failure; and yet in the Coffee Mountains I saw beautiful cotton

Country view

growing wild, in small lots, but the moment it was attended to and looked after, strange to say, it ceased to flourish.

It is upon, these rural places also that the Cascarilla cosmetic powder, so great a favorite with Cuban ladies, is prepared from the egg-shells; and the extent to which this is used may be imagined, when it is estimated that there are over one hundred thousand pounds consumed every year.

The last of the rural places we are called upon to notice is the "Hacienda de Crianza," or *sitio*, as it is called,—an uncultivated, unenclosed place, where the cattle are allowed to run wild, unattended except by the *montero*, who goes about on foot, or the half-savage *sabanero*, who, being mounted, rides in amongst the herd. Their united business is to scour the fields every day, and pick out the new-born calves, with their mothers, and take care of them for fifteen or twenty days at the houses or sheds; to see if there are any dead animals, or to pick out those ready to send to market or kill for consumption.

"The rural population of the island," says a Cuban author, "has rusticity, but not that boasted simplicity of the European laborer. Our *guajiro* (countryman) is astute though frank, boastful though brave,

Hacienda de Crianza

Guajiro

and superstitious if not religious. His ruling passions are gambling (particularly at cock-fights, of which he is very fond), and coffee, that he drinks at all hours; his favorite food, pork and the platano, usually roasted." His costume consists of a pair of loose pantaloons, girdled at the waist by a bit of leather, a shirt of fancy-colored linen, a handkerchief of silk or cotton tied around his neck, or, more frequently, about his head, upon which is a broad-brimmed hat of *yarey*,—a species of common palm-leaf,—while his usually bare feet are thrust into common leather pumps or slippers. Rarely does he wear a coat, even if he owns one, and his shirt is worn *al fresco*, more generally outside than inside his pants.

He never works regularly, nor does much else than direct the cultivation of his property, look after the cattle, or, perhaps, act as carter or teamster. Sometimes he may plow, or sow a little grain, or even pick fruit; but if he owns any negroes, he makes them do the work. Some of them are, in fact, too lazy to help themselves; and I have seen one of these fellows, near a country railroad station, plant himself in a chair to be amused by the train, while he lolled back and had his hair *combed* by one of his negro-women.

Too lazy to live

Sometimes he does a little trading on his own account, and may, perhaps, keep a *tienda mista* a sort of country-store and tavern, if his *finca* is on a public road. He travels on horseback, armed invariably with the *machete*, and often carrying a sun-umbrella, taking care to stop at every tavern on the road, where he is ready to talk with any one he meets, or accept an invitation to "*beber.*"

La guajira (country woman), is not so talkative as the husband, particularly with strangers, to whom her partially Castilian blood makes her, at first, ceremonious and dignified, even rising to receive them. She can mount a horse, though she usually rides with her

husband, sitting in front of him, upon the neck of the
horse almost, while his right arm encircles her. She
dresses in the most simple manner (often a little too
much so) in a *camison*, or frock, with a kerchief around
her neck; seldom wearing stockings, except on state
occasions,—of a ball, visit, etc., her head often being
covered with a huge straw hat when she moves about,
but otherwise dressed with the utmost care to display
to advantage her superb hair.

Country woman

These country people all have manners and
customs peculiar to themselves, even their food
being different from that of the cities; and it is amongst them one can
study *la cocina criolla* (the Cuban cuisine). They have but two meals
a day, always accompanied by coffee, which they also take on rising in
the morning, at night-time, and at any hour of the day they fancy, or
may have a guest.

Civilization has found its way even to the homes of these simple
people; and, on the richer and larger places, English beer is now
generally used, and to strangers even champagne is presented.

So natural a custom is it with these hospitable country people to
entertain the guest, that, does he happen to be present when a meal
is announced, he is not even honored with an invitation, but he is
expected, as the most natural thing in world, to seat himself at the
table and partake of their food, whatever it may be. To refuse to do
so, unless he has the excuse to make that he has lately eaten, would
be considered an offense.

As the service of the table, in most of the cities, at all the hotels,
and many of the best private houses partakes of the nature of French
cooking, it is only in the rural parts one can see the *bona fide* Cuban
dishes.

The daily meals of the more humble farmers consist of fried pork
and boiled rice in the morning, and, in lieu of bread, the roasted
plantain. At dinner, they make use of cow-beef, jerked beef, birds,
and roasted pig; but usually this meal consists of roasted plantains,
and the national dish of *ajiaco*, or what we should call an Irish stew.
This dish is to the island what *olla podrida* is to Spain. It is composed

of fresh meat, either beef or pork,—dried meat of either,—all sorts of vegetables, young corn, and green plantains. It is made with plenty of broth, thickened with a farinaceous root known as *malanga*, and has also some lemon-juice squeezed into it. It is, I assure the reader, toothsome, cheap, and nutritious,—quite equal to the French *pot au feu*. Boiled rice is never dispensed with at any meal, and the cooking of it is understood to perfection. It is used mixed in all their stews, or with a simple sauce of tomatoes. *El aporreado* is made of half raw meat, dressed with water, vineger, salt, etc., which operation is known as *perdigar* (or stewing in an earthen pan); then mashed and stirred together, it is fried slightly in a sauce (*mojo*) of lard, tomatoes, garlic, onions, and peppers. *Picadillos*, or hashes, are always good upon the island,—town or country,—even if one does not know who made them. The *tasajo brujo*, or jerked beef bewitched, so called from the fact that it grows so much larger in cooking, is the dish found almost everywhere, and cooked in many ways. It is almost always a savory dish the traveler need not be afraid of, particularly if he has had army experience. There are some other dishes, but with the knowledge of the above, the stranger will be safe to accept an invitation to dine with any of the *haciendados*, and it will also be seen that Cuban cookery is not such a fearful thing as we have been led to believe; for little or no oil is used, and the small quantity of garlic used is so disguised in other things that few people could tell it.

These country folks also have their special amusements as well as cookery. First upon the list stand the cock-fights (*peleas de gallos*), which have been already described.

Every village, or *pueblo*, has a patron saint, for whom there is a special *dia de fiesta*, which all the villagers and people in the vicinity celebrate with masses, etc., at the village church, and afterwards by games, dancing, and sports, the women taking part also as spectators if in no other way. But usually they are divided into two parties, each party being distinguished by the color of the ribbon it wears, and which gives its name to the band. Each party elects a queen, chosen for her grace, beauty, or good style, and the admirers of each are known as vassals, and they give their presence to the amusement going on. When the performers belonging to one party or the other are successful, the vanquished party with its queen and vassals has to render homage to the rival queen. The goose-fight, or *corrida de patos*, is another one of their sports, and a very cruel one it is; for in a plaza or smooth field two forked poles are set up, and from one to the other a rope is stretched; in the middle of this a live goose is hung, firmly tied by the feet. The place is now filled with spectators, while five, ten, or fifteen mounted *guajiros* pass at full gallop in front of the goose, and attempt to seize the head, which has been well greased, and separate it from the body in their full career. Of course many unsuccessful attempts are made, and the bird usually dies before the efforts are successful, but he who succeeds in this *glorious* attempt is declared *victor*.

Las loas (or prologues) are practiced in the country villages in their religious feasts and civil celebrations,—as processions of the Holy Virgin or the Patron Saint, etc. A little girl, dressed (or undressed) as an image, is conducted, publicly, in a small cart profusely decorated with banners, flowers, and branches; before her, march on horseback four or six men, in costumes of Indians, and behind, others clad as Moors. A band plays, and the procession, which is composed of almost all the people of the village, when arrived at the appointed place (*plaza*) stops, and the child stands up and recites or declaims her *loa*, a composition appropriate to the subject of the celebration.

Altares de Cruz,—the custom of forming altars in the houses in the first days of May, in order to celebrate the invention of the Holy Cross, is preserved very generally in the interior of the island, but with a character almost entirely profane. The altar is erected modestly in a sleeping-room of the house, on the 3rd of May, or day of Santa Cruz, and on every day of the first nine, the guests gather before it, to dance, sing, play, and eat and drink at times. On the first night, the master of the house delivers a branch of flowers to the guest that he chooses, and the latter contracts, in receiving it, the obligation to re-form the altar, and pay the expenses of the next night's entertainment, he himself taking the name of the godfather or *mayordomo*. The second night arrived, the godfather or godmother renews this performance of the branch upon another victim, and it thus happens that each altar has a new *mayordomo* for each night, and as every one endeavors to do better than his predecessor, it happens that the last night winds up the festival with a superb supper and a full orchestra.

Mamarrachos is the name given to the individuals on horseback, who, in a great part of the Vuelta Arriba, ride, masked and grotesquely costumed, through the streets, during the Carnival or other seasons of merry-making. Surprise parties, known as *asaltos*, are very numerous, not only amongst the country people but at the watering-places during the season.

The country dances, however, are something especially peculiar, many old-fashioned customs and figures being retained, although the usual waltzes and contra-dances are danced, too, under the name of *bailes de musica*, while the former are known as *changüis* or *guateques*, and are less formal, being the social meetings of intimate friends or neighbors.

The especial dance is the one known as the *zapateo*, and is peculiar to this island. It is danced to the music of the harp, the guitar, or the songs of the *guajiros*, by both women and men, and has a good many peculiar figures, the principal object appearing to me, to be for

El zapateo

Old-fashioned sugar mill

the women to see how many men they can tire out, as they give every now and then a signal to their *vis à vis* "to leave," when he is replaced by another. A low humming or singing is kept up by those present, broken every now and then by the loud plaudits of the spectators at the success of some dancer.

In many sections of the country one still finds sugar estates, almost as they were originally, in the possession of owners of moderate means and little intelligence, who have not availed themselves of the advantages afforded by improved machinery and scientific modes of making sugar.

Some of the places, again, are so poor in soil and product, having been worked for so many years without intermission, that the owners do not deem it worth while, even if they can afford the outlay, to put up new mills and machinery,—much preferring to try new land.

Still, the country is improving in its agricultural pursuits of all kinds, though in none has it made such rapid strides as in sugar-making. As an evidence of which, compare this view of the boiling house with that of the improved mills seen in the chapter on sugar-making.

Boiling house

Departure for home

And now, dear reader, my task is done. We have wandered together over the beautiful Island of Cuba, looked at its lovely scenery, mingled with its mixed population, dipped a little into its antiquities, history, and productions,—all, perhaps, in a desultory, too familiar way; but if, in parting here, you have obtained that which I started out to give,—a general knowledge of Cuba, its people, products, etc.,—I shall be satisfied; and, perhaps, you may be able to answer the question often asked: "What sort of a place would Cuba be if she did belong to the United States?" To which I can only say: Cuba with a free government, *plenty of ice*, and a large immigration, would become a wonderful garden.

But the prow of our good ship is northward turned, and we are standing on the deck taking our last look at the "ever faithful isle." Though our hearts are, perhaps, swelling with glad hopes of soon seeing the "loved ones at homes," yet there comes mingled with these a tinge of sadness at the thought that all our pleasant days of listless, easy life and interesting journeys are over; and though with renewed health and restored energy we are returning to take our part in the vigorous life of the cold and ever laboring north, yet we cannot but miss the warm tropic breezes that fanned our cheeks as we lay in the shade of the palm, the cocoa, or the banana tree, sucking the luscious orange, or blowing dreamy clouds of blue from our fragrant *tabacos*. And now, as, fast receding from those verdure-clad shores, we see the white spray dashing on the black rocks of the Morro, we turn away in pensive mood, murmuring those beautiful lines of Tennyson:

"Break, break, break,
At the foot of thy crags, O sea!
But the tender grace of a day that is dead,
Will never come back to me."

The Ceiba (cottonwood) tree

"Ye tropic forests of unfading green!
  Where the palm tapers and the orange glows,—
Where the light bamboo waves her feathery screen,
  And her far shade the matchless Ceiba throws;
Ye cloudless ethers of unchanging blue!
  Save where the rosy streaks of eve give way
To the clear sapphire of your midnight hue,
  The burnished azure of your perfect day!
Yet tell me not my native shores are bleak;
  That, flushed with liquid wealth, no cane-fields wave;
For Virtue pines, and *Manhood dares not speak*,
  And Nature's glories brighten round the slave."
                                    —Lord Morpeth.

The Island of Cuba was discovered by Christopher Columbus on his first voyage to that New World which his great mind had taught him must lie beyond the stormy seas of the Atlantic.

Having brought his anxious voyage to a successful termination, and having drawn fresh inspiration from his first discovery,—the island of San Salvador, one of the Bahama group,—he continued his explorations, under the belief that this new world was part of the far-famed region of Cathay, spoken of in the travels of Marco Polo.

Leaving, then, the little island of Isabella, another one of the Bahama group, at midnight, October 24, 1492, he, after three days' sailing, with winds that blew "most amorously," came in sight of the Island of Cuba on the morning of the 28th October.

So charming was the weather, that it would seem Providence had prepared it expressly for a man so great, so sensible to the attractions of nature, who, seeing spread before him at one view the majestic forests and mountains, as well as the smiling poetry of the fields and valleys of Cuba, and doubtless feeling the balmy influences of that wonderful air, exclaimed, "It is the most beautiful land that eyes have ever beheld."

He disembarked, on the same day, on the banks of the river to which he gave the name of San Salvador (now Maximo), emptying into the bay to the north-west of Nuevitas, now known as Sabinal, entering it, doubtless, by the narrow strait which to this day bears the name of "Boca de las Carabelas" (entrance of the vessels). Taking possession of the land for his sovereigns, he gave it the name of Juana, in honor of their eldest son.

Columbus remained some time upon the coasts of the island, visiting many ports, and among others, touching at the point of Yana, which he called Cabo de Palmas, where, misunderstanding something that some of the native Indians said while on one of his vessels, he (Columbus) was led to believe that he was on the main land, not far from the residence of the Tartar sovereign Cubley Khan, an error he was fully prepared to fall into from his own belief that he had discovered a part of India.

Retracing his steps to the east, around the coast of the island, after lingering in the beautiful bay of Nuevitas, he touched at Baracoa, giving, as he passed the extreme point of the island now known as Maisi, the name of Alpha and Omega, believing it to be the extreme point of Asia.

Finally, Columbus left the coast of Cuba to make the discovery of the island of Hayti, not returning to its shores for two years; but, in 1494, he revisited the island to explore its southern coasts, arriving, about the first of May, at the bay of Guantanamo, which he called Puerto Grande, and spending some months in visiting its different bays and points. [See Irving's "Columbus," vol. I].

Yet once again did Columbus visit these beautiful scenes (on his fourth voyage) before he returned to his adopted country to rest his bones in that peace which, living, his enemies refused to entirely yield him, embittering his latter days as they did, by their doubts and persecutions.

But his ashes now rest in, perhaps, the most fitting place after so many transfers from their original place of burial, never, it is hoped, to be again disturbed, but to be the shrine around which, may we also hope, shall cluster new life and new hopes for the beautiful island he so much admired when living.

Of the large number of inhabitants that the island possessed at the time of its discovery, there are to-day few or no actual descendants, though doubtless there are many of the natives of the island who may have a sprinkling of this Indian blood in their veins. Even the one or two villages that in all these generations seem to have retained some of the native Indian descendants together, as well as some of their customs, have almost entirely vanished, and at Caney and in the wild regions of the mountain lands of eastern Cuba there are now but a few left, still remarkable, however, for the thorough Indian characteristics of the men and the grace and gentleness of the women, so often alluded to by the early discoverers.

There seems to have been a blank (unless we except the voyage of Ocampo) in the history of the civilization of the island from the time Columbus left it on his last voyage until, in 1511, his son, Diego Columbus, Governor of Hispaniola, sent Diego Velasquez from St. Domingo, with four vessels and three hundred men, to conquer the island, which he did, landing with his forces in the port of Palmas, and though resisted by the natives, with their chief, Hatuey, defeating them, and taking lasting possession of the island.

Proceeding immediately to establish his authority, he divided off the lands in the island, as well as the natives, amongst his followers; and from that time, it would appear, a species of religious and industrial extermination began among these simple people, who, unaccustomed to hard labor or great physical exertion, from which their simple wants, sustained by the prolific nature of the vegetation of the island, had hitherto kept them, now found themselves slaves to the hardest of task-masters.

Velasquez founded many of the towns of the island, the first of which was Baracoa, then Bayamo, and in 1514, Trinidad, Santo Espiritu, Puerto Principe; next, in 1515, Santiago de Cuba, as also, in the same year, the town of Habana, though not on its present location.

In 1545 was also founded the town of San Juan de los Remedios, upon the north coast, looking even to-day as though it had not changed a particle since it was first founded; while Guanabacoa, founded in the same year, seems quite an active, growing place, probably from its near vicinity to Havana.

This period (1511-1607) is particularly interesting to the general reader from the fact that in it the explorations of Hernandez de Cadoba and Grijalva to Darien, Yucatan, etc., were inaugurated,— events which had so much to do with the spread of Spanish rule and discovery, paving the way as they did for the exploration of Mexico under Hernando Cortes, who, in the early history of Cuba, figures largely, as the Lieutenant of the Governor Velasquez, as the miner of copper in the Cobre mines, the ore of which he held in more value than the lives of the miners,—the poor Indian slaves; and even in a still more romantic light as the amorous admirer of the fair sex. This, however, is all overshadowed by the magnificence and brilliancy of the conquest of Mexico, which was originated, and the expedition for which prepared, in Cuba.

In 1524, Diego Velasquez died,—his death hastened, it is said, by the troubles brought upon him by his disputes with his insubordinate Lieutenant, Cortes; and whatever we may think of the causes of this insubordination and the after results thereof, it cannot be concealed that to Velasquez is due, at least, some honor and glory for having first with his brain originated these voyages of discovery, and then with his means and influence pushed them forward to execution.

In the history of the improvement of the island, his government will bear favorable comparison with many of the later governments; and while that great evil slavery was introduced into the island in his time, so also was the sugar-cane; and it may be that the wonderful success of the latter was in some degree influenced by the labor of the former.

Up to 1538, there seems to be nothing specially striking in the general history of the island, if we except the constant attacks with fire and sword of the *filibusteros*, or pirates of all nations, from which most all the sea-coast towns suffered more or less; but in that year there arrived at Santiago de Cuba, a man destined to play an important part in the history and discovery of the new world, and named as Provincial Governor of Florida as well as of Cuba,—I allude to Hernando de Soto, who brought with him ten large vessels, prepared and fitted out expressly for the conquest of the new Spanish territory of Florida.

After much care and preparation, this expedition started out from the city of Habana, the 12th of May, taking with it as part of its forces many of the residents of the island. Of the history of this expedition and its unfortunate results, a full account pertains rather to the history of our own country (see Bancroft's "United States"); but with it perished some of the best blood of the early Spanish adventurers, which sad result, in connection with the drain on the population of the island, caused by other expeditions, seems to have brought the advancement of affairs in Cuba to a standstill.

In this period, also, was promulgated that order, secured, it is believed, by the noble efforts of Padre Las Casas, prohibiting the enslaving of the aborigines; while, also, such had become its importance as a town, all vessels directed to and from Mexico were ordered to stop at Havana.

In the period of years that elapsed from 1607 to 1762, the island seems to have been in a perfect state of lethargy, except the usual changes of its many Governors, and the raids made upon it by pirates or by more legalized enemies in the form of French and English men-of-war.

In this latter year, however, occurred an event of much import, from the fact that after it, or upon its occurrence, the Government of Spain was led to see the great importance of Cuba, and particularly Havana, as the "Key to the New World,"—this event was the taking of Havana by the English.

On the 6th of June, 1762, there arrived off the port of Havana an English squadron of thirty-two ships and frigates, with some two hundred transports, bringing with them a force of nearly twenty thousand men of all arms, under command of the Duke of Albemarle. This formidable armament, the largest that America had ever seen, laid siege to the city of Havana, whose garrison consisted at this time of only about two thousand seven hundred regulars and the volunteers that took up arms immediately for the defense of the place.

The English, landing a force of twelve thousand men, took possession of Guanabacoa, then a small village, throwing a force forward to the heights to-day occupied by the Castillo del Principe, and the Spaniards having evacuated the heights where now stand the Cabañas fortifications, the English troops opened fire from these heights, both upon the Morro Castle and the city proper, they being ·exposed, from their less elevated position, to the plunging fire from the greater heights of the Cabañas. The great mistake, however, that appears to have been made by the Spaniards, was in blocking up the entrance of the port by the sinking of two vessels therein. This was done to prevent the entrance of the English ships to destroy the Spanish fleet inside the harbor, and the English now perceiving that, though they were shut out with their vessels from the harbor, so, also, was the Spanish fleet shut in from doing them any harm, availed themselves of every man to strengthen their land attack.

The garrison, however, made a very gallant and prolonged defense, notwithstanding the smallness of their numbers, and finally, surrendering, were permitted to march out with the honors of war, the English thus coming into possession of the most important defences on the coast, and, subsequently, taking possession of the town of Matanzas. Remaining in possession of this portion of the Island of Cuba for many months (until July 6, 1763), the English, by importing negro labor to cultivate the large tracts of wild land, and by shipping large quantities of European merchandize, gave a start to the trade and traffic of the island that pushed it far on its way to the state of prosperity it has now reached; but by the treaty of peace, at Paris, in February, 1763, was restored to Spain the portion of the island wrested from her by the English, and the day of this actual restitution, in Havana, was made a great day of festivity and rejoicing.

In this period (1762-1801), the island made rapid advances in improvement and civilization, many of the Captains-General of this period doing much to improve the towns and the people, beautifying the streets, erecting buildings, etc.

In 1763, also, a large emigration took place from Florida, and in 1795, the French emigrants, from Santo Domingo, came on to the island in large numbers, bringing with them improved modes of coffee-culture; while to the former the island is indebted for the hives of bees, which produce the large quantities of wax, for which the island is famous.

The literary culture of the island, too, made some advances at this period; for in 1793, the Royal Society for Improvement opened its sessions in Havana,—a society which has done much to increase and strengthen the material and literary prosperity of the island, while newspapers were established, among others, the *Diario de la Marina*, which is in existence to-day.

From 1801, rapid increase in the prosperity of the island has taken place; new systems of agriculture, and improved methods of sugar manufacture have been introduced, and an attempt at a general system of education has been made, and though at various times insurrections, some of them quite serious in their nature, have shown what the natural desire of the native population is for greater privileges and freedom, none have attained such magnitude, or been so universally participated in by the Creole inhabitants, as the rebellion now in existence on the island.

The history of the island shows, at various times, by these breakings out, that though the spirit of liberty was slumbering, it never has been entirely dead; for in 1823, there was a society of "Soles," as it was called, formed for the purpose of freeing the island, having at its head young D. Francisco Lemus, and having for its pretext that the island *was about to be sold to England.*

In 1829, there was discovered the conspiracy of the Black Eagle, as it was called (*Aguila Negra*), an attempt on the part of the population to obtain their freedom, some of the Mexican settlers in the island being prominent in it.

The insurrection, or attempt at one, by the blacks, in 1844, was remarkable for its wide-spread ramifications among the slaves of the island, as well as its thorough organization,—the intention being to murder all the whites on the island. Other minor insurrections there were, but it remained for Narciso Lopez, with a force of some three hundred men, to make the most important attempt, in which he lost his life, to free the island.

He landed with his troops in the district of Bahia Honda, 11th

August, 1851, and through either the treachery or cowardice of the natives, was not supported, and after some fighting and many hardships, was finally captured, himself and many of his followers being put to death.

Concerning the present rebellion, it has been very difficult indeed to get at the real facts of the case, as both sides appear to magnify matters very much, and it is, perhaps, natural that the Spanish authorities should "pooh, pooh" it,—it has always been their policy to blind public opinion.

In the number of "Lippincott" for April, 1868, in an article which was written by the author of this work, he took occasion to speak of the feelings of the Cubans against Spain which had been manifested to him. The "Diario de la Marina," the official organ, in reviewing that article, lightly remarked that its author did not understand the sentiment of the people of the island; and that this feeling was confined to only *few vulgar people*! Let us see.

Within six months after that review was written, there was flung to the breeze, in the Island of Cuba, the flag of liberty. By whom? By some of the richest, the most intelligent, the most influential men of the island; while, as soon as the insurrection got thoroughly under way, people of every grade flocked to the camps; and Dr. Simmons even mentions it as a fact that every physician except himself, had left Puerto Principe to join the patriots.*

It is not within the province of a volume like this to discuss thoroughly the troubles existing between Spain and Cuba, the causes which have led to the present rebellion, or the probable ending thereof. It may suffice for us to know that though the insurrection has continued now over two years, the participants in which are mostly either very poorly armed or entirely unarmed, except with a short knife or sabre; though there have been used in Cuba over fifty thousand regular Spanish troops and some seventy thousand volunteers, all of them splendidly armed and equipped, and with strong forts to back them, *the rebellion has not been put down yet*; and from authentic sources I learn that the patriots are not yet discouraged,—they say (to quote from a late letter) "Give us arms, ammunition, and some clothing, and we will hold our own for years to come." As it is the province of the American to foster free governments and unlimited liberties for all peoples in every quarter of the globe, let us, then, without wishing harm to our Spanish brethren in their effort for freedom, hope that the Cubans may soon be made happy and peaceful in their beloved Cuba Libre.**

But let us now take a more general view of Cuba with reference to its peculiarities of climate, productions, people, etc.

Cuba is the largest of the West India Islands. Its greatest length is about seven hundred and ninety miles; its width varies from twenty-eight to one hundred and twenty-seven miles; so that the island has a very elongated shape.

The area is about four thousand three hundred square miles. The coast line is about two thousand miles, but hardly one third of it is accessible to vessels; the remainder is surrounded by banks, reefs, and rocks. Only the south-eastern part of the island is mountainous,— that which lies between Cape Cruz, Cape Mayari, and the town of Holguin. This group is known as the "Sierra," or "Montaños de Maestra," or Cobre, and in its highest points rises more than seven thousand two hundred feet above the level of the sea, Turquino, the highest peak on the island, being it is said, eight thousand feet high. A few minor mountains occur in other parts, the high mountains being few in number, and confined in the eastern department to "Turquino," the "Gran Piedra," the "Ojo del Toro," and " the Yunque," and in the western department, to the "Pico de Potrerillo," near Trinidad, the "Loma de San Juan," "El Pan de Guajaibon," and the "Pan of Matanzas," the latter being usually the first land seen at sea when coming from the north.

Most of these mountains are thickly wooded almost to their very summits with the heavy woods of the country, and appear in an almost perpetual dress of verdure. In some of these, also, are found metallic substances, particularly copper. Silver is scarce, though it has been found in small quantities, as has also iron in very limited quantities, and stone coal; also, a species of bitumen, known as "chapapote."

Many of the mountains, however, abound in mineral waters of various qualities and of wonderful utility in the cure of disease.

To the north-east of Guantanamo there is an extensive range of hills, known as those of Quibijan and Baracoa, and in the hill of Moa, of this range, there is found a huge cavern, in which descends the Moa river, from a height of one hundred yards, forming a superb cascade.

There are no specially large rivers in Cuba,—some are navigable a few miles inland for small boats, others are used for irrigating the adjacent fields; but the waters of all, without exception, are delicious and pure for drinking purposes, some of the streams, particularly those running from the mountains, being clear and cool. They all run either north or south to the sea.

The climate of the island is, for the most part, temperate, compared with some other islands in the same latitude. No snow is ever known to fall, even in the mountains; hail storms are rare,—they occur only once in fifteen or twenty years, and always with a south-south-west wind; hurricanes are less frequent than in Jamaica, and sometimes do not occur for five or six years, and even then they vent their fury rather upon sea than land, occurring more particularly on the southern coast. Occasionally, during what are known as the cold months, there are cold winds, (*los nortes*), blowing from the north, which rarely last longer than forty-eight hours, and which, even by a northern man, would be deemed not half so uncomfortable as the March winds with us.

No month of the year is free from rain, but the greatest quantity falls in May, June, and July. Slight shocks of earthquakes are occasionally felt; but, judging from the one that I experienced, they serve only to get up a pleasant excitement.

In general in the torrid zone there are two seasons, known as the wet (*lluviosa*) and the dry (*seca*); but more properly three can be admitted in Cuba,—the dry, the wet, and that of the northers,—and they are very marked in their differences.

The first comprises the months of March, April, and May, though in the latter month the wet season sometimes begins, prolonging itself even into October, while the northers are experienced from November to February.

With the first rains begins the season of spring (*primavera*), during which it rains and thunders almost daily, and the temperature rises to a great height, with but little variation night or day; the showers, however, last sometimes only an hour or two, accompanied by thunder and lightning, which serve in some degree to dispel the intense heat existing before the rain.

In the interior of the island, the heat is never so extreme as on the coast, owing in great degree to the superior elevation, and there the terrible yellow fever (or *vomito*) is unknown. From ten to twelve in the morning are the hottest hours of the day, but about half-past two there always sets in the most delicious and refreshing sea breeze (*la virazon*), while at night copious and refreshing dews serve to invigorate the vegetation.

There are no diseases specially indigenous to Cuba, and the dreaded vomito is an exotic, having been introduced by convict labor from Mexico; and even this, in many cases where foreigners are attacked by it, is produced by gross imprudence in eating unripe fruit, and the drinking of spirituous or ardent liquors after eating freely of the banana fruit will frequently produce sickness, often ending fatally.

Extreme cases of longevity, both in men and women, are found all over the island, and I have seen negroes of eighty years of age very robust and at harder work than most men of fifty would care to do in this land.

When we come to understand the government and administration of Cuba, we can readily appreciate the intense desire pervading every *Cuban* breast for a *free Government*.

Starting upon the basis of the intense hatred existing between the native Cubans and their Spanish rulers (and that such a feeling did exist throughout every part of the island I had the firmest belief, since confirmed by their rebellion), taken in conjunction with the harsh government, it is easy to see why the natives were always ready for revolt and hardly a year passed that some attempt was not made at insurrection (though carried on in a disconnected way, and kept quiet by the Spanish authorities,) to culminate finally in the rebellion in which the Cubans are now involved, and which for over two years, they have carried on without its being put down by the Spaniards.

No greater offence can be given to a Cuban than to speak of or address him as a Spaniard, whom he unhesitatingly calls a thief (*picaro*), while, *vice versa*, the Spaniard of Castile speaks in the most contemptuous terms of the natives, applying to them indiscriminately the word "coward," saying "they would not fight." Time has shown, however, that if there are some who are false to their country, there are many others who, if they know not how to fight, are yet ready and willing to die in behalf of their "Cuba Libre."

No religion is tolerated in Cuba except the Roman Catholic religion, and the consequence is that the island is priest-ridden, sustained as the church is by the government, although it sometimes does step in and interfere, as lately, in the case of Consul Parsons, at Santiago de Cuba, whose body was refused Christian burial by the priests, until the Governor peremptorily ordered its decent interment.

The men seem to have no religion; the women go to church for pastime, it being their only hour of freedom from the shackles that custom throws around them.

Concerning the sincerity of the men, as a class, there is much dispute; I have often heard it called in question, doubtless on account of their extreme politeness in offering to you every thing you may admire of theirs; but this presupposes good breeding enough on the side of the party to whom the offer is made, to as politely refuse it.

Está á su disposicion, I take it, means nothing, but is merely a small coin passing current in good society; but when a Cuban takes one's hand, and adds to the above, with much emphasis, "frankly" (*francamente Señor*), in nine cases out of ten he means it, I think; if he don't, it does no harm to accept his offers as a punishment for his insincerity.

The Cubans, however, as a class, are a simple-hearted people, hospitable to all strangers, but for *los Americanos* nothing is too much for them to do. The men are, in the better classes, well bred and well educated, many of them having passed their earlier years either in the United States or Europe, and even the peasantry have a kindness and courtliness of manner that might put to blush the boorish manners of some of our own people; and while the young men of the cities do not seem to attain to a very full size or robust growth, some of the finest formed and best developed men I have ever seen, I found among the *paisanos* (countrymen), particularly on the Isle of Pines. Whether from the influences of the climate or the peculiarities of their government, which offers no paths of ambition to the aspiring youth, the men, generally, are listless, indifferent, and lacking in the energy peculiar to the people farther north. Many of them are, however, highly accomplished in either art, science, or literature; and, while Havana boasts of several scientific and artistic institutions and colleges, almost every small town possesses what is known as *El Liceo,*—an association of the young men of the place, which is encouraged by the presence of ladies, forming an attractive feature in the social life of the smaller places.

Women's relations, however, in Cuba, are very peculiar. They are absolute slaves to custom; they must never walk alone, not even attend church, without a *duenna*, and by no means must they receive male visitors alone. The majority of them are not educated, as we understand the word, though the native women, having more pride in this matter than their Castilian sisters, manage to pick up a little reading and writing; but it is rarely indeed that you ever see a woman reading a book in Cuba as an everyday matter of recreation or improvement. Their whole life (at least with the women of the cities), is passed in listless idleness, varied occasionally by a ball, a stroll of an evening at the "Retreta," or, if able, an airing in a volante on the Paseo. They begin their day by going to early morning mass: after which they pass the time lolling in rocking-chairs and fanning themselves, relieving the monotony perhaps, by a *siesta*.

While there are many exceptions to the above, in the houses of the rich and cultivated, yet I am at a loss to imagine what the women of Cuba would do under the auspices of a free government, which, having no occasion for the troops, would not maintain the military bands that now, in every town and on almost every evening, discourse such "sweet music," in the plazas or public squares. This is the great attraction for the sex on those evenings, but probably a change like the above might result in their being forced to books and to cultivating their minds for amusement—*Quien sabe?*

The slave-trade of Cuba has long been abolished, and the supply of labor in that respect is not up to the demand. Coolies have been introduced, and the plan has worked well for the planters, though it is death almost to the Coolies; but not enough of these have been imported, and the cargoes are immediately taken when landed.

What, then, is to become of the great labor interests of the island? Do the planters want slavery? Do they expect that they can retain it?

My answer to this is, they do not; but, hitherto, they have wanted a compensation for their slaves, and a system of free labor that would enable them to work their valuable estates. What effect the war will have upon their views remains yet to be seen; but it is now said that the whole island is in favor of free labor.

Probably the greatest farce ever enacted to choke off public criticism on the slavery in the island is the "Proclamation of Emancipation" lately issued by the home government, in which "all the babies and old men" are set free, thereby giving to the owners the picked, able-bodied for work, and relieving them of the expense of maintaining the infants and the aged.

In connection with this subject the question will be asked: Can foreign white labor succeed there? It has as yet never been tried. Some portions of the island offer superior advantages to white labor,—as, for instance, the magnificent climate of the Coffee Hills, on the eastern end of the island, where thousands and thousands of acres of the most fertile and naturally prolific land can be had for a song.

The lumber interest here, too, is valuable, though yet undeveloped; but, people those high, fine hills, covered with the various strange woods, with such a race as our hardy lumbermen from Maine, and how quickly would the dark recesses of those tangled forests give light to a new and healthy civilization.

Then again: Can not machinery be introduced to take the place of manual labor? It has been done, in many instances, successfully,—as witness the steam plough, now in operation in many parts of the island; also, all the best sugarmill machinery. And I think McCormick's invention of the reaper, applied to the cutting of the cane, will yet be made to answer in relieving the large gangs of negroes from that laborious and tedious work.

In the small towns, in the suburbs of large ones, and generally upon all the tobacco farms (*vegas*), and on all the lesser farms, the work is done by native white labor, the difference being in the system of labor which avoids the heat of noonday, and takes the cool hours of early morning and evening for work.

The island has some of the finest ports in the world; as, on the north coast, Havana, Nuevitas, Mariel, Nipe, Matanzas, Bahia Honda, and Cardenas; while on the south coast, there are Cienfuegos, Trinidad, Cuba, Guantanamo, and some few smaller ones, from all of which are shipped the valuable products of the island,—rum, sugar, molasses, coffee, tobacco, and many delicious fruits, all of which constitute the sources of the great wealth of the island.

The population of the island is about one million four hundred thousand, of which eight hundred thousand are whites, four hundred thousand slaves, and two hundred thousand free persons of color; which population, doubtless, would increase very fast by immigration, were there freedom of government, and religion, together with inducements to labor.

As there are no manufactories of any importance on the island, the natural source of supply of dry goods, hardware, machinery, furniture, carriages, and such agricultural products as are not cultivated there, is the United States of America.

By last reports, the exports of the island amounted to over sixty million dollars, and the imports to over fifty millions, the customs being over twelve millions. The total revenue of the island for the year 1860 was twenty million dollars, from which are to be deducted the expenses, amounting to nearly eleven million dollars, leaving a nice little plum for the home government, after paying all the expenses of an army actually useless, except it be to quell rebellion.

Every traveler in Cuba will be astonished at the excellent railroads of the principal routes, whether he notice the comfortable cars with their cool cane seats and lattice windows, the speed and punctuality with which the trains are run, the solidity of the construction of the roads, or, perhaps, the bright, pretty station-houses, which even we in our railroad country might copy, in their attractive and cleanly appearance. Some of the roads are very fine, as witness the two roads from Havana to Matanzas, particularly that *via* Guines, with its magnificent scenery; the road from Matanzas to Cardenas, from Havana to Guanajay, to Batabano, etc.

Before the present rebellion, there were constant additions being made to the railroads of the island; and it was the original intention, I understood, to have one long, central road running the entire length of the island, with branches on each side extending to the principal towns. Thus far, it is only half finished, but if ever completed, it will open a market for the lands and products of the interior, now almost debarred therefrom.

Of the productions of the island there is a great variety of animal and vegetable, and in fruits and flowers there is a great profusion, vegetation of every kind being wonderfully and naturally prolific. With knowledge, industry, and *the labor*, the Island of Cuba would be made the garden spot of the world. Most of the vegetables are produced all the year round, only in quantities more or less abundant, as it may happen; and while of many of these there are large quantities raised, yet there is not enough for home consumption. This is particularly the case with beans (*frijoles*) of various kinds; of peas (*garbanzos*), only a limited quantity is raised, most of those used being imported. Although there are few or no such fruits as we have in the north, yet there is abundance of various kinds quite as pleasing to the palate; and any country that grows the pine-apple, the banana, and the orange can well afford to do without the apple, pear, or peach.

While, as has been mentioned in another place in this book, horticulture has not reached a very high state in Cuba, yet there are a great many very beautiful plants, both native and foreign, that flourish and do well with a little care bestowed on them. But, strange to say, there are many delicate plants and flowers from more northern latitudes, that, in place of doing well under the mildness and warmth of this southern climate, do not succeed at all when transplanted here, the plants seeming never to flower or seed; and when planted from the seed brought out, are entirely infecund,—an effect produced, it is thought, from the nature of the climate to which they are translated.

Notes:

* "THE TRUTH ABOUT CUBA," a pamphlet issued for gratuitous circulation by A. S. Simmonds, M.D., for thirteen years a resident of the island. ** For an exhaustive article on the relations of Spain and Cuba, see "Puttnam's Magazine" for January, 1870.

appendix

TELEGRAPH LINES ON THE ISLAND OF CUBA

CENTRAL DIRECT LINE, to Bemba, Villa Clara, Sancti-Spiritu, Ciego de Avila, Puerto Principe, Guaimaro, Tunas, Bayamo, Jiguani y Santiago de Cuba, with

DETACHED LINE, to Bejucal, Batabano, Guines, Union, Bemba, Cardenas, Colon, Santo Domingo (colony of) y Villa Clara.

WESTERN LINE, to San Antonio, Guanajay, San Cristobal, Palacios, Paso Real, Consolacion y Pinar del Rio.

BRANCHES, to Matanzas, branch from La Union; Cienfuegos, Sagua, Remedios, Boca de Sagua y Caibarien, branch from Villa Clara; Trinidad, branch from Sancti-Spiritu.

LINES READY TO OPEN, to Cauto de los Dorados, Sibanicu, Nuevitas, Maternillos, Manzanillo, Holguin, Gibara, El Cristo y Cauto Embarcadero.

TARIFF.—From 1 to 10 words inclusive, $2.12; 10 to 20 words, $2.28; 20 to 30 words, $4.25; 30 to 40 words, $4.50; 40 to 50 words, $6.75.

From Havana to Santiago de Cuba, $2.50 for the first 10 words, and 25 cents for each additional word.

From Havana to Jamaica, $5.00 for the first 10 words, and 50 cents for each additional word.

The tolls, in all cases, are payable in gold.

Despatches are received for points beyond telegraph stations, and forwarded by special messengers at the rate of about $1.00 for every three miles, except the first three, for which the charge is $1.50.

The telegraph offices are open from 6 in the morning until 10 at night. Havana time is kept at all the stations.

COMPANY INTERNATIONAL, OCEAN—BETWEEN THE UNITED STATES AND HAVANA
OFFICE NO. 22 MERCADERES STREET, HAVANA

TARIFF.—From Havana to any point in the United States east of the Mississippi river, including St. Louis, 1 to 10 words, $5.00; every additional word, 40 cents.

From Havana to any point in the United States west of the Mississippi river, 1 to 10 words, $7.50; every additional word, 75 cents.

From Havana to Cayo Hueso, Florida, 1 to 10 words, $1.75; every additional word, 18 cents.

TABLE SHOWING THE RESULTS AND INCREASE OF POPULATION OF THE ISLAND OF CUBA FOR A PERIOD OF YEARS, COMMENCING WITH THE CENSUS OF 1774.

| | WHITES | | | PEOPLE OF COLOR | | | | | |
| | | | | FREE | | | SLAVES | | |
Year	Males	Females	Total	Males	Females	Total	Males	Females	Total
1774	55,576	40,864	96,440	16,152	14,695	30,847	28,771	15,562	44,333
1792	72,299	61,260	133,559	25,211	28,941	54,152	47,424	37,166	84,590
1817	130,519	109,311	239,830	55,885	55,173	114,058	124,324	74,821	199,145
1827	168,653	142,398	311,051	54,962	55,532	106,494	183,290	103,652	286,942
1830	332,352	112,365	310,978						
1841	227,144	191,147	418,291	77,703	77,135	152,838	281,250	155,245	436,495
1846	230,983	194,784	425,767	76,651	76,575	149,226	201,011	122,748	323,759
1849	245,695	211,438	457,133	84,623	84,787	164,410	199,177	124,720	323,897
1858	328,065	261,712	589,777	90,421	90,853	175,274	220,999	143,254	364,253
1860	615,234	209,497	367,758						
1861	468,087	325,397	793,484	118,806	118,687	232,493	218,722	151,831	370,553
1867			764,750			225,938			379,523

MORTALITY OF HAVANA COMPARED WITH THAT OF OTHER CITIES

The number of deaths, per annum, is:-In Havana, 1 to every 24.3 inhabitants; in Paris, 1 to every 36.3 inhabitants; In Madrid, 1 to every 30 inhabtants; In New York, 1 to every 40 inhabitants; In London, 1 to every 41.2 inhabitants; In Vienna, 1 to every 31.4 inhabitants.

TABLE OF CUBAN MEASURES.

LINEAL	Cuban Yards.	Spanish Yards.	English Yards.	Metres.
Cuban Yard,	1.	1.014	0.927	0.848
Havana Yard,	0.995	·1.009	0.922	0.844
Cord,	24.	24.336	22.128	20.352
League,	5000.	5070.	4635.	4220.

SQUARE.				
Cord,	576.	592.24	494.97	414.
Caballeria,	186.624	191,886.05	160,371.41	134,202.06

One arroba,			25 lbs.
A box of sugar contains from	17	to 22	arrobas.
A sack of coffee	6	" 8	"
A hogshead of mascabado sugar contains from	40	" 60	"
A sack of coal contains from	9	" 8	"
A (horse) load of tobacco contains			2 bales.
A load of bananas contains		275 large or 325 small ones.
A hogshead of molasses contains from		25 to 33 barrels.
A barrel of molasses contains		5½ American gallons.
A pipe of wine contains		600 bottles.
A garrafon of wine contains		25 "

Cuban money has been described in the first chapters of this volume. In addition to the coins mentioned there, there are some infinitesimal coins, such as *marcurdi, melisimos*, etc., which the traveler never sees. The people of the interior use, in emergencies, even chicken bones and bits of wood.

COMMERCE OF THE ISLAND OF CUBA

The commerce of Cuba has experienced great changes during the last century and the first quarter of the present, in consequence of the partial immunities conceded at various times from successive restrictions and freedom from the evil results of wars between Europe and America. Though in 1817 the Cuban ports were definitely opened to general commerce, it was not until 1825 that its new era of success began. From that date the commerce of Cuba has made great and rapid strides forward, as will be seen by the following table.

Periods of five years	Imports	Exports.	Per ct. Increase of imports.	Per ct. Increase of Exports
1826 to 1830	$15,412,689	$12,717,929	00.0	00.0
1831 to 1835	16,756,448	12,887,339	8.7	1.3
1836 to 1840	21,662,766	18,503,648	29.2	43.6
1841 to 1845	22,472,355	24,099,646	3.7	30.2
1846 to 1850	27,150,754	24,828,986	20.8	3.
1851 to 1855	30,498,390	31,498,516	12.3	26.

Taking one of these periods as an example we find that of this commerce there was done under the Spanish flag $8,945,989 imports, $3,545,818 exports; foreign flags, $21,552,401 imports, $27,952,698 exports. Of this there was done by the United States, $7,395,754 imports, $12,263,511 exports; England, $6,398,234 imports, $8,442,612 exports; France, $2,270,944 imports, $2,092,011 exports; Germany, $1,427,396 imports, $1,894,171 exports.

In the importations of the island there appears the following percentage of articles:

PROVISIONS—

Spanish wines,	4.95	per cent.	Spices	.34	per cent.
Spanish oil,	1.87	"	Fruits, dried & pressed,	.81	"
Rum, vinegar and all			Wheat flour,	10.20	"
other liquors,	3.01	"	Grains and other flours,	5.91	"
Meats,	6.33	"	Fish, .	2.37	"
Lard	3.66	"	Other provisions,	2.98	"
				42.43	per cent.

MERCHANDIZE—

Cotton goods,	8.62	per cent.	Linen goods,	9.62	"
Woolen "	1.66	"	Silk "	2.58	"
				22.48	per cent.

Coined Gold, 1.6 per cent. Coined Silver,   .   .09 "

                                                      2.5 per cent.

Skins or leather,	2.03	per cent.	Animals,	.72	"
Woods,	8.05	"	Railroad stuffs,	1.00	"
Machinery and ironmongery for ingenios,				1.30	"
Crockery, paper, jewelry, metals, etc,				19.57	"
				100.00	per cent.

In the Exports of the Island there appear the following articles and percentage :

Sugar, including molasses and rum	82.46	per cent.	Wax,	.80	per cent.
			Bees' honey	.25	"
Tobacco, manufactured,	4.55	"	Fruits, etc.,	.28	"
Tobacco, in leaf,	2.80	"	Animals,	.01	"
Copper,	3.45	"	Cacao, (chocolate) sponges,		
Coffee,	3.17	"	preserves, guano, etc.,	.70	"
Woods,	1.53	"		100.00	per cent.

The sugar interest is one that has grown enormously with the new machinery, and the percentage of tobacco has also vastly increased.

TABLE SHOWING PERCENTAGE OF THE COMMERCE DONE BY THE DIFFERENT PORTS OF THE ISLAND.

Havana,	62.64	per cent.	Jibara,	0.76	per cent.
Matanzas,	11.69	"	Remedios,	0.71	"
Cuba, .	7.95	"	Manzanillo,	0.61	"
Cardenas,	4.16	"	Baracoa,	0.26	"
Cienfuegos,	4.02	"	Sancti Spiritu,	0.10	"
Trinidad,	3.50	"	Santa Cruz,	0.14	"
Sagua la Grande,	2.28	"	Guantanamo,	0.10	"
Nuevitas,	1.02	"	Mariel,	0.01	"

In late years the commerce of some of these places has very much changed in the amount of business done at their points, particularly the new towns (comparatively), of Matanzas, Cardenas, Cienfuegos, Nuevitas, and Guantanamo. It is not possible to tell with exactitude what is the amount of business done in the Island at present, but the increase in the above figures has been enormous, the annual amount before the rebellion reaching the sum of nearly sixty millions of dollars of exports and the same of imports.

Everything is done to favor Spanish trade and place obstacles in the way of that of other nations; in fact their duties are almost prohibitory against many articles that the United States raises in great profusion, although the Island would, otherwise, be a splendid market for our people.

METHODS OF COMMUNICATION AND TRAVEL ON THE ISLAND OF CUBA

Without the assistance of railroad and steamboat routes, the communications on the Island of Cuba would be the worst in the world. The nature of the earth, and the abundance of the rains, that produce frequent inundations, and almost perpetual mud, in which horses and conveyances get stuck fast, do not permit of the construction of other roads than the expensive *calzadas* or *caminos reales*. Of these there are many, like those from Havana to Guines, or Regla to Guanabacoa, and particularly those outside the walls of Havana, which by the increase of population, and advance of city limits have become really streets to that part of the town. On all such roads the journeys can be made in the volante, but the moment these principal roads are left it becomes a matter of imperative necessity to go on horseback, as with other means travel would be impossible. Upon all these roads, though there are few or no inns or hotels, yet accommodations, though, perhaps, of the humblest, can always be had at the *fondas*, and at the *tenda mista*, a sort of cross-roads store. To the principal points on the island, however, access by easy and pleasant travel is obtained from the steamboats and railroad lines, and these are numerous, namely:

ON THE NORTH COAST

Line between Havana and Cardenas.—Every Tuesday and Friday, leaving at six o'clock in the evening, returning from Cardenas on Wednesdays and Saturdays. Office, No. 110 Calle de San Ygnacio.

Havana to Santiago de Cuba via the North Coast.—A line of steamers runs once a week, stopping at Nuevitas, Jibara, and Baracoa, reaching Cuba in about five days. This is a pleasant trip, affording the only means of seeing this part of the island pleasantly. Office, No. 6 Oficios street.

From Cuba to Santo Domingo and St. Thomas.—There are several steamer lines that touch at Cuba coming and going, affording easy means of reaching the British West Indies.

Havana to Caibarien and Sagua la Grande.—A steamer leaves Havana every Thursday at eleven o'clock in the morning for the above places, arriving on Saturday. Leaves Caibarien every Saturday, returning touching at Sagua la Grande, arriving at Havana on Monday. Office, No. 7 Baratillo street.

Cardenas to Caibarien.—A steamer leaves Cardenas every Saturday after the arrival of the steamer that leaves Havana Friday night, or the railroad train, stopping at La Teja, Ganuza, Sierra Morena, Las Pozas, Sagua la Grande, Boca de Sagua la Chica, arriving Sunday morning at Caibarien, which place it leaves, returning, the morning of Thursdays, reaching Cardenas on Wednesdays.

Havana to Bahia Honda, etc.—A steamer makes weekly trips between Havana, Bahia Honda, Rio Blanco, etc. Office, No. 28 Calle del Obispo.

STEAMERS OF THE SOUTH COAST

There are quite a number of these, sailing at different times, of which information can be obtained by inquiring at the offices of the respective lines. These are all first-class boats, their appointments being complete in every respect, and by them the traveler can reach Cienfuegos, Trinidad, Las Tunas, Santa Cruz, Manzanillo, and Santiago de Cuba. Offices, No. 16 Calle Amargura, Calle de los Oficios, Nos. 10 and 54.

Havana via Batabano to Island of Pines.—Steamers leave Batabano every Thursday, and return the following Monday. Leaving Havana at 5.45 o'clock in the morning the traveler can by night, with the aid of these steamers, be at Santa Fé, in the Isle of Pines. Office, in the café Dominica. (For steamers to points in the United States see Chapter I.)

CUBA TO SPAIN

Line of Ocean Mail Steamers leave Havana for Cadiz the 15th and 30th of each month. First cabin passage, two hundred dollars, gold; second cabin, one hundred and sixty dollars. Office, No. 2 Baratillo street.

Saint Nazaire to Vera Cruz.—Making stops at Havana and Saint Thomas. Office, No. 16 Obrapia street.

Havana to Saint Thomas and Southampton.—Royal line of English steamers, leaving about the 5th to the 7th of each month. Passage to Southampton, one hundred and ninety-two dollars and fifty cents; to Puerto Rico, fifty dollars.

Havana to Hamburg and Havre.—Hamburg American Line of Steamers to above place leave Havana about once a month. Passage, one hundred and fifty dollars, gold. Office, No. 5 Baratillo street.

Havana to Bremen.— North German Line makes regular trips to Northampton and Bremen. Passage one hundred and twenty-five dollars, gold. Office, Uppmann & Co., 64 Calle de Cuba.

The principal railroad lines on the Island of Cuba have been mentioned already in the different chapters of this work. A complete list of the principal lines, with their connections, branches, etc., can be found in May's "Mercantil Almanaque," elsewhere mentioned.

GAZETTEER OF THE ISLAND OF CUBA

The island is divided into two Grand Departments, known as the Eastern and the Western. The Western is again divided into the two Grand Districts (*Gobiernos*) of Havana and Matanzas, and into the Civil Districts (*Tenencias de Gobierno*) of Pinar del Rio, Bahia Honda, San Cristobal, Guanajay, San Antonio de los Baños, Guanabacoa, Santa Maria del Rosario, Santiago de las Vegas, Bejucal, Guines, Jaruco, Cardenas, Colon, Sagua la Grande, Villa Clara, Cienfuegos, Trinidad, Santo Espiritu, Moron, and San Juan de los Remedios. The Eastern Department is divided into the Grand Districts of Santiago de Cuba and Puerto Principe, and into the Civil Districts of Nuevitas, Las Tunas, Manzanillo, Bayamo, Jiguani, Holguin, Guantanamo, Baraca. The Civil or Sub-Districts are again divided into Districts (*Partidos*), of which there are one hundred and sixty-one in the island. The Head-quarters (*Cabeceras*) are those towns and cities which give their names to the Districts. The principal ones are Havana, Puerto Principe, Matanzas, Santiago de Cuba, Trinidad, Santo Espiritu, Guanabacoa, Villa Clara, Cienfuegos, Cardenas, Bayamo, and San Juan de los Remedios.

The following Gazetteer gives, opposite the name of each place, its class, the Sub-division or Civil District (*Tenencia de Gobierno* or *Distrito*) and District (*Partido*) to which it belongs, together with its population.

name	class	subdivision	district	population Whites	Free Cold	Slaves	Total
Abreus,	Town,	Cienfuegos,	Yaguaramas,	1,040	100	1,152	2,292
Aguacate,	Village,	Jaruco,	Bainoa,	303			
Aguada del Cura,	Hamlet,	Santiago de las Vegas,	Bauta,				
Alacranes,	District,	Guines,		6,894	943	8,853	16,690
Alacranes,	Village,	Guines,	Alacranes,	414	131	87	632
Alfonsos (Los),	Town,	Holguin,	Guabaciabo,	198	14	17	229
Alonso Rojas,	Little hamlet,	Pinar del Rio,	Consolacion,				
Alquizar,	District,	S. Antonio de los Baños,	Alquizar,	3,468	461	3,050	6,979
Alquizar,	Village,	S. Antonio de los Baños,		452	206	99	757
Altillo,	Town,	Holguin,	Mayari,	40	49	6	95
Alvarez (Narciso de),	District,	Sagua la Grande,	Alvarez,	1,291	115	258	1,664
Alvarez (Narciso de),	Little hamlet,	Sagua la Grande,					
Amaro,	District,	Cienfuegos,	Padre las Casas,	3,242	196	1,926	5,364
Arango,	Hamlet,	Tunas,	Unique,	643	51	601	1,295
Arenas,	Town,			257			
Arimao,	Village,	Cienfuegos,	Cumanayagua,	1,182	401	1,488	3,071

name	class	subdivision	district	population			
				Whites	Free Col'd	Slaves	Total
Arroyo Apolo,	Little town, *one of the suburbs of Havana*,						
Arroyo Arenas,	Town,	Santiago de las Vegas,	Cano,	361	52	25	438
Arroyo Blanco,	Town,	Santo Espiritu,	Jatibonico,				
Arroyo Hondo,	Town,	Holguin,	Mayari,				
Arroyo Naranjo,	District,	Havana,		1,254	96	635	1,985
Arroyo Naranjo,	Village,	Havana,	Arroyo Naranjo,	482	40	70	592
Artemisa,	District,	Guanajay,		3,793	609	2,862	7,264
Artemisa,	Village,	Guanajay,	Artemisa,	593	78	116	787
Auras,	Town,	Holguin,	Gibara,	114	20	19	153
Bacuranao,	District,	Guanabacoa,		1,734	127	432	2,293
Bacuranao,	Small village,	Guanabacoa,	Bacuranao,	123	4	20	147
Bacuranao (Playa de),	Town,	Guanabacoa,	Bacuranao,	110			
Baez,	District,	Villa Clara,		1,247	501	211	1,959
Bagazal,	Hamlet,	Cienfuegos,	Yaguaramas,	947	187	607	1,741
Bahia Honda,	Civil District,			5,840	818	6,115	12,773
Bahia Honda,	Village, *head-quarters of the Civil District of the same name,*			480	83	152	715
Bailen,	Small landing,	Pinar de Rio,	Consolacion del Sur,				
Bainoa,	District,	Jaruco,		3,021	384	2,213	5,618
Bainoa,	Small village,	Jaruco,	Bainoa,				
Baire,	District,	Jiguani,		7,200	2,278	302	9,780
Baire,	Village,	Jiguani,	Baire,	277	232	58	567
Baja,	District,	Pinar del Rio,		1,080	107	807	1,994
Baja,	Small village,	Pinar del Rio,	Baja,	81	6	52	139
Banaguises,	Small town,	Colon,	Macagua,				
Banao,	Small hamlet,	Puerto Principe,	Cubitas,				
Banes,	Town,	Guanajay,	Guayabal,	110	99	24	233
Baracoa,	Civil District, *City, head-quarters of the Civil District of the same name,*			4,530	4,799	1,471	10,800
Baracoa,	Little Town,	Santiago de las Vegas,	Bauta,	812	1,155	397	2,364
Barandilla,	Town,	Santiago de las Vegas,	Cano,				31
Bariay,	District,	Holguin,		3,390	292	206	3,888
Barrancas,	District,	Bayamo,		4,633	3,633	434	8,700

name	class	subdivision	district	Whites	Free Col'd	Slaves	Total (population)
Barrancas,	Town,	Bayamo,	Barrancas,	13	17	2	32
Batabano,	District,	Bejucal,		2,423	406	1,897	4,726
Batabano,	Village,	Bejucal,	Batabano,	572	211	94	877
Batabano,	Landing,	Bejucal,	Batabano,	541	108	93	742
Bauta,	District,	Santiago de las Vegas,					
Bayamo,	Civil District,			15,834	12,851	2,651	31,336
Bayamo,	*City, head-quarters of the Civil District of the same name,*			2,303	2,885	931	6,119
Bayate,	Town,	San Cristobal,	Candelaria,	36	9	11	56
Bejucal,	Civil District,			14,738	1,970	7,040	23,748
Bejucal,	*City, head-quarters of the Civil District of the same name*			2,562	498	425	3,485
Bemba,	Village,	Colon,	Jiquimas,	2,152	70	208	2,430
Bermeja (Vieja),	Town,	Matanzas,	Cabezas,	119	30	3	152
Blanquizal,	Town,	Cienfuegos,	Santa Isabel de las Lajas,	678	5	38	721
Boca (La),	Town,	Cardenas,	Camarioca,	79	5	34	118
Boca del Rio,	*Town, on the harbor of Sagua la Grande,*						
Bolondron,	Little village,	Guines,	Alcranes,	500			
Boyeros,	*Town, near Santiago de las Vegas,*			190	7	6	203
Braguetudos,	Town,	Holguin,	Mayari,	64	60	8	132
Buenaventura,	Town,	Bejucal,	Quivican,	136	24	12	172
Buena Vista,	Small town,	Colon,	Palmillas,				
Cabacu,	District,	Baracoa,		1,369	1,372	340	3,081
Cabagan,	District,	Trinidad,		671	420	284	1,375
Cabaniguan,	District,	Tunas,		2,233	845	215	3,293
Cabañas,	District,	Guanajay,		3,168	464	5,134	8,766
Cabañas,	Village,	Guanajay,	Cabañas,	382	125	58	565
Cabezas,	District,	Matanzas,		4,745	330	2,936	8,011
Cabezas,	Village,	Matanzas,	Cabezas,	260	33	27	320
Cacacum,	District,	Holguin,		1,527	385	86	1,998
Caibarien,	District,	Remedios,		1,916	425	737	3,078
Caibarien,	Village,	Remedios,	Caibarien,	1,427	312	139	1,878
Caiguanabo,	Small town,	Pinar del Rio,	Consolacion del Norte,				
Caimanera,	Small town,	Guantanamo,	Tiguabos,				37

name	class	subdivision	district	Whites	Free Col'd	population	
						Slaves	Total
Caimito,	Small village,	Colon,	Hanabana,	58	48	19	125
Caimito,	Village,	S. Antonio de los Baños,	Vereda Nueva,	459	20	39	518
Caimito,	Town,	Guines,	San Nicolas,	82	41	123	
Calabazal,	District,	Sagua la Grande,		5,027	433	2,841	8,301
Calabazal,	Small town,	Sagua la Grande,	Calabazal,				
Calabazal,	Village,	Santiago de las Vegas,	Ubajay,	410	95	132	637
Calvario,	District, *under the jurisdiction of Havana,*			1,068	125	305	1,498
Calvario,	Village,	Havana,	Calvario,	378	75	59	512
Calvo,	Town,	Guanabacoa,	Bacuranao,	163	13	65	241
Camajuani,	District,	Remedios,		3,437	397	1,800	5,634
Camarioca,	District,	Cardenas,		4,096	9	2,613	6,718
Camarioca,	Village,	Cardenas,	Camarioca,	76	13	21	110
Camarones,	District,	Cienfuegos,		4,308	816	3,267	8,391
Camarones,	Village,	Cienfuegos,	Camarones,	600	157	722	1,479
Camugiro,	District,	Puerto Principe,		2,321	236	1,164	3,721
Canasi,	Little village,	Matanzas,	Corral Nueva,	175	7	4	186
Canasi (Boca de),	Little town,	Matanzas,	Corral Nueva,				
Candelaria,	District,	San Cristobal,		2,590	451	1,544	4,585
Candelaria,	Village,	San Cristobal,	Candelaria,	165	29	33	227
Caney,	District,	Santiago de Cuba,		1,320	1,404	1,297	4,021
Caney,	Village,	Santiago de Cuba,	Caney,	334	239	107	680
Cangrejeras,	Town,	Santiago de las Vegas,	Bauta,	60			
Canimar,	Little town, *near the mouth of the river Canimar,*						
Cano (El),	District,	Santiago de las Vegas,		735	122	19	876
Cano (El),	Village,	Santiago de las Vegas,	El Cano,	34	4		38
Cantarranas,	Little town,	Santiago de las Vegas,	El Cano,				
Cantel,	Little town,	Cardenas,	Camarioca,				
Cañas,	Little town,	Matanzas,	Ceiba Mocha,				71
Cañas,	Town,	Guanajay,	Artemisa,	124	24	16	164
Caraballo,	Village,	Jaruco,	Bainoa,				387
Caracucey,	Town,	Trinidad,	Guinea,	124			
Cardenas,	Civil District,			24,452	1,460	24,553	50,465

name	class	subdivision	district	Whites	Free Cold	population	
						Slaves	Total
Cardenas,	City, *head-quarters of the Civil District of the same name,*			7,628	461	2,796	10,885
Cartagena,	District,	Cienfuegos,		5,742	681	2,799	9,222
Cartagena,	Village,	Cienfuegos,	Cartagena,	870	89	595	1,554
Casablanca,	Ward of Havana,						2,000
Cascorro,	Town,	Puerto Principe,	Sibanicu,	2,618	237	1,274	4,129
Casiguas,	District,	Jaruco,		32	2	7	41
Casiguas,	Town,	Jaruco,	Casiguas,	1,972	827	901	3,700
Casilda,	District,	Trinidad,		797	409	92	1,298
Casilda,	Village,	Trinidad,	Casilda,	3,273	266	1,578	5,117
Catalina (La),	District,	Guines,		1,242	78	1,252	2,572
Caunado,	District,	Puerto Principe,	Padre las Casas,	827	103	1,283	2,213
Caurege,	Town,	Cienfuegos,		916	1,697	472	3,085
Cauto Abajo,	District,	Bayamo,		40			
Cauto,	Town,	Santiago de Cuba,	Palma Soriano,	1,374	1,462	248	3,084
Cauto (Embarcadero de),	District,	Bayamo,	Cauto,	342	192	86	620
Cauto del Paso,	Village,	Bayamo,	Unique,	278			
Cayajabos,	Town,	Tunas,		2,947	418	2,815	6,180
Cayajabos,	District,	Guanajay,	Cayajabos,	171	54	81	306
Cayorroncano,	Village,	Guanajay,					
Ceiba (La),	Island,	Puerto Principe,					
Ceiba del Agua,	Little town,	Havana,	Puentes Grandes,	2,261	18	653	2,932
Ceiba del Agua,	District,	San Antonio de los Baños,		345	69	43	457
Ceiba Mocha,	Village,	San Antonio de los Baños,	Ceiba del Agua,	3,843	346	1,426	5,615
Ceiba Mocha,	District,	Matanzas,		744	27	119	890
Ceja de Pablo,	Village,	Matanzas,	Ceiba Mocha,	449	3,129	8,168	
Cercado,	District,	Sagua la Grande,	4,590				
Cerro Guayabo,	Little town,	Puerto Principe,	Cubitas,				
Chabaleta,	Little town, *on the harbor of Guantanamo,*	Holguin,	Mayari,	59	52		111
Chambas,	Town,	Moron,					
Chirigota (La),	District,	San Cristobal,	Santa Cruz de los Pinos,	72	20	8	100
Chorrera (La),	Town, *under the jurisdiction of Havana.*			36	7	5	48

name	class	subdivision	district	population			
				Whites	Free Col'd	Slaves	Total
Ciego Alonso,	Hamlet,	Cienfuegos,	Camarones,	1,024	158	1,184	2,366
Ciego de Avila,	District,	Moron,		2,436	326	264	3,026
Ciego de Avila,	Village,	Moron,	Ciego de Avila,	359	151	41	551
Ciego Montero,	Hamlet,	Cienfuegos,	Cartagena,	610	132	155	897
Cienfuegos,	Civil District,			29,701	7,207	17,126	54,034
Cienfuegos,	Town, *Head-quarters of the Civil District of the same name,*			6,086	2,387	1,477	9,950
Cifuentes,	Town,	Sagua la Grande,	Amaro,	2,706	118	4,905	7,729
Cimarrones,	District,	Cardenas,		580	37	108	725
Cimarrones,	Village,	Cardenas,	Cimarrones,	2,649	4,748	6,251	13,639
Cobre (El),	District,	Santiago de Cuba,	El Cobre,	1,190	1,553	828	3,571
Cobre (El),	Town,	Santiago de Cuba,		241	15	17	273
Cogimar,	Town,	Guanabacoa,	Bacuranao,	40	24	64	
Coliseo,	Town,	Matanzas,	Guamacaro,				
Coloma (La),	Shipping point,	Pinar del Rio,	Consolacion del Sur,				
Colon,	Civil district,			28,862	2,481	32,871	64,214
Colon,	Town, *Head-quarters of the Civil District of the same name,*			1,037	158	76	1,271
Colon,	Shipping point,	Pinar del Rio,	Consolacion del Sur,				
Condado (El),	Town,	Trinidad,	Sipiabo,	154	111	17	282
Consolacion del Norte,	District,	Pinar del Rio,		2,716	333	865	3,914
Consolacion del Sur,	District,	Pinar del Rio,		9,231	3,100	4,047	16,378
Corojo,	Little town,	Puerto Principe,	Cubitas,	1,021	156	248	1,425
Corral Falso,	Village,	Colon,	Macuriges,	48	15	27	90
Corralillo,	Little town,	Sagua la Grande,	Ceja de Pablo,				
Corralillo,	Town,	Santiago de las Vegas,	Bauta,				
Corral Nuevo,	District,	Matanzas,	Corral Nuevo,	4,895	575	4,439	9,819
Corral Nuevo,	Village,	Matanzas,	Catalina,	42	7	20	69
Corral Nuevo,	Village,	Guines,	Managua,	181	25	18	224
Cotorro (El),	Little town,	Santa Maria del Rosario,		538	135	356	1029
Cruces (Las),	Town,	Cienfuegos,	Camarones,	2,110	172	407	2,689
Cubitas,	District,	Puerto Principe,					
Cumanayagua,	District,	Cienfuegos,		4,542	1,596	2,298	8,936
Cumanayagua,	Village,	Cienfuegos,	Cumanayagua,	1,350	314	146	1,810

name	class	subdivision	district	population			
				Whites	Free Col'd	Slaves	Total
Cupeyes,	District,	Moron,		1,804	1,328	264	3,396
Datil (El),	District,	Bayamo,	Datil,	63	192	33	288
Datil (El),	Town,	Bayamo,					
Dayanguas,	Shipping point,	San Cristobal,	San Diego de los Baños,				
Derrocal,	Little town,	Puerto Principe,	Guaimaro,				
Dominico,	Town,	Holguin,	Mayari,	61	64		125
Enramada (La),	District,	Santiago de Cuba,		1,126	3,296	2,270	6,692
Ensenada,	Town,	Guanajay,	Cabañas,	33	19		52
Entrada (La),	Little town,	Puerto Principe,	Cubitas,				
Esperanza (La),	District,	Villa Clara,	La Esperanza,	5,827	1,538	1,059	8,424
Esperanza (La),	Village,	Villa Clara,	Lagunillas,	894	544	274	1,712
Esquina DE Tejas,	Little town,	Cardenas,					
Fray Benito,	District,	Holguin,	Guabaciabo,	4,359	149	597	5,105
Fusio,	Town,	Holguin,		163		4	167
Galafre,	Shipping point,	Pinar del Rio,	San Juan y Martinez,				
Gibara,	District,	Holguin,	Gibara,	6,619	836	852	8,370
Gibara,	Port,	Holguin,		1,082	346	182	1,610
Gongojas,	Town,	Cienfuegos,	Cartagena,	532	42	635	1,209
Gua,	District,	Manzanillo,		1,731	2,384	79	4,194
Guabaciabo,	District,	Holguin,		6,651	483	563	7,697
Guadalupe,	Little town,	Santo Espiritu,	Jatibonico,	158	217	140	515
Guagimico,	Hamlet,	Cienfuegos,	Cumanayagua,	3,239	523	574	4,336
Guaimaro,	District,	Puerto Principe,	Guaimaro,				500
Guaimaro,	Little village,	Puerto Principe,		3,380	222	6,083	9,685
Guamacaro,	District,	Matanzas,		5,220	331	7,307	12,858
Guamutas,	District,	Cardenas,					
Guamutas,	Little town,	Cardenas,	Guamutas,				
Guanabacoa,	Civil District,			15,283	4,096	6,834	26,213
Guanabacoa,	Town, *head-quarters of the Civil District of the same name,*			8,817	3,593	3,992	16,402
Guanabana,	Small town,	Matanzas,	Santa Ana,				
Guanabo,	District,	Jaruco,		2,090	265	817	3,072
Guanabo,	Village,	Jaruco,	Guanabo,	199	26	27	252

name	class	subdivision	district	Whites	Free Col'd	population	
						Slaves	Total
Guanabo (Boca de),	Town,	Jaruco,	Guanabo,				87
Guanaja,	Little hamlet,	Puerto Principe,	Cubitas,				
Guanajay;	Civil District,			19,177	3,521	17,145	39,843
Guanajay;	District,	Guanajay,		4,071	1,804	2,022	7,177
Guanajay;	Town, *head-quarters of the Civil District of the same name,*			2,654	881	451	3,986
Guanajayabo,	District,	Cardenas,		4,943	115	4,508	9,566
Guane,	District,	Pinar del Rio,		6,479	1,059	1,190	8,728
Guane,	Town,	Pinar del Rio,	Guane,	125	4	11	140
Guanimar,	Town,	S. Antonio de los Baños,	Alquizar,	52	4	16	72
Guanimar,	Town,	San Cristobal	Las Mangas,	482	154	406	1,042
Guaniquical,	District,	Trinidad,		5,268	5,515	8,638	19,414
Guantanamo,	Civil District,						
Guantanamo,	Port, *on the Bay of the same name,*						
Guara,	District,	Guines,		2,538	284	751	3,573
Guara,	Village,	Guines,	Guara,	314	91	27	432
Guaracabuya,	District,	Remedios,		2,831	431	711	3,973
Guaracabuya,	Little town,	Remedios,	Guaracabuya,				59
Guasimas,	Town,	Cardenas,	Camarioca,	129	61	51	241
Guatao,	Village,	Santiago de las Vegas,	Bauta,				
Guayabal,	District,	Guanajay,		2,346	273	2,040	4,659
Guayabal,	Town,	Guanajay,	Guayabal,	110	7		117
Guayabal	Town,	Puerto Principe,	Guaimaro,	2,563	191	1,515	4,269
Gueiba,	District,	Remedios,		2,449	238	171	2,858
Guinea,	District,	Trinidad,					
Guines,	Civil District,			33,227	4,138	25,097	62,462
Guines,	City, *head-quarters of the Civil District of the same name,*			6,820	1,413	2,386	10,619
Guinia,	Town,	Trinidad,	Cabagan,	559	115	27	701
Guiniao	District,	Baracoa,		1,272	840	199	3,311
Guira de Bolondron,	Little town,	Guines,	Alacranes,				
Guira de Melena,	District,	S. Antonio de los Baños,		3,800	567	3,764	8,131
Guira de Melena,	Village,	S. Antonio de los Baños,	Guira de Melena,	1,012	391	203	1,606
Guiro Boninges,	Town,	Bejucal,	La Salud,	189	36	906	1,131

name	class	subdivision	district	Whites	Free Col'd	population Slaves	Total
Guiro de Marrero,	Town,	Bejucal,	La Salud,	3,273	1,197	64	4,534
Guisa,	District,	Bayamo,		211	195	6	412
Guisa,	Town,	Bayamo,	Guisa,				
Habana,	Grand District,			122,892	40,144	27,296	190,332
Habana,	City, *Capital of the Island,*			108,754	37,623	22,807	169,184
Hanabana,	District,	Colon,		2,196	311	893	3,400
Hato Nuevo,	Town,	Cardenas,	Guamutas,	166	23	14	303
Hermita Vieja,	Little town,	Puerto Principe,	Cubitas,	100	25	25	150
Herradura (La),	Town,	San Cristobal,	San Diego de los Baños,				
Holguin,	Civil District,			40,852	7,045	4,226	52,132
Holguin,	City, *head-quarters of the Civil District of the same name,*						
Horno,	District,	Bayamo.		2,951	1,436	567	4,954
Horno,	Small town,	Bayamo,	Horno,	1,531	649	238	2,418
Hoyo Colorado,	Village,	Santiago de las Vegas,	Bauta,	487	122	609	1,218
Iguara,	District,	Santo Espiritu,		3,463	234	587	4,284
Isla de Pinos,	Civil District,			1,529	205	333	2,060
Jabaco,	Town,	Colon,	Jiquimas,	39	7	4	50
Jaimanita,	Town,	Santiago de las Vegas,	Cano,	55	8	4	67
Jamaica,	Town,	Jaruco,	San José de las Lajas,	27	9	6	42
Jaruco,	Civil District,			23,431	3,063	11,077	37,571
Jaruco,	City, *head-quarters of the Civil District of the same name*						
Jaruco (Boca de),	Town,	Jaruco,	Guanabo,	43		50	90
Jatibonico,	District,	Santo Espiritu,		1,069	270	260	1,599
Jibacoa,	District,	Jaruco,		3,996	861	303	5,160
Jibacoa,	Village,	Jaruco,	Jibacoa,	2,210	103	1,145	3,458
Jibaro,	District,	Santo Espiritu,	Jibaro,	549	59	112	720
Jibaro,	Hamlet,	Santo Espiritu,		2,293	290	1,938	4,521
Jicoteas,	Little town,	Moron,	Ciego de Avila,	242	93	48	383
Jiguani,	Civil District,			12,312	4,658	602	17,572
Jiguani,	Town, *head-quarters of the Civil District of the same name,*						
Jiquiabo,	Little town,	Sagua la Grande,	Narciso de Alvarez,	735	498	114	1,347
Jiquiabo,	Town,	Jaruco,	Guanabo,	33	12	13	58

name	class	subdivision	district	Whites	Free Col'd	Slaves	Total
						population	
Jiquimas,	District,	Colon,		10,823	770	11,203	22,796
Jiquimas,	Little town,	Trinidad,	Guaniquical,	210	530	40	780
Jojo,	District,	Baracoa,					
Jucaro,	Little town,	Cardenas,	Lagunillas,				
Jumagua,	Little town,	Sagua la Grande,	Sagua la Grande,				
Jumento,	Little town,	Trinidad,	Guaniquical,				
Justinicu,	District,	Santiago de Cuba,		1,044	5,912	7,890	14,846
Lagunillas,	District,	Cardenas,		2,558	145	5,468	8,171
Lagunillas,	Village,	Cardenas,	Lagunillas,	433	40	501	974
Lazaro Lopez,	Little town,	Moron,	Ciego de Avila,				
Limonar,	Town,	Matanzas,	Guamacaro,	89	28	81	198
Limonares,	Little town,	Puerto Principe,	Cubitas,				
Limones,	Town,	Cienfuegos,	Camarones,	803	96	500	1,399
Liza (La),	Town,	Santiago de las Vegas	Cano,	197	61	39	297
Lomitas,	Town,	Cienfuegos,	Camarones,	645	131	201	977
Luyano,	Village, *one of the suburbs of Havana,*						
Mabujado,	District,	Baracoa,		530	728	493	7,851
Macagua (La),	District,	Colon,		3,556	243	8,699	12,498
Macagua (La),	Little town,	Colon,	La Macagua,	28		5	33
Macuriges,	District,	Colon,		7,837	434	8,640	16,911
Madruga,	District,	Guines,		4,511	415	2,628	7,554
Madruga,	Village,	Guines,	Madruga,	673	178	147	998
Magarabomba,	District,	Puerto Principe.		1,108	170	930	2,208
Magarabomba,	Town,	Puerto Principe,	Magarabomba,	41	5	4	50
Maisi,	District,	Baracoa,		397	174	2	573
Majana,	Town,	San Cristobal,	Las Mangas,	54	4	7	65
Malezas,	District,	Villa Clara,		6,224	1,237	1,079	8,540
Manacas,	Hamlet,	Cienfuegos,	Padre las Casas,	560	149	419	1,128
Managua,	District,	S. Maria del Rosario,		2,589	482	1,170	4,241
Managua,	Village,	S. Maria del Rosario,	Managua,	132	47	33	212
Manati,	Town,	Holguin,	Yarigua,	30	5	35	
Mangas (Las),	District,	San Cristobal,		2,047	422	2,012	4,481

name	class	subdivision	district	Whites	Free Col'd	population Slaves	Total
Mangas (Las),	Village,	San Cristobal,	Las Mangas,	101	6	28	135
Maniabon,	District,	Holguin,		4,618	432	478	5,528
Manicaragua,	District,	Villa Clara,		3,791	1,327	247	5,365
Manicaragua,	Little town,	Villa Clara,	Manicaragua,	85		16	101
Mantilla,	Town,	Habana,	Calvario,	2,824	290	474	3,588
Mantua,	District,	Pinar del Rio,		407	56	74	537
Mantua,	Village,	Pinar del Rio,	Mantua,				
Manzanillo,	Civil District,			13,674	11,105	1,713	26,493
Manzanillo,	Town, *head-quarters of the Civil District of the same name.*			3,060	1,962	621	5,643
Maraguan,	District,	Puerto Principe,	Quemados,	3,799	345	2,346	6,490
Marianao,	Village,	Habana,		2,062	805	540	3,407
Mariel,	District,	Guanajay,		2,852	657	2,902	6,411
Mariel,	Village,	Guanajay,	Mariel,	617	229	111	957
Matanzas,	Grand District,			40,627	7,067	32,219	79,913
Matanzas,	City, *head-quarters of the Grand District of the same name,*			18,583	5,070	6,886	30,539
Mayajigua,	District,	Remedios,		2,354	682	255	3,291
Mayajigua,	Town,	Remedios,	Mayajigua,	2,373	340	1,455	4,168
Mayanabo,	District,	Nuevitas,	Mayari,	3,340	2,185	277	5,802
Mayari,	Village,	Holguin,	Cartagena,	250	217	52	519
Mayari Abajo,	Town,	Holguin,	Mayari,	1,497	247	500	2,244
Medidas,	Town,	Cienfuegos,		90	15	105	
Mejia,	District,	Holguin,					
Melena,	Village,	Guines,	Melena,	2,122	372	1,900	4,394
Melena,	Town,	Guines,	Ceiba Mocha,	820	206	506	1,532
Molinos (Los),	Town,	Matanzas,	Mantua,	206	7	9	277
Montezuelo,	Little town,	Pinar del Rio,	Cartagena,	215	54	29	298
Mordazo,	Town,	Cienfuegos,	Narciso del Alvarez,	482	40	70	592
Mordazo,	Little town,	Sagua la Grande,	Puentes Grandes,				
Mordazo,	Hamlet,						
Moron,	Civil district,	Habana,		6,268	737	528	7,533
Moron,	Village, *head-quarters of the Civil District of the same name,*						
Morrillo,	Little town,	Bahia Honda,	Las Pozas,	1,278	285	33	1,596

name	class	subdivision	district	population			
				Whites	Free Col'd	Slaves	Total
Mulata (La),	Little town,	Bahia Honda,	Las Pozas,	173	82	6	261
Navajas,	Little town,	Colon,	Macuriges,	2,229	205	341	2,775
Nazareno,	Little town,	Remedios,	Guaracabuya,	4,066	580	1,442	6,088
Nazareno,	Village,	Santa Maria del Rosario,	Managua,				1,000
Neiva,	District,	Santo Espiritu,		4,346	436	3,891	8,673
Niguas,	District,	Villa Clara,		662	115	227	1,004
Nueva Gerona,	Town, *head-quarters of the Government of the Isle of Pines,*						
Nueva Paz,	District,	Guines,		4,189	565	2,187	6,941
Nueva Paz,	Village,	Guines,	Nueva Paz,	1,816	225	167	2,208
Nuevitas,	Civil District,						
Nuevitas,	City, *head-quarters of the Civil District of the same name,*						
Padre las Casas,	District,	Cienfuegos,		2,612	561	3,353	6,520
Palacios,	District,	San Cristobal,		2,934	706	934	4,575
Palacios,	Village,	San Cristobal,	Palacios,	394	75	48	514
Palma (La),	Village,	Pinar del Rio,	Consolacion del Norte,	126	12	32	170
Palmarejo,	District,	Trinidad,		668	416	2,046	3,139
Palma Soriano,	District,	Santiago de Cuba,		2,864	4,078	2,383	9,326
Palma Soriano,	Village,	Santiago de Cuba,	Palma Soriano,	115	48	51	214
Palmillas,	District,	Colon,		3,041	531	2,833	6,407
Palmillas,	Village,	Colon,	Palmillas,				
Palmira,	Village,	Cienfuegos,	Padre las Casas,				
Parras,	Town,	Holguin,	Guabaciabo,	210	93	26	320
Paso Real de Guane,	Little town,	Pinar del Rio,	Guane,	582	258	1,050	1,896
Paso Real de San Diego,	Hamlet,	San Cristobal,	San Diego de los Baños,	71	3	14	88
Pepe Antonio,	District,	Guanabacoa,		205	58	58	321
Pepe Antonio,	Village,	Guanabacoa,	Pepe Antonio,	1,685	163	1,092	2,940
Perros (Los),	Little town,	Remedios,	Mayajigua,	115	37	17	169
Pijuan,	Little town,	Colon,	Macagua,	39	1	3	43
Pinar del Rio,	Civil District,			43,522	10,408	25,404	79,334
Pinar del Rio,	District,	Pinar del Rio,		11,104	3,111	4,419	18,604
Pinar del Rio,	City, *head-quarters of the Civil District of the same name,*			2,000	631	457	3,088
Pipian,	Hamlet,	Guines,	Madruga,	146	7	20	173

name	class	subdivision	district	Whites	Free Col'd	population	
						Slaves	Total
Playa DE Marianao,	Little town,	Havana,	Quemados,	568	148	647	1,363
Porcayo,	District,	Puerto Principe,		182	674	13	869
Portillo,	District.	Manzanillo,					
Porterillo,	Little town,	Villa Clara,					
Pozas (Las),	District,	Bahia Honda,	Juan de las Yaras,	2,556	412	986	3,954
Pozas (Las),	Village,	Bahia Honda,	Pozas,	480	74	33	587
Principe Alfonso,	Town,	Guines,	Nueva Paz,	152	30	39	221
Pueblo Nuevo,	Little town,	Puerto Principe,	Santa Cruz,				
Pueblo Nuevo,	Town,	San Cristobal,	Las Mangas,	59	4	9	72
Puente de Almendares,	Little town,	Habana,	Arroyo Naranjo,				
Puentes Grandes,	District,	Habana,	Puentes Grandes,	1,457	124	370	1,950
Puentes Grandes,	Village,	Habana,		1,000			
Puerta de la Guira,	Village,	Guanajay,	Artemisa,	223	17	20	260
Puerto Principe,	Grand District,			58,556	10,786	13,185	62,527
Puerto Principe,	City, *head-quarters of the Grand District of the same name*,			18,216	8,034	4,355	12,369
Punta de Cartas,	Shipping point,	Pinar del Rio,	San Juan y Martinez,				
Punta de Palmas,	Little town,	Pinar del Rio,	Pinar del Rio,				
Quemado de Guines,	District,	Sagua la Grande,	Quemado de Guines,	4,009	140	2,725	6,883
Quemado de Guines,	Little Village,	Sagua la Grande,		2,467	830	1,605	4,902
Quemados (Los),	District,	Habana,	Los Quemados,				
Quemados (Los),	Little Town,	Habana,	Los Quemados,				
Quemados Viejos,	Little town,	Guanajay,					
Quiebra Hacha,	Village,	Bejucal,	Mariel,	109	55	13	177
Quivican,	District,	Bejucal,	Quivican,	3,435	420	1,633	5,489
Quivican,	Village,			737	218	237	1,123
Rancho Veloz,	District,	Sagua la Grande,		1,297	221	3,721	5,289
Ranchuelo,	Little town,	Villa Clara,	San Juan de las Lleras,				
Recreo (El),	Little town,	Cardenas,	Guanajayabo,				
Regla,	Village, *on the Bay of Havana*,						8,000
Remedios,	Civil District,			28,593	4,924	9,223	42,740
Remedios,	Town, *head-quarters of the Civil District of the same name*,			4,800	1,881	956	7,637
Rincon,	Town,	Jaruco,	Guanabo,	86	24	16	126

name	class	subdivision	district	population			
				Whites	Free Col'd	Slaves	Total
Rincon,	Town,	Santiago de las Vegas,	Santiago de las Vegas,	56		29	85
Rio de Ay,	District,	Trinidad,		1,086	451	2,953	4,490
Rio Hondo,	Little town,	Pinar del Rio,	Consolacion del Sur,	226	41	36	303
Roque,	Village,	Colon,	Jiquimas,				
Sabalo,	Little town,	Pinar del Rio,	Guane,				
Saban. del Comendador,	District,	Matanzas,		2,079	217	6,068	8,364
Saban. del Comendador,	Village,	Matanzas,	Sabanilla del Comendador,	195	49	14	258
Saban illa,	Village,	Cienfuegos,	Cumanayagua,	1,476	206	183	1,865
Sagua de Tanamo,	District,	Guanatanamo,		2,526	1,664	594	4,784
Sagua de Tanamo,	Village,	Guanatanamo,	Sagua de Tanamo	173	173	90	436
Sagua la Grande,	Civil District,			30,420	2,416	19,150	52,986
Sagua la Grande,	Town, *head-quarters of the Civil District of the same name,*						7,000
Salad,	Town,	Cienfuegos,	Santa Isabel de las Lajas,	518	29	106	653
Salado,	Town,	Cienfuegos,	Cartagena,	527	23	295	485
Saltadero (El),	Village, *head-quarters of the Civil District of Guantanamo,*						
Salto	Town,	Cienfuegos,	Santa Isabel de las Lajas,	529	790	416	1,735
Salud (La),	District,	Bejucal,	La Salud,	767	91	457	1,137
Salud (La),	Village,	Bejucal,	Calvario,	2,782	189	1,945	4,925
San Augustin,	Town,	Habana,	Yarigua,	622	28	238	888
San Augustin,	Little town,	Holguin,	Guabaciabo,	15	30	45	
San Andres,	Town,	Holguin,		127	9	24	160
San Anton,	Town,	Cienfuegos,	Cumanayagua,	175	248	127	550
S.Antonio de las Vegas,	District,	Bejucal,		2,131	191	709	3,031
S. Antonio de las Vegas,	Village,	Bejucal,	San Antonio de las Vegas,	505	160	47	712
S. Antonio de los Baños,	Civil District,			21,127	2,022	10,737	33,886
S. Antonio de los Baños,	Town, *head-quarters of the Civil District of the same name.*			3,741	367	139	4,247
S. Ant. R. B. del Norte,	District,	Jaruco,		2,018	154	1,256	3,428
S. Ant. R. B. del Norte,	Village,	Jaruco,	S. Antonio R. B. del Norte,	324	60	60	444
San Cayetano,	Town,	Pinar del Rio,	Consolacion del Norte,	26	6	3	35
San Cristobal,	Civil District,			17,917	3,289	7,771	18,977
San Cristobal,	Village, *head-quarters of the Civil District of the same name,*			379	80	44	503
S. Diego de los Baños,	District,	San Cristobal.		6,147	1,224	2,090	9,461

name	class	subdivision	district	Whites	Free Cold	population	
						Slaves	Total
S. Diego de los Baños,	Village,	San Cristobal,	San Diego de los Baños,	769	147	242	1,158
S. Diego de lAs Niguas	Town,	Villa Clara,	Niguas,	81	4	14	99
S. Dieao de Nuñez,	District,	Bahia Honda,		2,113	195	3,188	5,496
S. Diego de Nuñez,	Village,	Bahia Honda,	San Diego de Nuñez,	671	99	72	842
San Felipe,	Hamlet,	Bejucal,	Quivican,	325	30	37	392
San Fernando,	Little town,	Villa Clara,	Manicaragua,				
San Francisco,	District,	Trinidad,		935	194	140	1,260
San Francisco de Paula,	Town,	Guanabacoa,	S. Miguel del Padron,	272	39	60	171
San Francisco de Paula,	Town,	Matanzas,	Ceiba Mocha,	199	15	18	232
San Geronimo,	Town,	Puerto Principe,	Urabo,	65	29	6	100
San José,	Town,	Holguin,	Mayari,	30	58	3	91
San José de las Lajas,	District,	Jaruco,		3,723	739	1,545	6,007
San José de las Lajas,	Village,	Jaruco,	S. José de las Lajas,	852	215	167	1,234
San José de los Ramos,	Town,	Colon,	Macagua,	37	6	43	
San Juan,	Little town,	Habana,	Arroyo Naranjo,				
San Juan,	Village,	Pinar del Rio,	S. Juan y Martinez,				
San Juan de las Lleras,	District,	Villa Clara,		5,366	1,491	1,457	8,314
San Juan de las Lleras.	Town,	Villa Clara,	S. Juan de las Lleras,				
San Juan y Martinez,	District,	Pinar del Rio,		8,078	1,777	2,737	12,529
San Lazaro,	Little town,	Puerto Principe,	Camugiro,				
San Luis,	Little village,	Pinar del Rio,	S. Juan y Martinez,				
San Matias,	Village,	Jaruco,	S. Antonio R. B. del Norte,	385	2	189	578
San Miguel,	Town,	Matanzas,	Guamacaro,	88	15	50	153
San Miguel,	Village,	Nuevitas,	Mayanabo,	493	106	36	635
San Miguel,	Little town,	Holguin,	Yarigua,				
San Miguel del Padron,	District,	Guanabacoa,		2,278	106	806	2,190
San Miguel del Padron,	Village,	Guanabacoa,	S. Miguel del Padron,	281	7	115	403
San Nicolas,	District,	Guines,		2,723	151	3,191	6,065
San Nicolas,	Village,	Guines,	San Nicolas,	225	52	104	381
San Nicolas de Moron,	Little town,	Santiago de Cuba,	Justinicu,				
San Patricio,	Hamlet,	Nuevitas,	Mayanabo,	136	8		144
San Pedro,	Little town,	Santiago de las Vegas,	Ubajay,	17		1	18

name	class	subdivision	district	Whites	Free Col'd	population	
						Slaves	Total
San Pedro,	Little town,	Trinidad,	Palmarejo,	3,062	309	4,641	8,012
San Pedro,	Little town,	Trinidad,	Guinea,	112	30	15	157
Santa Ana,	District,	Matanzas,					
Santa Ana,	Village,	Matanzas	Santa Ana,				
Santa Ana,	Town,	Santiago de las Vegas,	Bauta,	45	5	50	
Santa Clara,	Little town,	Pinar del Rio,	Consolacion del Sur,	137	3	20	160
Santa Cruz,	Town,	Jarcuo	Jibacoa,				
Santa Cruz,	District,	Puerto Principe,		1,543	603	893	2,939
Santa Cruz,	Village,	Puerto Principe,	Santa Cruz,	500			
Santa Cruz de los Pinos,	District,	San Cristobal,		2,201	338	922	3,461
Santa Cruz,	Town,	San Cristobal,	Santa Cruz,	23	12	6	41
Santa Fé,	Town,	Isle of Pines,					400
S. Isabel de Las Lajas,	District,	Cienfuegos,		3,252	382	1,930	5,564
S. Isabel de Las Lajas,	Village,	Cienfuegos,	Sta. Isabel de las Lajas,	1,287	257	1,329	2,873
S. Maria del Rosario,	Civil District,			5,045	828	2,173	8,046
S. Maria del Rosario,	*City, head-quarters of the Civil District of the same name,*			2,456	346	1,003	3,805
Santa Rita,	District,	Jiguani,	Santa Rita,	4,377	1,882	136	6,393
Santa Rita,	Town,	Jiguani,	Cartagena,	281	97	3	381
Santiago,	Town,	Cienfuegos,		415	63	190	668
Santiago de Cuba,	Grand District,			23,789	36,480	31,082	91,351
Santiago de Cuba,	*City, head-quarters of the Grand District of the same name,*			13,377	15,349	7,775	36,491
Santiago de las Vegas,	Civil District,			9,302	2,041	4,507	15,850
Santiago de las vegas,	*City, head-quarters of the Grand District of the same name,*			1,250	865	722	5,837
Santo (El).	Little town,	Sagua la Grande,	Calabazal,	5,131	271	1,333	6,735
Santo Domingo,	District,	Sagua la Grande,		25,188	5,808	8,685	42,681
Santo Domingo,	Little Village	Sagua le Grande,	Santo Domingo,	7,293	4,172	1,873	13,338
Santo Espiritu,	Civil District,			2,230	1,262	321	3,823
Santo Espiritu,	*City, head-quarters of the Grand District of the same name,*			3,968	210	648	4,826
Scibabo,	District,	Villa Clara,					
Saibanicu,	District,	Puerto Principe,					
Sibanicu,	Little village,	Puerto Principe,	Sibanicu,				
Sierra (La),	Hamlet,	Cienfuegos,	Cumanayagua,	201	150	214	565

name	class	subdivision	district	Whites	Free Col'd	Slaves	Total
						population	
Sierra Morena,	Little town,	Sagua la Grande,	Ceja de Pablo,	2,690	362	558	2,610
Sipiabo,	District,	Trinidad,					
Sipiabo,	Little town,	Trinidad,	Sipiabo,				
Socapa (La),	Town,	Santiago de Cuba,	El Cobre,	81	91	12	184
Soledad,	Town,	Cienfuegos,	Cartagena,	1,076	36	400	1,512
Tacamara,	District,	Holguin,		2,299	51	177	2,527
Taguayabon,	District,	Remedios,	Taguayabon	6,985	524	1,810	9,319
Taguayabon,	Little town,	Remedios,					
Tapaste,	District,	Jaruco,	Tapaste,	3,740	545	1,312	5,597
Tapaste,	Village,	J.aruco,		622	121	66	809
Teja (La),	Town,	Cardenas,	Guamutas,	279	56	47	382
Tejeria (La),	Town,	Pinar del Rio,	Guane				
Tiarriba,	Town,	Santiago de Cuba,	Justinicu,	52	136	22	210
Tiguabos,	District,	Guantanamo,	Tiguabos,	1,639	1,866	4,847	8,352
Tiguabos,	Little village,	Guantanamo,					
Toabaguey,	Little town,	Puerto Principe,	Cubitas,				
Trinidad,	Civil District			17,036	9,034	10,539	37,509
Trinidad,	*City, head quarters of the Civil District of the same name,*			7,003	5,972	2,680	15,665
Tuinucu,	District,	Santo Espiritu,		3,230	425	674	4,329
Tunas (Las),	Civil District,	Santo Espiritu,		4,089	2,254	480	6,823
Tunas (Las),	*Village, head-quarters of the Civil District of the same name,*			998	675	167	1,840
Tunas (Las),	Village,						
Ubajay,	District,	Santiago de las Vegas,	Jibara,	1,319	214	641	2,174
Ubajay,	Village,	Santiago de las Vegas,	Ubajay,	246	96	17	359
Union, (La),	Town,	Guines,	Alacranes,	548	91	111	750
Unique,	District,	Tunas,		858	634	95	1,687
Urabo,	District,	Puerto Principe,		543	170	349	1,062
Velasco,	Little town,	Holguin,	Maniabon				
Velazquez,	Little town,	Baracoa,	Cabacu,				
Vereda Nueva,	District,	San Antonio de los Baños,	Vereda Nueva,	3,498	304	1,184	4,986
Vereda Nueva,	Village,	San Antonio de los Baños,		1,250	121	154	1,525
Vicana,	Little town,	Sagua la Grande,	Calabazal,				

name	class	subdivision	district	population Whites	Free Col'd	Slaves	Total
Vicana,	District,	Manzanillo,		1,078	1,309	9	2,396
Vicana,	Town,	Manzanillo,	Gua,	120	210	47	377
Villa Clara,	Civil District,			34,579	11,200	6,865	52,644
Villa Clara,	City,	*head-quarters of the Civil District of the same name,*		5,098	2,753	740	8,591
Vueltas (Las),	Little town,		Taguayabon,				
Yaguajay,	District,	Remedies,		1,741	114	1,317	3,172
Yaguajay,	Town,	Remedios,	Yaguajay,	154	16	20	190
Yaguaramas,	District,	Cienfuegos,		3,164	784	2,002	5,950
Yaguaramas,	Village,	Cienfuegos,	Yaguaramas,	668	258	148	1,074
Yaguas (Las),	District,	Santiago de Cuba,		809	1,704	3,210	5,723
Yaka,	District,	Manzanillo,		3,007	1,061	100	4,168
Yara,	Village,	Manzanillo,	Yara,	323	182	44	549
Yarey,	Little town,	Holguin,	Yarigua,				
Yareyal,	District,	Holguin,		2,070	371	155	2,596
Yaribacoa,	District,	Manzanillo,		3,808	3,011	796	7,615
Yarigua,	District,	Holguin,		3,028	425	268	2,721
Yateras,	District,	Guantanamo,		574	1,195	2,761	4,530
Zarzal (El),	Town,	Manzanillo,	Yara,	366	312	4	682

In the above Gazetteer, for Cuba, *vid.* Santiago de Cuba; for Narciso de Alvarez, *vid.* Alvarez; for Nueva Filipina, *vid.* Pinar del Rio; for Palos (Los), *vid.* Nueva Paz; for Paso de Cauto, *vid.* Cauto de Paso; for San Gregorio de Mayari, *vid.* Mayari Abajo ; for San Juan de los Remedios, *vid.* Remedios; for Santa Catalino de Guasa ó el Saltadero, *vid.* Saltadero; for Santa Clara, *vid.* Villa-clara; for Vieja Bermeja, *vid.* Bermeja.

THE TOTAL POPULATION OF THE ISLAND ACCORDING TO DATA OF 1867

	WHITES	COLORED PEOPLE		TOTAL
		Free	Slaves	
Western Department,	601,656	129,880	313,288	1,044,824
Eastern Department,	163,094	96,058	66,235	325,387
Grand Total,	764,750	225,938	379,523	1,370,211

TABLE SHOWING THE COMPARATIVE VALUES IN DOLLARS OF SUBURBAN AND AGRICULTURAL PROPERTIES IN THE ISLAND OF CUBA, COMPILED FROM STATISTICS PUBLISHED BY THE "INTENDENCIA-GENERAL" FOR 1871

	CATTLE FARMS	SUBURBAN PROPERTIES	FARMS	TOTAL
Western Department,	3,049,169	13,786,365	87,240,400	104,075,934
Eastern Department,	2,237,011	2,473,695	17,646,601	22,357,307
Grand Total,	5,286,180	16,260,060	104,887,001	126,433,241

TABLE SHOWING THE NUMBER OF LANDED PROPERTIES ON THE ISLAND, IN 1866:

	TOBACCO FARMS	SMALL FARMS	CATTLE BREEDING FARMS	SUGAR ESTATES	COFFEE ESTATES	POTREROS.	TRUCK GARDENS
Western Department,..	4,228	53,475	2,034	1,167	454	5,269	19,628
Eastern Department,..	5,254	9,995	1,251	198	542	469	2,214
Total,	9,482	6,3470	3,285	1,365	966	5,738	21,842

In addition to the list given at the close of the preface there are a number of valuable books relating to the Island, published at different times, and to be picked up at the bookstores of Havana, viz.: ENSAYO HISTORICO DE LA ISLA DE CUBA. Por Pezuela. Hasta el Gobierno del General Tacon. One volume.—AVES DE LA ISLA DE CUBA. Por Lembeye, with illuminated drawings. One folio volume.—DICCIONARIO CASI RAZONADO DE VOCES CUBANAS. Por D. Estaban Pichardo. One volume.—MEMORIAS SOBRE EL ESTADO POLITICO, GOBIERNO Y ADMINISTRACION DE LA ISLA DE CUBA. Por D. José de la Concha, Governor General in 1853.—GEOGRAFIA DE LA ISLA DE CUBA. Por D. Estaban Pichardo. Three volumes.—TOPOGRAFIA MÉDICA DE LA ISLA DE CUBA. Por el Dr. D. Ramon, Piña y Peñuela.—LO QUE FUIMOS Y LO QUE SOMOS ò LA HABANA ANTIGUA Y MODERNA. Por Don José Maria de la Torre.—MEMORIAS DE LA SOCIEDAD ECONOMICA, and many pamphlets and periodicals published at different times upon subjects or matters of interest pertaining to the Island. All or most of these can be imported through any respectable book house.

A LIST OF SOME OF THE PRINCIPAL CIGAR
MANUFACTURERS,

Their residences, and the brands for which they are specially celebrated,— useful for dealers, and those smokers who, accidentally, come across any of these brands, and wish to order direct from the makers.

ACOSTA, FACUNDO (Bejucal).—Cleopatra, Facundo, Maravilla, Palmito, Tres Gracias.

—ALONSO, VALENTIN (Havana).—Alonso Fernandez, Flor de Mi gusto, Flor de Rio Seco, Flor de Valentin Alonso, Mis dos Hijas, Whitman.

—ALVAREZ, CASIMIRO (Santiago de las Vegas).—Celeste Imperio, Flor de CasiMiro Alvarez.

—ALVAREZ, JULIAN (Havana).—Camilo Muro, Flor de Franco P. Alvarez, Flor de Julian Alvarez, Francisco A. de Grande, Henry Clay, Primera Diana, Selecta.

—ALVEREZ, MYANO (Bejucal).—Clay, Calhoun and Webster, Nueva Empresa, Recreo.

—ALLONES, ANTONIO (Havana).—Confederacion, Confederacion Suiza, República Argentina, República de Chile, República Peruana, Rey del Mundo, Uruguay.

—AMARO Y CA., F. (Havana).—General Grant, Johnson, Orotava.

—AMAT, PAGUAGA Y CA. (Havana).—Avilesina, Boa, Gloria, Recinto de Nervion.

—ANDREU Y CA, JOSÉ (Havana).—Angelita, Designio, Inesita, San Francisco.

—ARANGO, VALENTIN (Havana).—Aguila Especial, Caliope, Cautiva, Flor de Solon, Flor de Valentin Arango, Stars and Stripes.

—ARGÜELLES Y HERMANOS, JOAQ. DE (Havana).—Argüelles y Her-manos, Flor de Arguelles y Hos, Flor de Joaq. Argüelles, Humboldt.

—ARRIGUNAGA, FERNANDO (Havana).—Flor de Arrigunaga, Flor del Arte, Jockey Club.

—BOCK Y CA. (Havana).—A. Bacallao y Ca., Aguila de Oro, Fausto, Flora Apiciana, Moscovita, Perla del Pacifico, Principe de Orange, Raleigh, Royal Engineers.

—BÁRCENAS, RAMON DE LAS (Havana).—Churruca, Lord Nelson, Manco de Lepanto, Sena.

—BASTARRECHEA, L.—Cachucha, Flor de Bastarrechea, Vega del Jagüey.

—BECI Y HERMANO, MANUEL (Havana).—Antoñica, Ermita, Rey de Würtemberg.

—CABARGA Y CA., A. (Havana).—Albertina, Cabarga y Lopez, Carona.

—CABARGA CA., J. DE (Havana).—Flor de los Tobacos Habanos, José de Cabarga y Ca.

—CANDEMIL, JOSÉ L. (Havana).—Coloso, Encanto, Encanto de Matilde, Estrella Fija, Gota de Agua, Know Something, Moctezuma, Plenty of Room, Reina de las Antillas, Reina del Golfo.

—CARBAJAL, L. (Havana).—Camelia del Japon, Carbajal y Carbajal, Dos Carbajales,Horcon, Peña la Deva.

—CARUNCHO, ANTO. (Havana).—Intimidad, Marqués de Caxia, Super Omnia.

—CASO Y CA. (Havana).—Flor de Cuba, Superior de Cuba.

—CASTILLO Y SUAREZ, JOSÉ (Havana).—Aguila Francesa, Figaro, Noriega, Primor Habanero, Pruébese, Rosa Habanera.

—CLISEN, JOSÉ J. (Havana). —Esmero, Fuego, Maria Antonieta, Vuelta al Rio.

—CODINA, JAIME (Havana).

—Cinto de Orion, Flor de Codina, Lirio, Redowa, Rifle.

—COMAS Y CA. (Bejucal).

—Corina, Cosecha de 1863, Flor de Aroma, Fundada Esperanza, Habana Industrial, Idea, Niña, Nuevo Mundo, Quinta Esencia.

—CONILL, JUAN (Bejucal).

—Juan Conill.

—CORDIER, ISIDRO (Pinar del Rio).

—Anela de Rio-Hondo.

—CORUJO, LUIS (Havana).—Camarioca, Comerciante, Flor de Corujo, Hija del Regimiento, Punch.

—COSTALES, BERNDO. (Santiago de las Vegas).—Clavel de Santiago, Flor de Mayo, Flor de Redo y Costales, Líbano.

—CUETO Y HERMANO, LUIS (Havana).—Aleázar, Aromáticos, Caimana, Chata, Chilena, Delicias Tropicales, Diamante, Elia, Emilia, Flor de José Cueto, Manuel Reina, Granadina, Merrimac y Monitor, Peninsular.

—CHINCHURRETA Y DUARTE (San Antonio de Los Baños).—Aralar, Cabinet, Chinchurreta y Duarte, Diógenes, Flor de Duarte y Ca., Flor de Manrico, Juan de Chinchurreta, Para la Grandeza, ¿ Qué sé yó? Resaláa.

—DIAZ, BANCES Y CA. (Havana).—A No. I, Almirante de Ruyter, Bellamar, Carolina, Flor de Diaz, Bances y Ca., Flor de P. Bances, Flor de Tomás Dias, Gen. McClellan, Mariscal Villars, Old Abe, Princesa Dagmar, Un grano fuí.

—DIAZ, LUIS (Santiago de las Vegas).—Arabella, Chile, Flor de Luis Diaz, Florida, Modelo de la Antigüedad.

—ESTRADA Y CA., A. (Havana).—Especialidad, Flor de Castelló y Ca., Luisa Miller, ¿ Para mi ? Paseo.

—FERNANDEZ TUNON, FRANCISCO (Havana).—Constancia, Pájaro del Océano, Torre de Tavira.

—FERRERIA Y HERMO, (Havana).—Eleccion, Orbe.—Fos y CA., V. (Pinar del Rio).—Catalana, Eldorado, Emperatriz Carlota, Ultramar.

—GARABALOSA, D. (Havana).—Ancla, Babilonia, Coloso de Santiago, Flor de D. Garbalosa, Flor de Jo e Rionda, Gibraltar, Guess, Isli, Langreo, Legalidad, María Stuart, Mejor de la Habana, Opera, Pensilvania, Perla de Santiago, Silistria.—

GARCIA Y MAZA (Havana).—Andrew Johnson, Rubí, Sultan.

—GARCIA Y CA., FELIX (Havana).—Alvaro de Bazan, Capitolio, Flor de Arroyave, Flor de Europa, Flor de Royales, Flor de Vigo, Júpiter, M. P. Mirat, Niña Adelina, Niño Eduardito, Victoria Regia.

—GARCIA, JOSÉ ANTO. (Havana).—Flor de J. A. García, Gobernador Stanley, Great Eastern, Iberia, Ingenuidad, J. A. García, Kladderadatsch, Legítima Ambrosia, Legítima de García, Nicotiana, Ponton, Raquel, Rosa de California, Telémaco.

—GARCIA Y LLERA, M. (Havana).—Alfonso, Apostólica, Aprobacion, Católica, Consuelo, Duque Ernesto, Manuel Garcia, Monitor, Nilo, Reina, Rey del Mar, Rivera, Romana.

—GONZALEZ, CASTRO Y CA. (Havana).—Josefina, Manola.

—GONZALEZ, EULOGIO (Havana).—Africana, Ella, Ernst Merck, Incógnita, Mi Madre, Mi Suegra,Mozart, Ramillete de Aromas, Rapidez.

—GONZALEZ, J. H. (Havana).—Aguila de Diamante, Central Park, Curiosidad, Dos Sofías, Florida Blanca, Mensagero, Scotch Fusilier Guards.

—JANÉ Y GENER (Havana).—Cruz de Malta, Escepcion, Monopolizacion, Vuelta-Abajo.

—LARRAÑAGA Y CA. (Havana).—Alexander II., Guipuzcoana, Por Larrañaga, Ready and Rough.—LOPEZ, ANTONIO (Havana).—Flor de Anto. Lopez y Ca., Paz de China, Prototipo, Rosa del Valle, Sublime de A. Lopez.

—LOPEZ Y FAJO (Havana).—Esmero de Arroyave, Esquisitos, Flor Agrícola, Flor de Fajo, Flor de Mata y García, Flor de Torres y Lopez, Jóven América, Sirena, Tiempo.

—LOPEZ Y TRUJILLO, DIEGO (Santiago de las Vegas).—Diego Lopez y Trujillo, Flor Chinesca, Flor de Santiago, Julia, Mina de Oro, Turca.

—LLERA, VENANCIO DE LA (Havana).—Consecuente, Flor de la Moda, Flor de Recalde y Llera, Popular, Rectitud.

—MARINAS, MANUEL (Havana).—Flor de Bengoechea, Flor de Marinas, Guillermo Tell, Incomparable, Inmejorable, Judit, Manuel Marinas, Montañesa, Perla del Tabaco, Primavera, Real, Reina de la Habana, Tino.

—MARRERO, MANUEL (Bejucal).—Aroma del Bálsamo, Bálsamo y Aroma, Black Warrior, Conchita, Palmeta, Para los Aficionados.

—MARTINEZ IBOR, VICENTE (Havana).—Criolla, Fin, Mas Selecta, Mina Cubana, Mis Tres Medallas, Príncipe de Gales, Tres Diosas.

—MATO, PEDRO (Santiago de las Vegas).—Dos Hermanos, General Grant, Peñon, Pureza de Mató, Sol de Santiago, Venturina, Visitadora.

—MENENDEZ Y SUAREZ (Havana).—Boschetti, Camagüeyana, Flor de Renduelas y Menendez, Flor el Todo, Flor Tropical, Infiesta y Castro, J. Menendez, Pedrera, Rio Feo.

—MESTRE, A. B. (Havana).—Elvira, Estrell de Chile.

—MORALES, M. A. (Havana).—Encanto de Cuba, Flor de J. Arés, Flor de J. M. M. Realidad.

—MORALES, JOSÉ, (Havana).—Aguila de Rusia, Celina, Flor de Canela, Flor de Morales, Lord Rivers, Matilde, Mayerbeer, Pelícano.

—MURIAS, GARCIA Y CA. (Havana)—Balmoral, Flor de los campos de Cuba, Meridiana, Palacio de Cristal, Reserva, Walter Scott.

—PANDO Y CA., J. (Havana).—Acuerdo, Alba, Caoba, Crema, Danubio, Dulzura, Fina, Flor de Albuerne, Lira de Oro.

—PARETS Y CA., SALVADOR, (Havana).—Army and Navy Club, Broderick, Caminante, Coloso de Rodas, Cometa, Cotorra, Creacion, Esperanza Realizada, Jardin, Jenny Lind, Magnífica, Parets y Pons, Perro, Postres, Rhin, Ritilla, Sancho Panza, Sebastopol, Tomeguin, Yumurri.

—PARTAGAS, JAIME, (Havana).—Balsámica, Flor de Tabacos.

—PEREZ DEL RIO, FO. (Havana).—Blason de Tabacos, Bouquet de Tabacos, Flor Escepcional, Flor de Inés, Flor del Sevillano, Flor de Tabacos de Gusto, General Prim, Legitimidad, Mérito, Rio de la Plata, Sevillano, Tabacos de Gala, Unica Flor de Rio.

—PRESMANES Y SOBRINO, (Havana).—Araucana, Flor de Presmanes y Sobrino, Fortuna de Navajas.

—PUMARIEGA, J. G. (Havana).—César, Flor de José G. Pumariega, Flor de Un dia, Incógnito, J. G. P., Palo Alto, Reformador, Rio Sella, Sublime de Pumariega.

—Rico MANUEL, (Santiago de las Vegas).—Benigno Rico, Habanos, Lima, Luna, Luna llena, Manuel Rico, Media Luna.

—RODRIGUEZ, ANDRÉS, (Havana).—Earl of Dunmore, Flor de S. Juan y Martinez, Granadier Guards, Isleñita Cubana, Tica de Bolton.

—RODRIGUEZ, ARIAS Y CA. (Havana).—Almendares, Felicidad de R. Rodriguez, Flor de R. Rodriguez, Ocasion, Puente de Agua Dulce, Relámpago, Rico Habano, Union Universal.

—ROGER Y CA., PEDRO, (Santiago de las Vegas).

—Ramo, Rosa de Santiago.

—ROMAY, JULIAN, (Havana).—Adela, Cisne, Competencia de Romay, Flor de Romay, Ria de Vigo, Rudesinda, Tres Primos.

—ROMERO, JUAN B. (Havana).—Cosmopolita, Española, Filántropa, Occidental.

—ROSALES Y TUERO, (Havana).—Australia, Comercial, Flor de Creta, Flor de Ramon Rosales y Ca., Flor de Tuero y Rosales, Indio, Ninfas del Parque, Ristori, Traviata.

—SALA, MANUEL DE LA, (Havana).—Bayamo, Buen Aroma, Dignidad, Eclectic, Engaña Bobos, Extra Malísima, Extra Superior, Flor de las Antillas, Flor Inesperada, Flor de lo Malo, Flo. de Sala, Guillermo II, Infra Omnia, Limeña, Malísima, Mejicana, Nada hay peor, No me Olvides, Our St. John, Si me compras te diviertes, Venenosa, Venezolana.

—SALAZAR Y CA., TOMAS, (Havana).—Buen Gusto, Feliz Habana, Flor de la Habana, Flor de Llavina, Flor de Salazar, Imperial, Laureles de la India, Hariscal, Regina, Rosa de Georgia, Rosalía, Serafina, Trieste, Verdi.

—SOLAR, FRANCO. G. (Havana).—Flor de Solar, Risita.

—TEMES, JOSÉ C. (Havana).—Bella Union, Firmeza, India, Pocahontas.

—TRUEBA, DIEGO (Havana).—Belencita, Bella de San Luis, Cometa Viela, Diego Trueba, Dolce Farniente, Sol Habanero, Suizos, Torre de Malakoff, Ultimatum, Vicálbaro.

—UNÁNUE Y HO. (Havana).—Arroyo Hondo, Flor del Valle, Irurac-Bat, Lealtad, Pinar del Rio, Por Unánue, Rio San Joaquin.

—UYMANN Y CA., H. (Havana).—Constelacion, Flor de la Leña, Flor del Pacífico, Francia, H. Upmann, Japon, Limpia. Bandera, Mil Hermosa.

—VALDÉS, José PABLO (Havana).—Afan, J. Pablo Valdés, Resolucion.

—VELEZ, MAXIMINO (Havana).—España, Flor de la Patria, Flor de Velez, Lord Palmerston, Pabellon Prusiano, Patria, Slug.

—VIDAL Y CA. (Havana).—Aurora, Bustamante, Florentina, Napoleon III, Nueva Empresa, Perfeccion, Pretension, San Roman.

—VILLAR, ALEJANDRO (Havana).—A. de Villar y Villar, Flor de Villar y Villar, Jorge Juan, Viriato.

—ZELLER, AMANDO (Havana).—Anzuelo, Columnas de Ambos Mundos, Fiel, Flor de Amando, Pilotos, Recuerdo, Zuavo.—ZUMALACARREGUI Y CA., JUAN M. (Havana).—Fatimita, Buenos Aires, Flor de Zumalacarregui, Introduccion, Modelo, Palmira, Vazcongado.